Lecture Notes in Artificial Intelligence   13603

Subseries of Lecture Notes in Computer Science

More information about this subseries at https://link.springer.com/bookseries/1244

Maosong Sun · Yang Liu ·
Wanxiang Che · Yang Feng ·
Xipeng Qiu · Gaoqi Rao ·
Yubo Chen (Eds.)

Chinese Computational Linguistics

21st China National Conference, CCL 2022
Nanchang, China, October 14–16, 2022
Proceedings

 Springer

Editors
Maosong Sun
Tsinghua University
Beijing, China

Yang Liu
Tsinghua University
Beijing, China

Wanxiang Che
Harbin Institute of Technology
Harbin, China

Yang Feng
Chinese Academy of Sciences
Institute of Computing Technology
Beijing, China

Xipeng Qiu
Fudan University
Shanghai, China

Gaoqi Rao
Beijing Language and Culture University
Beijing, China

Yubo Chen
Chinese Academy of Sciences
Institute of Automation
Beijing, China

ISSN 0302-9743   ISSN 1611-3349   (electronic)
Lecture Notes in Artificial Intelligence
ISBN 978-3-031-18314-0   ISBN 978-3-031-18315-7   (eBook)
https://doi.org/10.1007/978-3-031-18315-7

LNCS Sublibrary: SL7 – Artificial Intelligence

This Springer imprint is published by the registered company Springer Nature Switzerland AG
The registered company address is: Gewerbestrasse 11, 6330 Cham, Switzerland

Preface

Welcome to the proceedings of the 21st China National Conference on Computational Linguistics (CCL 2022). The conference and symposium were hosted and co-organized by Jiangxi Normal University, China.

CCL is an annual conference (bi-annual before 2013) that started in 1991. It is the flagship conference of the Chinese Information Processing Society of China (CIPS), which is the largest NLP academic and industrial community in China. CCL is a premier nation-wide forum for disseminating new scholarly and technological work in computational linguistics, with a major emphasis on computer processing of the languages in China such as Mandarin, Tibetan, Mongolian, Kazakh, Uyghur and their dialects. The Program Committee selected 86 papers (64 Chinese papers and 22 English papers) out of 293 submissions for publication. The acceptance rate is 29.35%. The 22 English papers cover the following topics:

- Linguistics and Cognitive Science (1)
- Fundamental Theory and Methods of Computational Linguistics (2)
- Information Retrieval, Dialogue and Question Answering (5)
- Text Generation and Summarization (1)
- Knowledge Graph and Information Extraction (3)
- Machine Translation and Multilingual Information Processing (2)
- Minority Language Information Processing (1)
- Language Resource and Evaluation (2)
- NLP Applications (5)

The final program for the 21st CCL was the result of intense work by many dedicated colleagues. We want to thank, first of all, the authors who submitted their papers, contributing to the creation of the high-quality program. We are deeply indebted to all the Program Committee members for providing high-quality and insightful reviews under a tight schedule, and extremely grateful to the sponsors of the conference. Finally, we extend a special word of thanks to all the colleagues of the Organizing Committee and secretariat for their hard work in organizing the conference, and to Springer for their assistance in publishing the proceedings in due time.

We thank the Program and Organizing Committees for helping to make the conference successful, and we hope all the participants enjoyed the CCL conference in Nanchang.

October 2022

Maosong Sun
Yang Liu
Wanxiang Che
Yang Feng
Xipeng Qiu

Organization

Program Committee

Conference Chairs

Maosong Sun   Tsinghua University, China
Yang Liu   Tsinghua University, China

Program Chairs

Wanxiang Che   Harbin Institute of Technology, China
Yang Feng   Institute of Computing Technology, CAS, China
Xipeng Qiu   Fudan University, China

Area Co-chairs

Linguistics and Cognitive Science

Weidong Zhan   Peking University, China
Jingxia Lin   Nanyang Technological University, Singapore

Basic Theories and Methods of Computational Linguistics

Kewei Tu   ShanghaiTech University, China
Tao Yu   The University of Hong Kong, China

Information Retrieval, Dialogue and Question Answering

Shaochun Ren   Shandong University, China
Jie Yang   Technische Universiteit Delft, Netherlands

Text Generation and Summarization

Xiaocheng Feng   Harbin Institute of Technology, China
Lifu Huang   Virginia Polytechnic Institute and State University, USA

Knowledge Graph and Information Extraction

Shizhu He   Institute of Automation, CAS, China
Yangqiu Song   The Hong Kong University of Science and Technology, China

Machine Translation and Multi-Language Information Processing

Jingsong Su   Xiamen University, China
Jiatao Gu   Meta, USA

Minority Language Information Processing

Aishan Wumaier   Xinjiang University, China
Huaque Cairang   Qinghai Normal University, China

Language Resources and Evaluation

Muyun Yang   Harbin Institute of Technology, China
Yunfei Long   University of Essex, England

Social Computing and Sentiment Analysis

Tieyun Qian   Wuhan University, China
Lidong Bing   Alibaba DAMO Academy, China

NLP Applications

Richong Zhang   Beihang University, China
Meng Jiang   University of Notre Dame, USA
Liang Pang   Institute of Computing Technology, CAS, China

Local Arrangement Chairs

Mingwen Wang   Jiangxi Normal University, China
Jiali Zuo   Jiangxi Normal University, China

Evaluation Chairs

Hongfei Lin   Dalian University of Technology, China
Zhenghua Li   Soochow University, China

Publication Chairs

Gaoqi Rao   Beijing Language and Culture University, China
Yubo Chen   Institute of Automation, CAS, China

Chair of Frontier Forum

Zhiyuan Liu   Tsinghua University, China

Workshop Chairs

Jiajun Zhang   Institute of Automation, CAS, China
Rui Yan   Peking University, China

Sponsorship Chairs

Qi Zhang   Fudan University, China
Tong Xiao   Northeastern University, China

Publicity Chair

Ruifeng Xu   Harbin Institute of Technology, China

Website Chair

Shujian Huang   Nanjing University, China

System Demonstration Chairs

Min Peng   Wuhan University, China
Weinan Zhang   Harbin Institute of Technology, China

Student Seminar Chairs

Xianpei Han   Institute of Software, CAS, China
Zhuosheng Zhang   Shanghai Jiao Tong University, China

Finance Chair

Yuxing Wang   Tsinghua University, China

Reviewers

Aihetamujiang Aihemaiti   XinJiang Technical Institute of Physics and Chemistry,
                              CAS, China
Bin Li   Nanjing Normal University, China
Bo Chen   Institute of Software, CAS, China
Chen Chen   Nankai University, China
Chi Chen   Tsinghua University, China
Chi Hu   Northeastern University, China
Fang Kong   Soochow University, China
Gang Jin   Hohhot Minzu College, China
Gaole He   Delft University of Technology, Netherlands
Gaoqi Rao   Beijing Language and Culture University, China
Guangming Huang   University of Essex, UK
Halidanmu Abudukelimu   Xinjiang University of Finance and Economics, China
Hao Huang   Xinjiang University, China
Heng Chen   Guangdong University of Foreign Studies, China
Heng Gong   Harbin Institute of Technology, China

Hongfei Jiang	Wobang Educational Technology (Beijing) Co., Ltd., China
Hongkun Hao	Shanghai Jiao Tong University, China
Hongshen Chen	JD, China
HuiChen Hsiao	National Taiwan Normal University, China
Jiafei Hong	National Taiwan Normal University, China
Jiahuan Li	Nanjing University, China
Jiawei Chen	University of Science and Technology of China, China
Jin Huang	University of Amsterdam, Netherlands
Jinguang Gu	Wuhan University of Science and Technology, China
Jingwei Cheng	Northeastern University, China
Jinhua Gao	Institute of Computing Technology, CAS, China
Junfan Chen	Beihang University, China
Junguo Zhu	Kunming University of Science and Technology, China
Junwei Bao	JD, China
Kaiyu Huang	Tsinghua University, China
Kehai Chen	Harbin Institute of Technology (Shenzhen), China
Kunyu Qi	Northwest Minzu University, China
Lei Lei	Shanghai Jiao Tong University, China
Leilei Kong	Foshan University, China
Liying Cheng	Singapore University of Technology and Design, Singapore
Luyi Bai	Northeastern University at Qinhuangdao, China
Mao Cunli	Kunming University of Science and Technology, China
Minxuan Feng	Nanjing Normal University, China
Pengzhi Gao	Baidu, China
Qian Li	Beihang University, China
Qianqian Dong	ByteDance AI Lab, China
Qinan Hu	Institute of Linguistics, CASS, China
Ren-feng Duann	National Taitung University, China
Rile Hu	Beijing Yuzhi Yunfan Technology Co., Ltd, China
Shaoru Guo	Institute of Automation, CAS, China
Shen Gao	Peking University, China
Shengxiang Gao	Kunming University of Science and Technology, China
Shi Feng	Northeastern University, China
Shuaichen Chang	The Ohio State University, USA
Shuyang Jiang	Peking University, China
Si Ha	Hohhot Minzu College, China
Sisi Huang	Huaqiao University, China
Wanqing Cui	University of Chinese Academy of Sciences, China
Wanyu Chen	National University of Defense Technology, China
Wei Hu	Nanjing University, China
Xiachong Feng	Harbin Institute of Technology, China
Xiang Ao	Institute of Computing Technology, CAS, China
Xiang Deng	The Ohio Student University, USA
Xiaocheng Feng	Harbin Institute of Technology, China

Xiaohui Guo	Beihang University, China
Xiaojing Bai	Language Centre, Tsinghua University, China
Xiaopeng Bai	East China Normal University, China
Xiaotong Jiang	Soochow University, China
Xingyu Chen	Shanghai Jiao Tong University, China
Xinwei Geng	Harbin Institute of Technology, China
Xiuying Chen	KAUST, Saudi Arabia
Yan Wang	Tencent AI Lab, China
Yanan Cao	Institute of Information Engineering, CAS, China
Yang Gao	Beijing Institute of Technology, China
Yi Cai	South China University of Technology, China
Yichong Huang	Harbin Institute of Technology, China
Yidong Chen	Xiamen University, China
Yixing Fan	Institute of Computing Technology, CAS, China
Yong Chen	Beijing University of Posts and Telecommunications, China
Yu Bai	Beijing Institute of Technology, China
Yu Bao	Byte Dance, China
Yubo Chen	Institute of Automation, CAS, China
Yufeng Chen	Beijing Jiaotong University, China
Yushi Hu	University of Washington, USA
Yusup Azragul	Xinjiang Normal University, China
Yuwei Huang	Baidu, China
Yuxin Huang	Kunming University of Science and Technology, China
Yuxuan Gu	Harbin Institute of Technology, China
Zhenguo Kang	Hebei Normal University, China
Zhiwei He	Shanghai Jiao Tong University, China
Zhongyuan Han	Foshan University, China
Zhoujun Cheng	Shanghai Jiao Tong University, China
Wugedele Bao	Hohhot Minzu College, China

Organizers

Chinese Information Processing Society of China

Tsinghua University

Jiangxi Normal University, China

Publishers

Lecture Notes in Artificial Intelligence, Springer

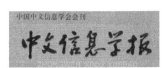

Journal of Chinese Information Processing

Science China

Journal of Tsinghua University (Science and Technology)

Sponsoring Institutions

Gold

Silver

PARATERA 并行®

Bronze

Contents

NLP Applications

Linguistics and Cognitive Science

Discourse Markers as the Classificatory Factors of Speech Acts

Da Qi[1]👤, Chenliang Zhou[1]👤, and Haitao Liu[1,2(✉)]👤

[1] Department of Linguistics, Zhejiang University, Hangzhou, China
{da.qi,cl.zhou,htliu}@zju.edu.cn
[2] Center for Linguistics and Applied Linguistics, Guangdong University of Foreign Studies, Guangzhou, China

Abstract. Since the debut of the speech act theory, the classification standards of speech acts have been in dispute. Traditional abstract taxonomies seem insufficient to meet the needs of artificial intelligence for identifying and even understanding speech acts. To facilitate the automatic identification of the communicative intentions in human dialogs, scholars have tried some data-driven methods based on speech-act annotated corpora. However, few studies have objectively evaluated those classification schemes. In this regard, the current study applied the frequencies of the eleven discourse markers (*oh, well, and, but, or, so, because, now, then, I mean,* and *you know*) proposed by Schiffrin [24] to investigate whether they can be effective indicators of speech act variations. The results showed that the five speech acts of *Agreement* can be well classified in terms of their functions by the frequencies of discourse markers. Moreover, it was found that the discourse markers *well* and *oh* are rather efficacious in differentiating distinct speech acts. This paper indicates that quantitative indexes can reflect the characteristics of human speech acts, and more objective and data-based classification schemes might be achieved based on these metrics.

Keywords: Speech act · Discourse marker · Hierarchical cluster analysis

1 Discourse Markers and the (Dis)agreement Continuum

A discourse marker (DM) is a word or phrase that people often use in the process of communication, and its main function is to coordinate and organize discourse to ensure the smooth flow of conversation. In addition, as a carrier of pragmatic information, it usually reflects speakers' mental states and communicative intentions, thus facilitating pragmatic inference [9]. In this regard, Fraser [8, p. 68] defined DMs as "linguistically encoded clues which signal the speaker's potential communicative intentions". Although scholars have never reached a consensus on the definition of DMs, no one would doubt their diverse discursive functions and the capability to transmit communicative intentions.

M. Sun et al. (Eds.): CCL 2022, LNAI 13603, pp. 3–16, 2022.
https://doi.org/10.1007/978-3-031-18315-7_1

When analyzing the functions of DMs, scholars also differ considerably in terms of their frameworks and research paradigms. Ariel [3] distinguished DMs from a semantic perspective: a DM either possesses a semantic meaning, which is interpreted in a particular context with some connection to its form (e.g., *and* and *I mean*); or it does not contain any semantic information (e.g., *well* and *oh*). However, Matei [17] pointed out that although some DMs contain rich semantic information, there are particular contexts in which the communicative intention it conveys is not related to the semantic information it carries. For example, in some cases, the DM *and* can be used as a discourse continuative, filler word, and buffer term, etc.

Some scholars analyzed the range of functions through the functional-cognitive approach, which shows that DMs have a specific rather than a completely arbitrary range of functions [7,21]. Ariel [3, pp. 242–243] also expressed support for the non-arbitrary nature of DM functions. She explicated this view in terms of the correspondence between form and function and argued that there are two probabilistically similar possibilities for the form-function correspondence, one in which a form corresponds to multiple functions and the other in which a function corresponds to multiple forms. She further claimed that these two possible relationships do not indicate syntactic arbitrariness but are characterized by unpredictability since the same form may evolve to express many innovative meanings. In this sense, functionalists argue that the universality of DM forms (as opposed to the uniformity of forms) is functionally driven.

The above investigations of DM functions have helped us to gain a deep and broad understanding of DMs' nature and their functional orientations in various contexts. However, as Matei [17] mentioned, there is a great deal of uncertainty in DMs' functions, and even those with a relatively fixed semantic meaning may produce new and rare uses in some contexts. In addition, the *one form - many functions* and *one function - many forms* nature of DMs, as well as the innovative nature of their functions, also make their functions perform in a variety of ways. Thus, it is difficult to assess all the functions of DMs through an in-depth analysis of the discourse material one by one (the workload is too large). If we want to characterize all aspects of certain DMs and explore the patterns of these linguistic units full of uncertainties and probabilities, it is better to apply an approach that is suitable for approximating all the features possessed by the DMs.

Another consideration in employing this approach is that human communicative intentions are themselves fraught with probabilities and uncertainties. As pointed out by the Speech Act Theory, there is not always a clear correspondence between the words people express and their functions, and speech acts are also characteristic of *one form - many functions* and *one function - many forms* as mentioned by Ariel [3,11]. A more extreme example, such as *Kennst du das Land wo die Zitronen blühen?* (Knowest thou the land where the lemon trees bloom?), can even express the communicative intention "I am a German soldier" [25]. By the same token, the various DMs proposed by previous authors, such as the eleven DMs by Schiffrin [24] (*oh, well, and, but, or, so, because, now, then, I mean,* and *you know*), may occur in various speech acts depending on the specific speech context.

To address the function of DMs and the probability and uncertainty of human communicative intentions, the present paper tries to introduce some basic probabilistic and statistical methods, such as the hierarchical cluster analysis (HCA), to quantitatively analyze the DMs contained in specific communicative intentions. Our aim is to examine whether certain indicators of DM (e.g., their percentage of frequency of occurrence in different speech acts) can effectively distinguish the communicative functions embodied in differing speech acts to propose a new research methodology for DM-related studies.

In the current study, the frequency of different DMs in differing speech acts was investigated as a possible defining feature for the distinction of communicative intentions. The reason for doing so is that DMs carry diverse pragmatic and contextual information [21]. In this regard, the frequency of DMs may reflect the pragmatic characteristics of different speech acts, which may help us better explore the patterns of human communicative intentions.

Since we want to examine whether the frequency of DMs can effectively distinguish different speech acts, these DMs should first be able to reflect the differences between speech acts that differ significantly, e.g., agreement and disagreement, thanks and apology, etc. Next, we may examine whether it can reflect the slight differences between similar speech acts. Therefore, in the current paper, we applied the continuum of (dis)agreement (*accept, partially accept, hedge, partially reject,* and *reject*) as the object of study to explore whether the frequency distribution of DMs can accurately capture the nuanced differences in speech acts.

When analyzing the agreement-disagreement continuum, scholars have mostly focused on the perception of agreement- and disagreement-like speech acts by people in specific types of discourses. For example, Mulkay [19] found that strong disagreement is easier to declare in writing than face to face after examining the written letters by biochemists. When investigating the arguments of mentally disabled people, Hewitt et al.'s [10] study showed that regarding conflict resolution as the primary goal of arguments detracts from the true nature of verbal conflicts - they reflect a social continuum of agreement and disagreement [12]. Trimboli and Walker [27] compared dyadic discussions following initial agreement and disagreement and found that disagreement was more competitive, characterized by high rates of verbalization, increased numbers of turns, more frequent interruptions, and reduced back channels.

From the studies above, it can be seen that agreement and disagreement are complex and influenced by various socio-cultural factors, but the specific mechanisms of their intricacies have been seldom studied, and a more systematic and comprehensive understanding has yet to be developed. In the current study, we attempted to employ the frequency of DMs as well as probabilistic and statistical methods to examine the speech acts of agreement and disagreement, complementing the existent findings in discourse analysis.

The research questions of this paper are as follows.

1. How is the frequency distribution of different DMs under the differing speech acts in the agreement-disagreement continuum?
2. Can the frequency of DMs effectively reflect the similarity and peculiarity of the different speech acts?

2   Methods and Materials

2.1   The Hierarchical Cluster Analysis (HCA)

The HCA is an algorithm for clustering the given data. It regards all the data input as a single cluster and then recursively divides each cluster into two subclasses. It enjoys a relatively long history in the study of communicative intentions, including the Speech Act Theory. In the 1960s, scholars had already proposed that human communicative behavior could be structured hierarchically [22,23]. Some researchers then innovatively employed hierarchical organizations for speech acts to analyze specific types of discourse, e.g., therapeutic discourse [15] or interpersonal behavior [6].

Furthermore, some pragmaticians in recent years started to analyze the data in their experiments with the HCA, especially when they probed into the relationship between existing classificatory schemes and people's perception of a given set of speech acts [11,16]. Though word frequency and other textual indices were not applied in their studies, it can be revealed that the HCA may be effective in speech act-related research.

As DMs indicate contextual information and pragmatic relationship, their frequency of use in utterances could be seen as an indicator of speech act. It is then plausible to examine whether these objective indices can be hierarchically clustered in a way that demonstrates the functional similarities and variations between different speech acts.

2.2   The Switchboard Dialog Act Corpus (SwDA)

The SwDA consists of 1,155 five-minute conversations, including around 205,000 utterances and 1.4 million words from the Switchboard corpus of telephone conversations [14,20]. The dialogs in this corpus all happened between two individuals of different ages, genders, and education levels, and the speech acts of speakers were annotated according to how participants might expect one sort of conversational units to be responded to by another. One of the SwDA's merits is that there can be more than one speech act within each utterance. This annotation scheme perfectly corresponds with the ideas of Labov and Fanshel, who criticized the one-utterance-to-one-speech act method of identifying speech acts in dialogs [15]. In this regard, the results obtained through the SwDA may be an accurate reflection of the speech act patterns in human beings' daily dialogs.

According to Jurafsky et al. [14], there are four sets of speech act hypercategories that have enough data and meaningful sub-categories - *Agreement, Understanding, Answer,* and *Information Request.* With the 27 kinds of speech acts and the 11 DMs in the four hyper-categories, statistical tests can be conducted to get reliable results. Moreover, traditional speech act classifications such as Searle's [26], though important, may have some defects, e.g., their abstractness and the overemphasis on speakers. Thus, the SwDA can serve as an ideal research material by virtue of the following attributes.

First, the corpus makes a more detailed and clear distinction between the speech acts of agreement and disagreement. According to Jurafsky et al.'s [14] classification criteria, speech acts expressing speakers' attitudes are distinguished into a continuum containing five subcategories - direct approval (Agree/Accept), partial approval (Maybe/Accept-part), hold before positive answers (Hedge), partial negation (Dispreferred Answers/Reject-part), and direct negation (Reject). All of them were annotated based on Allen and Core's [1] decision tree (see Fig. 1), which helped control the subjectivity and the disagreements of the annotators.

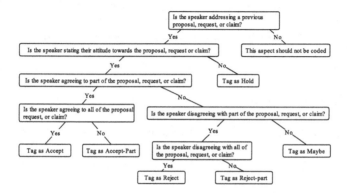

Fig. 1. The decision tree for annotating speech acts in the agreement-disagreement continuum.

Second, the SwDA was annotated based on a shallow discourse tag set, which can reduce the abstractness of the speech acts owing to the more direct description of human communicative intentions. In addition to that, eight labelers involved in the project spent about half an hour on labeling each conversation (the conversations lasted five minutes on average). The labeling accuracy and the impact of labelers' subjectivity was evaluated by the *Kappa statistic* [4,5,18], and the average pair-wise *Kappa* was .80, which indicated that the annotating results were acceptable [14].

We could thus explore not only whether the frequencies of DMs can effectively distinguish speakers' affective attitudes through the HCA, but also whether they can distinguish properties such as the degree of indirectness in communicative acts.

3   Results and Discussions

In this paper, the DM system (*oh, well, and, but, or, so, because, now, then, I mean,* and *you know*) proposed by Schiffrin [24] was employed to explore whether the frequencies of DMs can reflect the affinity relationship between different speech acts. This system, containing commonly occurring DMs and widely accepted by the academic community, can capture how the diverse DMs with distinctive functions demonstrate the similarities and peculiarities among different communicative intentions. As mentioned in Sect. 2, the current study analyzed the five speech acts in the SwDA that express agreement or disagreement because they present a typical continuum, which facilitates a more detailed examination of the results of data analysis.

The original text files of the five speech acts were firstly compiled. The five speech acts of *Agreement* contain altogether 24,816 words, among which Agree/Accept has 19,942 words, Maybe/Accept-part 528 words, Hedge 2,703 words, Dispreferred Answers 1,772 words, and Reject 942 words). Next, we applied Antconc 4.0.5 [2] to automatically get the total word count in the five speech acts, in which the frequency data of the eleven selected words/phrases proposed by Schiffrin [24] were extracted. Since the automatic process could not distinguish between the 11 words/phrases as DMs and other cases, the authors manually checked the automatically collected data to obtain the exact DM frequencies for follow-up analyses.

It should be noted here that the raw number of DM frequencies may affect the results of the statistical analysis due to the large variation in the total number of words in each speech act. In this regard, this paper calculated the percentages of each DM's frequency relative to the total word number to standardize the data. When converting the numbers to percentages, the authors distinguished two different kinds of DMs: one for single words (unigram), such as *oh, well,* etc., and the other for two consecutive words (bigram), *I mean* and *you know*. For the former types of DMs, we counted the percentages of DM frequencies relative to those of all unigrams in each speech act; for the latter, we calculated those of all bigrams, with the aim of making the standard uniform.

After collation and calculation, the frequency data of the eleven DMs proposed by Shiffrin [24] under each speech act were obtained, as shown in Table 1.

Table 1. The proportion of each DM to the total unigrams or bigrams under each speech act.

Speech act	oh	well	and	but	or	so	because	now	then	I mean	you know
Agree/Accept	0.0318	0.0117	0.0036	0.0015	0.0003	0.0011	0.0004	0.0004	0.0000	0.0031	0.0005
Maybe/Accept-part	0.0019	0.0455	0.0019	0.0019	0.0038	0.0000	0.0000	0.0000	0.0000	0.0000	0.0019
Hedge	0.0137	0.0396	0.0133	0.0074	0.0007	0.0067	0.0011	0.0037	0.0007	0.0033	0.0004
Dispreferred Answers	0.0045	0.0796	0.0034	0.0028	0.0000	0.0017	0.0000	0.0017	0.0006	0.0051	0.0006
Reject	0.0149	0.0658	0.0042	0.0138	0.0032	0.0011	0.0011	0.0021	0.0011	0.0053	0.0053

As can be seen from Table 1, there are significant differences in the proportion of DMs under each speech act, especially the difference between the proportion of *well* in the speech act of agreement and that of disagreement, in which the frequency of *well* is significantly higher than that in the speech act of agreement. In addition, the frequency of *well* in indirect speech acts is higher than that in the direct ones (Dispreferred Answers > Reject > Maybe/Accept-part > Hedge > Agree/Accept). This pattern may indicate a face-saving strategy at work in the politeness principle.

The following excerpts from the SwDA further illustrate the differences between agreement and disagreement as well as those between direct and indirect speech acts.

A. *Dispreferred Answers*
1) Well, I, I think, uh, my background is probably what absolutely turned me off with sixty minutes.
2) Well, I heard tonight on the news that he is willing to come down.
3) Well, I, I, I come from kind of a biased opinion because I'm a, a therapist and a drug and alcohol.
4) Well, that was, you know, with a, with a circular saw.

From the utterances containing *well* in the speech act of Dispreferred Answers, we can see that *well* mainly serves to provide a buffer for the subsequent words. In addition, since the speaker wants to express opposition to the words spoken by the hearer without completely opposing them, he or she tends to use the strategy of repetition (e.g., the repetition of *I* in A. 1) and A. 3)) or continue to apply other DMs as filler words to further moderate the illocutionary force of the speech act of opposition (e.g., *you know* in A. 4)). This phenomenon shows that people would frequently resort to the buffer DM *well* along with other means to minimize the force of opposition they are expressing.

B. *Reject*
1) Well, I don't think you can mail thing, guns through the mail.
2) Well, I doubt that.
3) Well, yes.

When expressing direct opposition to another speaker's opinions, the frequency of *well* is also higher due to the principle of politeness and the consideration of face-saving strategy. Although Reject and Agree/Accept are both direct speech acts, the use of buffer words like *well* in direct disagreement is still significantly higher than that in direct agreement (Reject: 0.0658 > Agree/Accept: 0.0117).

C. *Maybe/Accept-part*
1) Well, even if it's not technical. If it's, uh, some social thing or whatever. It doesn't matter.

D. *Hedge*
1) Well, uh, it's funny, when I tried, to make the call the other days,

E. *Agree/Accept*
1) Oh, well yeah.
2) Well, that's true.

Among the three speech acts concerning agreement (Agree/Accept, Maybe/Accept-part, and Hedge), the use of *well* is more convergent, serving as a simple tone buffer, and does not involve a strategy of face protection for the other interlocutor. According to previous studies on *well*, it is often employed as a delay device and a pragmatic marker of insufficiency, indicating the problems with the content of the current or the previous utterances, or as a face-threat mitigator, showing the conflicts in the interpersonal level [13]. Although *well* has a relatively fixed spectrum of discourse functions, its frequency of occurrence varies across discourses expressing different communicative intentions, depending on the specific context and the nature of probability within speakers' language use. Therefore, to accurately capture how the frequency of *well* in different speech acts reflects their affinities, it is best to apply a more suitable method to study these probabilistic linguistic units.

Moreover, from the above analysis, *well* is a DM that can effectively distinguish between agreement and disagreement; however, people cannot merely use *well* when expressing these communicative functions; DMs such as *you know* and *and* also frequently occur in these speech acts. In order to comprehensively and systematically grasp how the frequency of DMs reflects the differences of each speech act, we included in the present study a more comprehensive DM system (that proposed by Schiffrin). Meanwhile, to avoid the overwhelming workload caused by manual qualitative analysis, we adopted established statistical methods to grasp the characteristics embodied in DMs accurately. The *factoextra* and *cluster* packages in *R* were applied to perform an HCA on the data in Table 1. The results are shown in Fig. 2.

Figure 2a demonstrates that the clustering results based on the frequency of the eleven DMs neatly reflect the functions of the five speech acts under the *Agreement* hyper-category. The results show a tripartite classification, with Dispreferred Answers and Reject clustered together, Maybe/Accept-part and Hedge in the same cluster, and Agree/Accept in a separate cluster out of the above four speech acts. Hence, we can roughly get a "reject" cluster and an "accept" one in *Agreement*. Nevertheless, this result still has some imperfections: Agree/Accept is clustered out of the other four speech acts, while its function is similar to the "accept" category. After trying different method-distance combinations of the HCA, it was found that the aforementioned classification enjoys the highest probability of occurrence.

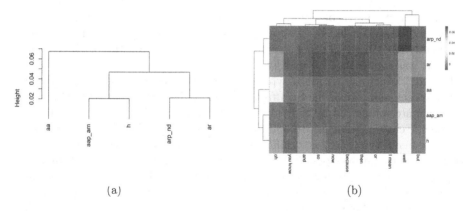

$$(a) \qquad\qquad\qquad (b)$$

Fig. 2. (a) The HCA results of the five speech acts in *Agreement*. (b) The HCA results of speech acts (in rows) using the Manhattan distance and the Ward.D2 method. *aa* is referred to as Agree/Accept, *aap_ am* is Maybe/Accept-part, *h* is Hedge, *arp_ nd* is Dispreferred Answers, and *ar* is Reject.

We then further altered the combination of clustering methods and distances and found that using the Manhattan distance together with the Ward.D2 method produced a clustering result consistent with the functional division of the speech acts in *Agreement* (see Fig. 2b)[1]. Moreover, the top panel in Fig. 2b displays the clustering result of each DM based on their frequency of use. The cluster of *well* and *but* further corroborates our previous analysis of *well*'s frequent appearance in the speech acts concerning disagreement.

After obtaining the above clustering results, we employed the *cluster* package in *R* to get the proportion of each DM in each cluster for a more detailed analysis. The distribution of DMs' frequency proportions when there are two clusters (henceforth Type A clustering) and three ones (henceforth Type B clustering) are shown in Table 2 and Table 3, respectively.

Table 2. The percentages of DM frequencies in different clusters (Type A).

Cluster	Oh	Well	And	But	Or	So	Because	Now	Then	You know	I mean
A	0.0158	0.0322	0.0063	0.0036	0.0016	0.0026	0.0005	0.0014	0.0002	0.0021	0.0009
B	0.0097	0.0727	0.0038	0.0083	0.0016	0.0014	0.0005	0.0019	0.0008	0.0052	0.0029

Note: Cluster A is the cluster of Agree/Accept, Maybe/Accept-part, and Hedge, and Cluster B is Dispreferred Answers and Reject.

---

[1] For all the clustering results using different methods and distance metrics, see Appendix A.

From the data in Table 2 and Table 3, the reason Agree/Accept is separated as an individual cluster in Fig. 2a is probably because *oh* appears significantly more frequently in it than in other speech acts. After analyzing the original corpus data, it was found that *oh* usually appears in expressions such as "Oh yes" or "Oh yeah", which constitute a typical feature of Agree/Accept compared with other speech acts. Also, the high frequency of *oh* indicates that most clustering methods are influenced by individual salient values, which lead to the changes in specific cluster branches. In addition, the results in Table 2 and Table 3 show that the frequency of *well* is significantly higher when it expresses negative views than when it expresses positive ones. Since the other DMs accounted for lower frequencies and contributed less to the clustering results, the results obtained in this study may indicate that the two DMs, *well* and *oh*, are more effective in distinguishing between the speech acts of agreement and disagreement. This result also further complements the previous studies on the principle of politeness and the face theory, providing new perspectives for future systematic research on pragmatic principles with large-scale corpus data.

Table 3. The percentages of DM frequencies in different clusters (Type B).

Cluster	oh	well	and	but	or	so	because	now	then	you know	I mean
C	0.0318	0.0117	0.0036	0.0015	0.0003	0.0011	0.0004	0.0004	0.0000	0.0031	0.0005
D	0.0078	0.0425	0.0076	0.0046	0.0023	0.0033	0.0006	0.0018	0.0004	0.0017	0.0011
E	0.0097	0.0727	0.0038	0.0083	0.0016	0.0014	0.0005	0.0019	0.0008	0.0052	0.0029

Note: Cluster C is the cluster of Agree/Accept, Cluster D is Maybe/Accept-part and Hedge, and Cluster E is Dispreferred Answers and Reject.

In summary, from the above analysis, it can be concluded that by employing a method that can accurately grasp the statistical patterns of linguistic units, we may be able to better capture the tendency of each speech act in using DMs and establish the connection between the two important constructions (*speech acts* and *DMs*) with the support from real data. This approach can complement well-developed qualitative analyses of DMs, provide more comprehensive and theoretically supported results (e.g., the DM classification system proposed by Schiffrin), and introduce the advantages of quantitative analysis (big data, objectivity, and accuracy) into the research related to pragmatics and discourse analysis.

4   Conclusions and Implications

In this study, we adopted a quantitative approach to analyze whether DMs, the discourse units that possess discursive and pragmatic information, can effectively distinguish the speech acts of different communicative functions. After calculating the frequencies of the 11 DMs proposed in Schiffrin [24], we conducted an HCA using R for the examination of such effects. The results showed that the frequencies of DMs were efficacious in differentiating the speech acts of agreement and disagreement. Moreover, the frequencies of DMs also well reflect the intricacies within the indirectness of the five speech acts in the agreement-disagreement continuum, corroborating that DMs are rather precise indicators of speech acts' differences.

The results also indicated that the frequencies of *well* and *oh* might be the key indicators to distinguish between the speech acts of agreement and disagreement, especially *well*, the frequencies of which echo the previous findings in the principle of politeness and the face theory. In this regard, the application of quantitative measures for testing and generalizing the existent theoretical framework may help the research related to pragmatics and discourse analysis develop in a scientific and precise direction. The deficiencies of traditional qualitative research in terms of data size can thus be supplemented by conducting research on the authentic data from large-scale corpus.

In addition, since the current study only examined the five speech acts under the continuum of agreement and disagreement, the patterns found may not fully reflect the patterns in all types of speech acts. Therefore, subsequent studies can further collect the natural corpus data of human conversations and examine more types of speech acts to further explore the effectiveness of DM frequency in reflecting human conversational behaviors. In this way, we may establish a more comprehensive framework for quantitative research in pragmatics and discourse analysis.

Acknowledgements. The authors are grateful to the three anonymous reviewers for providing helpful feedback on this paper.

Appendix A. The Clustering Results of the Frequencies of Discourse Markers in the Speech Acts of Agreement

(See Fig. 3).

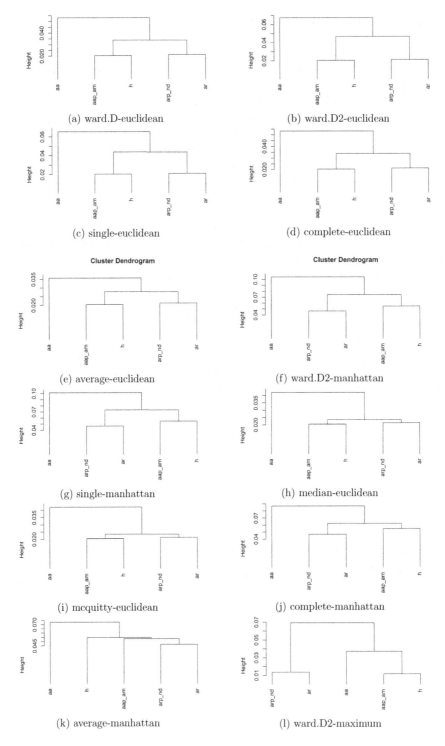

Fig. 3. The clustering results of the frequencies of DMs in the speech acts of *Agreement*.

References

1. Allen, J., Core, M.: Draft of DAMSL: dialog act markup in several layers (1997). http://www.fb10.uni-bremen.de/anglistik/ling/ss07/discourse-materials/DAMSL97.pdf
2. Anthony, L.: Antconc 4.0.5. Waseda University (2021)
3. Ariel, M.: Discourse markers and form-function correlations. In: Jucker, A.H., Ziv, Y. (eds.) Discourse Markers: Descriptions and Theory, pp. 223–260. John Benjamins, Philadelphia (1998)
4. Carletta, J.: Assessing agreement on classification tasks: the kappa statistic. Comput. Linguist. **22**(2), 249–254 (1996)
5. Carletta, J., Isard, A., Isard, S., Kowtko, J.C., Doherty-Sneddon, G., Anderson, A.H.: The reliability of a dialogue structure coding scheme. Comput. Linguist. **23**(1), 13–31 (1997)
6. D'Andrade, R.G., Wish, M.: Speech act theory in quantitative research on interpersonal behavior. Discourse Process. **8**(2), 229–259 (1985). https://doi.org/10.1080/01638538509544615
7. Fischer, K.: Frames, constructions, and invariant meanings: the functional polysemy of discourse particles. In: Fischer, K. (ed.) Approaches to Discourse Particles, pp. 427–447. Elsevier, Oxford (2006)
8. Fraser, B.: Pragmatic markers. Pragmatics **6**(2), 167–190 (1996). https://doi.org/10.1075/prag.6.2.03fra
9. Furkó, P.B.: Discourse Markers and Beyond: Descriptive and Critical Perspectives on Discourse-Pragmatic Devices Across Genres and Languages. Springer, Cham (2020). https://doi.org/10.1007/978-3-030-37763-2
10. Hewitt, L.E., Duchan, J.F., Segal, E.M.: Structure and function of verbal conflicts among adults with mental retardation. Discourse Process. **16**(4), 525–543 (1993). https://doi.org/10.1080/01638539309544852
11. Holtgraves, T.: The production and perception of implicit performatives. J. Pragmat. **37**(12), 2024–2043 (2005). https://doi.org/10.1016/j.pragma.2005.03.005
12. Jacobs, S., Jackson, S.: Argument as a natural category: the routine grounds for arguing in conversation. W. Jo. Speech Commun. **45**(2), 118–132 (1981). https://doi.org/10.1080/10570318109374035
13. Jucker, A.H.: The discourse marker well: a relevance-theoretical account. J. Pragmat. **19**(5), 435–452 (1993). https://doi.org/10.1016/0378-2166(93)90004-9
14. Jurafsky, D., Shriberg, L., Biasca, D.: Switchboard SWBD-DAMSL shallow-discourse-function annotation coders manual, draft 13 (1997). https://web.stanford.edu/~jurafsky/ws97/manual.august1.html
15. Labov, W., Fanshel, D.: Therapeutic Discourse: Psychotherapy as Conversation. Academic Press, New York (1977)
16. Liu, S.: An experimental study of the classification and recognition of Chinese speech acts. J. Pragmat. **43**(6), 1801–1817 (2011). https://doi.org/10.1016/j.pragma.2010.10.031
17. Matei, M.: Discourse markers as functional elements. Bull. Transilvania Univ. Braşov **3**(52), 119–126 (2010)
18. McHugh, M.L.: Interrater reliability: the kappa statistic. Biochemia Med. **22**(3), 276–282 (2012)
19. Mulkay, M.: Agreement and disagreement in conversations and letters. Text - Interdisc. J. Study Discourse **5**(3), 201–228 (1985). https://doi.org/10.1515/text.1.1985.5.3.201

20. Potts, C.: Switchboard Dialog Act Corpus with Penn Treebank links (2022). https://github.com/cgpotts/swda
21. Redeker, G.: Discourse markers as attentional cues at discourse transitions running head: discourse transitions. In: Fischer, K. (ed.) Approaches to Discourse Particles, pp. 339–358. Brill, Leiden, The Netherlands (2006). https://doi.org/10.1163/9780080461588_019
22. Scheflen, A.E.: Stream and Structure of Communicational Behavior: Context Analysis of a Psychotherapy Session. Eastern Pennsylvania Psychiatric Institute, Philadelphia (1965)
23. Scheflen, A.E.: On the structuring of human communication. Am. Behav. Sci. **10**(8), 8–12 (1967). https://doi.org/10.1177/0002764201000803
24. Schiffrin, D.: Discourse Markers. Studies in Interactional Sociolinguistics, Cambridge University Press, Cambridge (1987). https://doi.org/10.1017/CBO9780511611841
25. Searle, J.R.: Speech Acts: An Essay in the Philosophy of Language. Cambridge University Press, Cambridge (1969). https://doi.org/10.1017/CBO9781139173438
26. Searle, J.R.: A classification of illocutionary acts. Lang. Soc. **5**(1), 1–23 (1976). https://doi.org/10.1017/S0047404500006837
27. Trimboli, C., Walker, M.B.: Switching pauses in cooperative and competitive conversations. J. Exp. Soc. Psychol. **20**(4), 297–311 (1984). https://doi.org/10.1016/0022-1031(84)90027-1

Fundamental Theory and Methods
of Computational Linguistics

DIFM: An Effective Deep Interaction and Fusion Model for Sentence Matching

Kexin Jiang, Yahui Zhao[(⊠)], and Rongyi Cui

Department of Computer Science and Technology, Yanbian University, Yanji, China
{2020010075,yhzhao,cuirongyi}@ybu.edu.cn

Abstract. Natural language sentence matching is the task of comparing two sentences and identifying the relationship between them. It has a wide range of applications in natural language processing tasks such as reading comprehension, question and answer systems. The main approach is to compute the interaction between text representations and sentence pairs through an attention mechanism, which can extract the semantic information between sentence pairs well. However, this kind of methods fail to capture deep semantic information and effectively fuse the semantic information of the sentence. To solve this problem, we propose a sentence matching method based on deep interaction and fusion. We first use pre-trained word vectors Glove and character-level word vectors to obtain word embedding representations of the two sentences. In the encoding layer, we use bidirectional LSTM to encode the sentence pairs. In the interaction layer, we initially fuse the information of the sentence pairs to obtain low-level semantic information; at the same time, we use the bi-directional attention in the machine reading comprehension model and self-attention to obtain the high-level semantic information. We use a heuristic fusion function to fuse the low-level semantic information and the high-level semantic information to obtain the final semantic information, and finally we use the neural network to predict the answer. We evaluate our model on two tasks: text implication recognition and paraphrase recognition. We conducted experiments on the SNLI datasets for the recognizing textual entailment task, the Quora dataset for the paraphrase recognition task. The experimental results show that the proposed algorithm can effectively fuse different semantic information that verify the effectiveness of the algorithm on sentence matching tasks.

Keywords: Natural language sentence matching · Bilateral attention mechanism · Self-attention mechanism

1 Introduction

Natural language sentence matching is the task of comparing two sentences and identifying the relationship between them. It is a fundamental technique for a variety of tasks. For example, in the paraphrase recognition task, it is used to determine whether two sentences are paraphrased. In the text implication recognition task, it is possible to determine whether a hypothetical sentence can be inferred from a predicate sentence.

© The Author(s), under exclusive license to Springer Nature Switzerland AG 2022
M. Sun et al. (Eds.): CCL 2022, LNAI 13603, pp. 19–30, 2022.
https://doi.org/10.1007/978-3-031-18315-7_2

Recognizing Textual Entailment (RTE), proposed by Dagan [6], is a study of the relationship between premises and assumptions. It mainly includes entailment, contradiction, and neutrality. The main methods for recognizing textual entailment include the following: similarity-based methods [15], rule-based methods [11], alignment feature-based machine learning methods [18], etc. However, These methods can't perform well in recognition because they didn't extract the semantic information of the sentences well. In recent years, deep learning-based methods have been effective in semantic modeling, achieving good results in many tasks in NLP [12,13,23]. Therefore, on the task of recognizing textual entailment, deep learning-based methods have outperformed earlier approaches and become the dominant recognizing textual entailment method. For example, Bowman *et al.* used recurrent neural networks to model premises and hypotheses, which have the advantage of making full use of syntactic information [2]. After that, he first applied LSTM sentence models to the RTE domain by encoding premises and hypotheses through LSTM to obtain sentence vectors [3]. WANG *et al.* proposed mLSTM model on this basis, which focuses on splicing attention weights in the hidden states of the LSTM, focusing on the part of the semantic match between the premise and the hypothesis. The experimental results showed that the method achieved good results on the SNLI dataset [20].

Paraphrase recognition is also called paraphrase detection. The task of paraphrase recognition is to determine whether two texts hold the same meaning. If they have the same meaning, they are called paraphrase pairs. Traditional paraphrase recognition methods focus on text features. However, there are problems such as low accuracy rate. Therefore, deep learning-based paraphrase recognition methods have become a hot research topic. Deep learning-based paraphrase recognition methods are mainly divided into two types; 1) calculated word vectors by neural networks, and then calculated word vector distances to determine whether they were paraphrase pairs. For example, Huang *et al.* used an improved EMD method to calculate the semantic distance between vectors and obtain the interpretation relationship [7]. 2) Directly determining whether a text pair is a paraphrased pair by a neural network model, which is essentially a binary classification algorithm. Wang *et al.* proposed the BIMPM model, which first encodes sentence pairs by a bidirectional LSTM and then matches the encoding results from multiple perspectives in both directions [21]. Chen *et al.* proposed an ESIM model that uses a two-layer bidirectional LSTM and a self-attention mechanism for encoding, then it extracts features through the average pooling layer and the maximum pooling layer, and finally performs classification [5].

These models mentioned above have achieved good results on specific tasks, but most of these models have difficulty extracting deep semantic information and effectively fusing the extracted semantic information, in this paper, we propose a sentence matching model based on deep interaction and fusion. We use the bi-directional attention and self-attention to obtain the high-level semantic information. Then, we use a heuristic fusion function to fuse the low-level semantic information and the high-level semantic information to obtain the final semantic information. We conducted experiments on the SNLI datasets for the recognizing textual entailment task, the Quora dataset for the paraphrase recognition task. The results showed that the accuracy of the proposed algorithm on the SNLI test set is 87.1%, and the accuracy of the Quora test set is 86.8%. Our contributions can be summarized as follows:

- We propose a sentence matching model based on deep interaction and fusion. It introduces bidirectional attention mechanism into sentence matching task for the first time.
- We propose a heuristic fusion function. It can learn the weights of fusion by neural network to achieve deep fusion.
- We evaluate our model on two different tasks and Validate the effectiveness of the model.

2 BIDAF Model Based on Bi-directional Attention Flow

In the task of extractive machine reading comprehension, Seo *et al.* first proposed a bi-directional attention flow model BIDAF (Bi-Directional Attention Flow) for question-to-article and article-to-question [16]. Its structure is shown in Fig. 1.

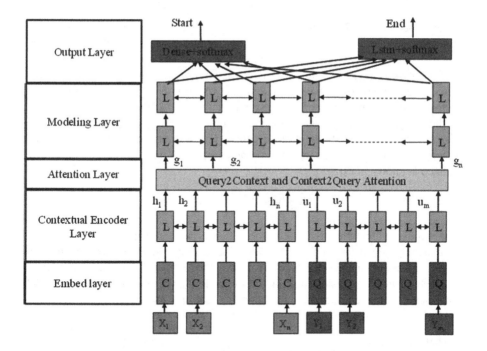

Fig. 1. Bi-directional attention flow model

The model mainly consists of an embed layer, a contextual encoder layer, an attention flow layer, a modeling layer, and an output layer. After the character-level word embedding and the pre-trained word vector Glove word embedding, the contextual representations X and Y of the article and the question are obtained by a bidirectional

LSTM, respectively. The bi-directional attention flow between them is computed, and it proceeds as follows:

a) The similarity matrix between the question and the article is calculated. The calculation formula is shown in Eq. 1.

$$K_{tj} = W^T [X_{:t}; Y_{:j}; X_{:t} \odot Y_{:j}] \tag{1}$$

where K_{tj} is the similarity of the t-th article word to the j-th question word, $X_{:t}$ is the t-th column vector of X, $Y_{:j}$ is the j-th column vector of Y, and W is a trainable weight vector.

b) Calculating the article-to-question attention. Firstly, the normalization operation is performed on the above similarity matrix, and then the weighted sum of the problem vector is calculated to obtain the article-to-problem attention, which is calculated as shown in Eq. 2.

$$x_t = soft \max (K)$$
$$\hat{Y}_{:t} = \sum_j x_{tj} Y_{:j} \tag{2}$$

c) Query-to-context (Q2C) attention signifies which context words have the closest similarity to one of the query words and are hence critical for answering the query. We obtain the attention weights on the context words by $y = softmax(max_{col}(K)) \in R^T$, where the maximum function max_{col} is performed across the column. Then the attended context vector is $\hat{x} = \sum_t y_t X_{:t}$. This vector indicates the weighted sum of the most important words in the context with respect to the query. $\hat{x}$ is tiled T times across the column, thus giving $\hat{X} \in R^{2d*T}$.

d) Fusion of bidirectional attention streams. The bidirectional attention streams obtained above are stitched together to obtain the new representation, which is calculated as shown in Eq. 3.

$$L_{:t} = \left[X_{:t}; \hat{Y}_{:t}; X_{:t} \odot \hat{Y}_{:t}; X_{:t} \odot \hat{X}_{:t} \right] \tag{3}$$

We builds on this work by looking at sentence pairs in a natural language sentence matching task as articles and problems for reading comprehension. We use the bi-directional attention and self-attention to obtain the high-level semantic information. Then, we use a heuristic fusion function to fuse the low-level semantic information and the high-level semantic information to obtain the final semantic information.

3   Method

In this section, we describe our model in detail. As shown in Fig. 2, our model mainly consists of an embedding layer, a contextual encoder layer, an interaction layer, a fusion layer, and an output layer.

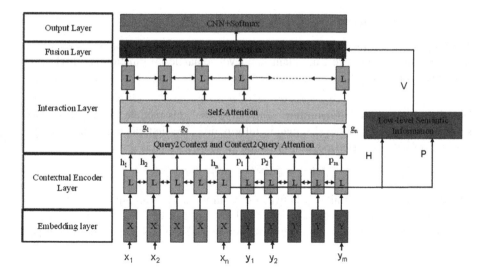

Fig. 2. Overview of the architecture of our proposed DIFM model. It consists of an embedding layer, a contextual encoder layer, an interaction layer, a fusion layer, and an output layer.

3.1   Embedding Layer

The purpose of the embedding layer is to map the input sentence A and sentence B into word vectors. The traditional mapping method is one-hot encoding. However, it is spatially expensive and inefficient, so we use pre-trained word vectors for word embedding. These word vectors are constant during training.

Since the text contains unregistered words, we also use character-level word vector embedding. Each word can be seen as a concatenation of characters and characters, and then we use LSTM to get character-level word vectors. It can effectively handle unregistered words.

We assume that the pre-trained word vector for word h is h_w, and character-level word vector is h_c, we splice the two vectors and use a two-tier highway network [25] to get the word vector representation of word h: $h = [h_1; h_2] \in R^{d_1+d_2}$, where d_1 is the dimension of Glove word embedding and d_2 is the dimension of character-level word embedding. Finally, we obtain the word embedding matrix $X \in R^{n*(d_1+d_2)}$ for sentence A and the word embedding matrix $Y \in R^{m*(d_1+d_2)}$ for sentence B, where n, m represent the number of words in sentence A and sentence B.

3.2   Contextual Encoder Layer

The purpose of the contextual encoder layer is to fully exploit the contextual relationship features of the sentences. We use bidirectional LSTM for encoding which can mine the contextual relationship features of the sentences. Then, we can obtain its representation $H \in R^{2d*n}$ and $P \in R^{2d*m}$, where d is the hidden layer dimension.

3.3   Interaction Layer

The purpose of the interaction layer is to extract the effective features between sentences. In this module, we can obtain low-level semantic information and high-level semantic information.

Low-Level Semantic Information. The purpose of this module initially fuses two sentences to get the low-level semantic information. We first calculate the similarity matrix S of the context-encoded information H and P, which is shown in Eq. 4.

$$S_{ij} = W_s^T[h; p; h \odot p] \tag{4}$$

where S_{ij} denotes the similarity between the i-th word of H and the j-th word of P, W_s is weight matrices, h is the i-th column of H, and p is the j-th column of P. Then, we calculate the low-level semantic information V of A and B, which is shown in Eq. 5.

$$V = P \cdot softmax(S^T) \tag{5}$$

High-Level Semantic Information. The purpose of this module is mine the deep semantics of the text, and to generate high-level semantic information. In this module, we frist calculate the bidirectional attention of H and P that is the attention of $H \to P$ and $P \to H$. It is calculated as follows.

$H \to P$: The attention describes which words in the sentence P are most relevant to H. The calculation process is as follows; firstly, each row of the similarity matrix is normalized to get the attention weight, and then the new text representation $Q \in R^{2d*n}$ is obtained by weighted summation with each column of P, which is calculated as shown in Eq. 6.

$$\alpha_t = softmax(S_{t:}) \in R^m$$
$$q_{:t} = \sum_j \alpha_{tj} P_{:j} \tag{6}$$

where $q_{:t}$ is the t-th column of Q.

$P \to H$: The attention indicates which words in H are most similar to P. The calculation process is as follows: firstly, the column with the largest value in the similarity matrix S is taken to obtain the attention weight, then the weighted sum of H is expanded by n time steps to obtain $C \in R^{2d*n}$, which is calculated as shown in Eq. 7.

$$b = softmax(\max_{col}(S)) \in R^n$$
$$c = \sum_t b_t H_{t:} \in R^{2d} \tag{7}$$

After obtaining the attention matrix Q of $H \to P$ and the attention matrix C of $P \to H$, we splice the attention in these two directions by a multilayer perceptron. Finally, we get the spliced contextual representation G, which is calculated as shown in Eq. 8.

$$G_{:t} = \beta(C_{:t}, H_{:t}, Q_{:t})$$
$$\beta(c, h, q) = [h; q; h \odot q; h \odot c] \in R^{8d} \tag{8}$$

Then, we calculate its self-attention [19], which is calculated as shown in Eq. 9.

$$E = G^T G$$
$$Z = G \cdot softmax(E)$$

$$(9)$$

Finally, we pass the above semantic information Z through a bi-directional LSTM to obtain high-level semantic information U.

3.4 Fusion Layer

The purpose of the fusion layer is to fuse the low-level semantic information V and the high-level semantic information U. We innovatively propose a heuristic fusion function, it can learn the weights of fusion by neural network to achieve deep fusion. We fuse V and U to obtain the text representation $L = fusion(U, V) \in R^{n*2d}$, where the fusion function is defined as shown in Eq. 10:

$$\widetilde{x} = \tanh(W_1[x; y; x \odot y; x - y])$$
$$g = sigmoid(W_2[x; y; x \odot y; x - y])$$
$$z = g \odot \widetilde{x} + (1 - g) \odot x$$

$$(10)$$

where W_1 and W_2 are weight matrices, and g is a gating mechanism to control the weight of the intermediate vectors in the output vector. In this paper, x refers to U and y refers to V.

3.5 Output Layer

The purpose of the output layer is to output the results. In this paper, we use a linear layer to get the results of sentence matching. The process is shown in Eq. 11.

$$y = softmax(\tanh(ZW + b))$$

$$(11)$$

where both W and b are trainable parameters. Z is the vector after splicing its first and last vectors.

4   Experimental Results and Analysis

In this section, we validate our model on two datasets from two tasks. We first present some details of the model implementation, and secondly, we show the experimental results on the dataset. Finally, we analyze the experimental results.

4.1 Experimental Details

Loss Function. In this paper, the cross-entropy loss function can be chosen as shown in Eq. 12.

$$loss = -\sum_{i=1}^{N}\sum_{k=1}^{K} y^{(i,k)} \log \hat{y}^{(i,k)}$$

$$(12)$$

where N is the number of samples, K is the total number of categories and $\hat{y}^{(i,k)}$ is the true label of the i-th sample.

Dataset. In this paper, we use the natural language inference datasets SNLI, and the paraphrase recognition dataset Quora to validate our model. The SNLI dataset contains 570K manually labeled and categorically balanced sentence pairs. The Quora question pair dataset contains over 400k pairs of data that each with binary annotations, with 1 being a duplicate and 0 being a non-duplicate. The statistical descriptions of SNLI and Quora data are shown in Table 1.

Table 1. The statistical descriptions of SNLI and Quora

Dataset	Train	Validation	Test
SNLI	550152	10000	10000
Quora	384290	10000	10000

Table 2. Values of hyper parameters

Hyper Parameters	Values
Glove dimension	300
Character embedding dimension	100
Hidden dimension	200
Learning rate	0. 0005
Optimizer	Adam
Dropout	0.2
Activation function	ReLU
Epoch	30
Batch size	128

Parameter Settings. This experiment is conducted in a hardware environment with a graphics card RTX5000 and 16G of video memory. The system is Ubuntu 20.04, the development language is Python 3.7, and the deep learning framework is Pytorch 1.8.

In the model training process, a 300-dimensional Glove word vector are used for word embedding, and the maximum length of text sentences is set to 300 and 50 words on the SNLI and Quora datasets, respectively. The specific hyperparameter settings are shown in Table 2.

4.2   Experimental Results and Analysis

We compare the experimental results of the sentence matching model based on deep interaction and fusion on the SNLI dataset with other published models. The evaluation metric we use is the accuracy rate. The results are shown in Table 3. As can be seen from Table 3, our model achieves an accuracy rate of 0. 871 on the SNLI dataset, which achieves better results in the listed models. Compared with the LSTM, it is improved by 0. 065. Compared with Star-Transformer model, it is improved by 0. 004. Compared with some other models, it is observed that our model is better than the others model.

Table 3. The accuracy (%) of the model on the SNLI test set. Results marked with [a] are reported by Bowman et al. [4], [b] are reported by Han et al. [9], [c] are reported by Shen et al. [17], [d] are reported by Borges et al. [1], [e] are reported by Guo et al. [8], [f] are reported by Mu et al. [14].

Model	Acc
300D LSTM encoders[a]	80.6
DELTA[b]	80.7
SWEM-max[c]	83.8
Stacked Bi-LSTMs[d]	84.8
Bi-LSTM sentence encoder[d]	84.5
Star-Transformer[e]	86.0
CBS-1+ESIM[f]	86.7
DIFM	**87.1**

We conduct experiments on the Quora dataset, and the evaluation metric is accuracy. The experimental results on the Quora dataset are shown in Table 4. As can be seen from Table 4, the accuracy of our method on the test set is 0.868. The experimental results improve the accuracy by 0.054 compared to the traditional LSTM model. Compared with the enhanced sequential inference model ESIM, it is improved by 0.004. The experimental results achieved good results compared to some current popular deep learning methods. Our model achieve relatively good results in both tasks, which illustrates the effectiveness of our model.

Table 4. The accuracy (%) of the model on the Quora test set. Results marked with [g] are reported by Yang et al. [22], [h] are reported by He et al. [10], [i] are reported by Zhao et al. [24], [j] are reported by Chen et al. [5].

Model	Acc
LSTM	81.4
RCNN[g]	83.6
PWIM[h]	83.4
Capsule-BiGRU[i]	86.1
ESIM[j]	85.4
DIFM	**86.8**

4.3 Ablation Experiments

To explore the role played by each module, we conduct an ablation experiment on the SNLI dataset . Without using the fusion function, which means that the low-level semantic information are directly spliced with the high-level semantic information. The experimental results are shown in Table 5.

Table 5. Ablation study on the SNLI validation dataset

Model	Acc(%)
DIFM	87.1
w/o character embedding	85.6 ($\downarrow$1.5)
w/o low-level semantic information	85.9 ($\downarrow$1.2)
w/o high-level semantic information	79.5 ($\downarrow$**7.6**)
w/o fusion	86.1 ($\downarrow$1.0)
w/o self-attention	58.8 ($\downarrow$1.3)
w/o $P \rightarrow H$	84.6 ($\downarrow$2.5)
w/o $H \rightarrow P$	86.2 ($\downarrow$0.9)

We first verify the effectiveness of character embedding. Specifically, we remove the character embedding for the experiment, and its accuracy drops by 1.5% points, proving that character embedding plays an important role in improving the performance of the model.

In addition, we verify the effectiveness of the semantic information and fusion modules. We removed low-level semantic information and high-level semantic information from the original model, and its accuracy dropped by 1.2% points and 7.6% points. At the same time, we remove the fusion function, and its accuracy drops by about 1.0% points. It shows that the different semantic information and the fusion function are beneficial to improve the accuracy of the model, with the high-level semantic information being more significant for the model.

Finally, we verify the effectiveness of each attention on the model. We remove the attention from P to H, the attention from H to P, and the self-attention module respectively. Their accuracy rates decreased by 2.5% points, 0.9% points, and 1.3% points. It shows that all the various attention mechanisms improve the performance of the model, with the P to H attention being more significant for the model.

The ablation experiments show that each component of our model plays an important role, especially the high-level semantic information module and the P to H attention module, which have a greater impact on the performance of the model. Meanwhile, the character embedding and fusion function also play an important role in our model.

5 Conclusion

we investigate natural language sentence matching methods and propose an effective deep interaction and fusion model for sentence matching. Our model first uses the bi-directional attention in the machine reading comprehension model and self-attention to obtain the high-level semantic information. Then, we use a heuristic fusion function to fuse the semantic information that we get. Finally, we use a linear layer to get the results of sentence matching . We conducted experiments on SNLI and Quora datasets. The experimental results show that the model proposed in this paper can achieve good results in two tasks. In this work, we find that our proposed interaction module and fusion module occupie the dominant position and have a great impact on our model. However, Our model is not as powerful as the pre-trained model in terms of feature extraction and lacks external knowledge. The next research work plan will focus on the following two points: 1) we use more powerful feature extractors, such as BERT pre-trained model as text feature extractors; 2) the introduction of external knowledge will be considered. For example, WordNet, an external knowledge base, contains many sets of synonyms, and for each input word, its synonyms are retrieved from WordNet and embedded in the word vector representation of the word to further improve the performance of the model.

Acknowledgements. This work is supported by National Natural Science Foundation of China [grant numbers 62162062]. State Language Commission of China under Grant No. YB135-76, scientific research project for building world top discipline of Foreign Languages and Literatures of Yanbian University under Grant No. 18YLPY13. Doctor Starting Grants of Yanbian University [2020-16], the school-enterprise cooperation project of Yanbian University [2020-15].

References

1. Borges, L., Martins, B., Calado, P.: Combining similarity features and deep representation learning for stance detection in the context of checking fake news. J. Data Inf. Qual. (JDIQ) **11**(3), 1–26 (2019)
2. Bowman, S., Potts, C., Manning, C.D.: Recursive neural networks can learn logical semantics. In: Proceedings of the 3rd Workshop on Continuous Vector Space Models and their Compositionality, pp. 12–21 (2015)
3. Bowman, S.R., Angeli, G., Potts, C., Manning, C.D.: A large annotated corpus for learning natural language inference. In: Conference on Empirical Methods in Natural Language Processing, EMNLP 2015, pp. 632–642. Association for Computational Linguistics (ACL) (2015)
4. Bowman, S.R., Gupta, R., Gauthier, J., Manning, C.D., Rastogi, A., Potts, C.: A fast unified model for parsing and sentence understanding. In: 54th Annual Meeting of the Association for Computational Linguistics, ACL 2016, pp. 1466–1477. Association for Computational Linguistics (ACL) (2016)
5. Chen, Q., Zhu, X., Ling, Z.H., Wei, S., Jiang, H., Inkpen, D.: Enhanced LSTM for natural language inference. In: Proceedings of the 55th Annual Meeting of the Association for Computational Linguistics (Volume 1: Long Papers), pp. 1657–1668 (2017)
6. Dagan, I., Glickman, O.: Probabilistic textual entailment: generic applied modeling of language variability. Learn. Methods Text Underst. Min. **2004**, 26–29 (2004)
7. Dong-hong, H.: Convolutional network-based semantic similarity model of sentences. J. South China Univ. Technol. (Nat. Sci.) **45**(3), 68–75 (2017)
8. Guo, Q., Qiu, X., Liu, P., Shao, Y., Xue, X., Zhang, Z.: Star-transformer. In: Proceedings of the 2019 Conference of the North American Chapter of the Association for Computational Linguistics: Human Language Technologies, Volume 1 (Long and Short Papers), pp. 1315–1325 (2019)

9. Han, K., et al.: Delta: a deep learning based language technology platform. arXiv preprint arXiv:1908.01853 (2019)
10. He, H., Lin, J.: Pairwise word interaction modeling with deep neural networks for semantic similarity measurement. In: Proceedings of the 2016 Conference of the North American Chapter of the Association for Computational Linguistics: Human Language Technologies, pp. 937–948 (2016)
11. Hu, C., Wu, C., Yang, Y.: Extended S-LSTM based textual entailment recognition. J. Comput. Res. Dev. **57**(7), 1481–1489 (2020)
12. Jin, J., Zhao, Y., Cui, R.: Research on multi-granularity ensemble learning based on korean. In: The 2nd International Conference on Computing and Data Science, pp. 1–6 (2021)
13. Li, F., Zhao, Y., Yang, F., Cui, R.: Incorporating translation quality estimation into chinese-korean neural machine translation. In: Li, S., et al. (eds.) CCL 2021. LNCS (LNAI), vol. 12869, pp. 45–57. Springer, Cham (2021). https://doi.org/10.1007/978-3-030-84186-7_4
14. Mu, N., Yao, Z., Gholami, A., Keutzer, K., Mahoney, M.: Parameter re-initialization through cyclical batch size schedules. arXiv preprint arXiv:1812.01216 (2018)
15. Ren, H., Sheng, Y., Feng, W.: Recognizing textualentailmentbasedonknowledgetopicmodels. J. Chin. Inf. Process. **29**(6), 119–127 (2015)
16. Seo, M., Kembhavi, A., Farhadi, A., Hajishirzi, H.: Bidirectional attention flow for machine comprehension. arXiv preprint arXiv:1611.01603 (2016)
17. Shen, D., et al.: Baseline needs more love: on simple word-embedding-based models and associated pooling mechanisms. In: Proceedings of the 56th Annual Meeting of the Association for Computational Linguistics (Volume 1: Long Papers), pp. 440–450 (2018)
18. Sultan, M.A., Bethard, S., Sumner, T.: Feature-rich two-stage logistic regression for monolingual alignment. In: Proceedings of the 2015 Conference on Empirical Methods in Natural Language Processing, pp. 949–959 (2015)
19. Vaswani, A., et al.: Attention is all you need. In: Proceedings of the 31st International Conference on Neural Information Processing Systems, pp. 6000–6010 (2017)
20. Wang, S., Jiang, J.: Learning natural language inference with LSTM. In: Proceedings of the 2016 Conference of the North American Chapter of the Association for Computational Linguistics: Human Language Technologies, pp. 1442–1451 (2016)
21. Wang, Z., Hamza, W., Florian, R.: Bilateral multi-perspective matching for natural language sentences. In: Proceedings of the 26th International Joint Conference on Artificial Intelligence, pp. 4144–4150 (2017)
22. Yang, D., Ke, X., Yu, Q.: A question similarity calculation method based on RCNN. J. Comput. Eng. Sci. **43**(6), 1076–1080 (2021)
23. Yang, F., Zhao, Y., Cui, R.: Recognition method of important words in korean text based on reinforcement learning. In: Sun, M., Li, S., Zhang, Y., Liu, Y., He, S., Rao, G. (eds.) CCL 2020. LNCS (LNAI), vol. 12522, pp. 261–272. Springer, Cham (2020). https://doi.org/10.1007/978-3-030-63031-7_19
24. Zhao, Q., Du, Y., Lu, T.: Algorithm of text similarity analysis based on capsule-BIGRU. J. Comput. Eng. Appl. **57**(15), 171–177 (2021)
25. Zilly, J.G., Srivastava, R.K., Koutník, J., Schmidhuber, J.: Recurrent highway networks. In: International Conference on Machine Learning, pp. 4189–4198. PMLR (2017)

ConIsI: A Contrastive Framework with Inter-sentence Interaction for Self-supervised Sentence Representation

Meng Sun and Degen Huang[✉]

Dalian University of Technology, Dalian, China
sunmeng20@mail.dlut.edu.cn, huangdg@dlut.edu.cn

Abstract. Learning sentence representation is a fundamental task in natural language processing and has been studied extensively. Recently, many works have obtained high-quality sentence representation based on contrastive learning from pre-trained models. However, these works suffer the inconsistency of input forms between the pre-training and fine-tuning stages. Also, they typically encode a sentence independently and lack feature interaction between sentences. To conquer these issues, we propose a novel **Con**trastive framework with **I**nter-sentence **I**nteraction (ConIsI), which introduces a sentence-level objective to improve sentence representation based on contrastive learning by fine-grained interaction between sentences. The sentence-level objective guides the model to focus on fine-grained semantic information by feature interaction between sentences, and we design three different sentence construction strategies to explore its effect. We conduct experiments on seven Semantic Textual Similarity (STS) tasks. The experimental results show that our ConIsI models based on BERT$_{base}$ and RoBERTa$_{base}$ achieve state-of-the-art performance, substantially outperforming previous best models SimCSE-BERT$_{base}$ and SimCSE-RoBERTa$_{base}$ by 2.05% and 0.77% respectively.

Keywords: Sentence representation · Inter-sentence interaction · Contrastive learning

1 Introduction

Learning good universal sentence representation is a fundamental task and benefits a wide range of natural language processing tasks such as text classification and machine translation, especially for large-scale semantic similarity computation and information retrieval. With the rise of pre-trained language models [16,27], many downstream tasks have achieved remarkable improvements. However, the native sentence representation derived from pre-trained language models without additional supervision are usually low-quality and can not be used directly [34]. Recently, contrastive learning has become a popular approach to improve the quality of sentence representation in a self-supervised way.

© The Author(s), under exclusive license to Springer Nature Switzerland AG 2022
M. Sun et al. (Eds.): CCL 2022, LNAI 13603, pp. 31–47, 2022.
https://doi.org/10.1007/978-3-031-18315-7_3

Contrastive learning is an approach of learning effective feature representation by positive pairs and negative pairs. It generally takes different views as positive or negative pairs for each sentence using various data augmentation ways. And it works by pulling semantically close positive instances together and pushing negative instances away. However, current approaches based on contrastive learning mainly suffer two problems: *train-tuned bias* and *fine-grained interaction deficiency*. Firstly, previous approaches typically input a single sentence to the encoder at a time, which is inconsistent with the pre-training stage of the language models. Most language models concatenate multiple sentences as the input form at the pre-training stage. We argue that the inconsistency of input forms between the pre-training and fine-tuning stages may harm the performance. Secondly, each sentence in a minibatch is encoded independently while training, which lacks fine-grained interaction information between sentences. According to previous works in text matching [25, 29, 39], modeling a proper interaction between input sentences can improve the performance of semantic feature embedding for representation-based models, but existing works on sentence representation ignore the importance of this interaction.

Therefore, to conquer these drawbacks of current contrastive learning based methods, we propose ConIsI, a **Con**trastive framework with **I**nter-**s**entences **I**nteraction for self-supervised sentence representation. Firstly, we present to construct a sentence pair as positive instance for each sentence to alleviate the train-tuned bias. By referring to an original sentence and a sentence pair as a positive pair, the model can not only obtain effective representation of a single sentence, but also mitigate the train-tuned bias between the pre-training and fine-tuning stages. Further, to solve the problem of lacking interaction between sentences, we propose a sentence-level objective to perform the inter-sentence interaction during encoding. We pass a pair of sentences as a text sequence into the encoder and the target semantic category of the two sentences is predicted. The sentence pair is sufficiently interacted through the internal interaction mechanism in Transformer-based block [37] during encoding. Through the inter-sentence interaction, the model can encode fine-grained semantic information and achieve further improvement. Moreover, for a minibatch of n sentences, there are $n \cdot (n-1)/2$ interactive computations. In order to ensure the training efficiency, we do not perform an interactive operation on all data due to too many possible combinations. Instead, we artificially construct a sentence for each original sentence to adjust the difficulty of the interactive objective, which only requires n interactive computations. We propose several models based on three sentence construction strategies, named ConIsI-o1, ConIsI-o2, and ConIsI-s, respectively. The overall model of our proposed ConIsI can be seen in Fig. 1.

Our contributions can be summarized as follows:

– We propose to construct each positive pair with an original sentence and a sentence pair based on contrastive learning, which not only learns effective representation by pulling semantically close samples together but also mitigates the train-tuned bias between pre-training and fine-tuning phases.

- We propose a simple but effective sentence-level training objective based on inter-sentence interaction. It alleviates the problem of interaction deficiency among sentences and enriches the semantic information of sentence representation. We also present three sentence construction strategies for interactive sentence pairs and analyze their effects.
- We conduct extensive experiments on seven standard Semantic Textual Similarity (STS) datasets. The results show that our proposed ConIsI-s-BERT$_{base}$ and ConIsI-s-RoBERTa$_{base}$ achieve 78.30% and 77.34% averaged Spearman's correlation, a 2.05% and 0.77% improvement over SimCSE-BERT$_{base}$ and SimCSE-RoBERTa$_{base}$ respectively, which substantially outperforms the previous state-of-the-art models.

2   Related Work

Sentence representation built upon the distributional hypothesis has been widely studied and improved considerably. Early works [20, 22, 28] inspired by word2vec [31] lead to strong results by predicting surrounding information of a given sentence. The emergence of pre-trained models such as BERT [16] shows much great potential for sentence representation. Recently, many works have explored how to learn better sentence embeddings from the pre-trained models.

Supervised Methods. A common supervised step of learning a model is fine-tuning with labeled data in downstream training sets. Several works build upon the success of using annotated natural language inference (NLI) datasets (including Stanford NLI [6] and Multi-Genre NLI [40]) for sentence representation, which projects it as a 3-way classification task (entailment, neutral, and contradiction) to get better sentence embeddings. Conneau et al. [14] use a BiLSTM-based model as encoder, and they train it on both Stanford NLI and Multi-Genre NLI datasets. Universal Sentence Encoder [9] uses the Stanford NLI dataset to enhance the unsupervised training by adopting a Transformer-based model. Sentence-BERT [34] that adopts a Siamese network [13] with a shared BERT encoder is also trained on Stanford NLI and Multi-Genre NLI datasets.

Unsupervised Methods. Some works focus on using the regularization method to improve the quality of raw sentence representation generated by original BERT. Bert-flow [24] puts forward a flow-based approach to solving the problem that native embeddings of BERT occupy a narrow cone in the vector space. Similarly, Bert-whitening [36] maps BERT's embeddings to a standard Gaussian latent space by whitening the native embeddings. They all try to alleviate the representation degeneration of pre-trained models and yield substantial improvement.

Self-supervised Methods. The sentence-level training objective in language models like BERT inspires a line of work over self-supervised sentence representation learning. BERT includes the next sentence prediction (NSP) task, which predicts whether two sentences are neighboring or not. However, Liu et al. [27] prove that NSP has minimal effect on the final performance and even does harm to the training model. Therefore, many works have proposed various self-supervised objectives for pre-training sentence encoders. Cross-Thought [38] and CMLM [43] are two similar approaches that present to predict surrounding tokens of given contextual sentences. And Lee et al. [23] propose to learn an objective that predicts the correct sentence ordering provided the input of shuffled sentences.

As a self-supervised learning method, contrastive learning with no need for scarce labeled data attracts much attention, and many excellent works have been proposed. Inspired by SimCLR [10] which applies data augmentation techniques on the same anchor such as image rotating, scaling, and random cropping to learn image representation in the computer vision community, some works pay attention to getting effective positive pairs by using similar approaches. In the natural language process community, many works apply textual augmentation techniques on the same sentence to obtain different views as positive pairs based on the SimCLR framework. Zhang et al. [45] extract global feature of a sentence as positive pairs, Clear [41] and ConSERT [42] take some token-level transformation ways such as word or subword deletion or replacement, and SimCSE [17] applys dropout mask of Transformer-based encoder to get positive pairs. And BSL [44] adopts BYOL [19] framework using back-translation data.

3   Methodology

In this section, we present ConIsI, a contrastive framework with inter-sentence interaction for self-supervised sentence representation, which contains two parts: (1) the ConIsI model of joint contrastive learning objective and inter-sentence interactive objective (Sect. 3.1), and (2) the strategies of sentence construction in the inter-sentence interactive objective (Sect. 3.2).

3.1   Model

The ConIsI model joints contrastive learning and inter-sentence interactive objectives. The inter-sentence interactive objective is a binary classification task that performs fine-grained interaction between sentences and predicts whether two sentences are in the same semantic category. The overall architecture is shown in Fig. 1.

Data Augmentation. To alleviate the train-tuned bias caused by different input forms, we perform sentence-level repetition operation to construct positive instances. For each sentence, our approach proposes to take a sentence pair as positive instance. Specifically, given a tokenized sentence $x = \{t_1, t_2, ..., t_l\}$ (l is the max sequence length), we define the sentence pair as $Y = \{t_1, t_2, ..., t_l, t_1, t_2, ..., t_l\}$, which is the concatenation of two original sentences. For each minibatch of sentences $\mathcal{B} = \{x_i\}_{i=1}^{N}$ (N is the batch size), we perform data augmentation operation on each sentence and then get the positive instances $\mathcal{B}_{\text{Aug}} = \{Y_i\}_{i=1}^{N}$.

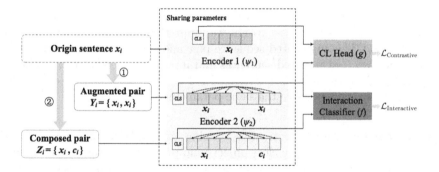

Fig. 1. The overall structure of the ConIsI model. It mainly consists of five components: the data augmentation operation (①), the text composition part (②), the encoder $\psi(\cdot)$ mapping the input data to the sentence representation space, the CL Head $g(\cdot)$ and the Interaction Classifier $f(\cdot)$ applying for the contrastive loss and the interactive loss respectively.

Sentence Pair Composition. To perform fine-grained interaction between sentences, we take a pair of sentences as a textual sequence to input into the encoder. The input two sentences can get fine-grained interaction with each other through Transformer-based block. Also, considering the training efficiency, we do not perform interaction on all sentences as there are too many combinations of sentence pairs. Instead, we construct the composed sentence pair $Z_i = \{x_i, c_i\}$ for each sentence x_i in $\mathcal{B}$. Specifically, we try to obtain a sentence c_i which belongs to a different semantic category from x_i. Then we concatenate the sentence x_i and the sentence c_i as a composed sentence pair Z_i. We perform the sentence pair composition operation on each sentence in minibatch $\mathcal{B} = \{x_i\}_{i=1}^{N}$ and then get the composed pairs $\mathcal{B}_{\text{Com}} = \{Z_i\}_{i=1}^{N}$. We explore three different sentence construction strategies to obtain c_i in Sect. 3.2.

Encoding. We take pre-trained checkpoints of BERT or RoBERTa as the encoder model to obtain sentence representation. For BERT, there are two input forms to fine-tune downstream tasks: one is the single sentence input, and the other is the sentence pair input. Previous works based on contrastive learning input a single sentence to the pre-trained model to learn sentence embeddings, which is inconsistent with the pre-training stage and suffers the train-tuned bias. To alleviate this problem and maintain the model's ability of encoding a single sentence meanwhile, we propose to adopt both two forms. The original sentence x_i is taken as a single sentence and input to the encoder 1. The augmented sentence pair Y_i and the composed sentence pair Z_i are taken as sentence pairs and input to the encoder 2. And to ensure that the augmented sentence pair has the same meaning as the original sentence, the max length of the tokenizer for the former is set double for the latter. The encoder 1 and the encoder 2 share the same parameters.

For RoBERTa whose input forms are a single sentence or several concatenated sentences separated by "$</s>$" token, we input the original sentence into the encoder 1. And The augmented sequence pair and the composed sentence pair are taken as two concatenated sentences and input to the encoder 2. Similarly, the max length of the tokenizer for encoder 2 is set double for that of encoder 1, and the two encoders share the same parameters.

Contrastive Learning. Contrastive learning aims to learn effective representation by pulling semantically close objects and pushing ones that are dissimilar away. We follow the SimCRL [10] contrastive framework and take a cross-entropy objective [12] in our approach.

For each minibatch $\mathcal{B} = \{x_i\}_{i=1}^N$, the contrastive loss is defined on $\mathcal{B}$ and the augmented instances $\mathcal{B}_{\text{Aug}} = \{Y_i\}_{i=1}^N$. Let $i \in \{1,..,N\}$ denote the index of an arbitrary instance in augmented set $\mathcal{B}_{\text{Aug}}$, and let $j \in \{1,..,N\}$ be the index of the other instance in $\mathcal{B}_{\text{Aug}}$. We refer to (x_i, Y_i) as a positive pair, while treating the other $N-1$ examples $Y_j (j \neq i)$ in $\mathcal{B}_{\text{Aug}}$ as negative instances for this positive pair. After the positive pair is encoded, we obtain the last hidden state of the special "[CLS]" token as the contextual representation of the corresponding sample, denoted as $h_{[\text{CLS}]}$.

$$
\begin{aligned}
h_{[\text{CLS}]}^x, h_1^x, ..., h_l^x, h_{[\text{SEP}]}^x = \psi_1(x) \\
h_{[\text{CLS}]}^Y, h_1^Y, ..., h_l^Y, h_{[\text{SEP}]}^Y, h_1^{Y'}, ..., h_l^{Y'}, h_{[\text{SEP}]}^Y = \psi_2(Y)
\end{aligned}
\tag{1}
$$

Then we add a predictor layer $g(\cdot)$ to map $h_{[\text{CLS}]}$ to the contrastive embedding space and obtain h, which is given as follows:

$$
h = Elu(BN_1(W_1 \cdot h_{[\text{CLS}]} + b_1))
\tag{2}
$$

where $W_1 \in R^{d \times d}$ is the weight matrix, $b_1 \in R^{d \times 1}$ is the bias vector, and d is the number of features in hidden layers. Both W_1 and b_1 are trainable parameters. BN_1 is the BatchNorm1d layer and Elu is the activate function.

Let h_i^x, h_i^Y and h_j^Y be the corresponding outputs of the head $g(\cdot)$. Then for x_i, we try to separate Y_i apart from all negative instances by minimizing the following,

$$
\ell_i^I = -log \frac{e^{sim(h_i^x, h_i^Y)/\tau}}{\sum_{j=1}^N e^{sim(h_i^x, h_j^Y)/\tau}}
\tag{3}
$$

where τ denotes the temperature parameter we set as 0.05. We choose cosine similarity $sim(\cdot)$ as the similarity calculation function between a pair of normalized outputs, $sim(h_1, h_2) = \frac{h_1^T h_2}{||h_1|| \cdot ||h_2||}$.

The contrastive loss is then averaged over all pairs,

$$
\mathcal{L}_{\text{Contrastive}} = \sum_{i=1}^N \ell_i^I / N
\tag{4}
$$

Interactive Classification. When applying a training objective after getting sentence embeddings in previous work, each sentence is encoded independently and can not see other sentences while encoding. Therefore, the semantic information contained in each sentence embeddings is insufficient. In contrast, modeling sentence pairs can effectively alleviate this problem. While encoding a sentence pair through the model, the two sentences can obtain fine-grained interaction information from each other. We propose to model an inter-sentence interaction objective between input sentences to enrich semantic information for sentence embeddings.

We encode the sentence pairs into the semantic category space for self-supervised classification. Different from contrastive learning objective, the interactive objective learns fine-grained semantic information through the interaction between sentences. The interactive loss is implemented on the augmented instance Y_i in B_{Aug} and the corresponding composed instance Z_i in B_{Com}. We refer to the two sentences $\{x_i, x_i\}$ in augmented pair Y_i as being in the same category, and the sentences $\{x_i, c_i\}$ in composed pair Z_i as being in different category. Our model passes Y_i and Z_i to the encoder 2 and obtains the last hidden state of the special "[CLS]" token as their sentence pair embeddings, respectively.

$$
\begin{aligned}
h^Y_{[CLS]}, h^Y_1, ..., h^Y_l, h^Y_{[SEP]}, h^{Y'}_1, ..., h^{Y'}_l, h^{Y'}_{[SEP]} &= \psi_2(Y) \\
h^Z_{[CLS]}, h^Z_1, ..., h^Z_l, h^Z_{[SEP]}, h^{Z'}_1, ..., h^{Z'}_l, h^{Z'}_{[SEP]} &= \psi_2(Z)
\end{aligned}
\tag{5}
$$

We use a predictor and linear layers to encode $h_{[CLS]}$ into the semantic category space to obtain r. $r \in R^d$ is the semantic category representation. The formulas are as follows:

$$
h = Elu(BN_2(W_2 \cdot h_{[CLS]} + b_2))
\tag{6}
$$

$$
r = W_3 \cdot h + b_3
\tag{7}
$$

where $W_2, W_3 \in R^{d \times d}$ are the weight matrixs, $b_2, b_3 \in R^{d \times 1}$ are the bias vectors, and d is the number of features in the hidden layers. W_2, W_3 and b_2, b_3 are all learnable parameters, and W_2, b_2 share the same parameters with W_1 and b_1 in $g(\cdot)$ respectively. BN_2 share the same parameters with BN_1 and Elu is the activate function.

Let r^Y_i and r^Z_i denote the corresponding outputs of the head $f(\cdot)$. Then we predict whether each pair is in the same category by optimizing the following objective,

$$
\ell^{II}_i = -log \frac{e^{r^Y_i}}{e^{r^Y_i} + e^{r^Z_i}}
\tag{8}
$$

Then the interactive loss for a mini-batch with N sentence pairs is as follows:

$$
\mathcal{L}_{Interactive} = \sum_{i=1}^{N} \ell^{II}_i / N
\tag{9}
$$

Overall Objective. Finally, our overall objective is,

$$\mathcal{L} = (1 - \lambda) \cdot \mathcal{L}_{\text{Contrastive}} + \lambda \cdot \mathcal{L}_{\text{Interactive}}$$

$$= (1 - \lambda) \cdot \sum_{i=1}^{N} \ell_i^I / N + \lambda \cdot \sum_{i=1}^{N} \ell_i^{II} / N \quad (10)$$

where ℓ_i^I, ℓ_i^{II} are defined in Eq. (3) and Eq. (8), respectively. λ is the balanced parameter between the contrastive loss and the interactive loss. During training, we jointly optimize a contrastive learning objective and an inter-sentence interactive objective over the original sentences, the augmented sentence pairs and composed sentence pairs. Then we fine-tune all the parameters using the joint objective.

3.2   Sentence Construction Techniques

Intuitively, two semantically opposite sentences are easier for the model to distinguish than two semantically closer sentences. As a self-supervised classification task, the difficulty of the interactive objective can significantly affect the performance of the model. Thus we propose different sentence construction techniques to control the complexity of the inter-sentence interactive objective. We try to construct a sentence c_i that is not in the same semantic category as the original sentence x_i in Sect. 3.1. We explore three sentence construction methods, two of which are constructing from the original sentence, and one is sampling from other sentences.

From Original Sentence. Since the bidirectional language models encode a word based on contextual information, sentences with high textual similarity usually are in high semantic similarity in representation. However, the sentences with high textual similarity may not actually be semantically similar. For example, "this is not a problem." and "this is a big problem." are two sentences with high textual similarity because of similar wording, but they are not semantically similar because of opposite meanings. The models usually fail to distinguish textual similarity and semantic similarity, which has been discussed deeply in the vision field [11,35]. As a result, a model may overestimate the semantic similarity of any pairs with similar wording regardless of the actual semantic difference between them. Therefore, we propose to construct sentences that are semantically different but are textually similar to the original sentence to improve the fine-grained semantic discrimination ability of the model.

Subword Replacement. The subword replacement mechanism randomly substitutes some sub-words in a sentence. Specifically, given a tokenized sub-word sequence $x = \{t_1, t_2, ..., t_l\}$ (l is the max sequence length) after processing by a sub-word tokenizer. Firstly, We mask a certain proportion of the tokenized sequence x at random. If the i-th token is chosen, then we replace the masked token with a random token 80% of the time, leaving the masked token unchanged 20% of the time.

Word Replacement. The word replacement mechanism works on full words in a sentence. Different from subword replacement, the word replacement mechanism randomly substitutes some full words with antonyms. If a word is chosen, then we replace the word with its antonym. We use the WordNet [32] to obtain the antonym of a word.

From Other Sentences. Different from constructing a new sentence from the original sentence, this method selects one other sentence from the training data at random. Specifically, for a given sentence x_i within the minibatch $\mathcal{B} = \{x_i\}_{i=1}^{N}$, we randomly select sentence x_k ($k \in [1, N], k \neq i$) as c_i for composed pair.

We apply the three sentence construction strategies to our ConIsI model, named ConIsI-o1, ConIsI-o2, and ConIsI-s. Among them, ConIsI-o1 and ConIsI-o2 represent the joint contrastive objective and interactive objective under the subword replacement and word replacement, respectively. ConIsI-s represents the jointing of contrastive learning and the interactive objective under the sampling from other sentences.

4 Experiments

4.1 Data

We train our model on the same one million sentences randomly sampled from English Wikipedia that are provided by SimCSE[1]. All our experiments are fully self-supervised and note that no STS sets are used for training.

We evaluate our approach on multiple Semantic Textual Similarity (STS) datasets: STS12-16 (STS12 - STS16) [1–5], STS Benchmark (STS-B) [8] and SICK-Relatedness (SICK-R) [30], which are seven standard STS benchmark datasets and are extensively used to measure the sentence embeddings and the semantic similarity of sentence pairs. These datasets are composed of pairs of sentences and one golden score between 0 and 5, where a higher score indicates a higher similarity between two sentences in Table 1. The statistics is shown in Table 2.

Table 1. The sentence samples of STS datasets.

Sentence1	Sentence2	Golden Score
A plane is taking off	An air plane is taking off	5.000
A cat is playing a piano	A man is playing a guitar	0.600
A man is playing a guitar	A man is playing a trumpet	1.714

---

[1] https://huggingface.co/datasets/princeton-nlp/datasets-for-simcse/resolve/main/wiki1mforsimcse.txt.

Table 2. The statistics of STS datasets.

	STS12	STS13	STS14	STS15	STS16	STSb	SICK-R	Total
Train samples	0	0	0	0	0	5479	4500	–
Valid samples	0	0	0	0	0	1500	500	–
Test samples	3108	1500	3750	3000	1186	1379	4927	–
Unlabeled texts	6216	3000	7500	17000	18366	17256	19854	89192

4.2 Evaluation Setup

Following previous work, we evaluate our method on STS tasks using the SentEval toolkit [15]. We take the "[CLS]" embedding generated by the last hidden layer of the encoder 1 in Fig. 1 as the sentence representation. To evaluate the sentence representation for a fair comparison, we follow the settings of Sentence-BERT [34] and SimCSE [17]: (1) we directly take cosine similarities for all STS tasks without training extra linear regressor on top of frozen sentence embeddings for STS-B and SICK-R; (2) we report Spearman's rank correlation coefficients rather than Pearson's; (3) and we take the "all" setting for STS12-STS16 which fuses data from different topics together to make the evaluation closer to real-world scenarios.

4.3 Training Details

We implement our ConIsI model with Huggingface's transformers package[2] 4.2.1 based on Python 3.8.12 and Pytorch 1.8.0 and run the model on Nvidia 3090 GPU. We start our experiments from pre-trained checkpoints of BERT or RoBERTa. All experiments use the Adam optimizer and the random seed is set as 42. The temperature parameter τ is set as 0.05, and the dropout rate is set as 0.1. Furthermore, the hyper-parameter settings of the models are shown in Table 3. Besides, We train our models for one epoch and evaluate the model every 125 training steps.

Table 3. Hyper-parameters settings for ConIsI-s models.

Model	Batch size	Max seq len	Learning rate	Hidden size	λ
ConIsI-s-BERT$_{base}$	64	32	3e-5	768	0.8
ConIsI-s-RoBERTa$_{base}$	64	32	3e-5	768	0.1
ConIsI-s-BERT$_{large}$	64	28	3e-5	1024	0.1

---

[2] https://github.com/huggingface/transformers.

4.4   Baselines

We compare our model with previous strong baseline models on STS tasks, including:

(1) Recent state-of-the-art self-supervised models using a contrastive objective: SimCSE [17], IS-BERT [45], ConSERT [42], Mirror-BERT [26], DeCLUTR [18], CT-BERT [7], BSL [44], SG-OPT [21];
(2) Post-processing methods like BERT-flow [24] and BERT-whitening [36];
(3) And naive baselines like averaged GloVe embeddings [33]; averaged first and last layer BERT embeddings.

4.5   Main Results

Table 4 shows the evaluation results on seven STS tasks. ConIsI-s-BERT$_{base}$ can significantly outperform SimCSE-BERT$_{base}$ and raise the averaged Spearman's correlation from 76.25% to 78.30%, which brings a 2.05% average improvement over the SimCSE-BERT$_{base}$ model on seven tasks. For the RoBERTa model, ConIsI-s-RoBERTa$_{base}$ can also improve upon SimCSE-RoBERTa$_{base}$ from 76.57% to 77.34%, a 0.77% increase. And for the ConIsI-s-BERT$_{large}$ model, we also achieve better performance, from 78.41% to 79.55%, a 1.14% increase. In general, our method achieves substantial improvement on the seven STS datasets over baseline models.

Table 4. Sentence embedding performance on STS tasks in terms of Spearman's correlation and "all" setting. ♣: results from [34]; §: results from [45]; †: results from [44]; ‡: results from [42]; ♭: results from [21]; ♮: results from [26]; ♭: results from [17]; *: results from ours.

Model	STS12	STS13	STS14	STS15	STS16	STS-B	SICK-R	Avg.
GloVe-embeddings♣	55.14	70.66	59.73	68.25	63.66	58.02	53.76	61.32
BERT$_{base}$♭	39.70	59.38	49.67	66.03	66.19	53.87	62.06	56.70
BERT$_{base}$-flow♭	58.40	67.10	60.85	75.16	71.22	68.66	64.47	66.55
BERT$_{base}$-whitening♭	57.83	66.90	60.90	75.08	71.31	68.24	63.73	66.28
IS-BERT$_{base}$§	56.77	69.24	61.21	75.23	70.16	69.21	64.25	66.58
BSL-BERT$_{base}$†	67.83	71.40	66.88	79.97	73.97	73.74	70.40	72.03
CT-BERT$_{base}$♭	61.63	76.80	68.47	77.50	76.48	74.31	69.19	72.05
ConSERT-BERT$_{base}$‡	64.64	78.49	69.07	79.72	75.95	73.97	67.31	72.74
SG-OPT-BERT$_{base}$♭	66.84	80.13	71.23	81.56	77.17	77.23	68.16	74.62
Mirror-BERT$_{base}$♮	69.10	81.10	73.00	81.90	75.70	78.00	69.10	75.40
SimCSE-BERT$_{base}$♭	68.40	82.41	74.38	80.91	78.56	76.85	**72.23**	76.25
*ConIsI-s-BERT$_{base}$	**70.92**	**84.35**	**76.67**	**83.53**	**78.94**	**82.15**	71.55	**78.30**
RoBERTa$_{base}$♭	40.88	58.74	49.07	65.63	61.48	58.55	61.63	56.57
RoBERTa$_{base}$whitening♭	46.99	63.24	57.23	71.36	68.99	61.36	62.91	61.73
DeCLUTR-RoBERTa$_{base}$♭	52.41	75.19	65.52	77.12	78.63	72.41	68.62	69.99
SimCSE-RoBERTa$_{base}$♭	70.16	81.77	73.24	**81.36**	80.65	80.22	68.56	76.57
* ConIsI-s-RoBERTa$_{base}$	**71.21**	**83.31**	**75.11**	81.13	**80.73**	80.50	69.39	**77.34**
SimCSE-BERT$_{large}$♭	70.88	84.16	76.43	84.50	**79.76**	79.26	73.88	78.41
* ConIsI-s-BERT$_{large}$	**72.33**	**86.14**	**77.42**	**84.83**	79.60	**81.76**	**74.78**	**79.55**

4.6 Ablation Study

In this section, we discuss the effects of different components. In our model, both the contrastive learning objective and the inter-sentence interactive objective are crucial because they are committed to obtaining the ability of normal semantic encoding and fine-grained semantic information, respectively. If we remove the inter-sentence interactive objective, the model becomes a SimCSE-like model with a different positive instance construction way, causing a drop of 1.30%. If we remove the contrastive learning objective, the performance of **Avg.** drops significantly by more than 10% (see Table 5). This results show that it is important to have common and fine-grained attributes that exist together in the sentence representation space. When compared with SimCSE-BERT$_{base}$, our proposed method of taking a sentence pair as positive instance brings an improvement of 0.75%. The result shows that the problem of train-tuned bias is alleviated by the input form of augmented sentence pair.

Table 5. Avg. results of seven STS tasks for ConIsI-s-BERT$_{base}$ model variants.

Model	Avg.
SimCSE-BERT$_{base}$	76.25
ConIsI-s-BERT$_{base}$	78.30
w/o fine-grained classification loss	77.00 (-1.30) $(+0.75)$
w/o contrastive loss	67.68 (-10.62)

4.7 Analysis

In this section, we conduct a series of experiments to validate our model better. We use BERT$_{base}$ or RoBERTa$_{base}$ model and all reported results are evaluated on the seven STS tasks.

Validation of Sentence Construction Strategies. We compare the three models ConIsI-o1, ConIsI-o2, and ConIsI-s to verify the effects of our proposed sentence construction strategies for the inter-sentence interactive objective.

Table 6 shows that our proposed sentence construction techniques for the inter-sentence interactive objective improve the performance of self-supervised sentence representation. Compared with SimCSE-BERT$_{base}$ and SimCSE-RoBERTa$_{base}$, the Spearman's correlation of ConIsI-o1-BERT$_{base}$ and ConIsI-o1-RoBERTa$_{base}$ on seven STS tasks have improved by 0.89% and 1.78% respectively, a 1.34% increase on average. The results of ConIsI-o2-BERT$_{base}$ and ConIsI-o2-RoBERTa$_{base}$ on seven STS tasks have improved by 1.10% and 1.56% respectively, a 1.33% increase on average. The results of ConIsI-s-BERT$_{base}$ and ConIsI-s-RoBERTa$_{base}$ have improved by 2.05% and 0.77% respectively, a 1.41% increase on average.

Table 6. Validation results of sentence construction strategies.

Model	Avg.	Model	Avg.
SimCSE-BERT$_{base}$	76.25	SimCSE-RoBERTa$_{base}$	76.57
*ConIsI-o1-BERT$_{base}$	77.14	*ConIsI-o1-RoBERTa$_{base}$	78.35
*ConIsI-o2-BERT$_{base}$	77.35	*ConIsI-o2-RoBERTa$_{base}$	78.13
*ConIsI-s-BERT$_{base}$	78.30	*ConIsI-s-RoBERTa$_{base}$	77.34

As the Table 6 shown, the ConIsI-o1-RoBERTa$_{base}$ and ConIsI-o2-RoBERTa$_{base}$ implemented by the strategies of "from original sentence" bring more remarkable improvement to the SimCSE-RoBERTa model, exceeding 1.5%. And the ConIsI-s models implemented by the strategy of "from other sentences" gets a lower boost to the SimCSE-RoBERTa model, but a greater improvement to the SimCSE-BERT model. That is, RoBERTa is more capable of encoding fine-grained features and distinguishing textual similarity and semantic similarity than BERT. In contrast, BERT focuses more on encoding common features in the sentence representation space. We argue that the pre-trained RoBERTa model pays more attention to fine-grained features because of the more refined optimization techniques than BERT in the pre-training phase. So ConIsI-o1-RoBERTa$_{base}$ and ConIsI-o2-RoBERTa$_{base}$ achieve better performance than ConIsI-s-RoBERTa$_{base}$. While ConIsI-s-BERT$_{base}$ achieves better performance than ConIsI-o1-BERT$_{base}$ and ConIsI-o2-BERT$_{base}$.

Overall, our proposed contrastive framework with inter-sentence interaction have improved performance compared with the previous best model SimCSE. The experimental results show that the three sentence construction strategies are effective for the ConIsI model. We take the ConIsI-s model's results as our final ConIsI model's performance.

Effect of Coefficient λ. λ is the weighted hyperparameter for contrastive loss and inter-sentence interactive loss involved in the final joint objective function Eq. (10). A smaller λ means a larger contrastive loss weight, indicating that the model pays more attention to common features. And a larger λ means a larger interactive loss weight, indicating that the model focuses more on fine-grained features. Our experiments find that λ plays an essential role in the joint objective, and the experimental results are shown in Table 7. When $\lambda = 0$, the model becomes a SimCSE-like model, and the result shows that our proposed method to take a sentence pair as the positive instance is effective, which brings an improvement over SimCSE-BERT$_{base}$ [17] by 0.75%. The results prove that the interactive objective is helpful to enhance the performance of the model under different λ. And when $\lambda = 0.8$, it achieves the best performance on the STS datasets and gets substantial improvement over that when $\lambda = 0$.

Table 7. Avg. results of seven STS tasks under different λ for ConIsI-s-BERT$_{base}$.

λ	0	0.1	0.2	0.3	0.4	0.5	0.6	0.7	0.8	0.9
Avg.	77.00	77.97	77.42	77.78	77.81	78.03	77.76	77.93	**78.30**	77.58

5 Conclusion

In this paper, we propose the ConIsI model, which joints contrastive learning and inter-sentence interactive training objective for optimization. We propose to perform a sentence repetition operation on each sentence and then take the augmented pair as a positive instance based on contrastive learning, which alleviates the train-tuned bias of language models. We also propose the inter-sentence interactive objective, which guides the model to focus on fine-grained semantic information by feature interaction between sentences. Moreover, we design three sentence construction strategies in the inter-sentence interactive objective. Experimental results show our proposed ConIsI achieves substantial improvement over the previous state-of-the-art models. In the future, we will further explore more effective inter-sentence interactive way to enrich semantic information in sentence representation, and we hope to apply our approach to other downstream tasks such as machine translation.

Acknowledgement. This research work was supported by the National Key R & D Program (2020AAA0108004) and the National Natural Science Foundation of China (U1936109, 61672127).

References

1. Agirre, E., et al.: SemEval-2015 task 2: semantic textual similarity, English, Spanish and pilot on interpretability. In: Proceedings of the 9th International Workshop on Semantic Evaluation (SemEval 2015), pp. 252–263 (2015)
2. Agirre, E., et al.: SemEval-2014 task 10: multilingual semantic textual similarity. In: Proceedings of the 8th International Workshop on Semantic Evaluation (SemEval 2014), pp. 81–91 (2014)
3. Agirre, E., et al.: SemEval-2016 task 1: semantic textual similarity, monolingual and cross-lingual evaluation. In: SemEval-2016. 10th International Workshop on Semantic Evaluation, 16–17 June 2016, San Diego, CA, pp. 497–511. ACL (Association for Computational Linguistics), Stroudsburg (2016)
4. Agirre, E., Cer, D., Diab, M., Gonzalez-Agirre, A.: SemEval-2012 task 6: a pilot on semantic textual similarity. In: * SEM 2012: The First Joint Conference on Lexical and Computational Semantics-Volume 1: Proceedings of the main conference and the shared task, and Volume 2: Proceedings of the Sixth International Workshop on Semantic Evaluation (SemEval 2012), pp. 385–393 (2012)
5. Agirre, E., Cer, D., Diab, M., Gonzalez-Agirre, A., Guo, W.: * SEM 2013 shared task: semantic textual similarity. In: Second Joint Conference on Lexical and Computational Semantics (* SEM), Volume 1: Proceedings of the Main Conference and the Shared Task: Semantic Textual Similarity, pp. 32–43 (2013)

6. Bowman, S., Angeli, G., Potts, C., Manning, C.D.: A large annotated corpus for learning natural language inference. In: Proceedings of the 2015 Conference on Empirical Methods in Natural Language Processing, pp. 632–642 (2015)

7. Carlsson, F., Gyllensten, A.C., Gogoulou, E., Hellqvist, E.Y., Sahlgren, M.: Semantic re-tuning with contrastive tension. In: International Conference on Learning Representations (2020)

8. Cer, D., Diab, M., Agirre, E., Lopez-Gazpio, I., Specia, L.: SemEval-2017 task 1: semantic textual similarity-multilingual and cross-lingual focused evaluation. arXiv preprint arXiv:1708.00055 (2017)

9. Cer, D., et al.: Universal sentence encoder for English. In: Proceedings of the 2018 Conference on Empirical Methods in Natural Language Processing: System Demonstrations, pp. 169–174 (2018)

10. Chen, T., Kornblith, S., Norouzi, M., Hinton, G.: A simple framework for contrastive learning of visual representations. In: International Conference on Machine Learning, pp. 1597–1607. PMLR (2020)

11. Chen, T., Luo, C., Li, L.: Intriguing properties of contrastive losses. In: Advances in Neural Information Processing Systems, vol. 34 (2021)

12. Chen, T., Sun, Y., Shi, Y., Hong, L.: On sampling strategies for neural network-based collaborative filtering. In: Proceedings of the 23rd ACM SIGKDD International Conference on Knowledge Discovery and Data Mining, pp. 767–776 (2017)

13. Chopra, S., Hadsell, R., LeCun, Y.: Learning a similarity metric discriminatively, with application to face verification. In: 2005 IEEE Computer Society Conference on Computer Vision and Pattern Recognition (CVPR 2005), vol. 1, pp. 539–546. IEEE (2005)

14. Conneau, A., Kiela, D., Schwenk, H., Barrault, L., Bordes, A.: Supervised learning of universal sentence representations from natural language inference data. In: Proceedings of the 2017 Conference on Empirical Methods in Natural Language Processing, pp. 670–680. Association for Computational Linguistics (2017)

15. Conneau, A., Kiela, D.: SentEval: an evaluation toolkit for universal sentence representations. In: Proceedings of the Eleventh International Conference on Language Resources and Evaluation (LREC 2018) (2018)

16. Devlin, J., Chang, M.W., Lee, K., Toutanova, K.: BERT: pre-training of deep bidirectional transformers for language understanding. In: NAACL-HLT (1) (2019)

17. Gao, T., Yao, X., Chen, D.: SimCSE: simple contrastive learning of sentence embeddings. In: Proceedings of the 2021 Conference on Empirical Methods in Natural Language Processing, pp. 6894–6910 (2021)

18. Giorgi, J., Nitski, O., Wang, B., Bader, G.: DeCLUTR: deep contrastive learning for unsupervised textual representations. In: Proceedings of the 59th Annual Meeting of the Association for Computational Linguistics and the 11th International Joint Conference on Natural Language Processing (Volume 1: Long Papers), pp. 879–895 (2021)

19. Grill, J.B., et al.: Bootstrap your own latent-a new approach to self-supervised learning. In: Advances in Neural Information Processing Systems, vol. 33, pp. 21271–21284 (2020)

20. Hill, F., Cho, K., Korhonen, A.: Learning distributed representations of sentences from unlabelled data. In: Proceedings of NAACL-HLT, pp. 1367–1377 (2016)

21. Kim, T., Yoo, K.M., Lee, S.G.: Self-guided contrastive learning for BERT sentence representations. In: Proceedings of the 59th Annual Meeting of the Association for Computational Linguistics and the 11th International Joint Conference on Natural Language Processing (Volume 1: Long Papers), pp. 2528–2540 (2021)

22. Kiros, R., et al.: Skip-thought vectors. In: Advances in Neural Information Processing Systems, pp. 3294–3302 (2015)

23. Lee, H., Hudson, D.A., Lee, K., Manning, C.D.: SLM: learning a discourse language representation with sentence unshuffling. In: Proceedings of the 2020 Conference on Empirical Methods in Natural Language Processing (EMNLP), pp. 1551–1562 (2020)

24. Li, B., Zhou, H., He, J., Wang, M., Yang, Y., Li, L.: On the sentence embeddings from pre-trained language models. In: Proceedings of the 2020 Conference on Empirical Methods in Natural Language Processing (EMNLP), pp. 9119–9130 (2020)

25. Li, D., et al.: VIRT: improving representation-based models for text matching through virtual interaction. arXiv preprint arXiv:2112.04195 (2021)

26. Liu, F., Vulić, I., Korhonen, A., Collier, N.: Fast, effective, and self-supervised: transforming masked language models into universal lexical and sentence encoders. In: Proceedings of the 2021 Conference on Empirical Methods in Natural Language Processing, pp. 1442–1459 (2021)

27. Liu, Y., et al.: RoBERTa: a robustly optimized bert pretraining approach. arXiv preprint arXiv:1907.11692 (2019)

28. Logeswaran, L., Lee, H.: An efficient framework for learning sentence representations. In: International Conference on Learning Representations (2018)

29. Lu, Y., et al.: Ernie-search: bridging cross-encoder with dual-encoder via self on-the-fly distillation for dense passage retrieval. arXiv preprint arXiv:2205.09153 (2022)

30. Marelli, M., et al.: A sick cure for the evaluation of compositional distributional semantic models. In: Lrec, pp. 216–223. Reykjavik (2014)

31. Mikolov, T., Sutskever, I., Chen, K., Corrado, G.S., Dean, J.: Distributed representations of words and phrases and their compositionality. In: Advances in Neural Information Processing Systems, pp. 3111–3119 (2013)

32. Miller, G.A.: WordNet: a lexical database for English. In: Human Language Technology: Proceedings of a Workshop Held at Plainsboro, New Jersey, 21–24 March 1993 (1993)

33. Pennington, J., Socher, R., Manning, C.D.: GloVe: global vectors for word representation. In: Proceedings of the 2014 Conference on Empirical Methods in Natural Language Processing (EMNLP), pp. 1532–1543 (2014)

34. Reimers, N., et al.: Sentence-BERT: sentence embeddings using Siamese BERT-networks. In: Proceedings of the 2019 Conference on Empirical Methods in Natural Language Processing, pp. 671–688. Association for Computational Linguistics (2019)

35. Robinson, J., Sun, L., Yu, K., Batmanghelich, K., Jegelka, S., Sra, S.: Can contrastive learning avoid shortcut solutions? In: Advances in Neural Information Processing Systems, vol. 34 (2021)

36. Su, J., Cao, J., Liu, W., Ou, Y.: Whitening sentence representations for better semantics and faster retrieval. arXiv preprint arXiv:2103.15316 (2021)

37. Vaswani, A., et al.: Attention is all you need. In: Advances in Neural Information Processing Systems, vol. 30 (2017)

38. Wang, S., et al.: Cross-thought for sentence encoder pre-training. In: Proceedings of the 2020 Conference on Empirical Methods in Natural Language Processing (EMNLP), pp. 412–421 (2020)

39. Wang, Z., Wang, W., Zhu, H., Liu, M., Qin, B., Wei, F.: Distilled dual-encoder model for vision-language understanding. arXiv preprint arXiv:2112.08723 (2021)

40. Williams, A., Nangia, N., Bowman, S.: A broad-coverage challenge corpus for sentence understanding through inference. In: Proceedings of the 2018 Conference of the North American Chapter of the Association for Computational Linguistics: Human Language Technologies, Volume 1 (Long Papers), pp. 1112–1122 (2018)
41. Wu, Z., Wang, S., Gu, J., Khabsa, M., Sun, F., Ma, H.: CLEAR: contrastive learning for sentence representation. arXiv preprint arXiv:2012.15466 (2020)
42. Yan, Y., Li, R., Wang, S., Zhang, F., Wu, W., Xu, W.: ConSERT: a contrastive framework for self-supervised sentence representation transfer. In: Proceedings of the 59th Annual Meeting of the Association for Computational Linguistics and the 11th International Joint Conference on Natural Language Processing (Volume 1: Long Papers), pp. 5065–5075 (2021)
43. Yang, Z., Yang, Y., Cer, D., Law, J., Darve, E.: Universal sentence representation learning with conditional masked language model. In: Proceedings of the 2021 Conference on Empirical Methods in Natural Language Processing, pp. 6216–6228 (2021)
44. Zhang, Y., He, R., Liu, Z., Bing, L., Li, H.: Bootstrapped unsupervised sentence representation learning. In: Proceedings of the 59th Annual Meeting of the Association for Computational Linguistics and the 11th International Joint Conference on Natural Language Processing (Volume 1: Long Papers), pp. 5168–5180 (2021)
45. Zhang, Y., He, R., Liu, Z., Lim, K.H., Bing, L.: An unsupervised sentence embedding method by mutual information maximization. In: Proceedings of the 2020 Conference on Empirical Methods in Natural Language Processing (EMNLP), pp. 1601–1610 (2020)

Information Retrieval, Dialogue and Question Answering

Data Synthesis and Iterative Refinement for Neural Semantic Parsing without Annotated Logical Forms

Shan Wu[1,3], Bo Chen[1], Xianpei Han[1,2], and Le Sun[1,2(✉)]

[1] Chinese Information Processing Laboratory, Chinese Academy of Sciences, Beijing, China
{wushan2018,chenbo,xianpei,sunle}@iscas.ac.cn
[2] State Key Laboratory of Computer Science Institute of Software,
Chinese Academy of Sciences, Beijing, China
[3] University of Chinese Academy of Sciences, Beijing, China

Abstract. Semantic parsing aims to convert natural language utterances to logical forms. A critical challenge for constructing semantic parsers is the lack of labeled data. In this paper, we propose a data synthesis and iterative refinement framework for neural semantic parsing, which can build semantic parsers without annotated logical forms. We first generate a naive corpus by sampling logic forms from knowledge bases and synthesizing their canonical utterances. Then, we further propose a bootstrapping algorithm to iteratively refine data and model, via a denoising language model and knowledge-constrained decoding. Experimental results show that our approach achieves competitive performance on GEO, ATIS and OVERNIGHT datasets in both unsupervised and semi-supervised data settings.

Keywords: Semantic parsing · Data synthesis · Unsupervised methods

1 Introduction

Semantic parsing is the task of translating natural language (NL) utterances to their formal meaning representations (MRs), such as lambda calculus [42,50], FunQL [23, 28], and SQL queries [5,8,16]. Currently, most neural semantic parsers [12,13] model semantic parsing as a sequence translation task via a encoder-decoder framework. For instance, given an utterance *"What is the length of river traverses state0"*, a SEQ2SEQ parsing model obtains its FunQL representation by sequentially generating its tokens `answer(length(river(traverse_2(state0))))`.

One of the key challenges in building a semantic parser is the scarcity of annotated data. Since annotating utterances with MRs is time consuming and requires specialized expert knowledge. Witnessed the data bottleneck problem, there are many learning algorithms have been proposed, such as denotation-based weak supervised learning [29,30], dual learning [6], transfer learning [18,37]. There are also many studies focus on the quick construction of training data, such as OVERNIGHT [40]. However, these works still require some degree of human efforts.

M. Sun et al. (Eds.): CCL 2022, LNAI 13603, pp. 51–65, 2022.
https://doi.org/10.1007/978-3-031-18315-7_4

In this paper, we propose a data synthesis and iterative refinement framework, which can build semantic parsers without labeled data. Inspired by the idea that, a simple and noise corpus can be synthesized by a grammar-lexicon method, like the one used in OVERNIGHT, and can be refined by leveraging external knowledges, like language models and knowledge base constraints. So, we first obtain a naive corpus based on synchronous context-free grammars and a seed lexicon. Then we improve the corpus with the knowledge of language models and knowledge base constraints by iteratively refining data and model to obtain mature corpus. Finally, we use the refined corpus to train the semantic parser. Figure 1 shows the overview of our method.

Specifically, to get the naive corpus, we sample logical forms from knowledge bases, and then synthesize their corresponding canonical utterances using a grammar-based synthesizing algorithm. For example, like in Overnight, we can synthesize an unnatural utterance *"what is length river traverse state0"* from `answer(length(river(traverse_2(state0))))`. Although the synthesized utterance *"what is length river traverse state0"* is different from the real-world utterance *"what is the length of river traverse state0"*, the naive corpus can provide a start for unsupervised learning, and can be used to pretrain a base semantic parser.

Then, to improve the synthesized naive corpus, we iteratively refine the model and the data via a bootstrapping process, using the knowledge of language models and knowledge base constraints. Due to the limitation of grammars and seed lexicon, the synthesized training instances in naive corpus are often noisy, differing from real-world utterances, and with limited diversity, which hinder the model from generalizing to natural data. To address these issues, we propose to iteratively refine the model and the synthesized data via a denoising language model and knowledge-constrained decoding. Firstly, we view synthesized canonical utterances as an artificial version of utterances which are often not as fluent as natural utterances, then leverage a denoising language model to rewrite the canonical utterances to be closer to natural utterances. Secondly, to address the noise problem, a knowledge-constrained decoding algorithm is employed to exploit constraints from knowledge bases, therefore meaning representations can be more accurately predicted even when semantic parser is not strong enough. Finally, the *data synthesization* and *semantic parsing* are iteratively refined to bootstrap both the corpus and the semantic parser: the refined corpus is used to train a better semantic parser, and the better semantic parser in turn is used to refine training instances.

The main contributions of this paper are:

- We propose a data synthesis and iterative refinement framework to build neural semantic parsers without labeled logical forms, in which we generate naive corpus from scratch and improve them with the knowledge of language models and knowledge base constraints via an iterative data-model refinement.
- Experimental results on GEO, ATIS and OVERNIGHT datasets show that our approach achieves competitive performance without using annotated data.

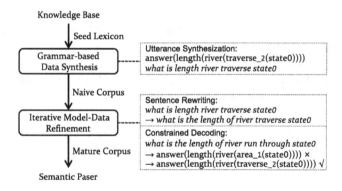

Fig. 1. The overview of our approach.

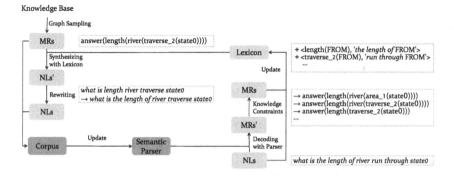

Fig. 2. The illustration of our approach. MRs denotes meaning representations, NLs denotes natural language sentences. The naive corpus is synthesized by seed lexicon. In each bootstrapping iteration, the corpus is refined via denoising language model and knowledge-constrained decoding. The data and the models are improved iteratively.

2 Background

2.1 Base Semantic Parsing Model

We employ the SEQ2SEQ semantic parser as our base model [12], which has shown its simplicity and effectiveness. Notice that our method is not specialized to SEQ2SEQ model and it can be used for any neural semantic parsers.

Encoder. Given a sentence $\mathbf{x} = w_1, w_2, ..., w_n$, the SEQ2SEQ model encodes $\mathbf{x}$ using a bidirectional RNN. Each word w_i is mapped to a fixed-dimensional vector by a word embedding function $\phi(\cdot)$ and then fed into a bidirectional LSTM [19]. The hidden states in two directions are concatenated $\mathbf{h}_i = [\overrightarrow{\mathbf{h}}_i; \overleftarrow{\mathbf{h}}_i]$, and the encoding of the whole sentence is: $\mathbf{h}_1, \mathbf{h}_2, ..., \mathbf{h}_n$.

Attention-Based Decoder. Given the sentence representation, the SEQ2SEQ model sequentially generates the tokens of its logical form. Specifically, the decoder is first initialized with the hidden states of encoder $\mathbf{s}_0 = [\overrightarrow{\mathbf{h}}_n; \overleftarrow{\mathbf{h}}_1]$. Then at each step t, let $\phi(y_{t-1})$ be the vector of the previous predicted logical form token, the current hidden state $\mathbf{s}_t$ is obtained from $\phi(y_{t-1})$ and $\mathbf{s}_{t-1}$. Then we calculate the attention weights for the current step t, with the i-th hidden state in the encoder:

$$\alpha_t^i = \frac{\exp(\mathbf{s}_t \cdot \mathbf{h}_i)}{\sum_{i=1}^n \exp(\mathbf{s}_t \cdot \mathbf{h}_i)} \tag{1}$$

and the next token is generalized from the vocabulary distribution:

$$\mathbf{c}_t = \sum_{i=1}^n \alpha_t^i \mathbf{h}_i$$

$$P(y_t | y_{<t}, \mathbf{x}) = \text{softmax}(\mathbf{W}_o[\mathbf{s}_t; \mathbf{c}_t] + \mathbf{b}_o) \tag{2}$$

where $\mathbf{W}_o \in \mathbb{R}^{|V_y| \times 3n}$, $\mathbf{b}_o \in \mathbb{R}^{|V_y|}$ and $|V_y|$ is the output vocabulary size.

Learning. Given a training corpus consisting of <utterance, logical form> pairs, the SEQ2SEQ model is trained by optimizing the objective function:

$$J = - \sum_{(\mathbf{x},\mathbf{y}) \in \mathbf{D}} \sum_{t=1}^m \log p(y_t | y_{<t}, \mathbf{x}) \tag{3}$$

where $\mathbf{D}$ is the corpus, $\mathbf{x}$ is the utterance, $\mathbf{y}$ is its logical form label.

2.2   SCFG for Data Synthesization

Wang, Berant, and Liang [40] use a synchronous context-free grammar(SCFG) to generate logical forms paired with canonical utterances, and use crowdsourcing to paraphrase these canonical utterances into natural utterances. The SCFG consists of a set of production rules (lexicon): $N \rightarrow \langle \alpha, \beta \rangle$, where N is a non-terminal, and α and β are sequence of terminal and non-terminal symbols. Any non-terminal symbol in α is aligned to the same non-terminal symbol in β, and vice versa. Therefore, SCFGs define a set of joint derivations of aligned pairs of strings. The seed lexicon in OVERNIGHT is specified by the builder containing types, entities, and properties in databases. Type checking is also performed to rule out some uninterpretable canonical utterances.

3   Approach

This section describes our data synthesis and iterative refinement method for semantic parsing. Firstly, we generate a naive training corpus by sampling meaning representations from knowledge bases and synthesizing their utterances using a grammar-based algorithm. Then, to reduce the noise and eliminate the gap with real corpus, we propose to iteratively refine the data and the model by rewriting synthesized utterances via a denoising language model and generating meaning representations via knowledge-constraint decoding. Figure 2 shows the overview of our approach and we describe all components in detail as follows.

3.1 Data Synthesis

In OVERNIGHT [40] and PARASEMPRE [3], they use simple grammars to generate logical forms paired with canonical utterances. To generate corpus from scratch, we also synthesize data via a grammar-based algorithm.

Specifically, we first sample MRs from knowledge bases via a graph sampling algorithm, then we synthesize their utterances by mapping predicates to words from a seed lexicon and composing these words using context free grammars. Different from the corpus generation method in OVERNIGHT, our method starts from not only grammar but also the knowledge base schema, and can be easier to extended to other datasets like GEO and ATIS.

Generating MRs via Graph Sampling. The graph sampling algorithm aims to sample meaning representations from knowledge bases. Given a knowledge base, Graph Sampling regards MRs as subgraphs of the knowledge base. To ensure the truthfulness and integrality of generated meaning representations, we sample subgraph-based MRs according to both the structure of MRs and the schemas of knowledge bases.

Specifically, to generate MRs, we start from the nonterminal token `root` and then recursively expand all nonterminal tokens in current MRs. For general/functional nonterminal tokens such as `root`, `argmax` and `count`, because they are domain-independent, we expand them using hand-crafted general production rules. For nonterminal tokens about entities and relations such as `river`, `state` and `city` for GEO, because they are domain dependent, we expand them by production rules sampled from knowledge base schemas.

To utilize the schema to produce MRs, we extend the original schema by adding the attribute value as value type nodes and the aggregation operations as self-loop edges. We provide the extended schema and sampling examples in the Fig. 3.

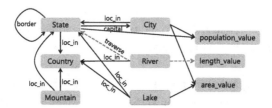

Fig. 3. The extended schema of GEO (partial). To sample the subgraph from the dotted edges, the root nonterminal token `root` is recursively extended by the production rules:
```
root → answer(length_value)
length_value → length(river_set)
river_set → river(river_attri)
river_attri → traverse_2(state_set)
state_set → state0,
```
generating the MR: `answer(length(river(traverse_2 (state0))))`

Based on the schema graph, the meaning representations can be effectively sampled by utilizing context-free grammar (i.e., the production rules) for grammatical correctness and knowledge base schemas for semantic correctness.

Synthesizing Utterances via SCFG-Based Algorithm. Based on canonical compositionality assumption in Wang, Berant, and Liang [40], we also use SCFG to generate utterances. We extend the context-free grammar in Graph Sampling to synchronous context-free grammar. For example in Fig. 2, based on the SCFG rules, we can synthesize the utterance "what is length river traverse state0" from the sampled MR:

$$\text{root} \rightarrow \langle \text{answer}(\text{FORM}), \text{what is FORM} \rangle$$
$$\text{FORM} \rightarrow \langle \text{length}(\text{FORM}), \text{length FORM} \rangle$$
$$\text{FORM} \rightarrow \langle \text{river}(\text{FORM}), \text{river FORM} \rangle$$
$$\text{FORM} \rightarrow \langle \text{traverse\_2}(\text{FORM}), \text{traverse FORM} \rangle$$
$$\text{FORM} \rightarrow \langle \text{state0}, \text{state0} \rangle$$

Seed Lexicon Construction. To synthesize utterances from sampled semantic representations, a lexicon is further needed for SCFG, which maps logical tokens to their natural language words. For OVERNIGHT, we simply use its original seed lexicon. For other datasets, we use the following simple way to build an initial lexicon:

For domain-general logical tokens we manually write their natural language templates. The number of domain-general rules is usually very small. Some examples of our domain-general rules are in Table 1.

Table 1. Examples of our domain-general rules on GEO (above) and ATIS (below). We write seed lexicon of domain-general grammar manually, the number of which is usually very small (only 5 needed in GEO and 12 in ATIS and 23 in OVERNIGHT).

Category	Domain-general rules	NL templates
Query	answer (FORM)	what is FORM
Count	count (FORM)	the number of FORM
Exclusion	exclude (FORM$_1$, FORM$_2$)	FORM$_1$ do not FORM$_2$
Superlative (max)	largest_one (VALUE (FORM))	FORM with largest VALUE
Filter (type)	$\lambda t \lambda s: (\$t\ \$s)$	$\$t\ \$s$
Filter (property)	$\lambda p \lambda v \lambda s: (\$p\ \$v\ \$s)$	$\$s$ whose $\$p$ is $\$v$
Comparative ($<$)	$\lambda p \lambda v \lambda s: (<\ (\$p\ \$v)\ \$s)$	$\$s$ whose $\$p$ is smaller than $\$v$
Superlative(max)	$\lambda p \lambda s: \text{argmax } \$s\ (\$p\ \$s)$	$\$s$ with largest $\$p$

For domain-dependent entity tokens and relation tokens, we simply use the words in their logical tokens, with a simple preprocessing which removes numbers and underlines. For example, the `area_1` denotes the words "area" and `departure_time` denotes the words "departure time".

Using the above SCFG with seed lexicon, an initial training corpus can be synthesized. Although, this seed lexicon is obviously with limited coverage and lack of diversity. This naive corpus can still provide a helpful start for semantic parsing. Next, we describe how to iterative refine the parsing mode and data.

3.2 Iterative Data-Model Refining

Due to the limitation of grammar and lexicon, the synthesized training instances in naive corpus are often noisy, differing from real-world sentences, and with limited diversity. To address these issues, we refine the corpus with the knowledge of language models and knowledge base constraints through a bootstrapping process: 1) we rewrite synthesized utterances via a denoising language model, so the utterances will be more fluent and closer to natural utterances; 2) we propose to exploit knowledge during decoding, so that meaning representations can be more accurately predicted even when the model is not strong enough; 3) we iteratively refine the data and the model via a bootstrapping process. After several iterations of refinement, we obtain the mature corpus and the final semantic parser.

Utterance Rewriting via Denoising Language Model. The synthesized utterances are often not fluent, differing from real-world sentences. For example, the synthesized utterance in Fig. 2: *"what is length river traverse state"* is very different to its natural expression *"what is the length of river traverses state0"*. And this discrepancy misleads models to learn incorrect patterns.

Thanks to the current powerful language models, we can use a denoising language model to rewrite synthesized utterances to more natural sentences. Specifically, we regard the synthesized utterances as a noisy version of natural expressions, and then denoise them via neural language model-based language denoising techniques [26].

Specifically, we train a language model based on GPT2.0 [34], which is then used to denoise by minimizing:

$$\mathcal{L}^{lm} = \mathbb{E}_{x \sim \mathbf{X}}[-\log P(x|C(x))] \tag{4}$$

where C is a noise model with some words dropped and swapped as in Lample et al. [26].

Generating High-Quality Lexicon via Knowledge-Constrained Decoding. To obtain high-quality lexicon, which can be used to synthesize better $\langle$MR, canonical utterance$\rangle$ pairs, we use the current parser to generate parallel data. Without manually annotated corpus, the initial semantic parser is often not strong enough, therefore it is difficult to find high-quality meaning representations. So we also apply knowledge-constrained decoding.

Like previous work [25,44,47], we decode the meaning representations under the grammar we mentioned in Graph Sampling. Only the grammatical logical forms are generated during the decoding. Additionally, we leverage knowledge base schemas to effectively filter out illegal logical forms. Given a semantic parser, we first obtain the top K meaning representations for each sentence. Then if there exists an executing program or search engine for logical forms, we will only keep the executable logical forms. Otherwise, we verify whether the logical form is well-typed under the knowledge base schema constraints, and only preserve the eligible logical forms.

After obtaining the higher quality parallel data, following Wong and Mooney [41], we apply the GIZA++ on the parallel data to get the alignments between words and grammar rules and induce a new SCFG lexicon.

Table 2. Accuracies on OVERNIGHT. The previous methods with superscript * means they use different unsupervised settings.

		Bas.	Blo.	Cal.	Hou.	Pub.	Rec.	Res.	Soc.	Avg.
Supervised										
SEQ2SEQ		84.3	57.9	78.1	69.9	76.2	80.7	78.0	80.5	75.7
RECOMBINATION [21]		85.2	58.1	78.0	71.4	76.4	79.6	76.2	81.4	75.8
CROSSDOMAIN [37]		86.2	60.2	79.8	71.4	78.9	84.7	81.6	82.9	78.2
SEQ2ACTION [9]		88.2	61.4	81.5	74.1	80.7	82.9	80.7	82.1	79.0
DUAL [6]		87.5	63.7	79.8	73.0	81.4	81.5	81.6	83.0	78.9
Unsupervised (with nonparallel data)										
Two-stage [7]		64.7	53.4	58.3	59.3	60.3	68.1	73.2	48.4	60.7
WmdSamples [7]		31.9	29.0	36.1	47.9	34.2	41.0	53.8	35.8	38.7
Mature Corpus + Samples		58.5	55.3	62.4	65.1	66.7	62.2	72.3	47.1	**61.2**
Unsupervised										
Cross-domain Zero Shot* [18]		-	28.3	53.6	52.4	55.3	60.2	61.7	-	-
GENOVERNIGHT [40]		15.6	27.7	17.3	45.9	46.7	26.3	61.3	9.7	31.3
Naive Corpus	EMBED BERT	15.9	24.6	18.6	44.1	46.9	27.0	62.2	9.7	31.1
	Glove	16.2	23.6	16.2	30.3	36.9	27.0	43.2	9.2	25.3
	Rand	13.8	21.1	15.6	28.2	21.9	27.0	31.1	8.2	20.9
Mature Corpus	EMBED BERT	**45.9**	**52.5**	**52.7**	**58.5**	**61.9**	**52.1**	**69.8**	**33.6**	**53.4**
	Glove	44.1	51.5	48.5	56.4	58.8	50.2	68.9	32.0	51.3
	Rand	35.1	43.2	36.5	44.7	46.9	46.5	65.0	25.6	42.9
	w/o Denoising	32.8	45.0	40.1	46.8	52.5	45.6	63.1	26.6	44.1
	w/o Constraint	29.0	39.7	35.3	37.8	41.9	42.8	64.7	23.4	39.3

Iterative Learning. It is obviously that the model promotion and the data refining can reinforce each other: better parsers can generate data of higher quality, and higher quality data can be used to train stronger models. Based on this intuition, we propose to iteratively refine model and data by leveraging the duality between them.

Specifically, in each data-model refining iteration, we: 1) first synthesize the utterances X' of the sampled MRs Y' using the current lexicon and the denoising model; 2) train a new semantic parser using the synthesized data; 3) parse the unlabeled utterances via knowledge-constrained decoding; 4) induce a new lexicon using both the highly confident automatically labeled data and the synthesized data.

We gradually increase the proportion of parsing data at each iteration. In the k-th iteration, we select the top $\delta \times (k+1)$ confident parsing pairs for lexicon learning. The confidence scores are calculated as the normalized likelihood:

$$Score(x, y) = \frac{1}{N_y} \log P(y|x) \tag{5}$$

4 Experiments

4.1 Experimental Settings

Datasets. We conduct experiments on three standard datasets: GEO, and ATIS, OVERNIGHT, which use different meaning representations and contain different domains.

GEO. This is a semantic parsing benchmark about U.S. geography [49]. The variable-free semantic representation FunQL [23] is used in this dataset. We follow the standard 600/280 train/test instance splits.

ATIS. This is a large dataset, which contains 5,410 queries to a flight booking system. Each question is annotated with a lambda calculus query. Following Zettlemoyer and Collins [51], we use the standard 4,473/448 train/test instance splits in our experiments.

OVERNIGHT. OVERNIGHT contains natural language paraphrases paired with lambda DCS logical forms across eight domains. We evaluate on the standard train/test splits as Jia and Liang [40].

In all our experiments, we only use the unlabeled sentences in each dataset. The standard accuracy is used to evaluate different systems, which is obtained as the same as Jia and Liang [21].

Synthesized Training Corpus. We generate training instances proportional to the original dataset sizes (1500 for GEO, 5000 for ATIS, and 1500 for each domain in OVERNIGHT). For OVERNIGHT, we use its original defined grammar and lexicon.

Denoising Language Model. We train an individual denoising language model for each dataset (each domain for OVERNIGHT). For each utterance in unlabeled queries, we sample 5 noisy sentences to construct the training pairs by dropping words randomly or slightly shuffling the utterance as Lample et al. [26]. The pretrained language model GPT2.0 is adapted on paraphrase generation dataset, then fine-tuned on denoising sentences with 15 epochs and the learning rate of 1e-5.

System Settings. We train all our models with 5 data-model refining iterations. In each iteration, the neural semantic parser is trained 15 epochs, with the initial learning rate of 0.001. We use Adam algorithm [24] to update parameters, with batch size is 20. Our model uses 200-dimensional hidden units and 200-dimensional word vectors for sentence encoding. We initialize all parameters by uniformly sampling within $[-0.1, 0.1]$. $BERT_{LARGE}$ [11] is used to get word representations. The beam size K during decoding is 5. The hyper-parameter δ is 0.1. Following Dong and Lapata [12], we handle entities with a Replacing mechanism, which replaces identified entities with their types and IDs.

4.2 Experimental Results

Overall Results. We compare our model with different settings:

1) **Naive Corpus** – the semantic parser is trained from the naive corpus, which is generated by meaning representation sampling and utterance synthesizing;

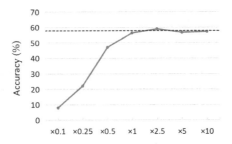

Fig. 4. Test accuracies on GEO with different size of synthesized data. The number of sampled meaning representations has increased from 0.1 times the amount of original data to 10 times. The dash line shows the accuracy of Golden MRs

2) **Mature Corpus** – the corpus is improved by iterative data-model refining;
3) **Supervised** – the model is trained using the original training corpus with the same settings.

For Overnight, we further compare with the Cross-domain Zero Shot [18] which is trained on other source domains and then generalized to new domains and GEN-OVERNIGHT [40] in which all the canonical utterances are also generated without manual annotation. With the nonparallel data: Two-stage [7] employs the cycle learning framework. WmdSamples [7] labels each input sentences with the most possible outputs in the unparallel corpus and deals with these faked samples in a supervised way. Our Mature Corpus + Samples method follows WmdSamples, using the parser built on the refined data to label each input.

The results are shown in Table 2 and Table 3. We can see that:

1) **Our learning framework is promising for resolving the training data bottleneck problem of semantic parsing.** In all datasets, our method outperforms other baselines in the same unsupervised settings. On OVERNIGHT, our method also surpasses the previous approaches in unsupervised data settings. These results verify that data synthesis and iterative data-model refinement is a promising method for semantic parsing without annotated logical forms.
2) **The iterative data-model refining is effective to bootstrap semantic parsers.** Compared with Naive Corpus, after corpus refinement our Mature Corpus gains 27.9 accuracy improvement in ATIS. This verifies the effectiveness of the data-model refining. We believe it results from: i) denoising language model can improve the quality of generated utterances and knowledge-constrained decoding can filter out invalid meaning representations; ii) the bootstrapping can leverage the duality between data and model for iterative refining.

Detailed Analysis

Effects of Utterance Denoising and Constrained Decoding. Table 2 and 3 show the accuracies by removing denoising language model (–Denoising) and by removing

Table 3. Accuracies on GEO and ATIS. The previous methods with superscript * means they use different unsupervised settings. Confidence-driven and Two-stage both use the nonparallel data.

	GEO	ATIS
Supervised		
SEQ2SEQ	88.2	84.2
Dong and Lapata [12]	87.1	84.6
Jia and Liang [21]	89.3	83.3
Susanto and Lu [39]	90.0	-
Xu et al. [45]	88.1	85.9
Chen, Sun, and Han [9]	88.9	85.5
Jie and Lu [22]	89.3	-
Guo et al. [17]	87.1	83.1
Unsupervised		
Confidence-driven*	66.4	-
Two-stage*	63.7	-
Naive Corpus	29.3	25.0
Mature Corpus		
EMBED BERT	**58.2**	**52.9**
GloVe	55.0	52.5
Rand	44.6	43.3
w/o Denoising	45.0	39.5
w/o Constraint	38.9	37.1

Table 4. Evaluation Accuracies on GEO and ATIS with the increase of iterations.

	GEO	ATIS
Iterative updating		
Iter.1	41.4	37.7
Iter.2	49.3	44.6
Iter.3	57.1	48.0
Iter.4	58.9	52.5
Iter.5	58.2	52.9

knowledge constraints during decoding (–Constraint). We can see that: 1) Both utterance denoising and constrained decoding are effective. In average on all three datasets, removing denoising results in 12.0 accuracy drop and removing constrained decoding results in 16.4 accuracy drop. 2) Constrained decoding is more helpful than denoising. We believe this is because the grammar and the knowledge-base can effectively improve the quality of automatically generated parallel data, from which a new lexicon is built and is further used to synthesize new parallel data.

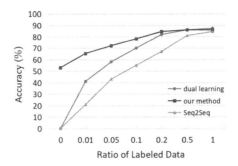

Fig. 5. Test accuracies on ATIS with different amounts of labeled data.

Effects of Word Embeddings. To analyze the effects of word embeddings settings, we compare our method with different settings of word embeddings: BERT – word representations are from the pretrained BERT$_{LARGE}$ [11]; GloVe – word embeddings are initialized by GloVe [31]; Rand – the word embeddings are initialized by uniformly sampling within the interval [-0.2, 0.2], and the unseen words are all presented as UNK token. We can see that the pretrained word embeddings can effectively improve the model. We believe this is because it empowers the model with better representation and helps the model generalize to similar words.

Effect of Data Synthesis. To analyze the effectiveness of synthesized data, we: 1) compare our models with Golden MRs – in which all utterances are synthesized from the manually labeled meaning representations in original corpus; 2) increase the amount of sampled meaning representations from ×0.1 to ×10 size of the original labeled data. The results on GEO are shown on Fig. 4.

We can see that: 1) the graph sampling algorithm can effectively sample meaning representations – compared with Golden-MRs, our method can achieve nearly the same performance with ×1 dataset. 2) The data synthesis is useful, when the size of data increases from ×0.1 to ×1, the performance gradually increases. We also noticed that when the data size exceeds the original data, the performance of the model does not improve much. We believe that this is because too much data generated with a certain amount of noise can no longer provide useful supervision information.

Effect of Iterative Bootstrapping. Table 4 shows the accuracies by increasing the number of iterations. We can see that: 1) the iterative data-model refining is effective: when we conduct more refining iterations, the performance gradually increases and stabilizes at a reasonable level – from 41.4 accuracy in Iter 1 to 58.9 in Iter 4 in GEO; 2) The bootstrapping process can reach its equilibrium within few iterations: for GEO in 5 iterations and for ATIS in 4 iterations.

Semi-supervised Learning. To investigate the effectiveness of our method given some additional labeled instances, we vary the amount of labeled data from 0 to all labeled data. Our model can use the labeled data to train semantic parser and induce lexicon in each iteration. Seq2Seq can only use the labeled data. Dual learning [6] forms a closed loop to learn unlabeled data in reinforcement learning. In Fig. 5, We can see that our model enhances semantic parsing over most settings. Especially, our model has obvious advantages when there is a small amount of labeled data.

5 Related Work

Neural Semantic Parsers. In recent years, neural semantic parsers have achieved significant progress. Neural parsers model semantic parsing as a sentence to logical form translation task [20–22,44], And many constrained decoding algorithms are also proposed [9,20,25,27];

Data Scarcity in Semantic Parsing. Witnessed the labeled data bottleneck problem, many techniques have been proposed to reduce the demand for labeled logical forms. Many weakly supervised learning are proposed [1,2,4,35], such as denotation-base learning [14,30], iterative searching [10]. Semi-supervised semantic parsing is also proposed, such as variational auto-encoding [48], dual learning [6], dual information maximization [46], and back-translation [38]. Constrained language models are also proposed to resolve few-shot semantic parsing [36,43].

Unsupervised Semantic Parsers. There are also some unsupervised semantic parsers, such as USP [32] proposes the first unsupervised semantic parse, and GUSP [33] builds semantic parser by annotating the dependency-tree nodes and edges. Wang et al. [15] select high confidence pairs for unsupervised learning. Two-stage [7] train unsupervised paraphrasing model with non-parallel data for semantic parsing.

6 Conclusions

We propose a data synthesis and iterative data-model refining algorithm for neural semantic parsing, which can build semantic parsers without labeled data. In our method, the naive corpus is generated from scratch by grammar-based method and knowledge base schemas, and the corpus is improved on bootstrapping to refine model and data with the knowledge of language models and knowledge bases constraints. Experimental results show our approach can achieve promising performance in unsupervised settings.

References

1. Agrawal, P., Dalmia, A., Jain, P., Bansal, A., Mittal, A.R., Sankaranarayanan, K.: Unified semantic parsing with weak supervision. In: ACL (2019)
2. Artzi, Y., Zettlemoyer, L.: Weakly supervised learning of semantic parsers for mapping instructions to actions. TACL 1, 49–62 (2013)
3. Berant, J., Liang, P.: Semantic parsing via paraphrasing. In: ACL (2014)
4. Berant, J., Chou, A., Frostig, R., Liang, P.: Semantic parsing on freebase from question-answer pairs. In: EMNLP (2013)
5. Bogin, B., Berant, J., Gardner, M.: Representing schema structure with graph neural networks for text-to-SQL parsing. In: ACL (2019)

6. Cao, R., Zhu, S., Liu, C., Li, J., Yu, K.: Semantic parsing with dual learning. In: ACL (2019)
7. Cao, R., et al.: Unsupervised dual paraphrasing for two-stage semantic parsing. In: ACL (2020)
8. Chang, S., Liu, P., Tang, Y., Huang, J., He, X., Zhou, B.: Zero-shot text-to-SQL learning with auxiliary task. In: AAAI (2020)
9. Chen, B., Sun, L., Han, X.: Sequence-to-action, end-to-end semantic graph generation for semantic parsing. In: ACL (2018)
10. Dasigi, P., Gardner, M., Murty, S., Zettlemoyer, L., Hovy, E.H.: Iterative search for weakly supervised semantic parsing. In: NAACL-HLT (2019)
11. Devlin, J., Chang, M.-W., Lee, K., Toutanova, K.: BERT: pre-training of deep bidirectional transformers for language understanding. In: NAACL-HLT (2019)
12. Dong, L., Lapata, M.: Language to logical form with neural attention. In: ACL (2016)
13. Dong, L., Lapata, M.: Coarse-to-fine decoding for neural semantic parsing. In: ACL (2018)
14. Goldman, O., Latcinnik, V., Nave, E., Globerson, A., Berant, J.: Weakly supervised semantic parsing with abstract examples. In: ACL (2018)
15. Goldwasser, D., Reichart, R., Clarke, J., Roth, D.: Confidence driven unsupervised semantic parsing. In: ACL (2011)
16. Guo, J., et al.: Towards complex text-to-SQL in cross-domain database with intermediate representation. In: ACL (2019)
17. Guo, J., et al.: Benchmarking meaning representations in neural semantic parsing. In: EMNLP (2020)
18. Herzig, J., Berant, J.: Decoupling structure and lexicon for zero-shot semantic parsing. In: EMNLP (2018)
19. Hochreiter, S., Schmidhuber, J.: Long short-term memory. Neural Comput. **9**, 1735–1780 (1997)
20. Iyyer, M., Yih, W., Chang, M.-W.: Search-based neural structured learning for sequential question answering. In: ACL (2017)
21. Jia, R., Liang, P.: Data recombination for neural semantic parsing. In: ACL (2016)
22. Jie, Z., Lu, W.: Dependency-based hybrid trees for semantic parsing. In: EMNLP (2018)
23. Kate, R.J., Wong, Y.W., Mooney, R.J.: Learning to transform natural to formal languages. In: IAAI (2005)
24. Kingma, D.P., Ba, J.: Adam: a method for stochastic optimization. In: ICLR (2015)
25. Krishnamurthy, J., Dasigi, P., Gardner, M.: Neural semantic parsing with type constraints for semi-structured tables. In: EMNLP (2017)
26. Lample, G., Ott, M., Conneau, A., Denoyer, L., Ranzato, M.: Phrase-based & neural unsupervised machine translation. In: EMNLP (2018)
27. Liang, C., Berant, J., Le, Q., Forbus, K.D., Lao, N.: Neural symbolic machines: learning semantic parsers on freebase with weak supervision. In: ACL (2017)
28. Lu, W., Ng, H.T., Lee, W.S., Zettlemoyer, L.S.: A generative model for parsing natural language to meaning representations. In: EMNLP (2008)
29. Misra, D., Chang, M.-W., He, X., Yih, W.: Policy shaping and generalized update equations for semantic parsing from denotations. In: EMNLP (2018)
30. Pasupat, P., Liang, P.: Inferring logical forms from denotations. In: ACL (2016)
31. Pennington, J., Socher, R., Manning, C.D.: Glove: global vectors for word representation. In: EMNLP (2014)
32. Poon, H., Domingos, P.M.: Unsupervised semantic parsing. In: EMNLP (2009)
33. Poon, H.: Grounded unsupervised semantic parsing. In: ACL (2013)
34. Radford, A., Wu, J., Child, R., Luan, D., Amodei, D., Sutskever, I.: Language models are unsupervised multitask learners (2019)
35. Reddy, S., Lapata, M., Steedman, M.: Large-scale semantic parsing without question-answer pairs. Trans. Assoc. Comput. Linguist. **2**, 377–392 (2014)

36. Shin, R., et al.: Constrained language models yield few-shot semantic parsers. In: Moens, M.-F., Huang, X., Specia, L., Yih, S.W. (eds.) Proceedings of the 2021 Conference on Empirical Methods in Natural Language Processing, EMNLP 2021, Virtual Event/Punta Cana, Dominican Republic, 7–11 November 2021, pp. 7699–7715. Association for Computational Linguistics (2021)
37. Su, Y., Yan, X.: Cross-domain semantic parsing via paraphrasing. In: EMNLP (2017)
38. Sun, Y., et al.: Neural semantic parsing in low-resource settings with back-translation and meta-learning. CoRR (2019)
39. Susanto, R.H., Lu, W.: Semantic parsing with neural hybrid trees. In: AAAI (2017)
40. Wang, Y., Berant, J., Liang, P.: Building a semantic parser overnight. In: ACL (2015)
41. Wong, Y.W., Mooney, R.J.: Learning for semantic parsing with statistical machine translation. In: NACL (2006)
42. Wong, Y.W., Mooney, R.J.: Learning synchronous grammars for semantic parsing with lambda calculus. In: ACL (2007)
43. Wu, S., et al.: From paraphrasing to semantic parsing: unsupervised semantic parsing via synchronous semantic decoding. In: Zong, C., Xia, F., Li, W., Navigli, R. (eds.) Proceedings of the 59th Annual Meeting of the Association for Computational Linguistics and the 11th International Joint Conference on Natural Language Processing, ACL/IJCNLP 2021, (Volume 1: Long Papers), Virtual Event, 1–6 August 2021, pp. 5110–5121. Association for Computational Linguistics (2021)
44. Xiao, C., Dymetman, M., Gardent, C.: Sequence-based structured prediction for semantic parsing. In: ACL (2016)
45. Xu, K., Wu, L., Wang, Z., Yu, M., Chen, L., Sheinin, V.: Exploiting rich syntactic information for semantic parsing with graph-to-sequence model. In: EMNLP (2018)
46. Ye, H., Li, W., Wang, L.: Jointly learning semantic parser and natural language generator via dual information maximization. In: ACL (2019)
47. Yin, P., Neubig, G.: A syntactic neural model for general-purpose code generation. In: ACL (2017)
48. Yin, P., Zhou, C., He, J., Neubig, G.: StructVAE: tree-structured latent variable models for semi-supervised semantic parsing. In: ACL (2018)
49. Zelle, J.M., Mooney, R.J.: Learning to parse database queries using inductive logic programming. In: AAAI (1996)
50. Zettlemoyer, L.S., Collins, M.: Learning to map sentences to logical form: structured classification with probabilistic categorial grammars. In: UAI (2005)
51. Zettlemoyer, L.S., Collins, M.: Online learning of relaxed CCG grammars for parsing to logical form. In: EMNLP-CoNLL (2007)

EventBERT: Incorporating Event-Based Semantics for Natural Language Understanding

Anni Zou[1,2,3], Zhuosheng Zhang[1,2,3], and Hai Zhao[1,2,3(✉)]

[1] Department of Computer Science and Engineering, Shanghai Jiao Tong University,
Shanghai, China
zhaohai@cs.sjtu.edu.cn
[2] Key Laboratory of Shanghai Education Commission for Intelligent Interaction
and Cognitive Engineering, Shanghai Jiao Tong University, Shanghai, China
[3] MoE Key Lab of Artificial Intelligence, AI Institute, Shanghai Jiao Tong University,
Shanghai, China

Abstract. Natural language understanding tasks require a comprehensive understanding of natural language and further reasoning about it, on the basis of holistic information at different levels to gain comprehensive knowledge. In recent years, pre-trained language models (PrLMs) have shown impressive performance in natural language understanding. However, they rely mainly on extracting context-sensitive statistical patterns without explicitly modeling linguistic information, such as semantic relationships entailed in natural language. In this work, we propose EventBERT, an event-based semantic representation model that takes BERT as the backbone and refines with event-based structural semantics in terms of graph convolution networks. EventBERT benefits simultaneously from rich event-based structures embodied in the graph and contextual semantics learned in pre-trained model BERT. Experimental results on the GLUE benchmark show that the proposed model consistently outperforms the baseline model.

Keywords: Event-based semantics · Graph convolution networks · Natural language understanding

1 Introduction

Recent years have witnessed deep pre-trained language models (PrLM) such as ELMo [28], BERT [8], XLNet [45] and ERNIE [38] significantly prospering the performance of a wide range of natural language understanding (NLU) tasks. The remarkable advancements brought by PrLM have shown the effectiveness of leveraging contextualized representation. However, they mainly rest on extracting context-sensitive statistical patterns without explicitly modeling linguistic information such as semantic relationships in natural language.

It is clear that natural language itself abounds with ample, multi-level linguistic information. Although PrLMs like BERT implicitly represent linguistic knowledge more or less [33], studies disclose that linguistic knowledge is far from fully

This work was supported in part by the Key Projects of National Natural Science Foundation of China under Grants U1836222 and 61733011.

absorbed [10,33]. Therefore, there emerges a series of derivatives of PrLM intending to fuse explicit linguistic knowledge so as to acquire better language representation, including syntactic [1,44,47] and semantic information [14,17,46].

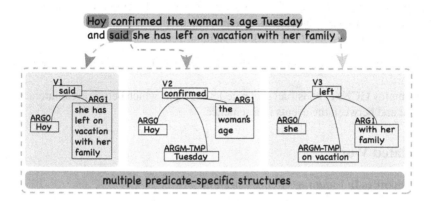

Fig. 1. An example showing how SRL parses sentences and the intuition of constructing event-based graph.

In cognition practice, human needs to distill semantics of different levels to gain a comprehensive understanding, whereas neural language models learn semantic representation to deal with downstream tasks [13]. Thus, effective learning of semantic knowledge plays a crucial role in NLU tasks and has gained growing attention recently. For instance, SemBERT [46] directly connects multiple predicate-argument structures acquired by semantic role labeler (SRL) to get the joint representation.

The essence of SRL [36] lies in that every sentence possesses multiple predicate-specific structures which can represent different frames of events, while semantic roles express the abstract role that arguments of a predicate can take in the event. Besides, the events inside a sentence have interactions with each other that serve together to present the overall semantic knowledge. As shown in Fig. 1, SRL parses every sentence with multiple predicate-specific structures which can serve as events inferring *who did what to whom, when and why*. Each event has an inner structure centered on the predicate to which several arguments are associated such as *Hoy[ARG0], the woman's age[ARG1]* and *Tuesday[ARGM-TMP]* connected to *confirmed[V]*. Meanwhile, the multiple events work together to give a comprehensive meaning of a sentence, like the events centered on *said, confirmed* and *left*. With regard to delving into the inner interactions between the events and effectively capturing multiple objects, we are motivated to build a graph to reveal the intrinsic structures between and inside the events.

Inspired by the above ideas, we propose EventBERT: an event-based semantic representation model which takes BERT as the backbone and refines with event-based structural semantics. Our EventBERT benefits simultaneously from rich event-based structures embodied in the graph and contextual semantics learned in the pre-trained BERT.

Our proposed model works in three steps: it first applies an off-the-shelf SRL toolkit to parse every sentence with semantic role labels; then it constructs event-based graphs and employs Graph Convolutional Networks (GCNs) [35] to propagate and aggregate information from neighboring nodes on the graph; at last, it combines the contextualized representation acquired by BERT encoder together with the graph-level representation to obtain an event-based contextualized representation.

The key contributions of our work are summarized as follows:

1) We extract event-based semantic knowledge from SRL to enrich language representation.
2) We employ GCNs to construct sentence-level graphs which better reveal interactions inside and between the events in a sentence.

2   Related Work

2.1   Semantics in Language Representation

Recent studies show that current prominent pre-trained language models have already incorporated semantic information to some extent [6], yet such implicit semantic information is far from enough for comprehensive natural language understanding [10]. Thus there emerges a research line that focuses on fusing semantic information into contextualized language representation. ERNIE2.0 [38] adopts three-stage masking in which entity-level masking helps to obtain a word representation containing richer semantic information. SemBERT [46] makes use of PropBank [27] to fuse semantic role tags into language representation. FMSR [16] utilizes FrameNet [2] to extract multi-level semantic information within sentences. SS-MRC [15] takes advantage of syntax and frame semantics in an attempt to carve out information from two complementary perspectives to obtain richer language representation.

Besides simply employing semantic knowledge, other recent works shift the focus to exploring deeper structural semantics. For instance, frame semantics and graph neural networks are leveraged to model sentences from both intra-sentence level and inter-sentence level [14]. SIFT is introduced to inject predicate-argument semantic dependencies into pre-trained language models via R-GCNs [42]. Structured knowledge is introduced through multi-tasking to get a unified model, which inspires the potential of leveraging structural information [43]. Unlike previous works that attempt to capture shallow semantic structures by semantic tags, our model digs deeper into semantics itself and aims to find the structured event-based information behind semantics, thus unveiling richer structural-semantic information inside the sentence.

2.2   Graph Modeling for Language Understanding

As natural language itself abounds with dependencies and intricate relations between different levels of language units, graph neural networks (GNNs), which model the units as nodes in the graph and learn the weight via the message passing between nodes of the graph [18,34,39], stand out by explicitly and intuitively capturing the relations. Besides, a number of extensions to the original graph neural networks have been developed, the most notable of which include graph convolutional networks (GCNs) [18], graph attention networks (GANs) [39] and the models from [22] and [29] utilizing gating mechanisms to facilitate optimization.

In response to the outstanding performance of GCNs, several efforts have been made in recent years to improve performance on natural language understanding using GCNs, including GraphRel [12] which considers the interaction between named entities and relations via relation-weighted GCNs to better extract relations, NumNet [32] which utilizes a numerically-aware graph to perform numerical reasoning, DFGN [30] which dynamically builds the entity graph by adding the edges with co-occurrence relations, HGN [11] which creates a hierarchical graph by constructing nodes on different levels of granularity and social information reasoning [21] which uses GCNs to capture the documents' social context.

Moreover, R-GCNs [35] have shown effectiveness in relational graph modeling. For example, Entity-GCN [7] employs R-GCNs to link mentions of candidate answers for multi-document question answering. DFGN [30] dynamically builds the entity graph by adding the edges with co-occurrence relations and softly masking out irrelevant entities. DGM [26] constructs two discourse graphs and uses R-GCNs to fully capture interactions among the elements. R-GCNs are employed to enhance reference dependencies for dialogue disentanglement [23]. In contrast with previous works, our work proposes a sentence-level graph that is finely designed to mine the relationships between multiple elements in a sentence, extract rich structural semantics and facilitate information flow over the graph as well.

3   Model

Figure 2 gives an overview of our proposed EventBERT, which consists of two major components:

1. Context Encoder which acquires deep and contextualized representations for raw input sequences by following BERT architecture;
2. Event-based Encoder which obtains richer structural-semantic representation by modeling event-based intra-sentence graphs.

We omit the details of BERT which is widely used and ubiquitous and leave readers to resort to [8] for more information.

3.1   Context Encoder

The raw input sentence $X = \{x_1, \ldots, x_n\}$ is a sequence of words in length n. It is first tokenized to a sequence of sub-words with [SEP] inserted at the end as the end marker and [CLS] inserted at the beginning to get a sentence-level representation: $X' = \{token_1, \ldots, token_m\}$. Then we pass it through the embedding block and encoder block of BERT to produce a context-informed representation $C = \{c_1, \ldots, c_m\} \in \mathbb{R}^{m \times d_{hs}}$ using the equation below:

$$C = BERT(X'), \tag{1}$$

where m denotes the length of sentence on sub-word level and d_{hs} stands for the dimension of hidden states.

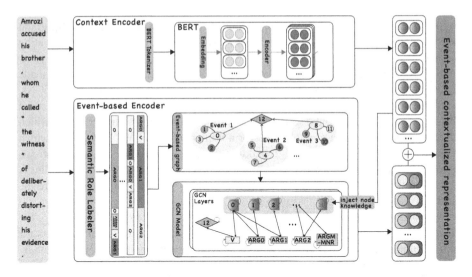

Fig. 2. The overall structure of EventBERT.

3.2 Event-Based Encoder

Semantic Role Labeler. The raw input sentence is simultaneously fed into Semantic Role Labeler [36] to fetch multiple predicate-specific structures tagged by PropBank semantic roles:

$$T = \{t_1, \ldots, t_d\}, \tag{2}$$

where d is the number of semantic structures for one sentence. Notably, t_i can be represented under the format $\{tag_1^i, tag_2^i, \ldots, tag_n^i\}$ and every tag span in t_i is recorded with its corresponding index in the context for further alignment.

Graph Construction. Figure 3 shows the process of graph construction: the predicates in the original input text are firstly extracted and an event subgraph is constructed with each predicate as the center; then a super event node (SEN) is applied to link all the predicates to collect the integral event information within the aggregated sentence; the Levi graph is finally constructed with reference to the method of [20], which is used to prepare the next stage of further computational operations on the graph.

For each sentence with the argument-predicate roles, we construct an event-based graph $G = (\mathcal{V}, \mathcal{E}, \mathcal{R})$ with span-level nodes $v_i \in \mathcal{V}$ and labeled edges $(v_i, r, v_j) \in \mathcal{E}$, where $r \in \mathcal{R}$ a relation type. Since every sentence has several semantic structures, here we take one structure as example and show the modeling method. Given $Seq_{tag} = \{tag_1, tag_2, \ldots, tag_n\}$ a word-level tag sequence,

1. We first transform it to a span-level sequence $Seq'_{tag} = \{tag'_1, tag'_2, \ldots, tag'_l\}$ by aggregating the same neighboring tags with $l \leq n$ representing the length of tags on span-level;
2. Then, we add a Super Event Node ($v = SEN$) to seize global graph information;

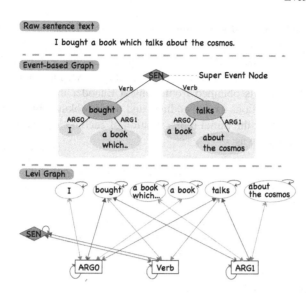

Fig. 3. The process of graph construction: from raw sentence text to event-based graph and corresponding Levi graph.

3. After that, we add other nodes and edges to G based on the following process:
   (a) we first find tag'_p which corresponds to predicate (*Verb* in e'),
   (b) we add a node $v = n_p$ and a directed edge $e = (n_p, Verb, SEN)$ with $r = Verb$,
   (c) for the rest tags referring to arguments of the predicate, tag'_q for example, we add a node $v = n_q$ and a directed edge linking to the predicate $e = (n_q, tag'_q, n_p)$ with relation $r = tag_q$;
4. Finally, the corresponding Levi graph [20] is extended from G to $G_L = (\mathcal{V}_L, \mathcal{E}_L, \mathcal{R}_L)$. For nodes $\mathcal{V}_L$, we add the nodes representing relations to the original: $\mathcal{V}_L = \mathcal{V} \cup \mathcal{R}$. For edges $\mathcal{E}_L$, we transform each edge $e = (n_q, tag'_q, n_p)$ in G into two corresponding edges: $e_1 = (n_q, tag'_q)$ and $e_2 = (tag'_q, n_p)$ in G_L. For $\mathcal{R}_L$, we follow the setting of [26] and refine it to five types: *default-in*, *default-out*, *reverse-in*, *reverse-out*, *self* according to the direction of edges towards the relation vertices, as is shown in Table 1.

Table 1. Relation types in our extended Levi graph

$\mathcal{R}_L$ in Levi graph	Illustration
default-in	The propagation path pointing to the node as the end point
default-out	The propagation path pointing to the node as the starting point
reverse-in	The propagation path in the opposite direction of *default-in*
reverse-out	The propagation path in the opposite direction of *default-out*
self	The propagation paths pointing to the node itself

Event-Based Contextualized Representation. We adopt Relational Graph Convolutional Networks (R-GCNs) [35] to implement explicit event graphs since traditional Graph Convolutional Networks (GCNs) cannot handle graphs containing edge features with multiple relations. For predicate and argument nodes, we inject the corresponding span-level encoding results obtained from Context Encoder in Sect. 3.1. For relation nodes, we regard the relations as embeddings and use a lookup table to get the initial representation. Given that the initial representation of each node v_i is h_i^0, the propagation process can be written as:

$$h_i^{(l+1)} = \text{ReLU} \left(\sum_{r \in \mathcal{R}_L} \sum_{v_j \in \mathcal{N}_r(v_i)} \frac{1}{c_{i,r}} w_r^{(l)} h_j^{(l)} \right), \tag{3}$$

where $h_i^{(l)} \in \mathbb{R}^{d^{(l)}}$ is the hidden state of node v_i in layer l with $d^{(l)}$ being the dimensionality of this layer's representations, $\mathcal{N}_r(v_i)$ denotes the set of neighbor indices of node v_i under the relation r, $c_{i,r}$ is a problem-specific normalization constant equal to $|\mathcal{N}_i^r|$, $w_r^{(l)}$ is the learnable parameters of layer l.

Since the importance of these relations cannot be treated the same, for example, the relation *Verb* is much more important than the relation *ARG2*, we introduce the gating mechanism [24]. The basic idea is to compute a value between 0 and 1 for message passing control as is shown in Eq. 4. Finally, the propagation process of R-GCNs under the gating mechanism is as follows:

$$g_j^{(l)} = \text{Sigmoid} \left(h_j^{(l)} W_{r,g}^{(l)} \right) \tag{4}$$

$$h_i^{(l+1)} = \text{ReLU} \left(\sum_{r \in \mathcal{R}_L} \sum_{v_j \in \mathcal{N}_r(v_i)} g_j^{(l)} \frac{1}{c_{i,r}} w_r^{(l)} h_j^{(l)} \right), \tag{5}$$

where $W_{r,g}^{(l)}$ is the learnable parameter under the l-th level relation type r.

With R-GCNs model, we obtain a graph-level semantic representation:

$$R = \{r_1, \ldots, r_f\} \in \mathbb{R}^{f \times d_{hs}} \tag{6}$$

where f is the number of nodes in the graph and d_{hs} is the same dimension as the representation C in Eq. 1 obtained from the context encoder.

At last, we concatenate R with the contextual sub-word-level representation C provided by Context Encoder and generate an event-based contextualized representation taking the mean value of both sub-word-level and graph-level information, which is then used as the new sequence representation for downstream tasks following the same way of [8].

4 Experiments

4.1 Setup

Datasets. We build EventBERT on the BERT backbone and fine-tune the model on GLUE (General Language Understanding Evaluation) benchmark [40] to evaluate the

Table 2. Comparisons between our models and baseline models on GLUE dev set.

Model	CoLA (mc)	SST-2 (acc)	MNLI (acc)	QNLI (acc)	RTE (acc)	MRPC (acc)	QQP (acc)	STS-B (pc)	Avg -
Base-size									
BERT$_{BASE}$	58.4	92.8	83.2	88.6	68.5	86.0	86.5	87.8	81.5
EventBERT$_{BASE}$	59.6	93.3	83.9	91.8	69.7	89.7	89.8	88.9	83.3(↑1.8)
Large-size									
BERT$_{LARGE}$	60.3	93.1	85.2	91.5	70.3	88.5	90.2	89.3	83.6
EventBERT$_{LARGE}$	63.1	94.0	85.3	92.6	71.4	89.5	90.6	89.5	84.5(↑0.9)

performance, which includes two single-sentence tasks CoLA [41], SST-2 [37]), three similarity and paraphrase tasks MRPC [9], STS-B [4], QQP [5], three inference tasks MNLI [25], QNLI [31], RTE [3]. We exclude the controversial and problematic dataset WNLI [19].

Evaluation Metrics. According to [40], different datasets in GLUE correspond to different evaluation metrics, which include accuracy (acc), Matthew's correlation (mc) and Pearson correlation (pc). Among the eight datasets, STS-B is reported by Pearson correlation, CoLA is reported by Matthew's correlation, and other tasks are reported by accuracy.

Implementation Details. For the experiments, we use an initial learning rate in {1e−5, 2e−5, 3e−5} with warm-up rate of 0.1 and L2 weight decay of 0.01. The batch size is selected in {16, 32}. The maximum number of epochs is set in [2, 5] depending on tasks. Texts are tokenized with maximum length of 256 for the tasks. We use 2 layers of R-GCNs in our model.

4.2   Results

Table 2 presents the results on the GLUE benchmark, which show that EventBERT achieves consistent gains over all the subtasks under both base and large models.

The results indicate that our model performs better on longer sentences as shown in Sect. 5.3. Furthermore, our analysis shows that EventBERT can effectively benefit from the fine-grained graph-like event-based structures, as illustrated in case studies in Sect. 5.4. The results also disclose that modeling intrinsic structures between and inside events is crucial for language understanding.

In addition, the experimental results show that EventBERT has a significant performance gain on small datasets such as CoLA and MRPC, which indicates that semantic information involving event modeling is more advantageous and competitive in smaller datasets. In practice or industry, large-scale annotated data is rare and scarce due to the high cost and required expensive human resources, so language models that dominate in small-scale datasets are more valuable and important for most NLP tasks.

5 Analysis

5.1 Ablation Study

We conduct the ablation study to investigate the effects of the gating mechanism and the addition of global nodes in the event-based encoder module. Results in Table 3 show that both the gating mechanism and global nodes are non-trivial.

5.2 Methods of Aggregation

During the period of concatenating and aggregating the graph level semantic representation R and the contextual representation C, we further analyze the influence of different methods of aggregation such as max-pooling and mean-pooling by comparing the models with the same hyper-parameters on three datasets CoLA, MRPC and RTE respectively. Results in Table 3 demonstrate that employing mean-pooling presents better performance.

5.3 Effectiveness of Semantic Structures

In order to dig deeper into the rationale behind the effectiveness of the model, we select two datasets QNLI and MRPC, representing large-scale and small-scale datasets respectively. We statistically calculate the accuracy of the corresponding models on different word-level sequence length intervals for EventBERT and baseline. Figure 4 shows that our model outperforms the baseline especially when the sequence is relatively long and our model performs better on longer sentences compared with shorter ones, which implies that modeling intrinsic semantic structures is potential to guide the model to learn richer structural semantics more than contextualized information. Thus, the analysis of word sequence lengths shows that EventBERT performs better on data with longer sequence lengths, which indicates that event-level modeling is promising and competitive for understanding long texts. Under many practical situations where available data are long texts, the idea of extracting event-level structural-semantic information is promising in many NLP tasks.

Table 3. Ablation study and comparison of aggregation methods on three datasets.

Model	CoLA (mc)	MRPC (acc)	RTE (acc)
Ablation study			
EventBERT$_{base}$	59.6	89.7	69.7
w/o gating	58.6	86.8	69.0
w/o global node	58.4	87.0	67.9
Aggregation methods			
BERT$_{base}$	58.4	86.0	68.5
w/ max-pooling	59.1	86.8	68.2
w/ mean-pooling	59.6	89.7	69.7

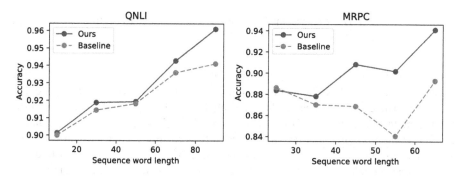

Fig. 4. Accuracy of different sequence word lengths on QNLI and MRPC.

5.4   Interpretability: Case Study

We select three cases in Classification, Sentence Similarity and Language Inference from SST-2, MRPC and QNLI respectively which are shown in Fig. 5, aiming to further explore the mechanism. It can be seen that our model can perceive explicit structural meaning to better understand the language. We will analyze each of the three cases in detail so as to analyze the advantages of EventBERT more intuitively.

Task	Example	Graph	Results
Classification	anchored by friel and williams 's exceptional performances , the film 's power lies in its complexity .		EventBERT: positive ✓ Baseline: negative ✗
Sentence Similarity	A: The Calgary woman , who is in her twenties, donated blood on Aug. 7 . B: The woman -- who has no symptoms of illness -- donated blood Aug. 7		EventBERT: not equivalent ✓ Baseline: equivalent ✗
Language Inference	A: Why was ABC forced to sell its interests in international networks in the 70s? B: As a result, ABC was forced to sell all of its interests in international networks, mainly in Japan and Latin America, in the 1970s.		EventBERT: not entailment ✓ Baseline: entailment ✗

Fig. 5. Examples selected from the dev set of SST-2, MRPC and QNLI where baseline fails but our model succeeds.

Classification. In the case from SST-2, our model succeeds in capturing and understanding the event *Friel and william's exceptional performances[ARG0] anchored[V]* *the film's power[ARG1]*, whereas the baseline does not manage to capture this meaning, thus leading to the failure.

Sentence Similarity. The case from MRPC demonstrates that our model grabs the distinct semantic structures centered on *is* and *has* and thus gives the right answer *not equivalent*. The event centered on the predicate *donate* belongs to the same structure, which contains the arguments *ARG0*, *ARG1* and *ARGM-TMP* having the same contents (i.e., *the woman donated blood*). Nevertheless, the remaining events which center on the predicate *is* and the predicate *has* in the sentence pair are semantically different as one structure includes the arguments *ARG1* and *ARG2* while the other contains only *ARG0* and *ARG1*.

In Sentence Similarity tasks, two sentences in a sentence pair are likely to have one or several events in common, such as the event centered *donate* in this case. However, a subtle difference in a key element in the semantic structure of the sentence may also lead to a very different semantics of the whole sentence, such as the events centered on *is* and *has*. Our proposed model EventBERT precisely appreciates the value of abstracting structural semantics, benefiting from capturing event-based semantic knowledge to perceive the differences between sentences and thus make more accurate judgments.

Language Inference. Referring to the case from QNLI, as can be seen from Fig. 5, the question and paragraph texts are broadly similar in terms of *sell*-centered structure, both containing the arguments labeled *ARG0*, *ARG1*, and *ARGM-TMP*. However, by means of graph modeling, it can be clearly and explicitly observed that the structures centered on *force* are distinct, with the structure in the interrogative sentence containing the argument *ARGM-CAU* and the corresponding structure in the paragraph texts containing the argument *ARGM-LOC* instead. It is worth noting that one of the most crucial steps in determining whether a paragraph entails the correct answer to a question is whether the corresponding semantic structure in paragraph texts has the span labeled with the semantic role referring to the interrogative in the question. For example, in this case, the interrogative *Why* is exactly the *ARGM-CAU* of the predicate *force*; whereas the structure centered on *force* in the paragraph lacks the corresponding argument content and is replaced by *ARGM-LOC* instead. Therefore, it can be easily inferred that the paragraph focuses on the location (i.e., *in Japan and Latin America*) while the question concentrates on the cause (i.e., *Why*), which exactly reflects that there is no answer span for the interrogative of the question.

It is known that interrogative in the question and corresponding answer span should belong to the same semantic role. EventBERT takes full advantage of extracting abstracted semantics based on predicates, thus conducting language inference tasks more efficiently.

5.5   Error Analysis

We select bad cases of the baseline model and further investigate the ones of which our EventBERT also fails to predict the correct answers. We study two cases respectively from MRPC and QNLI as is shown in Table 4. The first error is caused by EventBERT's identification of the argument *in a written statement* of the predicate *said* in the first sentence, which is not entailed in the second sentence. However, the lack of this argument does not affect the main semantic information. The second error is due to argument reference confusion for the special predicate *is*. For instance, the interrogative *What* is labeled as *ARG2* whereas the correct answer *Hypersensitivity* is labeled as *ARG1*. From the above error cases, it may suggest that our model needs to have a more accurate perception of semantic relationships, which is left for future studies.

Table 4. Errors in predictions for cases in MRPC and QNLI dev set. The words in magenta indicate the key predicate. The words in blue indicate the key arguments referred to the predicate.

Example	EventBERT	Golden answer
This decision is clearly incorrect, FTC Chairman Timothy Muris *said in a written statement*. The decision is clearly incorrect, FTC Chairman Tim Muris *said*	*Not equivalent*	Equivalent
What is the name for a response of the immune system that damages the body's native tissues? *Hypersensitivity is* an immune response that damages the body's own tissues	*Not entailment*	Entailment

6 Conclusion

In this work, we propose EventBERT, an event-based semantic representation model that builds on BERT architecture and incorporates event-based structural semantics in terms of graph network modeling for fine-grained language representation. Experiments on a wide range of NLU tasks show the effectiveness of our model by consistently surpassing the baseline. While most existing works focus on fusing accurate semantic signals to enhance semantic information, we open up a novel perspective to model intrinsic structural semantics for deeper comprehension and inference in an intuitive and explicit way.

References

1. Bai, J., et al.: Syntax-BERT: improving pre-trained transformers with syntax trees. arXiv preprint arXiv:2103.04350 (2021)
2. Baker, C.F., Fillmore, C.J., Lowe, J.B.: The Berkeley FrameNet project. In: 36th Annual Meeting of the Association for Computational Linguistics and 17th International Conference on Computational Linguistics, Montreal, Quebec, Canada, vol. 1, pp. 86–90. Association for Computational Linguistics (1998). https://doi.org/10.3115/980845.980860. https://aclanthology.org/P98-1013
3. Bentivogli, L., Clark, P., Dagan, I., Giampiccolo, D.: The fifth pascal recognizing textual entailment challenge. In: ACL-PASCAL (2009)

4. Cer, D., Diab, M., Agirre, E., Lopez-Gazpio, I., Specia, L.: SemEval-2017 task 1: semantic textual similarity-multilingual and cross-lingual focused evaluation. arXiv preprint arXiv:1708.00055 (2017)
5. Chen, Z., Zhang, H., Zhang, X., Zhao, L.: Quora question pairs (2018)
6. Clark, K., Khandelwal, U., Levy, O., Manning, C.D.: What does BERT look at? an analysis of BERT's attention. In: Proceedings of the 2019 ACL Workshop BlackboxNLP: Analyzing and Interpreting Neural Networks for NLP, Florence, Italy, pp. 276–286. Association for Computational Linguistics (2019). https://doi.org/10.18653/v1/W19-4828. https://aclanthology.org/W19-4828
7. De Cao, N., Aziz, W., Titov, I.: Question answering by reasoning across documents with graph convolutional networks. In: Proceedings of the 2019 Conference of the North American Chapter of the Association for Computational Linguistics: Human Language Technologies, (Long and Short Papers), Minneapolis, Minnesota, vol. 1, pp. 2306–2317. Association for Computational Linguistics (2019). https://doi.org/10.18653/v1/N19-1240. https://aclanthology.org/N19-1240
8. Devlin, J., Chang, M.W., Lee, K., Toutanova, K.: BERT: pre-training of deep bidirectional transformers for language understanding. In: Proceedings of the 2019 Conference of the North American Chapter of the Association for Computational Linguistics: Human Language Technologies, (Long and Short Papers), Minneapolis, Minnesota, vol. 1, pp. 4171–4186. Association for Computational Linguistics (2019). https://doi.org/10.18653/v1/N19-1423. https://aclanthology.org/N19-1423
9. Dolan, W.B., Brockett, C.: Automatically constructing a corpus of sentential paraphrases. In: IWP 2005 (2005)
10. Ettinger, A.: What BERT is not: lessons from a new suite of psycholinguistic diagnostics for language models. Trans. Assoc. Comput. Linguist. **8**, 34–48 (2020). https://doi.org/10.1162/tacl_a_00298. https://aclanthology.org/2020.tacl-1.3
11. Fang, Y., Sun, S., Gan, Z., Pillai, R., Wang, S., Liu, J.: Hierarchical graph network for multi-hop question answering. arXiv preprint arXiv:1911.03631 (2019)
12. Fu, T.J., Li, P.H., Ma, W.Y.: GraphRel: modeling text as relational graphs for joint entity and relation extraction. In: Proceedings of the 57th Annual Meeting of the Association for Computational Linguistics, pp. 1409–1418 (2019)
13. Geeraerts, D., Cuyckens, H.: Introducing cognitive linguistics. In: The Oxford Handbook of Cognitive Linguistics (2007)
14. Guan, Y., Guo, S., Li, R., Li, X., Tan, H.: Frame semantic-enhanced sentence modeling for sentence-level extractive text summarization. In: Proceedings of the 2021 Conference on Empirical Methods in Natural Language Processing, Punta Cana, Dominican Republic, pp. 4045–4052. Association for Computational Linguistics, Online (2021). https://doi.org/10.18653/v1/2021.emnlp-main.331. https://aclanthology.org/2021.emnlp-main.331
15. Guo, S., Guan, Y., Li, R., Li, X., Tan, H.: Incorporating syntax and frame semantics in neural network for machine reading comprehension. In: Proceedings of the 28th International Conference on Computational Linguistics, Barcelona, Spain, pp. 2635–2641. International Committee on Computational Linguistics (Online) (2020). https://doi.org/10.18653/v1/2020.coling-main.237. https://aclanthology.org/2020.coling-main.237
16. Guo, S., Guan, Y., Li, R., Li, X., Tan, H.: Frame-based multi-level semantics representation for text matching. Knowl.-Based Syst. **232**, 107454 (2021). https://doi.org/10.1016/j.knosys.2021.107454. https://www.sciencedirect.com/science/article/pii/S0950705121007164
17. Guo, S., et al.: A frame-based sentence representation for machine reading comprehension. In: Proceedings of the 58th Annual Meeting of the Association for Computational Linguistics, pp. 891–896. Association for Computational Linguistics, Online (2020). https://doi.org/10.18653/v1/2020.acl-main.83. https://aclanthology.org/2020.acl-main.83

18. Kipf, T.N., Welling, M.: Semi-supervised classification with graph convolutional networks. arXiv preprint arXiv:1609.02907 (2016)
19. Levesque, H., Davis, E., Morgenstern, L.: The Winograd schema challenge. In: Thirteenth International Conference on the Principles of Knowledge Representation and Reasoning (2012)
20. Levi, F.W.: Finite geometrical systems: six public lectures delivered in February, 1940, at the University of Calcutta. University of Calcutta (1942)
21. Li, C., Goldwasser, D.: Encoding social information with graph convolutional networks for-political perspective detection in news media. In: Proceedings of the 57th Annual Meeting of the Association for Computational Linguistics, pp. 2594–2604 (2019)
22. Li, Y., Tarlow, D., Brockschmidt, M., Zemel, R.: Gated graph sequence neural networks. arXiv preprint arXiv:1511.05493 (2015)
23. Ma, X., Zhang, Z., Zhao, H.: Structural characterization for dialogue disentanglement. In: Proceedings of the 60th Annual Meeting of the Association for Computational Linguistics (Volume 1: Long Papers), Dublin, Ireland, pp. 285–297. Association for Computational Linguistics (2022). https://aclanthology.org/2022.acl-long.23
24. Marcheggiani, D., Titov, I.: Encoding sentences with graph convolutional networks for semantic role labeling. In: Proceedings of the 2017 Conference on Empirical Methods in Natural Language Processing, Copenhagen, Denmark, pp. 1506–1515. Association for Computational Linguistics (2017). https://doi.org/10.18653/v1/D17-1159. https://aclanthology.org/D17-1159
25. Nangia, N., Williams, A., Lazaridou, A., Bowman, S.R.: The RepEval 2017 shared task: multi-genre natural language inference with sentence representations. In: RepEval (2017)
26. Ouyang, S., Zhang, Z., Zhao, H.: Dialogue graph modeling for conversational machine reading. In: Findings of the Association for Computational Linguistics: ACL-IJCNLP 2021, pp. 3158–3169. Association for Computational Linguistics, Online (2021). https://doi.org/10.18653/v1/2021.findings-acl.279. https://aclanthology.org/2021.findings-acl.279
27. Palmer, M., Gildea, D., Kingsbury, P.: The proposition bank: an annotated corpus of semantic roles. Computat. Linguist. 31(1), 71–106 (2005). https://doi.org/10.1162/0891201053630264. https://aclanthology.org/J05-1004
28. Peters, M.E., et al.: Deep contextualized word representations. In: Proceedings of the 2018 Conference of the North American Chapter of the Association for Computational Linguistics: Human Language Technologies, (Long Papers), New Orleans, Louisiana, vol. 1, pp. 2227–2237. Association for Computational Linguistics (2018). https://doi.org/10.18653/v1/N18-1202. https://aclanthology.org/N18-1202
29. Pham, T., Tran, T., Phung, D., Venkatesh, S.: Column networks for collective classification. In: Thirty-First AAAI Conference on Artificial Intelligence (2017)
30. Qiu, L., et al.: Dynamically fused graph network for multi-hop reasoning. In: Proceedings of the 57th Annual Meeting of the Association for Computational Linguistics, Florence, Italy, pp. 6140–6150. Association for Computational Linguistics (2019). https://doi.org/10.18653/v1/P19-1617. https://aclanthology.org/P19-1617
31. Rajpurkar, P., Zhang, J., Lopyrev, K., Liang, P.: SQuAD: 100,000+ questions for machine comprehension of text. In: EMNLP (2016)
32. Ran, Q., Lin, Y., Li, P., Zhou, J., Liu, Z.: NumNet: machine reading comprehension with numerical reasoning. arXiv preprint arXiv:1910.06701 (2019)
33. Rogers, A., Kovaleva, O., Rumshisky, A.: A primer in BERTology: what we know about how BERT works. Trans. Assoc. Comput. Linguist. 8, 842–866 (2020). https://doi.org/10.1162/tacl_a_00349. https://aclanthology.org/2020.tacl-1.54
34. Scarselli, F., Gori, M., Tsoi, A.C., Hagenbuchner, M., Monfardini, G.: The graph neural network model. IEEE Trans. Neural Netw. 20(1), 61–80 (2008)

35. Schlichtkrull, M., Kipf, T.N., Bloem, P., van den Berg, R., Titov, I., Welling, M.: Modeling relational data with graph convolutional networks. In: Gangemi, A., et al. (eds.) ESWC 2018. LNCS, vol. 10843, pp. 593–607. Springer, Cham (2018). https://doi.org/10.1007/978-3-319-93417-4_38

36. Shi, P., Lin, J.J.: Simple BERT models for relation extraction and semantic role labeling. arXiv abs/1904.05255 (2019)

37. Socher, R., et al.: Recursive deep models for semantic compositionality over a sentiment treebank. In: EMNLP (2013)

38. Sun, Y., et al.: Ernie 2.0: a continual pre-training framework for language understanding. In: Proceedings of the AAAI Conference on Artificial Intelligence, vol. 34, pp. 8968–8975 (2020)

39. Velickovic, P., Cucurull, G., Casanova, A., Romero, A., Lio, P., Bengio, Y.: Graph attention networks. Stat **1050**, 20 (2017)

40. Wang, A., Singh, A., Michael, J., Hill, F., Levy, O., Bowman, S.: GLUE: a multi-task benchmark and analysis platform for natural language understanding. In: Proceedings of the 2018 EMNLP Workshop BlackboxNLP: Analyzing and Interpreting Neural Networks for NLP, Brussels, Belgium, pp. 353–355. Association for Computational Linguistics (2018). https://doi.org/10.18653/v1/W18-5446. https://aclanthology.org/W18-5446

41. Warstadt, A., Singh, A., Bowman, S.R.: Neural network acceptability judgments. arXiv preprint arXiv:1805.12471 (2018)

42. Wu, Z., Peng, H., Smith, N.A.: Infusing finetuning with semantic dependencies. Trans. Assoc. Comput. Linguist. **9**, 226–242 (2021). https://doi.org/10.1162/tacl_a_00363

43. Xie, T., et al.: UnifiedSKG: unifying and multi-tasking structured knowledge grounding with text-to-text language models. arXiv preprint arXiv:2201.05966 (2022)

44. Xu, Z., et al.: Syntax-enhanced pre-trained model. In: Proceedings of the 59th Annual Meeting of the Association for Computational Linguistics and the 11th International Joint Conference on Natural Language Processing (Volume 1: Long Papers), pp. 5412–5422. Association for Computational Linguistics, Online (2021). https://doi.org/10.18653/v1/2021.acl-long.420. https://aclanthology.org/2021.acl-long.420

45. Yang, Z., Dai, Z., Yang, Y., Carbonell, J., Salakhutdinov, R.R., Le, Q.V.: XLNet: generalized autoregressive pretraining for language understanding. In: Advances in Neural Information Processing Systems, vol. 32 (2019)

46. Zhang, Z., et al.: Semantics-aware BERT for language understanding. In: Proceedings of the AAAI Conference on Artificial Intelligence, vol. 34, pp. 9628–9635 (2020)

47. Zhang, Z., Wu, Y., Zhou, J., Duan, S., Zhao, H., Wang, R.: SG-Net: syntax-guided machine reading comprehension. In: Proceedings of the AAAI Conference on Artificial Intelligence, vol. 34, pp. 9636–9643 (2020)

An Exploration of Prompt-Based Zero-Shot Relation Extraction Method

Jun Zhao[1], Yuan Hu[1], Nuo Xu[1], Tao Gui[1(✉)], Qi Zhang[1(✉)], Yunwen Chen[2], and Xiang Gao[2]

[1] School of Computer Science, Shanghai Key Laboratory of Intelligent Information Processing, Fudan University, Shanghai, China
{zhaoj19,yuanhu20,tgui,qz}@fudan.edu.cn, xun22@m.fudan.edu.cn
[2] DataGrand Information Technology (Shanghai) Co., Ltd., Shanghai, China
{chenyunwen,gaoxiang}@datagrand.com

Abstract. Zero-shot relation extraction is an important method for dealing with the newly emerging relations in the real world which lacks labeled data. However, the mainstream two-tower zero-shot methods usually rely on large-scale and in-domain labeled data of predefined relations. In this work, we view zero-shot relation extraction as a semantic matching task optimized by prompt-tuning, which still maintains superior generalization performance when the labeled data of predefined relations are extremely scarce. To maximize the efficiency of data exploitation, instead of directly fine-tuning, we introduce a prompt-tuning technique to elicit the existing relational knowledge in pre-trained language model (PLMs). In addition, very few relation descriptions are exposed to the model during training, which we argue is the performance bottleneck of two-tower methods. To break through the bottleneck, we model the semantic interaction between relational instances and their descriptions directly during encoding. Experiment results on two academic datasets show that (1) our method outperforms the previous state-of-the-art method by a large margin with different samples of predefined relations; (2) this advantage will be further amplified in the low-resource scenario.

Keywords: Relation extraction · Semantic matching · Deep learning

1 Introduction

Relation extraction (RE) aims to extract the relation between entity pairs from unstructured text. The extracted relation facts can benefit various downstream applications such as knowledge graph completion [25], web search [27] and dialog systems [18]. However, many effective RE methods [7,26] work within predefined relation sets. They failed to deal with a real-world environment where new relations will emerge after the training phase. These fast-growing new relations make it impossible for us to gather labeled training data for all of them. To recognize the newly emerging relations lacking labeled data, zero-shot RE is of the utmost practical interest.

J. Zhao and Y. Hu—Equal contribution.

M. Sun et al. (Eds.): CCL 2022, LNAI 13603, pp. 81–95, 2022.
https://doi.org/10.1007/978-3-031-18315-7_6

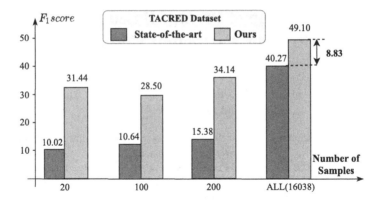

Fig. 1. When shifting to some special domains (e.g. medicine, finance) where large-scale labeled data are not available, the performance of these methods on new relations decreases significantly. By inducing the knowledge in the pre-trained language model, our method can approach the results of previous state-of-the-art method ZS-BERT [1] using only 200 labeled data. When using all data, our method improves the F1 score by 8.83%.

Despite the great potential of zero-shot RE in real-world applications, there have been relatively few studies focusing on this challenging task. To enable models to predict unseen relations, previous works usually model zero-shot relation extraction as a well-designed task form. Levy et al. [15] consider relation extraction as a machine reading comprehension. They first associate a few question templates for each relation and then determine which relation satisfies the given sentence and question by model prediction. However, a reasonable and effective question template usually needs careful design, which cannot meet the extraction needs of rapidly growing new relations [1]. Therefore, instead of manually constructing question templates, subsequent works [1, 19] take advantage of the readily available textual description to represent the new relations, and formulate zero-shot RE as a semantic matching task achieving superior results.

However, current methods usually require a large number of in-domain labeled data of predefined relations to train the model parameters. The learned relational knowledge is mainly from labeled data itself. As a result, when shifting to some special domains where large-scale labeled data are not available, the performance of these methods on new relations decreases significantly. An experimental illustration is shown in Fig. 1. Fortunately, pre-trained language models (PLMs) such as BERT [4] and GPT [21], can learn a wealth of linguistic [20], local syntactic [12] and long-range semantic [13] from large-scale corpora by self-supervised learning. An interesting question is whether we can reduce the dependence on labeled data of predefined relations with the help of knowledge in PLMs?

To answer this question, in this work, we propose a prompt-based zero-shot RE method. Different from previous methods, in which the learned relational knowledge mainly comes from the labeled data of predefined relations, we leverage prompt to stimulate the rich knowledge distributed in PLMs to reduce dependence on these labeled data. Specifically, we model zero-shot RE as a semantic matching task between relational instance and description. In order to induce the knowledge in PLMs, we fuse the original input with the prompt template to formulate a cloze-style task. Then, we count the probability distribution of the model output and take the words with significant differences between classes as label words. In addition, each predefined relation corresponds to **many** instances and **one** description. The significant quantity gap makes the two-tower methods unable to effectively model the semantics of relation description. Therefore, we directly model the semantic interaction between instances and descriptions during training. Based on the reformulated input and these selected label words, we optimize a semantic matching model, which predicts whether the relation and the textual description match. Experimental results show that our method has very significant advantages when the large-scale labeled data of predefined relations are not available.

To summarize, the main contributions of our work are as follows: (1) We propose a prompt-based zero-shot relation extraction method, which maintains high generalization ability when using even one labeled data per predefined relations. (2) We design comprehensive experiments to analyze the impact of predefined relations and prompt composition on the generalization performance of the model in the low-resource scenario, which may enlighten the following work. (3) Experiment results on two academic datasets show that our method outperforms the previous state-of-the-art method by a large margin and this advantage will be further amplified in low resource scenarios.

2   Related Work

2.1   Knowledge in Pretrained Language Model

Contextual word representations derived from pre-trained language models have recently been shown to provide significant improvements to the state of the art for a wide range of NLP tasks, motivating a growing body of research investigating what aspects of linguistic knowledge they are able to learn from unlabeled data. Peters et al. [20] showed that different neural architectures (e.g., LSTM, CNN, and Transformers) can hierarchically structure linguistic information that varies with network depth. [3, 8, 13] show that such hierarchy exists as well for BERT models that are not trained using the standard language modeling objective. More recently, many studies [12, 23] probe the knowledge within PLMs from various perspectives and find that the existing models trained on language modeling and translation produce strong representations for syntactic phenomena. Together, these results suggest that pre-trained language models entail comprehensive linguistic knowledge, which accounts for its great performance on downstream tasks and proves its potential to represent the samples of zero-shot relation extraction tasks, which has limited training data.

2.2   Prompt-Based Optimization

Since the advent of prompt tuning, it has soon become the prevailing paradigm of natural language processing. Prompt tuning is based on language models that estimate the probability of text. It modifies the original input of downstream tasks to a prompt with unfilled positions, and predicts the output based on the slot-filling result by language models [17]. This method has been proven to be helpful on various NLP tasks, including text classification [9], entity typing [6], text generation [16], and also multi-modal tasks [24]. Current studies have made some attempts to derive knowledge from PLMs with prompts. Jiang et al. [14] proposed mining-based and paraphrasing-based methods to automatically generate high-quality prompts, which boosted the performance of knowledge-driven tasks. Zhong et al. [29] conducted a set of control experiments to disentangle the efforts of training data and pre-trained knowledge. Inspired by these works, compared with direct fine-tuning, using the limited labeled data to derive the existing relational knowledge in the pretrained model is a better choice.

3 Method

We reformulate the task of zero-shot relation extraction as a semantic matching task optimized by prompt-tuning. In this section, we will introduce our proposed method in detail. We start by defining the problem we will tackle. Then we introduce how we reformulate zero-shot relation extraction, our prompt design and the selection of label tokens. Finally, we introduce the strategy of making predictions with our model.

3.1 Problem Definition

For the zero-shot relation extraction task, we expect the model $\mathcal{M}$ to predict the right relation of two annotated entities within the text, where the candidate relations are unseen during training.

Formally, let $R_s = \{r_s^1, \ldots, r_s^n\}$ denotes the set of predefined relations. Each relation in R_s has a corresponding textual description, composing the set of relation descriptions $D_s = \{d_s^1, \ldots, d_s^n\}$. In the train set $S_s = \{S_s^1, \ldots, S_s^N\}$, each sample $S_s^i = (x^i, r_s^i)$ consists of a relational instance x^i and its relation label $r_s^i \in R_s$, in which the relational instance x^i is a piece of text s^i with annotated entities e_1^i and e_2^i, namely $x^i = \langle s^i, e_1^i, e_2^i \rangle$. Similarly, the set of unseen relations for testing is denoted as $R_u = \{r_u^1, \ldots, r_u^m\}$, together with the corresponding description set $D_u = \{d_u^1, \ldots, d_u^m\}$. Note that all relations in R_u are unseen during training, i.e. $R_s \cap R_u = \varnothing$. The test set is denoted as $S_u = \{S_s^1, \ldots, S_u^M\}$, in which each test sample $S_u^j = (x^j, r_u^j)$.

3.2 Task Reformulation

In our work, we model zero-shot relation extraction as a semantic matching task where we need to recognize the semantic equivalence relations between relational instances and the description of their corresponding relation labels. Specifically, we pair each test sample with the description of every candidate relation, and label them with match/not_match to form semantic matching samples. And we set it to have half the probability of pairing the training sample with the non-corresponding relation description and half the probability of pairing it with the corresponding relation description.

Table 1. An example of the reformulation of zero-shot relation extraction task. Each original sample is paired with various descriptions to form new samples.

Input		Label
Original Sample	Prompt	
Cloud Nothings was formed in Cleveland .	[CLS] [CT] Premise : *input text* [SEP] [CT] Hypothesis : *relation description* . Answer : [MASK] [SEP]	Place of Foundation
Reformulated Samples		
[CLS] [CT] Premise : Cloud Nothings was formed in Cleveland [SEP] [CT] Hypothesis : location where a group or organization was formed . Answer : [MASK] [SEP]		match
[CLS] [CT] Premise : Cloud Nothings was formed in Cleveland [SEP] [CT] Hypothesis : musical instrument that a person plays . Answer : [MASK] [SEP]		not_match
[CLS] [CT] Premise : Cloud Nothings was formed in Cleveland [SEP] [CT] Hypothesis : league in which team or player plays or has played in . Answer : [MASK] [SEP]		not_match
[CLS] [CT] Premise : Cloud Nothings was formed in Cleveland [SEP] [CT] Hypothesis : heritage designation of a historical site . Answer : [MASK] [SEP]		not_match

Therefore, the number of positive and negative semantic examples in the training set is roughly equal. As shown in Table 1, the pair is labeled as match only when the description matches the corresponding relation label of the relational instance.

Formally, taking the training sample $S_s^i = (x^i, r_s^i)$ for example, we can derive a semantic matching sample $\{(x^i, d_s^k, y^k)\}$ from it, where

$$y^k = \begin{cases} \text{match} & r_s^i = r_s^k \\ \text{not\_match} & otherwise, \end{cases} \tag{1}$$

We denote the newly derived train set for semantic matching as $S_s' = \{(x^i, d_s^k, y^{ik})\}_{i=1...N}$. Note that from each test sample we will derive m semantic matching samples. The test set is denoted as $S_u' = \{(x^j, d_u^l, y^{jl})\}_{j=1...M, l=1...m}$. In summary, the above efforts convert the original problem to a semantic matching task, which is basically a 2-classification task that we could handle.

Is the Two-Tower Architecture Suitable for this Task? The state-of-the-art zero-shot methods [1, 19] adopt a two-tower architecture to implement the above semantic matching model. However, encoding instances and descriptions in isolation is not a good choice. Assuming that we use 10 relations and 100 instances of each relation to train a two-tower model, there are 1000 different inputs for instance encoder and only 10 inputs for the description encoder. This significant gap makes it difficult for description encoder to learn semantics effectively. Different from the two-tower architecture, the proposed method directly models the semantic interaction between instances and description during encoding. We will show the significant improvement brought by this change in the experiments.

3.3 Model with Prompt Tuning

To model the semantic matching between relational instances and descriptions, we take advantage of pre-trained language models together with prompt tuning. Noticeably, for zero-shot relation extraction, the most critical issue during training is that very few relation descriptions are exposed to the model. Furthermore, all of the descriptions in the test set are unseen in training. Thus, the rich linguistic knowledge of PLM is necessary to ensure that the model understands the descriptions with limited training. Additionally, to tackle the discrepancy of PLM between the pre-training and fine-tuning stage, prompt tuning is necessary to reformulate downstream tasks as cloze-style tasks that BERT is good at. We believe that prompt tuning provides an effective way to fully export knowledge from pre-trained language models and also enables few-shot

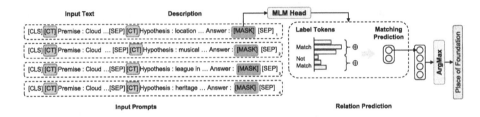

Fig. 2. An overview of the process of relation prediction. The [MASK]ed positions within input prompts are firstly filled by language model, then the logits of label tokens are collected to predict the matching probability of input text and description. Lastly, we collect the matching probabilities for each pair and estimate the distribution of relational labels based on them.

learning of the task. Due to the discussions, we build our model based on BERT, which learns the objectives by prompt tuning.

Prompt Design. For each reformulated sample (x, d, y), we fill the original text of relational instance and the description into a prompt. We define the prompt x' for relational instance x and relation description d as

$$x' = [\text{CLS}] [\text{CT}] \; s' \; [\text{SEP}] [\text{CT}] \; d'$$
$$[\text{MASK}] [\text{SEP}]$$
$$\text{where} \; s' = \text{Premise:} \; s$$
$$d' = \text{Hypothesis:} \; d \; \text{Answer:}, \tag{2}$$

where s is the input text, which is the original text of x; s' and d' denotes the prompt-formulated input text and description respectively; [CT] denotes T different continuous tokens that make up the template. Examples of input prompts could be seen in Table 1. The design of prompt aims to fully utilize the ability of BERT as a rich knowledge base, and the introduction of continuous tokens in template aims to enhance the representation ability of the prompt, since these tokens could be optimized in the whole embedding space.

Label Token Selection. Following the common settings of prompt tuning on classification task, we also determine label tokens for each category (namely match or not_match) for consequential prompt tuning. Basically, for the two categories, the probability distributions of masked language modeling should be different and distinguishable. Thus, retrieving label tokens is the process of capturing features that indicate the distribution associated with a certain category. We solve the problem by estimating the distributions and retrieving tokens that have the most significant difference of probability among distributions.

Formally, we partition the reformulated train set S'_s by category of label y. The matched and unmatched samples are denoted as $S_{sm} = \{(x, d, y) \in S'_s | y = \text{match}\}$ and $S_{sn} = \{(x, d, y) \in S'_s | y = \text{not\_match}\}$, respectively. The prompts of samples are then fed to BERT. For sample (x, d, y), the estimated distribution of the [MASK] token is calculated as

$$P(w|x, d) = \text{softmax}(W(\text{MLM}(x')) + b),\tag{3}$$

where w denotes every token in vocabulary, $P(w|x, d)$ indicates the estimated MLM distribution of the sample, MLM denotes the output embedding of [MASK] token, W and b denote trainable weights of linear projection.

The MLM distribution of categories is estimated by averaging the predicted distributions among samples in the category:

$$P_m(w) = \frac{1}{|S_{sm}|} \sum_{(x,d,y)}^{S_{sm}} P(w|x, d),\tag{4}$$

$$P_n(w) = \frac{1}{|S_{sn}|} \sum_{(x,d,y)}^{S_{sn}} P(w|x, d),\tag{5}$$

where $P_m(w)$ and $P_n(w)$ indicate the estimated MLM distribution of the category match and not_match, $|S_{sm}|$ and $|S_{sn}|$ denote the number of matched and unmatched samples, respectively.

Finally, for each category, the tokens with top-K possibility difference between the MLM distribution within and without the category are selected as the label tokens. The possibility difference of each word is divided by their estimated occurrence possibility to ensure fair comparison.

$$\{w_m^1, \ldots, w_m^K\} = \underset{w}{\text{topK}} \frac{P_m(w) - P_n(w)}{P_m(w) + P_n(w)},\tag{6}$$

$$\{w_n^1, \ldots, w_n^K\} = \underset{w}{\text{topK}} \frac{P_n(w) - P_m(w)}{P_m(w) + P_n(w)}.\tag{7}$$

In Eqs. 6 and 7, K is the number of tokens selected for each category, $\{w_m^1, \ldots, w_m^K\}$ and $\{w_n^1, \ldots, w_n^K\}$ denote the selected label tokens of the category of $\{$match and not_match$\}$ respectively.

3.4 Training and Inference

In this part, we introduce our strategy to derive relation predictions from the semantic matching model, along with the training objectives.

Similar to other prompt-based methods, the output possibilities of label tokens are collected to perform a 2-classification on label y. The possibility of categories is proportional to the production possibility of label words. As shown in Eq. 8, in implementation, we achieve this by adding the output logits of label tokens and applying softmax on them:

$$P(y = c|x, d) = \text{softmax}\left(\sum_{k=1}^{K} \log P(w_c^k|x, d)\right),\tag{8}$$

where $c \in \{\texttt{match}, \texttt{not\_match}\}$.

The prediction of relation label for relational instance x_i is done by collecting the possibilities of match between x_i and the descriptions of every candidate relation $R^k \in R$. As in Eq. 9, the matching possibilities of x_i and all candidate relations are collected as logits and are put to a softmax function to predict the distribution of the relation label.

$$p^{ik} = P(y^{ik} = \texttt{match}|x^i, D^k), \qquad (9)$$

$$P(r^k|x^i) = \frac{\exp(p^{ik})}{\sum\limits_{r^k \in R} \exp(p_{ik})}. \qquad (10)$$

Lastly, the model is trained on cross-entropy loss L_{CE} to maximize the log-likelihood of all training samples.

$$L_{CE} = \sum_{i=1}^{N} \mathrm{CrossEntropy}(r_s^i, \{p_s^{ik}\}_{k=1}^n). \qquad (11)$$

As for making prediction on unseen samples, i.e. evaluating model on test sets, for each test sample S_u^j, the predicted relation distribution of relational instance x_j is illustrated in Eqs. 12 and 13. We pick the relation with the highest possibility as the predicted result.

$$p^{jl} = P(y^{jl} = \texttt{match}|x^j, d_u^l), \qquad (12)$$

$$P(R_u^l|x^j) = \frac{\exp(p^{jl})}{\sum\limits_{r_u^j \in R_u} \exp(p_{ik})}, \qquad (13)$$

$$\hat{r}_u^j = \underset{l}{\mathrm{argmax}} P(R_u^l|x^j). \qquad (14)$$

4 Experimental Setup

In this section, we describe the datasets for training and evaluating the proposed method. We also detail the baseline models for comparison. Finally, we clarify the implementation details and hyperparameter configuration of our method.

4.1 Datasets

Our main experiments are conducted on two relation extraction datasets: FewRel and TACRED. The original statistics of the two datasets are listed in Table 2.

FewRel [10]. There are 80 relations included in FewRel, a high-quality RE dataset with 56,000 instances from Wikipedia. To be consistent with the previous state-of-the-art method, we rearrange the dataset. To be specific, we choose 65 relations as labeled set with predefined relation and select 15 relations as the unlabeled set with unseen relations.

TACRED [28]. TACRED is a human-annotated relation extraction dataset that contains 106,264 examples with 42 kinds of relations(including "no_relation"). The instances of special class "no_relation" is removed, and we use the remaining 21,773 instances for training and evaluation.

We also add a low-resource setting, which means the size of training data is small. Under the setting, the development set is provided, with about 5 examples per relation. As shown in Table 3 and Table 4, the three different values of n represents the number of data used for training are only 20, 100 and 200 respectively. For the setting, We randomly sample training data from each relation category roughly evenly. Note that when sampling 20 training data, the number of relation categories in the training set of both datasets is also reduced to 20. For both of the two datasets, we use the Macro-F1 score as the main metric to evaluate the model's performance.

Table 2. Original statistics of datasets FewRel and TACRED. %N/A is the proportion of label "no_relation" and "-" represents there is no N/A instances.

Dataset	# Inst	# relations	% N/A
FewRel	56000	80	–
TACRED	106264	42	79.5%

4.2 Compared Methods

To verify the effectiveness of our proposed method, we select the following models for comparison. The state-of-the-art method ZS-BERT [1] adopted the two-tower architecture, this method encodes sentences and relation descriptions separately and uses nearest neighbor search as the matching function to obtain the prediction of unseen relations. When comparing with R-BERT [26] and Attentional Bi-LSTM [30], two supervised relation extraction (SRE) models, we take the same way as ZS-BERT [1] so that SRE models can carry out zero-shot prediction. Specifically, we change the last layer to a fully-connected layer with tanh activation function. Based on the input instance embedding and relation description's embedding, the nearest neighbor search will be applied to generate the zero-shot prediction. We also compare our method with ESIM [2], a semantic matching model. To have a fair comparison, the strategy to generate relation predictions from the semantic matching model is the same as ours. Finally, we introduce BERT(CLS) [5] to intuitively show the performance improvement brought by modeling the semantic interaction between instances and descriptions during encoding.

4.3 Implementation Details

We adopt BERT-base-cased as the encoder and all experiments are conducted using a NVIDIA GeForce RTX 3090 with 24 GB memory. The number of continuous tokens is $t = 4$. We use AdamW for optimization, in which the initial learning rate is 3e−5. Taking into account the randomness of network initialization and random selection of n training instances, we run our experiment 5 times and the results we report are the average results. Other results of compared methods are gotten when the parameters remain the same as its own published source code. We follow Soares et al. [22] to augment each instance with four reserved word pieces to mark the begin and end of each entity. The relation descriptions of FewRel are obtained from [11] and TACRED's are obtained from the TAC-KBP relation ontology guidelines[1].

5   Results and Discussion

Table 3. Main results on FewRel. The best results are bold. n is the number of provided training data and m represents unseen relations' number.

FewRel ($m = 15$)												
Method	n = 20			n = 100			n = 200			n = all		
	Prec.	Rec.	F_1	Prec.	Rec.	F_1	Prec.	Rec.	F_1	Prec.	Rec.	F_1
Att Bi-LSTM [30]	14.19	13.88	14.03	15.75	19.8	17.55	20.83	26.00	23.13	38.13	32.05	34.82
ESIM [2]	0.60	5.45	1.08	0.90	6.56	1.58	7.66	7.38	7.52	36.97	32.51	34.60
R-BERT [26]	8.40	8.38	8.39	13.61	15.90	14.67	16.05	18.58	17.22	32.25	25.58	28.53
ZS-BERT [1]	6.04	6.36	6.20	6.34	7.93	7.05	8.35	9.59	8.93	35.54	38.19	36.82
BERT(CLS) [5]	**44.95**	33.65	38.49	49.99	47.20	48.55	**53.14**	52.13	52.62	**67.62**	59.12	63.09
Ours	44.94	**45.72**	**45.33**	**50.21**	**51.72**	**50.96**	52.49	**53.98**	**53.23**	64.48	**62.45**	**63.45**

Table 4. Main results on TACRED. The best results are bold. n is the number of provided training data and m represents unseen relations' number.

TACRED ($m = 11$)												
Method	n = 20			n = 100			n = 200			n = all		
	Prec.	Rec.	F_1	Prec.	Rec.	F_1	Prec.	Rec.	F_1	Prec.	Rec.	F_1
Att Bi-LSTM [30]	14.33	11.38	12.68	13.73	10.64	11.99	15.68	21.70	18.20	25.20	20.17	22.41
ESIM [2]	9.09	0.15	0.29	8.54	9.41	8.96	1.52	9.15	2.61	26.99	18.38	21.87
R-BERT [26]	14.59	7.27	9.70	18.93	12.12	14.78	23.62	19.67	21.47	44.66	45.86	45.25
ZS-BERT [1]	10.79	9.35	10.02	12.53	9.25	10.64	14.98	15.79	15.38	38.08	42.72	40.27
BERT(CLS) [5]	25.53	19.78	22.29	9.34	10.55	9.91	**37.97**	**34.43**	**36.11**	**51.90**	44.71	48.03
Ours	**32.40**	**30.54**	**31.44**	**38.12**	**22.75**	**28.50**	34.56	33.73	34.14	51.85	**46.63**	**49.10**

5.1   Main Results

The main results of our experiments on FewRel and TACRED are listed in Table 3 and Table 4. **First**, as can be seen, the method we propose steadily outperforms compared methods, and even the previous state-of-the-art method [1] performs much worse than our method when targeting at different number of training instances. The reason

---

[1] https://tac.nist.gov/2015/KBP/ColdStart/guidelines/TAC_KBP_2015_Slot_Descriptions_V1.0.pdf.

is that the two-tower model which the previous state-of-the-art method [1] encodes the input instances and candidate relations with large quantitative differences separately, and we argue that this modeling choice is insufficiently expressive for modeling the semantic matching between instances and relation descriptions. What's more, the simple matching function (ZS-BERT uses nearest neighbor search) is incapable of capturing the complicated interactions between input sentences and relation descriptions. Our proposed method yields rich interactions between the input instance and candidate relation description, as they are jointly encoded to obtain a final representation. At the layers of transformer, every word in the candidate relation description can attend to every word in the input instance, and vice-versa, so our proposed method can produce a candidate-sensitive input representation, which the ZS-BERT cannot. **Second**, it can be apparently found that the baseline's performance decreases significantly when the number of labeled data decreases, which indicates that large number of in-domain labeled data of predefined relations is a prerequisite for their good performance. While our method manage to derive the original knowledge in PLMs with prompt so that our method still performs well when the labeled data is scarce. For FewRel, our MACRO-F1 score reaches 45.33% training with 20 instances, which is better than the result of previous state-of-the-art using the complete train dataset. Such results verify the strong ability of low-resource learning for our proposed method.

5.2 Cross Domain Analysis

Through the analysis of main results, we have concluded that large-scale labeled data of predefined relations is a prerequisite for the existing model to achieve good generalization performance on unseen relations. An ensuing question is: when we deal with the problem of a field that lacks labeled data, can we solve this problem by using labeled data with existing relations in common fields? To answer this question, we conducted experiments on two constructed cross-domain zero-shot relation extraction tasks.i.e.,: FewRel to TACRED and TACRED to FewRel. Specifically, pre-defined relations and their labeled instances come from the source domain training dataset, and we evaluate performance on the target domain testing dataset.

Table 5 shows the results. By comparing with the in-domain experimental results in the main experiment, we can find: the change of domain does increase the semantic gap between the pre-defined and unseen relations. As a result of that: For FewRel to TACRED, the experimental result of our method is reduced from 49.10% to 39.36%, and for TACRED to FewRel, the result is reduced from 63.45% to 54.99%. But our performance still outperforms compared methods, which shows the proposed method's generalization on unseen relations.

5.3 Influence of Pre-defined Relation Number

In this subsection, we study the effect of the number of seen predefined relations in the train dataset. And we conduct the experiment on FewRel. For FewRel, the original number of predefined relations is 65, we sample 33, 17, 9, 5 classes from the original train dataset in turn, which correspond to 50%, 25%, 12.5%, 6.25% of the original classes represented by the scale on the horizontal axis in the figure. The results of Fig. 3

Table 5. Results on two constructed cross-domain tasks.

Method	FewRel_TACRED			TACRED_FewRel		
	n=all			n=all		
	Prec.	Rec.	F_1	Prec.	Rec.	F_1
Att Bi-LSTM [30]	21.86	27.72	24.44	31.27	39.26	34.82
ESIM [2]	22.67	18.91	20.62	19.38	11.93	14.77
R-BERT [26]	23.10	28.49	23.98	15.31	14.70	15.00
ZS-BERT [1]	35.90	29.78	32.55	17.69	11.81	14.16
Ours	**41.26**	**37.62**	**39.36**	**60.01**	**50.74**	**54.99**

Table 6. Results on different prompts.

Prompt	FewRel	TACRED
[PRE] Question : [HYP] . true or false ? Answer : [MASK]	63.11	47.19
[PRE] Question : [HYP] ? [MASK]	61.09	48.79
[PRE] Is [HYP] true ? Answer : [MASK]	**63.58**	47.72
Does [HYP] agree with [PRE] ? [MASK]	62.44	45.73
Ours	63.45	**49.10**

prove that the number of pre-defined relations does matter. As the number decreases, the knowledge learned from the training set also decreases, which can weaken the model's generalization of unseen relations. So the performance of our proposed method also gets worse. Nevertheless, our method can still be said to perform well. For FewRel, When we reduce the number of predefined relation types to 5, our performance still outperforms the previous state-of-the-art, which can validate the effectiveness of our proposed method.

5.4 Analysis on Different Prompt Forms

To explore the impact of different forms of prompt on the performance of the proposed method, we conducted experiments on two datasets based on different prompts. Because the continuous tokens' position relative to [HYP] and [PRE] doesn't change, it is omitted from the table. As is shown in Table 6, inappropriate forms may lead to worse results, but on the other hand, a suitable prompt form can also improve model performance since it can help elicit the existing knowledge in PLMs. Among all the prompt forms, the form we have chosen is relatively well-behaved. Moreover, the prompt's performance is not necessarily the same as our intuition, in other words, the prompt we think good is not necessarily good for PLMs and we think the automatic generation of prompts is a promising research direction.

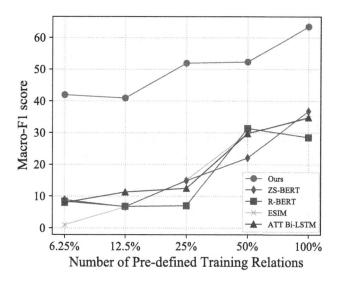

Fig. 3. Model results with different number of predefined training relations on FewRel.

6   Conclusions

In this work, we introduce a prompt-based zero-shot relation extraction method, which still maintains superior generalization performance under low-resource settings. We clarify the limitations of the two-tower architecture in previous state-of-the-art methods, and directly model the interaction between instances and descriptions during encoding, which breaks the performance bottleneck of the previous model. The introduce of prompt-tuning effectively elicit the knowledge in PLMs and significantly reduces the dependence on predefined relations. We believe that these are the reasons why our method achieves excellent results. Experiment results on two academic datasets show that our method outperforms the previous state-of-the-art method by a large margin and this advantage will be further amplified in low resource scenarios.

References

1. Chen, C.Y., Li, C.T.: Zs-bert: towards zero-shot relation extraction with attribute representation learning. arXiv preprint arXiv:2104.04697 (2021)
2. Chen, Q., Zhu, X., Ling, Z.H., Wei, S., Jiang, H., Inkpen, D.: Enhanced LSTM for natural language inference. In: Proceedings of the 55th Annual Meeting of the Association for Computational Linguistics (Volume 1: Long Papers), pp. 1657–1668. Association for Computational Linguistics, Vancouver, Canada (2017). https://doi.org/10.18653/v1/P17-1152, https://aclanthology.org/P17-1152
3. Clark, K., Khandelwal, U., Levy, O., Manning, C.D.: What does BERT look at? an analysis of bert's attention. CoRR abs/1906.04341 (2019). http://arxiv.org/abs/1906.04341
4. Devlin, J., Chang, M.W., Lee, K., Toutanova, K.: Bert: pre-training of deep bidirectional transformers for language understanding. arXiv preprint arXiv:1810.04805 (2018)

5. Devlin, J., Chang, M.W., Lee, K., Toutanova, K.: BERT: pre-training of deep bidirectional transformers for language understanding. In: Proceedings of the 2019 Conference of the North American Chapter of the Association for Computational Linguistics: Human Language Technologies, Volume 1 (Long and Short Papers), pp. 4171–4186. Association for Computational Linguistics, Minneapolis, Minnesota (2019). https://doi.org/10.18653/v1/N19-1423, https://aclanthology.org/N19-1423

6. Ding, N., et al.: Prompt-learning for fine-grained entity typing. arXiv preprint arXiv:2108.10604 (2021)

7. Du, J., Han, J., Way, A., Wan, D.: Multi-level structured self-attentions for distantly supervised relation extraction. arXiv preprint arXiv:1809.00699 (2018)

8. Goldberg, Y.: Assessing bert's syntactic abilities. CoRR abs/1901.05287 (2019). http://arxiv.org/abs/1901.05287

9. Han, X., Zhao, W., Ding, N., Liu, Z., Sun, M.: Ptr: prompt tuning with rules for text classification. arXiv preprint arXiv:2105.11259 (2021)

10. Han, X., et al.: Fewrel: a large-scale supervised few-shot relation classification dataset with state-of-the-art evaluation. In: Proceedings of the 2018 Conference on Empirical Methods in Natural Language Processing, pp. 4803–4809 (2018)

11. Han, X., Zhu, H., Yu, P., Wang, Z., Yao, Y., Liu, Z., Sun, M.: FewRel: a large-scale supervised few-shot relation classification dataset with state-of-the-art evaluation. In: Proceedings of the 2018 Conference on Empirical Methods in Natural Language Processing, pp. 4803–4809. Association for Computational Linguistics, Brussels, Belgium (2018). https://doi.org/10.18653/v1/D18-1514, https://aclanthology.org/D18-1514

12. Hewitt, J., Manning, C.D.: A structural probe for finding syntax in word representations. In: Proceedings of the 2019 Conference of the North American Chapter of the Association for Computational Linguistics: Human Language Technologies, Volume 1 (Long and Short Papers), pp. 4129–4138. Association for Computational Linguistics, Minneapolis, Minnesota (2019). https://doi.org/10.18653/v1/N19-1419, https://aclanthology.org/N19-1419

13. Jawahar, G., Sagot, B., Seddah, D.: What does BERT learn about the structure of language? In: Proceedings of the 57th Annual Meeting of the Association for Computational Linguistics, pp. 3651–3657. Association for Computational Linguistics, Florence, Italy (2019). https://doi.org/10.18653/v1/P19-1356, https://aclanthology.org/P19-1356

14. Jiang, Z., Xu, F.F., Araki, J., Neubig, G.: How can we know what language models know? Trans. Assoc. Comput. Linguist. **8**, 423–438 (2020). https://doi.org/10.1162/tacl_a_00324, https://aclanthology.org/2020.tacl-1.28

15. Levy, O., Seo, M., Choi, E., Zettlemoyer, L.: Zero-shot relation extraction via reading comprehension. In: Proceedings of the 21st Conference on Computational Natural Language Learning (CoNLL 2017), pp. 333–342. Association for Computational Linguistics, Vancouver, Canada (2017). https://doi.org/10.18653/v1/K17-1034, https://aclanthology.org/K17-1034

16. Li, X.L., Liang, P.: Prefix-tuning: optimizing continuous prompts for generation. arXiv preprint arXiv:2101.00190 (2021)

17. Liu, P., Yuan, W., Fu, J., Jiang, Z., Hayashi, H., Neubig, G.: Pre-train, prompt, and predict: a systematic survey of prompting methods in natural language processing. arXiv preprint arXiv:2107.13586 (2021)

18. Madotto, A., Wu, C.S., Fung, P.: Mem2Seq: effectively incorporating knowledge bases into end-to-end task-oriented dialog systems. In: Proceedings of the 56th Annual Meeting of the Association for Computational Linguistics (Volume 1: Long Papers), pp. 1468–1478. Association for Computational Linguistics, Melbourne, Australia (2018). https://doi.org/10.18653/v1/P18-1136, https://aclanthology.org/P18-1136

19. Obamuyide, A., Vlachos, A.: Zero-shot relation classification as textual entailment. In: Proceedings of the First Workshop on Fact Extraction and VERification (FEVER), pp. 72–78. Association for Computational Linguistics, Brussels, Belgium (2018). https://doi.org/10.18653/v1/W18-5511, https://aclanthology.org/W18-5511

20. Peters, M.E., Neumann, M., Zettlemoyer, L., Yih, W.t.: Dissecting contextual word embeddings: architecture and representation. In: Proceedings of the 2018 Conference on Empirical Methods in Natural Language Processing, pp. 1499–1509. Association for Computational Linguistics, Brussels, Belgium (2018). https://doi.org/10.18653/v1/D18-1179, https://aclanthology.org/D18-1179

21. Radford, A., Narasimhan, K., Salimans, T., Sutskever, I.: Improving language understanding by generative pre-training (2018)

22. Soares, L.B., FitzGerald, N., Ling, J., Kwiatkowski, T.: Matching the blanks: distributional similarity for relation learning. arXiv preprint arXiv:1906.03158 (2019)

23. Tenney, I., et al.: What do you learn from context? probing for sentence structure in contextualized word representations. In: International Conference on Learning Representations (2019). https://openreview.net/forum?id=SJzSgnRcKX

24. Tsimpoukelli, M., Menick, J., Cabi, S., Eslami, S., Vinyals, O., Hill, F.: Multimodal few-shot learning with frozen language models. arXiv preprint arXiv:2106.13884 (2021)

25. Wang, Z., Zhang, J., Feng, J., Chen, Z.: Knowledge graph embedding by translating on hyperplanes. In: Proceedings of the AAAI Conference on Artificial Intelligence, vol. 28 (2014)

26. Wu, S., He, Y.: Enriching pre-trained language model with entity information for relation classification. In: Proceedings of the 28th ACM International Conference on Information and Knowledge Management, pp. 2361–2364 (2019)

27. Xiong, C., Power, R., Callan, J.: Explicit semantic ranking for academic search via knowledge graph embedding. In: Proceedings of the 26th International Conference on World Wide Web, pp. 1271–1279. WWW 2017, International World Wide Web Conferences Steering Committee, Republic and Canton of Geneva, CHE (2017). https://doi.org/10.1145/3038912.3052558

28. Zhang, Y., Zhong, V., Chen, D., Angeli, G., Manning, C.D.: Position-aware attention and supervised data improve slot filling. In: Proceedings of the 2017 Conference on Empirical Methods in Natural Language Processing, pp. 35–45. Association for Computational Linguistics, Copenhagen, Denmark (2017). https://doi.org/10.18653/v1/D17-1004, https://aclanthology.org/D17-1004

29. Zhong, Z., Friedman, D., Chen, D.: Factual probing is [MASK]: learning vs. learning to recall. In: Proceedings of the 2021 Conference of the North American Chapter of the Association for Computational Linguistics: Human Language Technologies, pp. 5017–5033. Association for Computational Linguistics, Online (2021). https://doi.org/10.18653/v1/2021.naacl-main.398, https://aclanthology.org/2021.naacl-main.398

30. Zhou, P., et al.: Attention-based bidirectional long short-term memory networks for relation classification. In: Proceedings of the 54th Annual Meeting of the Association for Computational Linguistics (Volume 2: Short Papers), pp. 207–212 (2016)

Abstains from Prediction: Towards Robust Relation Extraction in Real World

Jun Zhao[1], Yongxin Zhang[1], Nuo Xu[1], Tao Gui[1(✉)], Qi Zhang[1(✉)], Yunwen Chen[2], and Xiang Gao[2]

[1] School of Computer Science, Shanghai Key Laboratory of Intelligent Information Processing, Fudan University, Shanghai, China
{zhaoj19,yongxinzhang20,tgui,qz}@fudan.edu.cn,
xun22@m.fudan.edu.cn
[2] DataGrand Information Technology (Shanghai) Co., Ltd., Shanghai, China
{chenyunwen,gaoxiang}@datagrand.com

Abstract. Supervised learning is a classic paradigm of relation extraction (RE). However, a well-performing model can still confidently make arbitrarily wrong predictions when exposed to samples of unseen relations. In this work, we propose a relation extraction method with rejection option to improve robustness to unseen relations. To enable the classifier to reject unseen relations, we introduce contrastive learning techniques and carefully design a set of class-preserving transformations to improve the discriminability between known and unseen relations. Based on the learned representation, inputs of unseen relations are assigned a low confidence score and rejected. Off-the-shelf open relation extraction (OpenRE) methods can be adopted to discover the potential relations in these rejected inputs. In addition, we find that the rejection can be further improved via readily available distantly supervised data. Experiments on two public datasets prove the effectiveness of our method capturing discriminative representations for unseen relation rejection.

Keywords: Relation extraction · Rejection option · Deep learning

1 Introduction

Relation extraction aims to predict the relation between entities based on their context. The extracted relational facts play a vital role in various natural language processing applications, such as knowledge base enrichment [5], web search [32], and question answering [12].

To improve the quality of extracted relational facts and benefit downstream tasks, many efforts have been devoted to this task. *Supervised relation extraction* is a representative paradigm built upon the closed world assumption [8]. Benefiting from artfully designed network architectures [14,24,36] and valuable knowledge in pretrained language model [1,6,30,31], models effectively capture semantic-rich representations and achieves superior results. However, conventional supervised relation extraction

---

J. Zhao and Y. Zhang—Equal contribution.

© The Author(s), under exclusive license to Springer Nature Switzerland AG 2022
M. Sun et al. (Eds.): CCL 2022, LNAI 13603, pp. 96–111, 2022.
https://doi.org/10.1007/978-3-031-18315-7_7

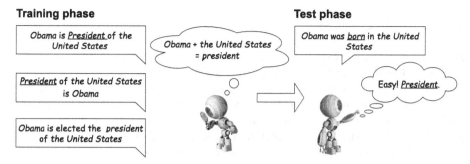

Fig. 1. Neural models tend to use the simplest way to meet the supervised objective (*Shortcut phenomenon* [9]), which would lead to negative predictions on unseen relations. Hence, for the unseen relations, we hope neural models can reject prediction through embracing sufficient features.

suffer from the lack of large-scale labeled data. To tackle this issue, *distantly supervised relation extraction* has attracted much attention. The existing works mainly focus on how to alleviate the noise generated in the automatic annotation. Common approaches include selecting informative instances [19], incorporating extra information [35], and designing sophisticated training [22].

Although a supervised relation classifier achieves excellent performance on known relations, real-world inputs are often mixed with samples of unseen relations. A well-performing model can still confidently make arbitrarily wrong predictions when dealing with these unseen relations [25,27]. The unrobustness is rooted in the *Shortcut* feature [9] of neural networks. Models optimized by a supervised objective does not actively learn features beyond the bare minimum necessary to discriminate between known relations. As shown in Fig. 1, if there is only president relation in the training data between Obama and the United States, the model tends to predict the president relation when it encounters them again. However, entities are not equivalent to relation definitions. Models severely biased to the extraction of overly simplistic features can easily fail to generalize to discriminate between known and unseen relations. As shown in Table 1, when the unseen relations appears in the test set, the supervised RE models' F_1-score drops by at least 30 points.

Table 1. Supervised RE models' performance when encountering new relations. These models are from previous papers [15,21,26]. Ori: all relations in the test set are present in the training set. Mix: 50% of the relations in the test set do not appear in the training set.

Model/Dataset	SpanBERT	Roberta	CP
Ori (F_1-score)	0.919	0.928	0.936
Mix (ΔF_1-score)	0.317↓	0.310↓	0.310↓

In this work, we propose a robust relation extraction method in real world settings. By integrating rejection option, the classifier can effectively detect whether inputs express unseen relations instead of making arbitrary bad predictions. Specifically, we introduce contrastive training techniques to achieve this goal. A set of carefully designed class-preserving transformations are used to learn sufficient features, which can enhance the discriminability between known and unknown relation representations. The classifier built on the learned representation is confidence-calibrated. Thereby samples of unseen relations are assigned a low confidence score and rejected. Off-the-shelf OpenRE methods can be used to discover potential relations in these samples. In addition, we find the rejection can be further improved via the readily available distantly-supervised data. Experimental results show the effectiveness of our method capturing discriminative representations for unseen relation rejection.

To summarize, the main contributions of our work are as follows: (1) We propose a relation extraction method with rejection option, which is still robust when exposed to unseen relations. (2) We design a set of class-preserving transformations to learn sufficient features to discriminate known and novel relations. In addition, we propose to use readily available distantly-supervised data to enhance the discriminability. (3) Extensive experiments on two academic datasets prove the effectiveness of our method capturing discriminative representations for unseen relation rejection.

2 Related Work

2.1 Relation Extraction

Relation extraction has advanced for more than a couple of decades. Supervised/Distantly supervised relation extraction is oriented at predefined relational types. Researchers have explored different network architectures [36], training strategies [22] and external information [35]. Superior results have been achieved. Open relation extraction is oriented at emerging unknown relation. Well-designed extraction forms (e.g. sequence labelling [7], clustering [38]) are used to deal with relations without pre-specified schemas. Different from them, we consider a more general scenario, in which known and unknown relations are mixed in the input. We effectively separate them by a rejection option, which enables us to use the optimal paradigm to deal with the corresponding relations.

2.2 Classification with Rejection Option

Most existing classification methods are based on the closed world assumption. However, inputs are often mixed with samples of unknown classes in real-world applications. The approaches used to handle it roughly fall into one of two groups. The first group calculates the confidence score based on the classifier output. The score can be used to measure whether an input belongs to unknown classes. Maximum softmax probability (MSP) [11] is a represetative method and Liang et al. [17] further improve MSP by introducing temperature scaling. Furthermore, Shu et al. [29] build a multi-class classifier with a 1-vs-rest final layer of sigmoids to reduce the open space risk. The second group considers classification with rejection option as an outlier detection problem.

Off-the-shelf outlier detection algorithms [2,20,28] are leveraged. Different optimization objectives such as large margin loss [18], gaussian mixture loss [33] are adopted to learn more discriminative representations to facilitate anomaly detection. Recently, Zhang et al. [34] propose to learn the adaptive decision boundary (ADB) that serves as the basis for judging outliers.

3 Approach

In this paper, we propose a robust relation extraction method in real world settings. By integrating rejection option, the classifier can effectively detect whether inputs express unseen relations instead of making arbitrary bad predictions. Off-the-shell OpenRE methods can be used to discover potential relations in these rejected samples.

The problem setting in this work is formally stated as follows. Let $\mathcal{K} = \{\mathcal{R}_1, ..., \mathcal{R}_k\}$ be a set of known relations and $\mathcal{U} = \{\mathcal{R}_{k+1}, ..., \mathcal{R}_n\}$ be a set of unseen relations where $\mathcal{K} \cap \mathcal{U} = \emptyset$. Let $\mathcal{X}$ be an input space. Given the training data $\mathcal{D}^\ell = \{(x_i^\ell, y_i^\ell)\}_{i=1,...,N}$ where $x_i^\ell \in \mathcal{X}$, $y_i^\ell \in \mathcal{K}$, we target constructing a mapping rule $f : \mathcal{X} \rightarrow \{\mathcal{R}_1, ..., \mathcal{R}_k, \mathcal{R}^*\}$ where $\mathcal{R}^*$ denotes rejection option. Let $\mathcal{D}^u = \{(x_i^u, y_i^u)\}_{i=1,...,M}$ be the testing dataset where $y_i^u \in \mathcal{K} \cup \mathcal{U}$. An desirable mapping rule f should meet the following objective as much as possible:

$$f(x) = \begin{cases} y_i^u & y_i^u \in \mathcal{K} \\ \mathcal{R}^* & y_i^u \in \mathcal{U}. \end{cases}$$

3.1 Method Overview

We approach the problem by introducing contrastive learning techniques. As illustrated in Fig. 2, the proposed method comprises four major components: relation representation encoder $g(\cdot)$, confidence-calibrated classifier $\eta(\cdot)$, class-preserving transformations $\mathcal{T}$, and the OpenRE module.

Our overview starts from the first two components. There is no doubt that an encoder and classifier are the basic components of a supervised relation extractor. However, the supervised training objective does not encourage the model to learn features beyond the bare minimum necessary to discriminate between known relations. Consequently, the classifier can misclassify unseen relations to known relations with high confidence.

In order to calibrate the confidence of the classifier, we introduce contrastive learning techniques. Given training batch $\mathcal{B}$, an augmented batch $\widetilde{\mathcal{B}}$ is obtained by applying random transformation $t \in \mathcal{T}$ to mask partial features. Then the supervised contrastive learning objective max/minimize the representation agreement according to whether their relations are the same. By doing this, the model is forced to find more features to discriminate between relations and the classifier can be calibrated. Based on the confidence-calibrated classifier, unknown relations are rejected if the maximum softmax probability of the classifier does not exceed a preset threshold θ.

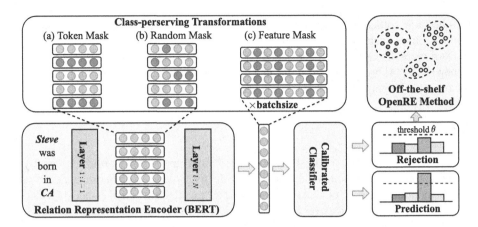

Fig. 2. An overview of the proposed method. Three steps are included: (1) Contrastive training techniques and a set of class-preserving transformations are utilized to learn sufficient features. (2) The classifier extract known relations and rejects samples of unseen relations according to these features. (3) Off-the-shelf OpenRE method (SelfORE) is incorporated to discovery unseen relations in these rejected samples.

In order to discriminate unknown relations rather than just detect their existence, we further integrate the off-the-shelf OpenRE method into our framework. The samples rejected by the classifier are sent to the OpenRE module to detect potential unknown relations.

3.2   Relation Representation Encoder

Given a relation instance $x_i^\ell = (\boldsymbol{w}_i, h_i, t_i) \in \mathcal{D}^\ell$ where $\boldsymbol{w}_i = \{w_1, w_2, ..., w_n\}$ is the input sentence and $h_i = (s^h, e^h)$, $t_i = (s^t, e^t)$ mark the position of head and tail entities, relation representation encoder $g(\cdot)$ aims to encode contextual relational information to a fixed-length representation $\boldsymbol{r}_i = g(x_i) \in \mathbb{R}^d$. We opt for simplicity and adopt the commonly used BERT [4] to obtain $\boldsymbol{r}_i$ while various other choices of the network architecture are also allowed without any constraints. Formally, the process of obtaining $\boldsymbol{r}_i$ is:

$$\boldsymbol{h}_1, ..., \boldsymbol{h}_n = \text{BERT}(w_1, ..., w_n) \tag{1}$$

$$\boldsymbol{h}_{ent} = \text{MAXPOOL}(\boldsymbol{h}_s, ..., \boldsymbol{h}_e) \tag{2}$$

$$\boldsymbol{r}_i = \langle \boldsymbol{h}_{head} | \boldsymbol{h}_{tail} \rangle , \tag{3}$$

where $\boldsymbol{h}_1, ..., \boldsymbol{h}_n$ is the result of the input sentence after BERT encoding, subscript s and e represent the start and end positions of the entity, $\boldsymbol{h}_{ent}$ represents the result of the maximum pooling of the entity, $\boldsymbol{h}_{ent}$ can be divided into head entity $\boldsymbol{h}_{head}$ and tail entity $\boldsymbol{h}_{tail}$, and $\langle \cdot | \cdot \rangle$ is the concatenation operator.

3.3 Confidence-Calibrated Classifier

In order to alleviate overconfidence to unseen relations, we introduce contrastive learning techniques to calibrate classifier. A well-calibrated classifier should not only accurately classify known relations, but also give low confidence to unseen relations, that is, $\max_y p(y|x)$.

Given a training batch $\mathcal{B} = (x_i^\ell, y_i^\ell)_{i=1}^B$, we obtain an augmented batch $\widetilde{\mathcal{B}} = (\widetilde{x}_i^\ell, y_i^\ell)_{i=1}^B$ by applying random transformation $t \in \mathcal{T}$ on $\mathcal{B}$. For brevity, the superscript ℓ is omitted in the subsequent elaboration of this section. For each labeled sample $(\widetilde{x}_i, y_i)$, $\widetilde{\mathcal{B}}$ can be divided into two subsets $\widetilde{\mathcal{B}}_{y_i}$ and $\widetilde{\mathcal{B}}_{-y_i}$. $\widetilde{\mathcal{B}}_{y_i}$ denotes a set that contains samples of relation y_i and $\widetilde{\mathcal{B}}_{-y_i}$ contains the rest. The supervised contrastive learning objective is defined as follows:

$$\mathcal{L}_{cts}^{sup}(\mathcal{B}, \mathcal{T}) = \frac{1}{2B} \sum_{j=1}^{2B} \mathcal{L}_{cts}(\widetilde{x}_i, \widetilde{\mathcal{B}}_{y_i} \setminus \{\widetilde{x}_i\}, \widetilde{\mathcal{B}}_{-y_i}) \tag{4}$$

$$\mathcal{L}_{cts}(x, \mathcal{D}^+, \mathcal{D}^-) = -\frac{1}{|\mathcal{D}^+|} log \frac{\sum_{x' \in \mathcal{D}^+} q(x, x')}{\sum_{x' \in \mathcal{D}^+ \cup \mathcal{D}^+} q(x, x')} \tag{5}$$

$$q(x, x') = \exp(sim(z(x), z(x'))/\tau), \tag{6}$$

where $|\mathcal{D}|$ denotes the number of samples in $\mathcal{D}$, $sim(x, x')$ denotes the cosine similarity between x and x' and τ denotes a temperature coefficient. Following Chen et al. [3], we use a additional projection layer t to obtain the contrastive feature $z(x) = t(g(x))$.

Benifiting from contrastive training, the encoder $g(\cdot)$ learns rich features to discriminate between known and novel relations. Accordingly, we train a confidence-calibrated classifier $\eta(\cdot)$ upon $g(\cdot)$ as follows:

$$\mathcal{L} = \mathbb{E}_{(x,y) \sim \mathcal{D}^\ell}[\mathcal{L}_{ce}(\eta(g(x_i)), y)], \tag{7}$$

where $\mathcal{L}_{ce}$ is the cross entropy loss. In addition, we can easily obtain a large number of training data $\mathcal{D}^{dist}$ through distant supervision. None of the y_i^{dist} in $\mathcal{D}^{dist}$ are known relation, that is, $\{y_i^{dist}\} \cap \{y_j^\ell\} = \emptyset$. These data are only used as negative examples, so the noise in the data will not be a problem. We force the classifier output distribution of negative examples to approximate the uniform distribution by optimizing the cross-entropy between them. Using $\mathcal{D}^{dist}$, we optimize model by following objective instead of Eq. 7.

$$\mathcal{L}^{dist} = \mathcal{L} + \lambda \mathbb{E}_{x \sim \mathcal{D}^{dist}}[\mathcal{L}_{ce}(\eta(g(x)), y_{uni})], \tag{8}$$

where $\mathcal{L}$ refers to the optimization objective of Eq. 7. λ is the hyperparamters that balances the known relation data and distantly supervised data. We can achieve good results simply by setting λ to 1 without adjustment. y_{uni} represents a uniform distribution.

Based on the confidence-calibrated classifier, we specify the rejection rule $f(\cdot)$ as follows:

$$f(x_i) = \begin{cases} y & max_y p(y|x_i) > \theta \\ \mathcal{R}^* & Otherwise, \end{cases} \tag{9}$$

where θ is a threshold hyperparameters, the posterior probability $p(y|x_i)$ is the output of classifier η and $\mathcal{R}^*$ denotes the rejection option.

3.4   Class-Preserving Transformations

Transformations is the core component of contrastive learning. Our intuition in designing transformation is that feature masks at different views force the model to find more features to discriminate between known relations. These new features can play a vital role in recognizing unseen relations. Why do the above methods work? As shown in Fig. 1, due to the *shortcut* phenomenon, the model is more inclined to remember the relations between entities and it would make mistakes when predicting new relations between the same entity pair. Intuitively through the mask mechanism, the model could mask out some features that belong to Obama and the United States, and then it will have to find more other features to distinguish *the president of* from other relations. Therefore it will not learn the *Shortcut* bias of *Obama + the United States = the president of*. In this work, we design three class-preserving transformations to mask partial features as follows.

Token Mask. Token mask works in the process of sentence encoding. In this transformation, we randomly mask a certain proportion of tokens to generate a new view of relation representation.

Random Mask. Random mask also works in the process of sentence encoding. Instead of completely masking representation of selected tokens, each dimension of the representation of each word is considered independently in this transformation.

Feature Mask. Feature mask works after sentence encoding. Given a relation instance $x_i^\ell \in \mathcal{D}^\ell$, we first obtain its relation representation $r_i = g(x_i)$. Then we randomly mask a certain proportion of feature dimensions of r_i to generate a new view.

It is certain that a more complicated and diverse transformations will bring additional improvement. This will be one of our future work.

3.5   OpenRE Module

We introduce the OpenRE module for the integrity of the framework, although it is not our main concerns. Based on the rejection rules f described in Sect. 3.3, we can classify samples of known relations while rejecting unseen relations. In this section, we take a step forward. By integrating the off-the-shelf OpenRE method, we try to discover the potential unseen relations in the rejected samples instead of only detecting their existence. We adopt SelfORE [13], a clustering-based OpenRE method, as the building block of our OpenRE module. Various other methods can also be used as the alternative to SelfORE without any constraints. More details about OpenRE methods can be found in the related papers. Overall, the method proposed in this paper is detailed in Algorithm 1.

4   Experimental Setup

In this section, we describe the datasets for training and evaluating the proposed method. We also detail the baseline models for comparison. Finally, we clarify the implementation details.

Algorithm 1. Robust Relation Extraction

Input: known relation dataset $\mathcal{D}^\ell$, distantly supervised dataset $\mathcal{D}^{dist}$ (optional), testing dataset $\mathcal{D}^u$, transformation set $\mathcal{T}$, model parameters Θ, Φ for encoder and classifier, OpenRE module $\mathcal{O}$ and learning rate α.

1 **Training Phase**
2 **repeat**
3   sample a training batch $\mathcal{B}$ from $\mathcal{D}^\ell$;
4   obtain transformed batch $\tilde{\mathcal{B}} = t(\mathcal{B}), t \sim \mathcal{T}$;
5   enrich representation by contrastive training (Eq. 4): $\Theta = \Theta - \alpha \nabla_\Theta \mathcal{L}_{cts}^{sup}$;
6   sample a distant batch $\mathcal{B}^{dist}$ from $\mathcal{D}^{dist}$;
7   optimize classifier by supervised training (Eqs. 7 or 8):
8     $\{\Theta, \Phi\} = \{\Theta, \Phi\} - \alpha \nabla_{\{\Theta, \Phi\}} \mathcal{L}^{dist}$;
9 **until** *convergence*;
10 **Testing Phase**
11 Filter the unseen relations subset $\mathcal{D}^{rej}$ from $\mathcal{D}^u$ by the rejection rule f (Eq. 9);
12 Output predictions $\{y_i^u\}$ for the rest samples of known relations;
13 Run the OpenRE module $\mathcal{O}$ to obtain potential relations in $\mathcal{D}^{rej}$;

4.1 Datasets

We conduct our experiments on two well-known relation extraction datasets. In addition, a distantly supervised dataset are used in a auxiliary way.

FewRel. Few-Shot Relation Classification Dataset [10]. FewRel is a human-annotated dataset containing 80 types of relations, each with 700 instances. We use the top 40 relations as known and the middle 20 relations as unseen. Since the relations of FewRel dataset is exactly the same as that of FewRel-Distance, we hold out the last 20 relations for the use of distant supervision. The training set contains 25600 randomly selected samples of known relations. In order to evaluate the rejection performance to the unseen relations, the test/validation set contains 3200/1600 samples composed of known and unseen relations.

TACRED. The TAC Relation Extraction Dataset [37]. TACRED is a human-annotated large-scale relation extraction dataset that covers 41 relation types. Similar to the setting of FewRel, we use the top 31 relations as known and the rest 10 relations as unseen. The training set consists of 18113 randomly selected samples of known relations. The size of validation set and test set are 900 and 1800 respectively, including known and unseen relations. It should be noted that 50% of the unseen relation samples in the validation set and test is `no_relation`.

FewRel-distant. FewRel-distant contains the distantly-supervised data obtained by the authors of FewRel before human annotation. We use this dataset as the distantly supervised data in our experiments.

4.2 Baselines and Evaluation Metrics

MSP [11]. MSP assumes that correctly classified examples tend to have greater maximum softmax probabilities than examples of unseen classes. Thereby the maximum softmax probabilities are used as confidence score for unseen classes detection.

MSP-TC [17]. MSP-TC uses maximum softmax probabilities with temperature scaling and small perturbations to enhance the separability between known and unseen classes, allowing for more effective detection.

DOC [29]. DOC builds n 1-vs-rest sigmoid classifiers for n known classes respectively. The maximum probability of these binary classifiers is considered as the confidence score for unseen classes detection.

LMCL [18]. Large margin cosine loss (LMCL) aims to learn a discriminative deep representations. It forces the model to not only classify correctly but also maximize inter-class variance and minimize intra-class variance. Based on the learned representations, local outlier factor (LOF) is used to detect unseen classes.

ADB [34]. Labeled known classes samples are first used for representation learning. Then the learned representations are utilized to learn the adaptive spherical decision boundaries for each known classes. Samples outside the hypersphere will be rejected for recognition.

Evaluation Metrics. We follow previous work [18,34] and take all the unseen relations as one rejected class. The accuracy and macro F1 metrics are used as the scoring function to evaluate the unseen relation detection.

4.3   Implementation Details

We use the Adam [16] as the optimizer, with a learning rate of $1e - 4$ and batch size of 100 for all datasets. If the results don't improve on the validation set for 10 epochs, we stop the training to avoid overfitting. All experiments are conducted using a NVIDIA GeForce RTX 3090 with 24 GB memory.

5   Results and Analysis

In this section, we present the experimental results of our method on FewRel and TACRED datasets to demonstrate the effectiveness of our method.

5.1   Main Results

Our experiments in this section focus on the following three related questions.

Can the Proposed Method Effectively Detect Unseen Relations? To answer this question, we consider all the known relations as one predicted class and the rest unseen relations as one rejected class. Table 2 reports model performances on FewRel, TACRED datasets, which shows that the proposed method achieves state-of-the-art results on unseen relation detection. Benefiting from the contrastive training objectives and the carefully designed transformations, the *Shortcut* phenomenon is effectively alleviated, and the model learns sufficient features to discriminate between known and unseen relations. Therefore, the proposed method consistently outperforms the compared baselines by a large margin in different mixing-ratio settings.

Table 2. Main results of unseen relation detection with different known class proportions (25%, 50% and 75%) on two relation extraction datasets. Compared with the best results of all baselines, our method improves F_1-score by an average of 2.6%, 3.5% on FewRel and TACRED dataset, respectively.

Dataset	Method	25%		50%		75%	
		Accuracy	F_1-score	Accuracy	F_1-score	Accuracy	F_1-score
FewRel	MSP [11]	0.805	0.781	0.786	0.786	0.797	0.774
	MSP-TC [17]	0.802	0.772	0.769	0.769	0.786	0.768
	DOC [29]	0.794	0.768	0.781	0.781	0.784	0.761
	LMCL [18]	0.810	0.785	0.740	0.740	0.835	0.777
	ADB [34]	0.801	0.800	0.837	0.799	0.837	0.784
	Ours	**0.888**	**0.852**	**0.844**	**0.824**	**0.838**	**0.827**
TACRED	MSP [11]	0.758	0.691	0.698	0.688	0.734	0.650
	MSP-TC [17]	0.789	0.687	0.674	0.670	0.765	0.671
	DOC [29]	0.793	0.687	0.707	0.678	0.775	0.681
	LMCL [18]	0.737	0.705	0.667	0.684	0.785	0.654
	ADB [34]	0.772	0.714	0.711	0.710	0.767	0.699
	Ours	**0.827**	**0.758**	**0.723**	**0.742**	**0.788**	**0.715**

Table 3. Macro F_1-score of known relation classification with different proportion of known relations.

Dataset	Method	25%	50%	75%
FewRel	MSP	0.730	0.769	0.814
	MSP-TC	0.675	0.771	0.764
	DOC	0.737	0.780	0.805
	LMCL	0.765	0.767	0.809
	ADB	0.778	0.770	0.810
	Ours	**0.827**	**0.793**	**0.828**
TACRED	MSP	0.610	0.619	0.668
	MSP-TC	0.378	0.438	0.639
	DOC	0.628	0.627	0.686
	LMCL	0.616	0.615	0.687
	ADB	0.625	**0.640**	0.665
	Ours	**0.637**	0.633	**0.688**

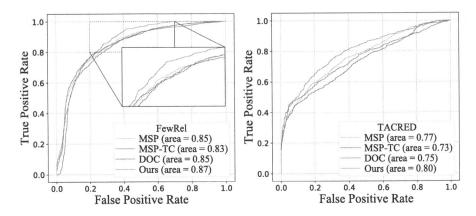

Fig. 3. ROC curves on two datasets.

Does the Detection of Unseen Relations Impair the Extraction of Known Relations? Integrating the rejection option can make the classifier more robust in real applications. However, we do not want the unseen relations detection impair known relations classification, which is the basic function of the classifier. From table 3 we can observe that the proposed model not only effectively detect unseen relations, but also accurately classify known relations. This demonstrate that the designed transformation will not affect the original relational semantics, so the rich features obtained by comparative learning remain discriminability for the known relations.

Can the Model Achieve Superior Performance Under Different Threshold Settings? We show the receiver operating characteristic (ROC) curve in Fig. 3. The area under ROC curve (AUROC) summarize the performance of a classifier detecting unseen relations across different thresholds. From Fig. 3 we can observe that the AUROC of the proposed method is the largest. Therefore, the proposed method has certain advantages under different threshold settings.

5.2   Ablation Study

To understand the effects of each component of the proposed model, we conduct an ablation study on it and report the results (Macro-F_1) on the two dataset in Table 4. The results show that the detection of unseen relations is degraded if any transformation is removed. It indicates that (1) These transformations force model learn sufficient features through mask mechanism from different views. The learned features are beneficial for the detection of unseen relations. (2) Since the transformations are from different views, they can be superimposed and further enhance the detection of unseen relations. In addition, we find that distantly supervised data can significantly improve the detection of unseen relations. Because there are a large number of diverse relations in the external knowledge base, we can easily construct a large number of negative samples. So this improvement can be seen as a free lunch.

Table 4. Abalation study of our method.

Dataset	Method	25%	50%	75%
FewRel	W/o Feature mask	0.845	0.807	0.816
	w/o Random mask	0.846	0.814	0.809
	w/o Token mask	0.833	0.810	0.803
	w/o Distant	0.810	0.805	0.815
	Ours	**0.852**	**0.824**	**0.827**
TACRED	w/o Feature mask	0.753	0.728	0.703
	w/o Random mask	0.740	0.735	0.706
	w/o Token mask	0.750	0.738	0.706
	w/o Distant	0.716	0.700	0.684
	Ours	**0.758**	**0.742**	**0.715**

5.3 Relation Representation Visualization

To intuitively show the influence of the rich features learned through contrastive training, we visualize the relational representation with t-SNE [23]. We select five semantically similar known relations from FewRel dataset, and randomly select 40 samples for each of them. 100 hard samples of unseen relations misclassified by MSP method are selected to show the superiority of our method. From the visualization results in Fig. 4, we can observe that, before training (upper left), the relation representations are scattered in the semantic space. After supervised training (upper right), samples can be roughly divided by relation, but different relations are still close to each other. This is consistent with the *Shortcut* feature in neural network. We note that samples of unseen relations are mixed with known relation samples. After contrastive training (down left), model learns sufficient features to discriminate unseen relations. Therefore, samples of unseen relations are effectively separated. Finally, a best relation representation are obtained by applying both supervised and contrastive optimization (down right).

5.4 A Case Study on OpenRE

Table 5. Extracted and golden surface-form relation names on TACRED.

Extracted surface-form	Golden surface-form
university	schools_attended
was found	founded
charges with	charges
died in	country_of_death
was born in	date_of_birth

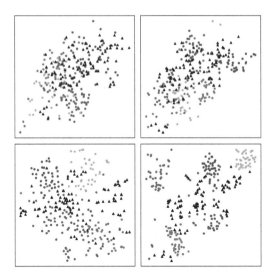

Fig. 4. Visualization of the relation representation after t-SNE dimension reduction. The representations are colored with their ground-truth relation labels. Black triangles indicate unknown relations. These four from top left to bottom right sequentially illustrate the relation representation of initial state, after supervised optimization, after contrastive optimization, after both of them.

For the samples rejected by the classifier, the off-the-shelf OpenRE method can be used to discovery potential unseen relations. In this section, we provide a brief case study to show the discovered unseen relations by SelfORE [13]. OpenRE module outputs the cluster assignment of these rejected samples. We extract the relation names using the frequent n-gram in each cluster and the extraction results are shown in Table 5. By integrating the OpenRE module, our method complete (1) the classification of known relations, (2) the rejection of unseen relations, (3) discovery of unseen relations. Based on the above process, robust relation extraction in real applications is realized.

6   Conclusions

In this work, we introduce a relation extraction method with rejection option to improve the robustness in real-world applications. The proposed method employs contrastive training techniques and a set of carefully designed transformations to learn sufficient features. The classification of known relations and rejection of unseen relations can be done with these features. Unseen relations in the rejected samples can be discovered by incorporating off-the-shelf OpenRE methods. Experimental results show that our method outperforms SOTA methods for unseen relation rejection.

References

1. Baldini Soares, L., FitzGerald, N., Ling, J., Kwiatkowski, T.: Matching the blanks: distributional similarity for relation learning. In: Proceedings of the 57th Annual Meeting of the Association for Computational Linguistics, pp. 2895–2905. Association for Computational Linguistics, Florence, Italy (2019). https://doi.org/10.18653/v1/P19-1279, https://aclanthology.org/P19-1279
2. Breunig, M.M., Kriegel, H.P., Ng, R.T., Sander, J.: Lof: identifying density-based local outliers. SIGMOD Rec. **29**(2), 93–104 (2000). https://doi.org/10.1145/335191.335388
3. Chen, T., Kornblith, S., Norouzi, M., Hinton, G.E.: A simple framework for contrastive learning of visual representations. CoRR abs/2002.05709 (2020), https://arxiv.org/abs/2002.05709
4. Devlin, J., Chang, M., Lee, K., Toutanova, K.: BERT: pre-training of deep bidirectional transformers for language understanding. CoRR abs/1810.04805 (2018), http://arxiv.org/abs/1810.04805
5. Distiawan, B., Weikum, G., Qi, J., Zhang, R.: Neural relation extraction for knowledge base enrichment. In: Proceedings of the 57th Annual Meeting of the Association for Computational Linguistics, pp. 229–240 (2019)
6. Du, J., Han, J., Way, A., Wan, D.: Multi-level structured self-attentions for distantly supervised relation extraction. In: Proceedings of the 2018 Conference on Empirical Methods in Natural Language Processing, pp. 2216–2225. Association for Computational Linguistics, Brussels, Belgium (2018). https://doi.org/10.18653/v1/D18-1245, https://aclanthology.org/D18-1245
7. Fader, A., Soderland, S., Etzioni, O.: Identifying relations for open information extraction. In: Proceedings of the 2011 Conference on Empirical Methods in Natural Language Processing, pp. 1535–1545. Association for Computational Linguistics, Edinburgh, Scotland, UK (2011). https://aclanthology.org/D11-1142
8. Gallaire, H., Minker, J. (eds.): On Closed World Data Bases, pp. 55–76. Springer, US, Boston, MA (1978). https://doi.org/10.1007/978-1-4684-3384-5_3, https://doi.org/10.1007/978-1-4684-3384-5_3
9. Geirhos, R., et al.: Shortcut learning in deep neural networks. Nat. Mach. Intell. **2**(11), 665–673 (2020)
10. Han, X., et al.: FewRel: a large-scale supervised few-shot relation classification dataset with state-of-the-art evaluation. In: Proceedings of the 2018 Conference on Empirical Methods in Natural Language Processing, pp. 4803–4809. Association for Computational Linguistics, Brussels, Belgium (2018). https://doi.org/10.18653/v1/D18-1514, https://aclanthology.org/D18-1514
11. Hendrycks, D., Gimpel, K.: A baseline for detecting misclassified and out-of-distribution examples in neural networks. In: 5th International Conference on Learning Representations, ICLR 2017, Toulon, France, 24–26 April 2017, Conference Track Proceedings. OpenReview.net (2017). https://openreview.net/forum?id=Hkg4TI9xl
12. Honovich, O., Choshen, L., Aharoni, R., Neeman, E., Szpektor, I., Abend, O.: Q^2: evaluating factual consistency in knowledge-grounded dialogues via question generation and question answering. CoRR abs/2104.08202 (2021). https://arxiv.org/abs/2104.08202
13. Hu, X., Wen, L., Xu, Y., Zhang, C., Yu, P.S.: Selfore: self-supervised relational feature learning for open relation extraction. CoRR abs/2004.02438 (2020). https://arxiv.org/abs/2004.02438
14. Huang, Y.Y., Wang, W.Y.: Deep residual learning for weakly-supervised relation extraction. CoRR abs/1707.08866 (2017). http://arxiv.org/abs/1707.08866

15. Joshi, M., Chen, D., Liu, Y., Weld, D.S., Zettlemoyer, L., Levy, O.: SpanBERT: Improving Pre-training by Representing and Predicting Spans. arXiv e-prints arXiv:1907.10529 (2019)
16. Kingma, D.P., Ba, J.: Adam: a method for stochastic optimization. In: ICLR (Poster) (2015). http://arxiv.org/abs/1412.6980
17. Liang, S., Li, Y., Srikant, R.: Enhancing the reliability of out-of-distribution image detection in neural networks. In: International Conference on Learning Representations (2018). https://openreview.net/forum?id=H1VGkIxRZ
18. Lin, T.E., Xu, H.: Deep unknown intent detection with margin loss. In: Proceedings of the 57th Annual Meeting of the Association for Computational Linguistics, pp. 5491–5496. Association for Computational Linguistics, Florence, Italy (2019). https://doi.org/10.18653/v1/P19-1548, https://aclanthology.org/P19-1548
19. Lin, Y., Shen, S., Liu, Z., Luan, H., Sun, M.: Neural relation extraction with selective attention over instances. In: Proceedings of the 54th Annual Meeting of the Association for Computational Linguistics (Volume 1: Long Papers), pp. 2124–2133 (2016)
20. Liu, F.T., Ting, K.M., Zhou, Z.H.: Isolation forest. In: 2008 Eighth IEEE International Conference on Data Mining, pp. 413–422 (2008). https://doi.org/10.1109/ICDM.2008.17
21. Liu, Y., et al.: RoBERTa: A Robustly Optimized BERT Pretraining Approach. arXiv e-prints arXiv:1907.11692 (2019)
22. Ma, R., Gui, T., Li, L., Zhang, Q., Zhou, Y., Huang, X.: SENT: sentence-level distant relation extraction via negative training. CoRR abs/2106.11566 (2021). https://arxiv.org/abs/2106.11566
23. van der Maaten, L., Hinton, G.: Visualizing data using t-sne. J. Mach. Learn. Res. **9**(86), 2579–2605 (2008). http://jmlr.org/papers/v9/vandermaaten08a.html
24. Miwa, M., Bansal, M.: End-to-end relation extraction using LSTMs on sequences and tree structures. In: Proceedings of the 54th Annual Meeting of the Association for Computational Linguistics (Volume 1: Long Papers), pp. 1105–1116. Association for Computational Linguistics, Berlin, Germany (2016). https://doi.org/10.18653/v1/P16-1105, https://aclanthology.org/P16-1105
25. Nguyen, A.M., Yosinski, J., Clune, J.: Deep neural networks are easily fooled: High confidence predictions for unrecognizable images. CoRR abs/1412.1897 (2014). http://arxiv.org/abs/1412.1897
26. Peng, H., et al.: Learning from Context or Names? An Empirical Study on Neural Relation Extraction. arXiv e-prints arXiv:2010.01923 (2020)
27. Recht, B., Roelofs, R., Schmidt, L., Shankar, V.: Do imagenet classifiers generalize to imagenet? In: International Conference on Machine Learning, pp. 5389–5400. PMLR (2019)
28. Schölkopf, B., Platt, J.C., Shawe-Taylor, J., Smola, A.J., Williamson, R.C.: Estimating the Support of a High-Dimensional Distribution. Neural Comput. **13**(7), 1443–1471 (2001). https://doi.org/10.1162/089976601750264965
29. Shu, L., Xu, H., Liu, B.: DOC: deep open classification of text documents. In: Proceedings of the 2017 Conference on Empirical Methods in Natural Language Processing, pp. 2911–2916. Association for Computational Linguistics, Copenhagen, Denmark (2017). https://doi.org/10.18653/v1/D17-1314, https://aclanthology.org/D17-1314
30. Verga, P., Strubell, E., McCallum, A.: Simultaneously self-attending to all mentions for full-abstract biological relation extraction. In: Proceedings of the 2018 Conference of the North American Chapter of the Association for Computational Linguistics: Human Language Technologies, Volume 1 (Long Papers), pp. 872–884. Association for Computational Linguistics, New Orleans, Louisiana (2018). https://doi.org/10.18653/v1/N18-1080, https://aclanthology.org/N18-1080
31. Wu, S., He, Y.: Enriching pre-trained language model with entity information for relation classification. In: Proceedings of the 28th ACM International Conference on Information and Knowledge Management, pp. 2361–2364 (2019)

32. Xiong, C., Power, R., Callan, J.: Explicit semantic ranking for academic search via knowledge graph embedding. In: Proceedings of the 26th International Conference on World Wide Web, pp. 1271–1279 (2017)
33. Yan, G., et al.: Unknown intent detection using Gaussian mixture model with an application to zero-shot intent classification. In: Proceedings of the 58th Annual Meeting of the Association for Computational Linguistics, pp. 1050–1060. Association for Computational Linguistics, Online (2020). https://doi.org/10.18653/v1/2020.acl-main.99, https://aclanthology.org/2020.acl-main.99
34. Zhang, H., Xu, H., Lin, T.E.: Deep open intent classification with adaptive decision boundary. In: Proceedings of the AAAI Conference on Artificial Intelligence, vol. 35, pp. 14374–14382 (2021)
35. Zhang, N., et al.: Long-tail relation extraction via knowledge graph embeddings and graph convolution networks. In: Proceedings of the 2019 Conference of the North American Chapter of the Association for Computational Linguistics: Human Language Technologies, Volume 1 (Long and Short Papers), pp. 3016–3025. Association for Computational Linguistics, Minneapolis, Minnesota (2019). https://doi.org/10.18653/v1/N19-1306, https://aclanthology.org/N19-1306
36. Zhang, Y., Qi, P., Manning, C.D.: Graph convolution over pruned dependency trees improves relation extraction. In: Proceedings of the 2018 Conference on Empirical Methods in Natural Language Processing, pp. 2205–2215. Association for Computational Linguistics, Brussels, Belgium (2018). https://doi.org/10.18653/v1/D18-1244, https://aclanthology.org/D18-1244
37. Zhang, Y., Zhong, V., Chen, D., Angeli, G., Manning, C.D.: Position-aware attention and supervised data improve slot filling. In: Proceedings of the 2017 Conference on Empirical Methods in Natural Language Processing, pp. 35–45. Association for Computational Linguistics, Copenhagen, Denmark (2017). https://doi.org/10.18653/v1/D17-1004, https://aclanthology.org/D17-1004
38. Zhao, J., Gui, T., Zhang, Q., Zhou, Y.: A relation-oriented clustering method for open relation extraction (2021)

Using Extracted Emotion Cause to Improve Content-Relevance for Empathetic Conversation Generation

Minghui Zou, Rui Pan, Sai Zhang$^{(\boxtimes)}$, and Xiaowang Zhang

College of Intelligence and Computing, Tianjin University, Tianjin 300350, China
{zzzxzmh,ruipan,zhang_sai,xiaowangzhang}@tju.edu.cn

Abstract. Empathetic conversation generation intends to endow the open-domain conversation model with the capability for understanding, interpreting, and expressing emotion. Humans express not only their emotional state but also the stimulus that caused the emotion, i.e., emotion cause, during a conversation. Most existing approaches focus on emotion modeling, emotion recognition and prediction, and emotion fusion generation, ignoring the critical aspect of the emotion cause, which results in generating responses with irrelevant content. Emotion cause can help the model understand the user's emotion and make the generated responses more content-relevant. However, using the emotion cause to enhance empathetic conversation generation is challenging. Firstly, the model needs to accurately identify the emotion cause without large-scale labeled data. Second, the model needs to effectively integrate the emotion cause into the generation process. To this end, we present an emotion cause extractor using a semi-supervised training method and an empathetic conversation generator using a biased self-attention mechanism to overcome these two issues. Experimental results indicate that our proposed emotion cause extractor improves recall scores markedly compared to the baselines, and the proposed empathetic conversation generator has superior performance and improves the content-relevance of generated responses.

Keywords: Empathetic conversation generation · Emotion cause · Content relevance · Semi-supervised training

1 Introduction

Open-domain conversation generation has made remarkable progress over recent years, relying on deep learning and neural networks [5, 19, 27, 32]. However, previous works primarily centre around improving the linguistic quality of the generated responses, such as grammatical correctness, content variety, and topic relevance, neglecting the important factor of emotion [31]. The information conveyed

---

M. Zou and R. Pan–Equal contribution.

© The Author(s), under exclusive license to Springer Nature Switzerland AG 2022
M. Sun et al. (Eds.): CCL 2022, LNAI 13603, pp. 112–129, 2022.
https://doi.org/10.1007/978-3-031-18315-7_8

by humans during communication contains not only syntactic and semantic information but also emotional information. Emotion is one of the essential cognitive behaviors in humans, and artificial intelligence has the objective of enabling machines to mimic human intelligent behaviors. As an important research branch of AI, one of the long-term goals of dialogue systems is to enable machines to perceive, comprehend and express emotions. In addition, studies [13–15] have shown that introducing emotional information into conversation systems can improve user engagement and satisfaction, make human-computer conversation more natural, and reduce the number of conversation terminations.

As a new research hotspot for the NLP community, most existing approaches on empathetic conversation generation focus on identifying the emotion category of the input sequence and generating a response based on the predicted emotion label. Song et al. [23] introduce an external emotion lexicon into the generation module to achieve explicit and implicit emotion expression. Li et al. [9] create a coarse-grained and fine-grained emotion representation for the input sequence by using an emotion classifier to identify the input sequence's emotion category and an external emotion lexicon to identify the emotion terms. Majumder et al. [12] improve the empathetic expression in the generated response by mimicking the input sequence's emotion while taking into account their emotional polarity. Firdaus et al. [3] incorporate multiple emotions to varying degrees in the generation of responses to make the model more anthropomorphic.

Table 1. Examples of empathetic conversation.

Input 1	My son really needs to cut down on the amount of sugary snacks he has!
Emotion	Disappointed
EmpDG	That is so disgusting! I bet he is a very disgusting situation
GPT2	I know how you feel. I have a son who is 6 and a daughter who is 5
Input 2	I feel so lonely sometimes because all my friends live in a different country
Emotion	Lonely
EmpDG	I am sorry you had to go through that
GPT2	Oh no! I hope you are ok!

Existing works mainly focus on emotion-related issues, focusing less on content-relevance. However, a case study of the responses generated by the existing models shows that the existing models do not guarantee the content-relevance of the generated responses very well. As shown in Table 1, in case 1, EmpDG [9] generates an emotionally irrational and irrelevant response, whereas GPT2 [16] can express empathy for the user's emotion, but the generated response deviates from the conversation's topic (from diet to age); in case 2, EmpDG and GPT2 both focus too much on the user's lonely emotion but fail to develop the conversation around the user's specific situation, resulting in the generation of a safe response, which is also irrelevant to the situation.

We suggest there are two main reasons: Firstly, as Gao et al. [4] pointed out, existing works deal with emotions on a surface level and do not consider the underlying causes of the emotion, making it difficult to comprehend user's complicated emotions and badly affecting the subsequent links of emotion prediction and empathetic conversation generation. Secondly, emotion category is a strong supervisory signal, and overemphasizing its importance in the process of generating responses can easily lead to the generation of safe responses for specific emotion categories. For examples in Table 1, if the model can accurately capture the emotion cause in the input sequence (as highlighted in red) and incorporate them into the process of generating responses, the model will have the ability to understand the user's emotion better and generate responses with more relevant content by developing topics around the facts conveyed by the user during the generation process.

To this end, we propose an empathetic conversation generation model enhanced by emotion cause to improve the content-relevance of generated responses. Specifically, our model involves two components, an emotion cause extractor and an empathetic conversation generator. In order to accurately identify emotion cause in the absence of large-scale labeled data, we present a semi-supervised training method to optimize the emotion cause extractor. To integrate the extracted emotion cause into the empathetic conversation generator and minimize the damage to the general language knowledge already learned by the pre-trained language model, we introduce a biased self-attention mechanism to enhance the model's attention to the emotion cause when generating responses.

The contributions of our work are summarized as follows:

- To compensate for the scarcity of large-scale word-level emotion-cause labeled datasets, a semi-supervised training method using labeled and unlabeled data for joint training is proposed.
- To integrate the extracted emotion cause into the generation process, a biased self-attention mechanism that does not introduce new additional parameters is proposed.
- Experimental results indicate that our proposed model performs superior to the baselines and improves the content-relevance of the generated responses.

2   Related Work

Empathetic conversation generation has made great progress in recent years. Several works [18,20,21,23,26,30] attempt to make dialogue models more empathetic and have achieved promising results. Song et al. [23] introduce an external emotion lexicon into the generation module to achieve explicit and implicit emotion expression. Shen et al. [20] present a novel framework that extends the emotional conversation generation through a dual task and alternatively generates the responses and queries. Welivita et al. [26] combine dialogue intent modeling and neural response generation to obtain more controllable and empathetic responses. Zheng et al. [30] propose a multi-factor hierarchical framework to model communication mechanism, dialog act and emotion in a hierarchical way. Sabour et al. [18] introduce external commonsense information to absorb additional information about the situation and help the model better understand the user's emotion.

Emotion cause extraction is intended to discover the stimulus reasons behind the user's emotion [2,7]. Although there has been a lot of excellent works in this research direction [1,24,28], most of the existing datasets are at the sentence/sub-sentence level [6]. There is still a lack of a large-scale word-level emotion-cause labeled dataset up till now.

Most existing approaches on empathetic conversation generation only consider superficial emotional information in the dialogue context but ignore deeper emotional causes. Recently, some researches [4,6] have attempt to investigate emotion cause in empathetic conversation generation, resulting in more relevant and empathetic responses. Since there is no large-scale word-level emotion-cause labeled dataset, Gao et al. [4] train an emotion cause extractor using a sentence-level labeled dataset and then automatically construct a word-level labeled dataset. Kim et al. [6] use a Bayesian conditional probability formula based on the emotion category of the dialogue context to train an emotion cause extractor in a weakly supervised way. In order to incorporate emotion cause into the process of generating responses, Gao et al. [4] introduce a soft gating mechanism and a hard gating mechanism to make model boost the attention on emotion cause; while Kim et al. [6] introduce the RSA framework, which is essentially a Bayesian conditional probability-based response rewriting module based on the original decoder.

3   Task Formulation

Emotion Cause Extraction. Given an input sequence $X_e = (x_1, x_2, ..., x_k)$, the goal is to predict the emotion cause probability $C = (c_1, c_2, ..., c_k)$ that indicates whether the token is an emotion cause. Specifically, we add special tokens [CLS] and [SEP] at the beginning and end of the sequence, respectively (as shown in Fig. 1).

Empathetic Conversation Generation. Given an input sequence $X_g = (x_1, x_2, ..., x_n)$, the goal is to generate a response $Y = (y_1, y_2, ..., y_m)$ that is empathetic and relevant to the conversation. Specifically, follow the previous works [4,10,22], we concatenate all utterances in the dialogue context together as input and separate utterances by [SEP] tokens (as shown in Fig. 1).

4   Approach

Our proposed emotion-cause-enhanced empathetic conversation generation model consists of two main modules: Emotion Cause Extractor and Empathetic Conversation Generator. The overview is shown in Fig. 1. Since there is no large-scale word-level emotion cause dataset available, we present a semi-supervised

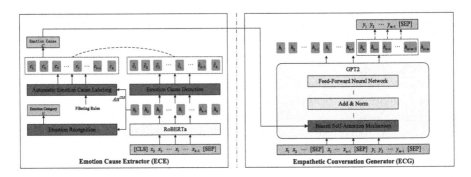

Fig. 1. The overview of our proposed ECE and ECG.

training method to obtain the emotion cause extractor using small-scale labeled data jointly trained with large-scale unlabeled data. To involve the emotion cause in the generation process, we introduce multiplicative signals to implement the biased self-attention mechanism. The multiplicative signal enhances the model's attention to the emotion cause in the generation process and improves the content-relevance of the generated responses.

4.1 Emotion Cause Extractor

The RoBERTa model [11] created by stacking the Transformer encoder [25] can better model contextual information in both directions. We construct the Emotion Cause Extractor (ECE for short) based on the RoBERTa to identify the emotion categories of the input sequence and its emotion causes. Thus the tasks of the ECE can be divided into emotion recognition and emotion cause detection.

Emotion Recognition. Emotion recognition is a classification problem aiming to predict the emotion category of the input sequence. Given a input sequence X_e, the forward propagation process of the model can be defined as:

$$H_h^E = \text{RoBERTa}(X_e) \tag{1}$$

$$P = \text{softmax}\left(W_e H_{h,1}^E + b_e\right) \tag{2}$$

where H_h^E denotes the output of the last hidden layer, and $H_{h,1}^E$ denotes the output of the first token (i.e., [CLS]) in the last hidden layer. W_e and b_e denote the parameters of the feed-forward neural network.

After obtaining the probability distribution P of emotion category, the emotion category of the X_e can be defined as $\mathcal{E} = \text{argmax}(P)$.

We employ the following loss function to optimize the parameters:

$$\mathcal{L}_{emo}(P) = -\sum_{i \in labels} t(i) \log p_i \tag{3}$$

where $labels \in \{1, 2, ..., s\}$ denotes emotion categories, and $t(i)$ denotes the ground truth distribution corresponding to the input sequence.

It is noted that the input representation of the RoBERTa contains both word embedding and positional embedding:

$$H_0^E = X_e W_e^W + X_e^P W_e^P \tag{4}$$

where W_e^W denotes the word embedding matrix, X_e^P denotes the absolute position of tokens in X_e, and W_e^P denotes the positional embedding matrix.

Emotion Cause Detection. Emotion cause detection is a sequence labeling problem that aims to predict whether each token in the input sequence is the emotion cause, i.e., a word-level $\{0, 1\}$ labeling problem. Since no large-scale word-level emotion cause dataset is available, this section proposes a semi-supervised training method using small-scale labeled data jointly with large-scale unlabeled data.

For the labeled data, given an input sequence X_e, the context-aware word representation is obtained by encoding using the RoBERTa. Then, a layer of the feed-forward neural network is used for $\{0, 1\}$ sequence labeling:

$$H_h^E = \text{RoBERTa}(X_e) \tag{5}$$

$$\widehat{C} = \text{softmax}\big(W_c H_h^E + b_c\big) \tag{6}$$

where $\widehat{C}$ represents the emotion cause probability of each token, W_c and b_c denote the parameters of the feed-forward neural network.

The loss function applied for parameter learning is as follows:

$$\mathcal{L}_{cau}\big(\widehat{C}\big) = -\sum_{i=1}^{k} \log \text{P}\big(\widehat{C}_i\big) \tag{7}$$

where k indicates the length of the input sequence, and $\text{P}(\cdot)$ denotes obtaining the probability corresponding to the ground truth label of each token.

For the unlabeled data, we observe that the model needs to pay attention to the emotion cause when predicting the emotion category of the input sequence. Thus the attention weight distribution of the model in predicting emotion categories can be used to predict whether each token is an emotion cause or not. Given an input sequence X_e, emotion recognition is performed using the RoBERTa to obtain the attention weight distribution Att^{CLS} of the first [CLS] token in the last hidden layer. Then, simple filtering based on the rules (including removing punctuation, special words, stop words, etc.) is applied, and the tokens with *top-k* weights are selected as the emotion cause of the input sequence. In this way, emotion cause labels can be automatically constructed for unlabeled data, and the rest of the processing is similar to labeled data.

However, the above method of automatic emotion cause labeling requires converting each token from vector to text at the realization and then performing rule-based filtering. This leads to the fact that the computational graph of automatic emotion cause labeling module is not fully linked with that of emotion cause detection module, i.e., the loss function $\mathcal{L}_{cau}$ of emotion cause detection is not derivable for Att^{CLS}, and cannot be directly involved in the optimization of Att^{CLS}. Thus we propose an additional auxiliary loss function to link the computational graph and introduce the regularization constraint by computing the vector inner product of Att^{CLS} and $\widehat{C^1}$:

$$\mathcal{L}_{aux}\left(Att^{CLS}, \widehat{C}\right) = Att^{CLS} \cdot \widehat{C^1} \tag{8}$$

where $\widehat{C^1} = \widehat{C}\left[1, :\right]$ denotes the probability that each token is the emotion cause.

In summary, we employ the following loss function to optimize the emotion cause extractor:

$$\mathcal{L}^{ECE} = \lambda_1 \mathcal{L}_{emo} + \lambda_2 \mathcal{L}_{cau} + \lambda_3 \mathcal{L}_{aux} \tag{9}$$

where λ_i indicates the weight of each loss function (we set $\lambda_1 = 1/3$, $\lambda_2 = \lambda_3 = 1$).

4.2   Empathetic Conversation Generator

Conversation Generation. Given a input sequence X_g and the corresponding probability of emotion cause C, the goal of the Empathetic Conversation Generator (ECG for short) is to maximize the probability $P\left(Y|X_g, C\right)$. The empathetic conversation generator proposed in this section is implemented based on the GPT2 [16]. Forward propagation process of the GPT2 in conversation generation task can be defined as:

$$H_h^G = \text{GPT2}(X_g) \tag{10}$$

$$\widehat{Y} = \text{softmax}\left(W_g H_h^G + b_g\right) \tag{11}$$

where W_g and b_g denote the parameters of the feed-forward neural network.

The loss function is as follows:

$$\mathcal{L}^{ECG}\left(\widehat{Y}\right) = -\sum_{i=1}^{m} \log \text{P}\left(\widehat{Y}_i\right) \tag{12}$$

where m denotes the length of the sequence, and $\text{P}(\cdot)$ denotes obtaining the probability corresponding to the ground truth.

It is noted that the input representation of the GPT2 contains three parts: word embedding, positional embedding and role embedding:

$$H_0^G = X_g W_g^W + X_g^P W_g^P + X_g^R W_g^R \tag{13}$$

where X_g^R denotes the role identifier of each token in the input sequence X_g (used to distinguish different speakers), and W_g^R denotes the role embedding matrix.

Biased Self-attention Mechanism. In order to integrate the emotion cause into the generation progress of the GPT2, it is typical to introduce a new attention mechanism layer. However, considering that the GPT2 has large-scale, trained parameters, if a new attention mechanism layer is introduced in the fine-tuning phase, it may greatly impact the original parameters and destroy the general knowledge already learned by the GPT2. Therefore we chose to introduce multiplicative signals based on emotion cause on top of the original self-attention mechanism of the GPT2 to enhance the model's attention to emotion cause during generation. Meanwhile, the above possible problems are avoided since no additional parameters are introduced.

Moreover, considering that deep neural networks are biased toward modelling syntactic information at the bottom level and semantic information at the top level, the first few layers of the GPT2 network do not require special attention for the emotion cause. We use the layer number information to scale the above multiplicative signals. As the number of layers increases, the multiplicative signals based on the emotion cause gradually strengthen.

The original self-attention mechanism of the GPT2 is defined as:

$$\text{MaskedAttention}(Q, K, V) = \text{softmax}\left(\frac{QK^T}{\sqrt{d_k}} \odot M - \lambda\left(I - M\right)\right) V \quad (14)$$

where $\odot$ denotes the multiplication of the corresponding elements of the matrix, λ denotes an infinite scalar (generally taken as $\lambda = 10000$). M denotes the lower triangular matrix with all non-zero elements being 1, I denotes the matrix where all elements are 1.

Our proposed biased self-attention mechanism based on the emotion cause can be defined as:

$$\text{MaskedScore}(Q, K) = \text{softmax}\left(\frac{QK^T}{\sqrt{d_k}} \odot M - \lambda\left(I - M\right)\right) \quad (15)$$

$$\text{BiasedScore}(Q, K) = \text{Normalize}\left(\text{MaskedScore}(Q, K) \odot \left(I + \frac{h_i}{h} C\right)\right) \quad (16)$$

$$\text{Normalize}(X) = \frac{x_{i,j}}{\sum_i x_{i,j}} \quad (17)$$

$$\text{BiasedAttention}(Q, K, V) = \text{BiasedScore}(Q, K) V \quad (18)$$

where C represents the probability of each token being an emotion cause, $h_i \in \{1, 2, ..., h\}$ denotes the serial number of the self-attention layer, $\text{Normalize}(\cdot)$ denotes the function for normalization by row.

4.3   Training Strategy

Our proposed model is trained using a two-stage training strategy.

In the first stage, the ECE is trained using a semi-supervised training method, as shown in Algorithm 1.

Algorithm 1: The training process of ECE

   Input: ECE, EmoCause-1 dataset and EmpDialog dataset
1 Loading the RoBERTa and randomly initializing other parameters;
2 **for** *training iteration* **do**
3   **for** *data* $\in$ *EmoCause-1* **do**
4   Train ECE in a supervised method;
5   **end**
6   **for** *data* $\in$ *EmpDialog* **do**
7   Construct emotion cause labels automatically;
8   Train ECE in a supervised method based on the emotion cause labels;
9   **end**
10 **end**
   Output: ECE

In the second stage, the ECG is trained based on the emotion cause extracted by the ECE, and the parameters of the ECE are frozen in this stage. The training process is shown in Algorithm 2.

Algorithm 2: The training process of ECG

   Input: ECG, ECE and EmpDialog dataset
1 Loading the ECE;
2 Loading the GPT2 and randomly initializing other parameters;
3 **for** *training iteration* **do**
4   **for** *data* $\in$ *EmpDialog* **do**
5   Extract the emotion cause of the input sequence using ECE;
6   Integrate the extracted emotion cause into ECG using biased self-attention mechanism;
7   Update the parameters of the ECG;
8   **end**
9 **end**
   Output: ECG

---

5 Experiments

5.1 Datasets

We use the following two datasets to conduct experiments.

EmpatheticDialogues (EmpDialog for short) is a dataset for empathetic conversation generation created by Rashkin et al. [17]. The dataset, which contains 19,533 conversations in the training set, 2770 conversations in the validation set and 2547 conversations in the test set, is collected and created by the Amazon Mechanical Turk platform. EmpDialog defines 32 emotion categories, and each conversation is created based on an emotional category and a situation description. An example of the EmpDialog dataset is shown in Table 2.

Table 2. An example of the EmpDialog dataset.

Label	Hopeful
Situation	I have been making goals each week for earning money. I'm hoping to save enough to start renovations on my house
Conversation	Speaker: I have big renovation plans for my house. I've made a money plan and have kept to it so far
	Listener: Well at least you have a plan. Are you planning to start the renovation soon?
	Speaker: Yes, hopefully it will all go as planned. So far so good
	Listener: Awesome. I'm sure it's going to turn out great

EmoCause is a word-level emotion cause dataset created by Kim et al. [6] based on the validation and test sets of EmpDialog. The dataset is also collected and created by the Amazon Mechanical Turk platform. The workers are asked to vote for each token in a given *situation* to determine whether it is the emotion cause. EmoCause have 2770 validation data and 2547 test data. An example of the EmoCause dataset is shown in Table 3.

Table 3. An example of the EmoCause dataset.

Label	Hopeful
Situation	I have been making goals each week for earning money. I'm hoping to save enough to start renovations on my house
Cause	Goals, earning, money

As described in Subsect. 4.3 our proposed model is trained in two stages and the experimental data used in different stages are different.

Experimental Data for ECE: The experimental data used by ECE are obtained from EmpDialog and EmoCause. First, the validation set of Emo-Cause is randomly divided into two equal parts (denoted as EmoCause-1 and EmoCause-2). Then, the training set (unlabeled) of EmpDialog is combined with EmoCause-1 (labeled) to form the training set used in the experiments, EmoCause-2 is used as the validation set for experiments, and the test set of EmoCause is used as the test set for experiments.

Experimental Data for ECG: The experimental data used in ECG are derived from EmpDialog, and the division of the training set, validation set and test set is the same as the original dataset.

5.2 Comparison Methods

For ECE, we chose the following three models as baselines: (1) **EmpDG** [9]: a Transformer-based model that creates the coarse and fine-grained emotion representation by emotion classification and external emotion lexicon. In addition, it uses two discriminators to interact with user feedback. Here, we select the coarse-grained tokens as the emotion cause. (2) **RoBERTa_Att:** a RoBERTa-based [11] model that is trained on the emotion recognition task, we obtain emotion cause by the attention weight distribution of the first special token [CLS]. (3) **GEE** [6]: a BART-based [8] model that uses a Bayesian conditional probability formula based on the emotion category labels of context to predict emotion cause.

For ECG, we chose the following three models as baselines: (1) **EmpDG** [9]: the same as mentioned above. (2) **RecEC** [4]: a Transformer-based model that incorporates emotion cause into response generation with gating mechanisms. It constructs emotion cause labels using a pre-trained sentence-level emotion cause extractor. (3) **GPT2** [16]: a GPT2-based model that is fine-tuned on the conversation generation task.

5.3   Evaluation Metrics

For ECE, we conducted the automatic evaluation to evaluate with the following metrics: emotion classification accuracy (Accuracy for short) and emotion cause recall rate (Recall for short).

For ECG, we used automatic evaluation and manual evaluation to verify the effectiveness. The metrics used for the automatic evaluation included Perplexity, Distinct-1, Distinct-2, and emotion classification accuracy (Accuracy for short), well-known metrics commonly used to evaluate conversation generation. Additionally, we introduced BERTscore [29] to measure the cosine similarity between the generated response and the gold response. BERTscore contains three more specific metrics, namely recall rate (R_{BERT}), precision rate (P_{BERT}) and F1 score (F_{BERT}).

The manual evaluation included both quantitative and qualitative components. The quantitative component required scorers to score on three dimensions of Empathy, Relevance, and Fluency, with each dimension being scored in an increasing value domain from 1 to 5. The qualitative component required scorers to rank the response generated by different models in order of preference. The manual evaluation randomly selected 100 test data and disrupted the responses generated by different models. Afterwards, these responses are distributed to 3 scorers for scoring, and the final results are averaged. The above approach fully ensures the fairness of the manual evaluation.

5.4   Parameter Settings

ECE is constructed based on RoBERTa-base, and ECG is constructed based on GPT2-base. Table 4 is drawn to show the parameter settings in detail.

5.5   Experimental Results and Analysis

Table 5 shows the experimental results of different emotion cause extractors. Our ECE performs optimally in all metrics compared to the comparison methods.

Table 4. Parameter setting of ECE and ECG.

	ECE	ECG
Initial learning rate	0.00002	0.00002
Gradient reduce strategy	ReduceLROnPlateau	ReduceLROnPlateau
Gradient clip threshold	1	1
Gradient accumulation threshold	1	2
Batch size	64	8
Early stopping strategy	Top-5 Recall	Perplexity
Early stopping threshold	5	5

Table 5. Results on comparative experiments of the different Emotion Cause Extractors.

Model	Accuracy	Top-1 Recall	Top-3 Recall	Top-5 Recall
EmpDG	0.31	0.134	0.362	0.493
Roberta_Att	0.58	0.148	0.399	0.596
GEE	0.40	0.173	0.481	0.684
ECE (Ours)	**0.58**	**0.227**	**0.565**	**0.727**

Compared with the Roberta_Att, ECE maintains its original strong competitiveness in emotion classification accuracy while achieving remarkable improvement in emotion cause recall rate. These achievements demonstrate that our proposed semi-supervised training method can effectively narrow the gap between emotion recognition and emotion cause detection and significantly improve the emotion cause detection ability of the model.

Table 6. Results on ablation study of the ECE.

Training dataset	Accuracy	Top-1 Recall	Top-3 Recall	Top-5 Recall	Training method
Train	0.56	0.147	0.410	0.607	Unsupervised
Valid	0.56	0.246	0.514	0.556	Supervised
Merge (ours)	**0.58**	**0.227**	**0.565**	**0.727**	Semi-supervised
Merge w/o $\mathcal{L}_{aux}$	0.58	0.208	0.523	0.709	Semi-supervised

We design the ablation study to further analyze the effectiveness of our proposed semi-supervised training method. In Table 6, the "train" (or "valid") in Training Dataset represents that ECE uses only the training (or validation) set of EmoCause for unsupervised (or supervised) training. Similarly, "merge" represents that ECE uses the training set of EmpDialog with EmoCause-1 for semi-supervised training. Note that in the "valid" set of experiment, the test set of EmoCause is used as the validation set, which is actually not a regular practice and is only required here to meet the need of the ablation experiments because we do not have more labeled data.

The experimental results in Tabel 6 show that the supervised training method is outstanding on Top-1 Recall and Top-3 Recall compared with the unsupervised training method. Still, the supervised training method is significantly weaker than the unsupervised training method on Top-5 Recall. This phenomenon declares that the supervised training method is superior to the unsupervised training method in performance, but it can easily cause overfitting and lead to instability. In contrast, the semi-supervised training method has the advantage of combining the two. On the one hand, supervised training can be used to provide a clear, task-appropriate optimization goal for emotion cause detection. On the other hand, the labeled data can guide the processing of automatic emotion cause labeling and the unlabeled data can avoid overfitting that may result from using only labeled data. In addition, an ablation study on $\mathcal{L}_{aux}$ under the semi-supervised training method also validates the effectiveness of our proposed auxiliary loss function.

Table 7. Results on Automatic Evaluation of the ECG. It should be noted that the particularly large Perplexity of RecEC is because the model is trained with F_{BERT} as the optimization target for the early stop strategy.

Model	Perplexity	Distinct-1	Distinct-2	P_{BERT}	R_{BERT}	F_{BERT}	Accuracy
EmpDG	34.311	0.018	0.069	0.252	0.213	0.232	0.314
RecEC	177.825	0.019	0.090	0.225	0.177	0.201	0.412
GPT2	14.132	**0.027**	**0.112**	0.304	0.238	0.271	/
ECG (Ours)	**14.063**	0.025	0.109	**0.307**	**0.240**	**0.273**	**0.598**

Table 7 demonstrates the automatic evaluation results of different empathetic conversation generation models. Our ECG achieves remarkable improvements in all metrics compared with EmpDG and RecEC, which are Transformer-based models. ECG also makes a small improvement in all metrics except Distinct compared with the pre-trained language model GPT2. The above phenomenon suggests that our ECG can improve the quality of the generated responses by introducing attention to emotion cause on the basis of pre-trained language models. Regarding the poor performance of ECG on Distinct, it may be due to the limitations caused by the emotion cause in the generation process.

Table 8. Results on Manual Evaluation of the ECG.

Model	Empathy	Relevance	Fluency
EmpDG	2.927	2.763	4.497
RecEC	2.893	2.790	4.677
GPT2	3.213	3.257	4.753
ECG (Ours)	**3.383**	**3.553**	**4.763**

Table 8 shows the manual evaluation results of different empathetic conversation generation models. The improvement in Empathy and Relevance of the

Table 9. Preference test (%) between any two method.

Pref. (%)	EmpDG	RecEC	GPT2	ECG (Ours)
EmpDG	/	47.1	26.7	29.9
RecEC	52.9	/	38.2	31.0
GPT2	73.3	61.8	/	42.5
ECG (Ours)	**70.1**	**69.0**	**57.5**	/

responses generated by ECG is remarkable, which indicates that introducing attention to the emotion cause in the generation process can promote the model's understanding of user emotion and generate more content-relevant emotional responses. Table 9 presents the preferences of scorers for different models. The scorers' preference for our ECG is greater than the other models, which verifies the validity of the ECG.

5.6   Case Study

Table 10. Two cases of responses generated by different models.

Input	I recently went to eat a restaurant that was not very clean. The whole place had an odd odor and made me uncomfortable
Emotion	Disgusted
EmpDG	I would have cried right now
RecEC	Oh no! I hate when people do that
GPT2	Oh no! Did you clean it up?
ECG (Ours)	That's not good. Did you complain to the manager?
Input	My son was just born, My first boy after 6 girls!
Emotion	Joyful
EmpDG	Wow, That is amazing. How old is your son?
RecEC	Oh that's great. Is he a big boy?
GPT2	Wow! That's amazing! I bet you are proud of him!
ECG (Ours)	Congratulations! That is a very exciting time for you and your family

To further illustrate that focusing on the emotion cause helps improve the content-relevance of the generated responses, we show two cases in Table 10. In the first case, ECE identifies the emotion cause in user input (as highlighted in red) and understands the stimulus behind the user's disgusted emotion is the poor environment of the restaurant, which prompts ECG to generate an empathetic response expressing sympathy and concerning for subsequent development (as highlighted in cyan). In the second case, ECE recognizes the emotion cause in user input (as highlighted in red) and understands the stimulus behind the user's joyful emotion is the long-awaited birth of a son, prompting ECG to generate an empathetic response that congratulates to the user and fits the user's family situation (as highlighted in cyan).

Comparing the responses generated by different models in the above two cases, it can be seen that our proposed model can accurately capture the emotion cause in user input and effectively incorporate it into the generation process, showing stronger content-relevance compared to other baselines, which further illustrates the important role of the emotion cause in the content-relevance of generated responses.

6   Conclusion

In this paper, we present an empathetic conversation generation model enhanced by the emotion cause to make the generated responses more content-relevant. Our proposed model comprises an emotion cause extractor and an empathetic conversation generator. To compensate for the scarcity of large-scale word-level emotion-cause labeled datasets, we suggest a semi-supervised training method that simultaneously uses labeled and unlabeled data for training. To integrate the extracted emotion cause into the generation process, we propose a biased self-attention mechanism that does not introduce new additional parameters. Experimental results indicate that our proposed model performs superior to the baselines and the generated responses of our model are more empathetic and content-relevant.

Acknowledgements. This work was supported by the Joint Project of Tianjin University-Bohai Bank Joint Laboratory for Artificial Intelligence Technology Innovation and Bayescom.

References

1. Bao, Y., Ma, Q., Wei, L., Zhou, W., Hu, S.: Multi-granularity semantic aware graph model for reducing position bias in emotion cause pair extraction. In: Findings of the Association for Computational Linguistics: the 60th Conference of the Association for Computational Linguistics (ACL), Dublin, Ireland, pp. 1203–1213. Association for Computational Linguistics (2022)
2. Chen, Y., Lee, S.Y.M., Li, S., Huang, C.: Emotion cause detection with linguistic constructions. In: Proceedings of the 23rd International Conference on Computational Linguistics (COLING), Beijing, China, pp. 179–187. Tsinghua University Press (2010)
3. Firdaus, M., Chauhan, H., Ekbal, A., Bhattacharyya, P.: More the merrier: towards multi-emotion and intensity controllable response generation. In: Proceedings of the 35th AAAI Conference on Artificial Intelligence (AAAI), pp. 12821–12829. AAAI Press, Virtual Event (2021)

4. Gao, J., et al.: Improving empathetic response generation by recognizing emotion cause in conversations. In: Findings of the Association for Computational Linguistics: the 26th Conference on Empirical Methods in Natural Language Processing (EMNLP), Punta Cana, Dominican Republic, pp. 807–819. Association for Computational Linguistics (Virtual Event) (2021)
5. Huang, M., Zhu, X., Gao, J.: Challenges in building intelligent open-domain dialog systems. ACM Trans. Inf. Syst. **38**(3), 1–32 (2020)
6. Kim, H., Kim, B., Kim, G.: Perspective-taking and pragmatics for generating empathetic responses focused on emotion causes. In: Proceedings of the 26th Conference on Empirical Methods in Natural Language Processing (EMNLP), Punta Cana, Dominican Republic, pp. 2227–2240. Association for Computational Linguistics (Virtual Event) (2021)
7. Lee, S.Y.M., Chen, Y., Huang, C.R.: A text-driven rule-based system for emotion cause detection. In: Proceedings of the NAACL HLT 2010 Workshop on Computational Approaches to Analysis and Generation of Emotion in Text, Los Angeles, USA, pp. 45–53. Association for Computational Linguistics (2010)
8. Lewis, M., et al.: BART: denoising sequence-to-sequence pre-training for natural language generation, translation, and comprehension. In: Proceedings of the 58th Annual Meeting of the Association for Computational Linguistics (ACL), pp. 7871–7880. Association for Computational Linguistics, Online (2020)
9. Li, Q., Chen, H., Ren, Z., Ren, P., Tu, Z., Chen, Z.: EmpDG: multi-resolution interactive empathetic dialogue generation. In: Proceedings of the 28th International Conference on Computational Linguistics (COLING), Barcelona, Spain, pp. 4454–4466. International Committee on Computational Linguistics (Online) (2020)
10. Lin, Z., Madotto, A., Shin, J., Xu, P., Fung, P.: MoEL: mixture of empathetic listeners. In: Proceedings of the 24th Conference on Empirical Methods in Natural Language Processing and the 9th International Joint Conference on Natural Language Processing (EMNLP-IJCNLP), Hong Kong, China, pp. 121–132. Association for Computational Linguistics (2019)
11. Liu, Y., et al.: RoBERTa: a robustly optimized BERT pretraining approach. arXiv preprint arXiv:1907.11692 (2019)
12. Majumder, N., et al.: MIME: mimicking emotions for empathetic response generation. In: Proceedings of the 25th Conference on Empirical Methods in Natural Language Processing (EMNLP), pp. 8968–8979. Association for Computational Linguistics, Online (2020)
13. Martinovski, B., Traum, D.: The error is the clue: breakdown in human-machine interaction. In: Proceedings of the International Speech Communication Association Tutorial and Research Workshop on Error Handling in Spoken Dialogue Systems, Château-d'Oex, Vaud, Switzerland, pp. 11–16. ISCA Archive (2003)
14. Prendinger, H., Ishizuka, M.: The empathic companion: a character-based interface that addresses users' affective states. Appl. Artif. Intell. **19**(3–4), 267–285 (2005)
15. Prendinger, H., Mori, J., Ishizuka, M.: Using human physiology to evaluate subtle expressivity of a virtual quizmaster in a mathematical game. Int. J. Hum. Comput. Stud. **62**(2), 231–245 (2005)
16. Radford, A., et al.: Language models are unsupervised multitask learners. OpenAI blog **1**(8), 9 (2019)
17. Rashkin, H., Smith, E.M., Li, M., Boureau, Y.: Towards empathetic open-domain conversation models: a new benchmark and dataset. In: Proceedings of the 57th Conference of the Association for Computational Linguistics (ACL), Florence, Italy, pp. 5370–5381. Association for Computational Linguistics (2019)

18. Sabour, S., Zheng, C., Huang, M.: CEM: commonsense-aware empathetic response generation. In: Proceedings of the 36th AAAI Conference on Artificial Intelligence (AAAI), pp. 11229–11237. AAAI Press, Virtual Event (2022)

19. Serban, I.V., Lowe, R., Charlin, L., Pineau, J.: Generative deep neural networks for dialogue: a short review. arXiv preprint arXiv:1611.06216 (2016)

20. Shen, L., Feng, Y.: CDL: curriculum dual learning for emotion-controllable response generation. In: Proceedings of the 58th Annual Meeting of the Association for Computational Linguistics (ACL), pp. 556–566. Association for Computational Linguistics, Online (2020)

21. Shen, L., Zhang, J., Ou, J., Zhao, X., Zhou, J.: Constructing emotional consensus and utilizing unpaired data for empathetic dialogue generation. In: Findings of the Association for Computational Linguistics: the 26th Conference on Empirical Methods in Natural Language Processing (EMNLP), Punta Cana, Dominican Republic, pp. 3124–3134. Association for Computational Linguistics (Virtual Event) (2021)

22. Shin, J., Xu, P., Madotto, A., Fung, P.: Generating empathetic responses by looking ahead the user's sentiment. In: Proceedings of the 45th International Conference on Acoustics, Speech, and Signal Processing (ICASSP), Barcelona, Spain, pp. 7989–7993. IEEE (2020)

23. Song, Z., Zheng, X., Liu, L., Xu, M., Huang, X.: Generating responses with a specific emotion in dialog. In: Proceedings of the 57th Conference of the Association for Computational Linguistics (ACL), Florence, Italy, pp. 3685–3695. Association for Computational Linguistics (2019)

24. Turcan, E., Wang, S., Anubhai, R., Bhattacharjee, K., Al-Onaizan, Y., Muresan, S.: Multi-task learning and adapted knowledge models for emotion-cause extraction. In: Findings of the Association for Computational Linguistics: The Joint Conference of the 59th Annual Meeting of the Association for Computational Linguistics and the 11th International Joint Conference on Natural Language Processing (ACL-IJCNLP), pp. 3975–3989. Association for Computational Linguistics, Online Event (2021)

25. Vaswani, A., et al.: Attention is all you need. In: Proceedings of the 30th Conference on Annual Conference Neural Information Processing Systems (NeurIPS), Long Beach, USA, pp. 5998–6008. MIT Press (2017)

26. Welivita, A., Pu, P.: A taxonomy of empathetic response intents in human social conversations. In: Proceedings of the 28th International Conference on Computational Linguistics (COLING), Barcelona, Spain, pp. 4886–4899. International Committee on Computational Linguistics (Online) (2020)

27. Wolf, T., Sanh, V., Chaumond, J., Delangue, C.: TransferTransfo: a transfer learning approach for neural network based conversational agents. arXiv preprint arXiv:1901.08149 (2019)

28. Xia, R., Ding, Z.: Emotion-cause pair extraction: a new task to emotion analysis in texts. In: Proceedings of the 57th Conference of the Association for Computational Linguistics (ACL), Florence, Italy, pp. 1003–1012. Association for Computational Linguistics (2019)

29. Zhang, T., Kishore, V., Wu, F., Weinberger, K.Q., Artzi, Y.: BERTScore: evaluating text generation with BERT. In: Proceedings of the 8th International Conference on Learning Representations (ICLR), Addis Ababa, Ethiopia. OpenReview.net (2020)

30. Zheng, C., Liu, Y., Chen, W., Leng, Y., Huang, M.: CoMAE: a multi-factor hierarchical framework for empathetic response generation. In: Findings of the Association for Computational Linguistics: The Joint Conference of the 59th Annual Meeting of the Association for Computational Linguistics and the 11th International Joint Conference on Natural Language Processing (ACL-IJCNLP), pp. 813–824. Association for Computational Linguistics, Online (2021)
31. Zhou, H., Huang, M., Zhang, T., Zhu, X., Liu, B.: Emotional chatting machine: emotional conversation generation with internal and external memory. In: Proceedings of the 32nd AAAI Conference on Artificial Intelligence (AAAI), New Orleans, USA, pp. 730–739. AAAI Press (2018)
32. Zhou, L., Gao, J., Li, D., Shum, H.: The design and implementation of Xiaoice, an empathetic social chatbot. Comput. Linguist. **46**(1), 53–93 (2020)

Text Generation and Summarization

To Adapt or to Fine-Tune: A Case Study on Abstractive Summarization

Zheng Zhao[(✉)] and Pinzhen Chen

University of Edinburgh, Edinburgh EH8 9AB, UK
{zheng.zhao,pinzhen.chen}@ed.ac.uk

Abstract. Recent advances in the field of abstractive summarization leverage pre-trained language models rather than train a model from scratch. However, such models are sluggish to train and accompanied by a massive overhead. Researchers have proposed a few lightweight alternatives such as smaller adapters to mitigate the drawbacks. Nonetheless, it remains uncertain whether using adapters benefits the task of summarization, in terms of improved efficiency without an unpleasant sacrifice in performance. In this work, we carry out multifaceted investigations on fine-tuning and adapters for summarization tasks with varying complexity: language, domain, and task transfer. In our experiments, fine-tuning a pre-trained language model generally attains a better performance than using adapters; the performance gap positively correlates with the amount of training data used. Notably, adapters exceed fine-tuning under extremely low-resource conditions. We further provide insights on multilinguality, model convergence, and robustness, hoping to shed light on the pragmatic choice of fine-tuning or adapters in abstractive summarization.

Keywords: Summarization · Pre-trained language models · Transfer learning

1 Introduction

In the current era of research, using large pre-trained language models (PLM) and fine-tuning these models on a downstream task yields dominating results in many tasks [2,6,15,23]. The scope of our work is on abstractive summarization, which is the task of generating a concise and relevant summary given a long document. Recent works have demonstrated the success of fine-tuning PLMs on summarization [17,24,26]. Nonetheless, such a paradigm becomes increasingly expensive with the ever-growing sizes of PLMs, since both the training time and space requirement increase along with the number of parameters. The issue becomes more severe when multiple languages or domains are introduced, as separate models need to be trained and saved depending on the setup.

Houlsby et al. [10] proposed lightweight adapters as an alleviation of the large overhead of fine-tuning PLM on a downstream task. While many researchers have followed and adopted their idea, experiments are rarely done on summarization; from both quantitative and qualitative perspectives, it remains a myth of which direction one should pick in practice. In this work, we perform a thorough exploration of using adapters with a PLM on the task of abstractive summarization by examining different scenarios.

© The Author(s), under exclusive license to Springer Nature Switzerland AG 2022
M. Sun et al. (Eds.): CCL 2022, LNAI 13603, pp. 133–146, 2022.
https://doi.org/10.1007/978-3-031-18315-7_9

Our experiments are designed along three dimensions: 1) languages involved: monolingual, cross-lingual, and multilingual; 2) data availability: high, medium, low, and scarce; 3) knowledge being transferred: languages, domains as well as tasks. Through comprehensive experimental results, we demonstrate that with a realistic availability of resources, fine-tuning a PLM is superior to using adapters for the purpose of obtaining the best text quality. However, the game changes under low-resource settings: adapters have shown better, if not, on par performances compared to fine-tuning, especially in domain adaption.

2   Related Work

Fine-tuning a PLM with downstream task-specific objectives is a useful paradigm. It not only speeds up training, but also transfers the knowledge from abundant pre-training data to lower-resourced tasks. Whilst it has been proven successful in the field of summarization [14,24,26,28], this strategy requires optimizing and updating all parameters in the fine-tuned model, and is particularly expensive when a number of (sub-)tasks need to be approached.

To mitigate these problems, Houlsby et al. [10] proposed to insert small neural modules named "adapters" to each layer of the PLM sequentially, and only update the adapters during fine-tuning while freezing most of the PLM parameters. When dealing with different sub-tasks – languages, domains, etc. – it is especially storage-efficient as only adapter weights need to be saved instead of the whole fine-tuned model. Several adapter architectures have been designed since then. Pfeiffer et al. [22] suggested simply placing adapters after the feed-forward block in each layer of the PLM, instead of adding adapters after both the multi-head attention and feed-forward block as proposed in the original work. Apart from adding adapters sequentially, He et al. [9] designed an adapter that is parallel to the PLM.

Recent research that had utilized adapters in the task of summarization, argued that the low availability of opinion summarization datasets often leads to the standard fine-tuning method overfitting on tiny datasets [1]. Thus, they presented an efficient few-shot fine-tuning method based on adapters for opinion summarization. They added adapters to pre-trained models, trained the adapters on a large unlabelled customer reviews dataset, then fine-tuned them on the human-annotated corpus. Their method outperformed standard fine-tuning methods on various datasets. In addition, they showed that the proposed method can generate better-organized summaries with improved coherence and fewer redundancies in the case of summary personalization. Chen and Shuai [3] created a meta-transfer learning framework for low-resource abstractive summarization, aiming to leverage pre-trained knowledge to improve the performance of the target corpus with limited examples. They inserted adapter modules into their model to perform meta-learning and leverage pre-trained knowledge simultaneously. Their methods are particularly effective under manually constructed low-resource settings on various summarization datasets with diverse writing styles and forms.

In comparison, our work investigates fine-tuning and using adapters in summarization, by comparing the performance of models using the fine-tuning strategy with models using adapters in the case of language adaptability, data availability, and knowledge transfer. For language adaptability, we examine the case of monolingual, cross-lingual, and multilingual summarization. For data availability, we study models trained under low, medium, and high resource scenarios. Lastly, for knowledge transfer, we investigate several factors: languages, domains, and tasks. To the best of our knowledge, adapters have not been tested in these scenarios.

3   Methodology

3.1   Method Overview

Our aim is to study two fine-tuning variants for summarization under several settings using a PLM: the *fine-tuning* paradigm, and the *adapter* strategy. Fine-tuning initializes a PLM from a pre-trained checkpoint, then trains and updates the whole model on a summarization dataset. On the other hand, the adapter strategy also initializes a PLM from a pre-trained checkpoint, with adapter modules then inserted into the model. During training, we only update the adapter, the layer normalization parameters, and the final output layer.

We use mBART [18] as our backbone PLM for settings involving non-English languages. It is a sequence-to-sequence model pre-trained on large-scale monolingual corpora in 25 languages, with a denoising autoencoding objective. The model is designed to do multilingual machine translation tasks. After training it on a summarization dataset, the model is capable of doing monolingual, cross-lingual, and multilingual summarization. For English-only settings, we use BART [15] as the PLM. Similar to mBART, BART is also a sequence-to-sequence model pre-trained on large-scale corpora with denoising autoencoder architecture.

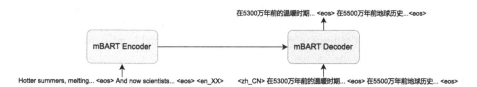

Fig. 1. An illustration of our mBART based model for cross-lingual summarization from English to Chinese.

We have two types of models: mBART-FT which employs the fine-tune strategy, and mBART-Adapt which uses the adapt strategy. In order to recognise the source and target languages, following Liu et al. [18], our models take a special separator token between each sentence, a language code token at the end of the source document, and at the beginning of the target summary. We provide a cross-lingual demonstration for our model in Fig. 1. In addition for English-only experiments, we propose BART-FT and BART-Adapt which use the fine-tuning strategy and the adapter strategy, respectively.

3.2   Adapter Variants

As mentioned earlier, there are various adapter variants. We experiment with two variants: one with sequential connections [10], and one with parallel connections [9]. We display an illustration of these variants in Fig. 2. After trying out different learning rates and reduction factors (the ratio between PLM's hidden dimension and adapter's bottleneck dimension), we discover that sequential adapters always outperform the parallel ones in our tasks. Thus we use the sequential adapter for all of our mBART/BART-Adapt models.

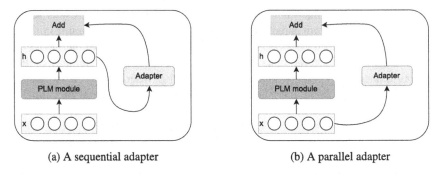

(a) A sequential adapter   (b) A parallel adapter

Fig. 2. An illustration of adapter variants, adapted from He et al. [9]. "PLM module" denotes a certain sub-layer in the PLM (e.g. attention or feed-forward) that is frozen.

3.3   Evaluation

The evaluation metrics are F1 scores of ROUGE-1/2/L [16]. Since we deal with multiple languages, we use the multilingual ROUGE implemented in a previous paper.[1] We stick to the toolkit's default settings, e.g., sentence segmentation and word stemming.

4   Language Experiments

4.1   Experimental Setup

We test our proposed paradigm on NCLS[2], WikiLingua[3], and XL-Sum[4] datasets particularly designed for cross-lingual and multilingual summarization [8,14,27]. These datasets are either machine-translated or crawled from the web.

NLCS is built by machine-translating an existing English (en) dataset (CNN/Daily Mail by Nallapati et al. [19]) to Chinese (zh), and vice versa (Sina Weibo by Hu et al. [11]). A translated document is only kept if its round-trip translation reaches a certain

---

[1] https://github.com/csebuetnlp/xl-sum/tree/master/multilingual_rouge_scoring.
[2] https://github.com/znlp/ncls-corpora.
[3] https://github.com/esdurmus/wikilingua.
[4] https://github.com/csebuetnlp/xl-sum.

Table 1. Statistics of datasets and languages for the language adaption experiment.

Dataset	Language	train/valid/test	Source
NCLS	zh→en	1.7m/3.0k/3.0k	Sina Weibo
	en→zh	365k/3.0k/3.0k	CNN/Daily Mail
Wiki-Lingua	en→ar	20.4k/2.9k/5.8k	wikiHow
	en→vi	13.7k/2.0k/3.9k	
	en↔ja	8.9k/1.3k/2.5k	
XL-Sum	gu	9.1k/1.1k/1.1k	BBC
	fr	8.7k/1.1k/1.1k	
	ne	5.8k/0.7k/0.7k	
	ko	4.4k/0.6k/0.6k	
	si	3.2k/0.5k/0.5k	

threshold score. Plain translations and human-corrected translations are supplied as separate test sets; we use the human-corrected set in this work. WikiLingua is constructed by extracting and aligning article-summary pairs from wikiHow. We experiment with three languages that resemble medium and low-resource scenarios: Arabic (ar), Vietnamese (vi), and Japanese (ja).

Different from the cross-lingual datasets, XL-Sum is monolingual. It consists of professionally annotated article-summary pairs from BBC in many languages. The datasets come in various sizes for a number of languages, as shown in Table 1. This dataset allows for multilingual experiments since the data come from the same domain and are not centred on English. We experiment on five low-resource languages: Gujarati (gu), French (fr), Nepali (ne), Korean (ko), and Sinhala (si). For the monolingual scenario, we directly use the monolingual summarization data to train the model. For the cross-lingual setting, since machine translation is a cross-lingual task, we also directly train the model using the cross-lingual summarization data. Lastly, in a multilingual configuration, we simply mix summarization data in different languages, and train the model using the mixed data.

Our experiments are based on a public mBART checkpoint[5]. Fine-tuning an mBART model updates around 610M parameters in total; the addition of adapters introduces 50M parameters, yet only this 8% are being optimized during training. We use the Adam optimizer for training [12], with a learning rate of 1e-5 for mBART, and 1e-4 for mBART with adapters. We set the adapter reduction factor to 2, which means that the bottleneck dimension in an adapter is half of the hidden dimension in mBART. We perform hyperparameter searches on the following: learning rate and reduction factor, and monitor ROUGE scores on the validation set to select the best value. We provide further details of the grid search in Appendix A.

All models are trained on 4 NVIDIA A100 GPUs with a batch size of 12 on NCLS, and 4 on WikiLingua and XL-Sum. The model convergence time is from 1 to 30 h depending on the dataset used. We use PyTorch [20] for our model implementation.

---

[5] https://huggingface.co/facebook/mbart-large-cc25.

Table 2. Results for cross-lingual summarization.

(a) High-resource, NCLS.

Lang.	mBART-FT			mBART-Adapt		
	R1	R2	RL	R1	R2	RL
zh→en	**46.46**	**30.18**	**42.26**	41.41	22.73	36.56
en→zh	**45.22**	**22.49**	**34.38**	40.74	16.83	29.27

(b) Medium and low-resource, WikiLingua.

Lang.	mBART-FT			mBART-Adapt		
	R1	R2	RL	R1	R2	RL
en→ar	**25.85**	**7.35**	**21.01**	24.68	7.26	20.40
en→vi	**33.63**	**15.17**	**26.65**	30.98	13.94	24.59
en→ja	**35.70**	**12.34**	**28.34**	34.06	11.43	27.08
ja→en	**35.24**	**12.38**	**28.09**	33.14	11.54	26.46

Table 3. Results for low-resource multilingual and monolingual summarization on XL-Sum.

Lang.	Multilingual						Monolingual					
	mBART-FT			mBART-Adapt			mBART-FT			mBART-Adapt		
	R1	R2	RL	R1	R2	RL	R1	R2	RL	R1	R2	RL
gu	**20.18**	**6.96**	**18.09**	20.12	6.82	17.99	**20.23**	**6.43**	**17.67**	19.20	5.95	16.96
fr	**33.53**	**14.37**	**26.11**	33.44	14.01	25.63	**33.29**	**13.68**	**25.13**	32.37	13.02	24.73
ne	**24.70**	**9.52**	**22.23**	23.26	8.55	20.94	**24.06**	**9.05**	**21.62**	23.31	8.36	21.01
ko	17.73	**8.76**	16.27	**18.82**	8.12	**17.23**	**19.73**	9.12	**18.07**	19.05	**9.24**	17.73
si	**26.95**	**13.51**	**22.36**	25.68	12.69	21.80	**25.59**	12.25	**21.92**	24.99	**12.30**	21.44

We use the Huggingface library [25] and AdapterHub [21] for mBART and adapter implementation.

4.2 Results

We first provide results on high-recourse cross-lingual summarization on NCLS in Table 2a. We can see that mBART-FT achieves significantly higher ROUGE scores than mBART-Adapt in both Chinese-to-English as well as English-to-Chinese settings. We then list result numbers on medium and low-recourse cross-lingual summarization on WikiLingua in Table 2b. Similar to the behaviour under the high-resource setting, mBART-FT consistently achieves better ROUGE performance than mBART-Adapt, regardless of the source or target languages. However, we spot that the difference in ROUGE scores is smaller for language pairs with lower resources, which suggests a positive correlation between the gap in performance and training data availability.

In Table 3, we show results of both multilingual (left) and monolingual (right) summarization on XL-Sum. In a multilingual setup, a single model is trained on five languages. whereas in a monolingual setup, five individual models are trained on the five languages separately. We can first see that mBART-FT generally surpasses mBART-Adapt, in both multilingual and monolingual setups. In addition, multilingual models generally outperform monolingual models by a small margin. This behaviour is corroborated by Hasan et al. [8]'s work that mixing multiple languages altogether during training can result in a positive transfer among them [5].

It is straightforward from our work, that, for summarization tasks with high data availability, it is not worth trading performance for efficiency with adapters. For low-resource scenarios, adapters achieve similar results as fine-tuning, and can therefore be a convenient choice for fast training and compact disk storage. When multiple low-resource languages are concerned, especially if they are related languages, it might be beneficial to build a multilingual model instead of individual monolingual models.

4.3 Convergence

To measure the convergence difference between mBART-FT and mBART-Adapt, we plot validation set ROUGE-1 scores against epochs for two previous experiments (high-resource zh→en and low-resource ja→en) in Fig. 3. Plotting stops when validation does not improve. We measure convergence in terms of epochs, rather than wall-time. In our experiments, we find that wall-time per epoch for mBART-FT is about merely 1.5 times that for mBART-Adapt, since validation takes a large portion especially when the dataset is small.

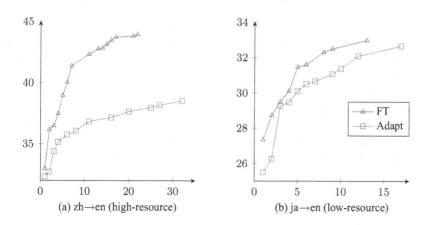

(a) zh→en (high-resource)   (b) ja→en (low-resource)

Fig. 3. Validation ROUGE-1 (y-axis) against epochs (x-axis) for mBART-FT and mBART-Adapt in different data conditions.

As Fig. 3(a) shows, with sufficient resources, mBART-FT and mBART-Adapt started with similar ROUGE scores, then the gap quickly increases, suggesting a faster and better convergence rate for fine-tuning. We also observe that mBART-FT converged within fewer epochs. Furthermore, Fig. 3(b) suggests that, in a low-resource condition, even though mBART-FT surpasses mBART-Adapt in terms of ROUGE, they both have similar convergence rates with the gap reduced. These trends indicate that in a high-resource scenario fine-tuning is preferred, whereas in a low-resource scenario, adapters can be used to reduce overhead while maintaining performance.

5   Domain Adaptation Experiments

5.1   Experimental Setup

In addition to multilinguality, we conduct extra experiments on domain adaptation, which is typically tackled using the same pre-training then fine-tuning paradigm. In our setting, we adapt CNN/Daily Mail to XL-Sum, both in English, with various data sizes. Although both datasets are news articles, they differ hugely in writing styles. We start with a BART model [15] fine-tuned on the CNN/Daily Mail dataset for summarization; it is available as a public model checkpoint.[6]

To further understand the impact of data availability, we artificially and iteratively make the training data 10 times smaller. This results in five data conditions with sizes ranging from merely 31 to 306.5k. We make sure that larger training splits are supersets of the smaller splits. The validation and test sets remain unchanged at 11.5k as provided in the original dataset. In addition to the XL-Sum dataset, which is in the news domain, we also experimented with adapting CNN/Daily Mail to the BookSum[7] [13] dataset, a collection of narratives from the literature domain such as novels, plays, and stories. Their human written summaries have three levels of granularity, and we use the paragraph-level summaries for our experiment. Unlike the CNN/Daily Mail dataset, we only experiment on the full size of the BookSum dataset.

The English BART checkpoint has in total 139M parameters to be fine-tuned, while adapters have 14.2M parameters (10%). As an additional parameter-controlled fine-tuning variant, we choose to freeze the entire BART but the last decoder layer, which has 9.5M parameters. The final decoder layer makes up 7% of the entire model, and has a comparable amount of trainable parameters to an adapter. Similar to the previous setting, we use the Adam optimizer with a learning rate of 1e-5 for BART-FT, and 1e-4 for BART-Adapt. We use a batch size of 4 on XL-Sum, and 8 on BookSum. All other hyperparameter settings are identical to those in the language adaptation experiment.

5.2   Results

We report the experiment results in Table 4. The pattern is that for medium to large CNN/Daily Mail data sizes, BART-FT outperforms BART-Adapt significantly. The two methods tie at around 300-3000 training sizes. BART-Adapt wins notably when there are only a handful of examples. This implies that adapters only stand out when the amount of data is extremely limited. In this case, we doubt the importance of training efficiency in adapters when the data size is so small. Instead, we argue that a potential benefit of using adapters is to reduce overfitting. As for BookSum, we can observe that numbers are very similar for both models with BART-FT slightly outperforming

---

[6] https://huggingface.co/ainize/bart-base-cnn.

[7] https://github.com/salesforce/booksum.

Table 4. Results for domain adaptation from CNN/Daily Mail to XL-Sum on English (top) with artificially constrained data sizes, and to BookSum (bottom) with full data size.

Domain	Data size		BART-FT			BART-Adapt			BART-FT-LastLayer		
			R1	R2	RL	R1	R2	RL	R1	R2	RL
XL-Sum	original	306.5 k	**34.48**	**14.73**	**28.93**	32.94	13.46	27.60	30.20	11.69	25.17
	medium	30.65 k	**30.63**	**11.38**	**25.31**	30.15	11.10	25.05	26.70	8.67	21.94
	small	3065	27.27	**8.91**	**22.27**	**27.32**	8.79	22.20	23.06	6.21	18.76
	tiny	307	24.10	**6.52**	19.38	**24.29**	6.41	**19.50**	19.13	4.12	15.54
	micro	31	19.69	4.26	15.73	**20.74**	**4.65**	**16.45**	16.30	2.20	11.43
BookSum	111.6 k		**20.27**	**4.01**	15.50	20.22	3.95	**15.57**	19.33	3.56	14.93

Table 5. Examples of gold and generated summaries (from models trained on the full dataset) with their corresponding articles selected from the XL-Sum (English) dataset. Summary phrases italicized and highlighted in red denote hallucinations.

Article: Lewis Williams, 20, died on 11 January from a shotgun wound suffered in Wath Road, Mexborough. South Yorkshire Police said two men aged 20 and 49 were arrested on Friday in connection with his death, bringing the total number of arrests to eight …

Gold Summary: Two more people have been arrested in connection with a fatal shooting.

BART-FT Summary: Two more people have been arrested in connection with the fatal shooting of a man in South Yorkshire.

BART-Adapt Summary: *Eight* more people have been arrested in connection with the death of a man in South Yorkshire.

Article: BBC News Officials say the country's Olympic Committee will "oversee participation of women athletes who can qualify". The decision will end recent speculation as to whether the entire Saudi team could have been disqualified on grounds of gender discrimination …For the desert kingdom, the decision to allow women to compete in the Olympics is a huge step, overturning deep-rooted opposition from those opposed to any public role for women …

Gold Summary: Saudi Arabia is to allow its women athletes to compete in the Olympics for the first time.

BART-FT Summary: Saudi Arabia is to allow women to compete in next year's Olympic and Paralympic Games.

BART-Adapt Summary: Saudi Arabia is to allow women to take part in the *2012 Winter* Olympics, officials say.

Article: The vehicle was seen at about 03:45 BST at the fast food giant's branch in Catterick, North Yorkshire. A 19-year-old man was arrested at the site, a short distance from the local golf club, on suspicion of theft and driving while unfit through drink. Police said it was the "most unusual job" of the night but officers managed to "avoid a high-speed pursuit" …

Gold Summary: A stolen golf buggy was seized after being spotted at a McDonald's drive-thru.

BART-FT Summary: A suspected stolen car was spotted at a McDonald's drive-thru.

BART-Adapt Summary: A man has been arrested after a car was seen driving into a McDonald's branch.

BART-Adapt. We argue adapters can do well in domain adaption despite the domain difference as long as there are sufficient training data. Finally, we notice the performance of fine-tuning only the last decoder layer is nowhere near BART-FT or BART-Adapt; this implies the practicability of adapters in summarization.

5.3 Qualitative Analysis

To understand the quality of generated summaries between BART-FT and BART-Adapt, we examined a set of randomly selected model outputs from the XL-Sum dataset. We show some examples in Table 5. We find that summaries generated by the two models are roughly the same in terms of informativeness, grammaticality, and fluency. Despite summaries being similar in these aspects, we find that BART-Adapt summaries are more prone to hallucinations, which is a well-known problem in abstractive summarization that summaries are not factual with respect to the source or general knowledge.

Table 6. Results for task adaption from CNN/Daily Mail to DialogSum and SAMSum.

Task	Data size	Model	R1	R2	RL
DialogSum	12.5k	BART-FT	**47.40**	**24.66**	**39.03**
		BART-Adapt	47.24	24.57	38.56
SAMSum	14.7k	BART-FT	**49.52**	**24.91**	40.64
		BART-Adapt	49.38	24.69	**40.99**

Table 7. Results for robustness analysis of task adaption experiments. Results are directly obtained by using the trained model from the other task without any further training. *denotes the model trained on SAMSum, and **denotes the model trained on DialogSum.

Task	Data size	Model	R1	R2	RL
DialogSum	12.5k	BART-FT*	35.60	16.59	29.69
		BART-Adapt*	**36.35**	**17.03**	**30.25**
SAMSum	14.7k	BART-FT**	**40.91**	**14.82**	**32.32**
		BART-Adapt**	40.42	14.65	32.28

6 Task Transfer Experiments

6.1 Experimental Setup

In previous settings, we conduct experiments with the fine-tuning paradigm on the subject of language and domain adaption. We also conduct experiments on task adaption to further verify our findings. In particular, we experiment with adapting a news summarization model to dialogue summarization. Dialogue summarization is often considered a much different task from monologic texts (e.g. news in our case) summarization due to its unique challenges. Chen et al. [4] pointed out that: information flow is reflected in the dialogue discourse structures, summaries are required to be objective, and dialogue is acted at the pragmatic level. For these reasons, we choose to work with the DialogSum [4] and the SAMSum [7] datasets. We follow the previous setting and start with a BART model already fine-tuned on the CNN/Daily Mail dataset, then further train the model on these two datasets separately. We use a batch size of 8 for both DialogSum and SAMSum. All other hyperparameter settings are identical to those in the domain adaptation experiment.

6.2 Results

We report the experiment results in Table 6. We can observe that despite the dataset, BART-FT almost always beats BART-Adapt. However, we can notice that the performance gap is rather small, possibly due to the small dataset sizes. This is consistent with our earlier findings that adapters are on par with fine-tuning when the amount of training data is limited.

6.3 Model Robustness

In addition to model performance, we also examine the robustness of models with either fine-tuning or adapters. In particular, we evaluate the model in a zero-shot manner where we directly test the DialogSum model on the SAMSum dataset, and vice versa. We present the results in Table 7. We can first observe that performance drops significantly compared to those in Table 6. Moreover, BART-Adapt has better performance than BART-FT on the DialogSum dataset, and it achieves very similar results on the SAMSum dataset. This suggests that adapters are more robust in a zero-shot setup with fewer data; the reason could be less overfitting introduced by a limited number of parameters in adapters.

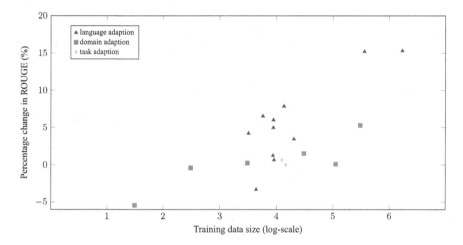

Fig. 4. The effect of the training data size on ROUGE difference between the fine-tuning and adapter strategy. We display how much percent FT is better than using adapters. Note that data points from different tasks (with different shapes and colors) are not strictly comparable.

6.4 Effect of Data Availability on Performance

Our results suggest that fine-tuning generally surpasses adapters under all three settings (language, domain, and task adaption). In addition, we observe that the amount of training data affects the performance gap between the two methods. To further validate this observation, we plot the percentage change in ROUGE performance (between those of fine-tuning and those of adapters) against the training size (log-scale) and we provide the visualization in Fig. 4. We use the average number of ROUGE-1/2/L to represent the performance. From the plot, we can see that percentage change in ROUGE has an obvious positive relationship with the training data size which means that as the amount of training data increases, the performance gap between BART-FT and BART-Adapt increases as well. Looking at the tasks individually, we can see that for language adaption tasks with relatively small amounts of data, this trend is not very notable. The trend is most salient on domain adaption tasks since we manually controlled the data size for the experiment for adapting CNN/Daily Mail to XL-Sum.

7   Conclusions and Future Work

With large PLMs coming to light, we investigate fine-tuning and adapter strategies for transfer learning in abstractive summarization. We demonstrated that the performance gap between the two strategies is positively correlated with the availability of training resources, despite the languages being tested. Further analysis on domain adaptation and task adaption produces agreeing observations. We conclude that for realistically large summarization datasets, full fine-tuning will guarantee the best output quality. On the other hand, when resources are scarce, the advantages of adapters emerge in the niche market.

Most summarization datasets are web-crawled or machine-translated, resulting in non-optimal data quality. We plan to perform more qualitative analysis on the model outputs such as linguistic interpretation and human evaluation. In addition, we only experimented with fine-tuning and using adapters on mBART and BART for abstractive summarization, so there is room for research on other large PLMs, as well as other NLP tasks in the future.

Acknowledgements. We thank the reviewers of the paper for their feedback. Zheng Zhao is supported by the UKRI Centre for Doctoral Training in Natural Language Processing (grant EP/S022481/1). Pinzhen Chen is supported by a donation to Kenneth Heafield. This work does not necessarily reflect the opinion of the funders.

A   Model Configurations

We tuned the hyperparameters using the validation set. We list the hyperparameters in Table 8, and highlight the selected ones in bold if multiple values are tried out. Instead of an expensive grid search on all combinations, we searched for the best configurations one by one. We performed a single run for each experiment.

Table 8. Model and training configurations.

Configuration	Value
training toolkit	PyTorch [20]
stopping criterion	validation ROUGE
learning rate	1e-3, 5e-3, **1e-4** (mBART+Adapt), 5e-4, **1e-5** (mBART-FT), 5e-5
optimizer	Adam [12]
beta1, beta2	0.9, 0.999
weight decay	1e-6
loss function	cross-entropy
decoding batch size	1
decoding beam size	5
decoding len. penalty	1.0
adapter reduction factor	1, **2**, 8, 16
trainable parameters	mBART-FT: 610M
	mBART-Adapt: 50M

References

1. Brazinskas, A., Nallapati, R., Bansal, M., Dreyer, M.: Efficient few-shot fine-tuning for opinion summarization. Findings of the Association for Computational Linguistics: NAACL 2022 (2022)
2. Brown, T., et al.: Language models are few-shot learners. In: 34th Conference on Neural Information Processing Systems (2020)
3. Chen, Y.S., Shuai, H.H.: Meta-transfer learning for low-resource abstractive summarization. In: Proceedings of the AAAI Conference on Artificial Intelligence (2021)
4. Chen, Y., Liu, Y., Zhang, Y.: DialogSum challenge: summarizing real-life scenario dialogues. In: Proceedings of the 14th International Conference on Natural Language Generation (2021)
5. Conneau, A., et al.: Unsupervised cross-lingual representation learning at scale. In: Proceedings of the 58th Annual Meeting of the Association for Computational Linguistics (2020)
6. Devlin, J., Chang, M.W., Lee, K., Toutanova, K.: BERT: pre-training of deep bidirectional transformers for language understanding. In: Proceedings of the 2019 Conference of the North American Chapter of the Association for Computational Linguistics: Human Language Technologies (2019)
7. Gliwa, B., Mochol, I., Biesek, M., Wawer, A.: SAMSum corpus: a human-annotated dialogue dataset for abstractive summarization. In: Proceedings of the 2nd Workshop on New Frontiers in Summarization (2019)
8. Hasan, T., Bhattacharjee, A., Islam, M.S., Mubasshir, K., Li, Y.F., Kang, Y.B., Rahman, M.S., Shahriyar, R.: XL-sum: Large-scale multilingual abstractive summarization for 44 languages. Findings of the Association for Computational Linguistics: ACL-IJCNLP 2021 (2021)
9. He, J., Zhou, C., Ma, X., Berg-Kirkpatrick, T., Neubig, G.: Towards a unified view of parameter-efficient transfer learning. In: International Conference on Learning Representations (2022)
10. Houlsby, N., et al.: Parameter-efficient transfer learning for NLP. In: Proceedings of the 36th International Conference on Machine Learning (2019)
11. Hu, B., Chen, Q., Zhu, F.: LCSTS: a large scale Chinese short text summarization dataset. In: Proceedings of the 2015 Conference on Empirical Methods in Natural Language Processing (2015)
12. Kingma, D.P., Ba, J.: Adam: a method for stochastic optimization. In: International Conference on Learning Representations (2015)
13. Kryscinski, W., Rajani, N., Agarwal, D., Xiong, C., Radev, D.: Booksum: a collection of datasets for long-form narrative summarization. arXiv (2021)
14. Ladhak, F., Durmus, E., Cardie, C., McKeown, K.: WikiLingua: a new benchmark dataset for cross-lingual abstractive summarization. In Findings of the Association for Computational Linguistics: EMNLP 2020 (2020)
15. Lewis, M., et al.: BART: denoising sequence-to-sequence pre-training for natural language generation, translation, and comprehension. In: Proceedings of the 58th Annual Meeting of the Association for Computational Linguistics (2020)
16. Lin, C.Y.: ROUGE: a package for automatic evaluation of summaries. Text Summarization Branches Out (2004)
17. Liu, Y., Lapata, M.: Text summarization with pretrained encoders. In: Proceedings of the 2019 Conference on Empirical Methods in Natural Language Processing and the 9th International Joint Conference on Natural Language Processing (2019)
18. Liu, Y., et al.: Multilingual denoising pre-training for neural machine translation. Transactions of the Association for Computational Linguistics (2020)

19. Nallapati, R., Zhou, B., dos Santos, C., Gülçehre, c., Xiang, B.: Abstractive text summarization using sequence-to-sequence RNNs and beyond. In: Proceedings of The 20th SIGNLL Conference on Computational Natural Language Learning (2016)
20. Paszke, A., et al.: Pytorch: an imperative style, high-performance deep learning library. In: 33rd Conference on Neural Information Processing Systems (2019)
21. Pfeiffer, J., et al.: AdapterHub: a framework for adapting transformers. In: Proceedings of the 2020 Conference on Empirical Methods in Natural Language Processing (2020)
22. Pfeiffer, J., Vulić, I., Gurevych, I., Ruder, S.: MAD-X: an adapter-based framework for multitask cross-lingual transfer. In: Proceedings of the 2020 Conference on Empirical Methods in Natural Language Processing (2020)
23. Raffel, C., et al.: Exploring the limits of transfer learning with a unified text-to-text transformer. J. Mach. Learn. Res. 21(140), 1–67 (2020)
24. Rothe, S., Narayan, S., Severyn, A.: Leveraging pre-trained checkpoints for sequence generation tasks. Trans. Assoc. Comput. Linguis. 8, 264–280 (2020)
25. Wolf, T., et al.: Transformers: state-of-the-art natural language processing. In: Proceedings of the 2020 Conference on Empirical Methods in Natural Language Processing (2020)
26. Zhang, J., Zhao, Y., Saleh, M., Liu, P.: PEGASUS: pre-training with extracted gap-sentences for abstractive summarization. In: Proceedings of the 37th International Conference on Machine Learning (2020)
27. Zhu, J., et al.: NCLS: neural cross-lingual summarization. In: Proceedings of the 2019 Conference on Empirical Methods in Natural Language Processing and the 9th International Joint Conference on Natural Language Processing (2019)
28. Zou, Y., Zhang, X., Lu, W., Wei, F., Zhou, M.: Pre-training for abstractive document summarization by reinstating source text. In: Proceedings of the 2020 Conference on Empirical Methods in Natural Language Processing (2020)

Knowledge Graph and Information Extraction

MRC-Based Medical NER with Multi-task Learning and Multi-strategies

Xiaojing Du, Yuxiang Jia$^{(\boxtimes)}$, and Hongying Zan

School of Computer and Artificial Intelligence, Zhengzhou University,
Zhengzhou, China
zzu_dxj@163.com, {ieyxjia,iehyzan}@zzu.edu.cn

Abstract. Medical named entity recognition (NER), a fundamental task of medical information extraction, is crucial for medical knowledge graph construction, medical question answering, and automatic medical record analysis, etc. Compared with named entities (NEs) in general domain, medical named entities are usually more complex and prone to be nested. To cope with both flat NEs and nested NEs, we propose a MRC-based approach with multi-task learning and multi-strategies. NER can be treated as a sequence labeling (SL) task or a span boundary detection (SBD) task. We integrate MRC-CRF model for SL and MRC-Biaffine model for SBD into the multi-task learning architecture, and select the more efficient MRC-CRF as the final decoder. To further improve the model, we employ multi-strategies, including adaptive pre-training, adversarial training, and model stacking with cross validation. Experiments on both nested NER corpus CMeEE and flat NER corpus CCKS2019 show the effectiveness of the MRC-based model with multi-task learning and multi-strategies.

Keywords: Medical NER · MRC · Multi-task learning · Multi-strategies

1 Introduction

With the fast development of medical digitalization, more and more medical documents are generated, including electronic medical records, medical reports, etc. Medical information extraction, including medical named entity recognition (NER), becomes increasingly important to applications like knowledge graph construction, question answering system, and automatic electronic medical record analysis. Medical NER is a task to automatically recognize medical named entities, like body (bod), disease, clinical symptom (sym), medical procedure, medical equipment, drug, medical examination item, etc., from medical texts. Medical named entities are usually long, nested and polysemous, which pose great challenges to medical NER. For example, in Fig. 1, the two "bod" entities "延髓" (medulla oblongata) and "脊髓" (spinal cord) are nested in the "sym" entity "延髓和脊髓受损" (damage to the medulla oblongata and spinal cord).

M. Sun et al. (Eds.): CCL 2022, LNAI 13603, pp. 149–162, 2022.
https://doi.org/10.1007/978-3-031-18315-7_10

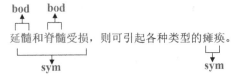

Damage to the medulla oblongata and spinal cord **can cause various** types of paralysis.

Fig. 1. An example with nested entity

To tackle both flat and nested NER, like [13], we take NER as a machine reading comprehension (MRC) problem. In addition, from different views, NER can be treated as a sequence labeling (SL) task or a span boundary detection (SBD) task. We integrate MRC-CRF model for SL and MRC-Biaffine model for SBD into the multi-task learning (MTL) architecture. There is no nested NEs composed of entities of the same type in the datasets, so we select the more efficient MRC-CRF as the final decoder. To further improve the model, we employ multi-strategies (MS), including adaptive pre-training, adversarial training, and model stacking with cross validation. The main contributions of this paper are as follows:

- We improve MRC-CRF for medical NER with Biaffine through a multi-task learning architecture, which is a lighter way than traditional ensemble learning.
- We propose multi-strategies to improve the NER model, including adaptive pre-training, adversarial training, and model stacking with cross validation.
- Experimental results on both the nested NER corpus CMeEE [20] and the flat NER corpus CCKS2019 [7] show the effectiveness of the proposed model.

2　Related Work

Just like NER in other application domains, medical NER borrows methods from NER in general domain. The methods evolve from rule-based methods, traditional machine learning-based methods, deep learning-based methods, to the present mainstream pre-training-based methods.

Pre-trained models like BERT [4,12,17], ELMo [11,14,18], etc., have become a standard module to encode the input texts. To better represent a text, RNN [3], LSTM [4], GRU [17], CNN [8] and other neural networks are usually employed after the pre-trained model. Taking the NER as a sequence labeling problem, CRF [10] is finally used to generate the sequence labels.

For Chinese, characters [14], radicals, strokes [11,16] and glyphs [24] can provide useful information besides words. Thus such linguistic units are encoded together with words using LatticeLSTM [22], ELMo [11,14,18] and other networks. Domain data can be used to improve medical NER. [15] pre-train a Med-BERT based on medical texts to boost the performance significantly. [2] integrate domain dictionary and rules with Bi-LSTM-CRF.

Multi-task learning is another way to improve the performance. NER model can be enhanced by parameter sharing with models of other tasks. [3] take NER and POS tagging as two tasks. [16] take NER on two different datasets as two tasks. To tackle nested NER problem and encode knowledge from entity types, NER is formulated as a machine reading comprehension task [13], and two binary classifiers are used to detect the span of a named entity. To enhance the information interaction between the head and tail of an entity, [1] introduce biaffine to MRC. [25] ensemble sequence labeling and span boundary detection by voting strategies while [23] ensemble CRF and MRC.

3 The MRC-MTL-MS Model

MRC model extracts answer fragments from paragraphs by a given question. Suppose X is the input text, for each entity type y, designing a query q_y, extracting a subsequence x of type y from X, and we can get the triple (q_y, x, X), which is exactly the $(question, answer, context)$ a MRC model needs. The model only calculates the loss of context during training, and masks the loss of query and padding.

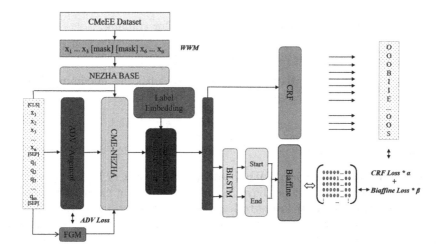

Fig. 2. The architecture of the proposed NER model

3.1 Multi-task Learning (MTL)

The overall architecture of the model is shown in Fig. 2. The multi-task learning architecture consists of the main task of sequence labeling by CRF and the auxiliary task of span boundary detection by Biaffine. For each entity type y, the input to the model is context X followed by query q_y, which is proved experimentally better than reversed concatenating way. The input is encoded by an adaptive pre-trained model CME-NEZHA, then goes through a Conditional LayerNorm guided by entity label embedding to further untilize entity type knowledge, and finally is decoded by CRF and Biaffine respectively.

Sequence Labeling with CRF. Suppose $h = (h_1, h_2, ..., h_N)$ is the encoded hidden layer sequence after Conditional LayerNorm, and $y = (y_1, y_2, ..., y_N)$ is the tag sequence, as shown in Fig. 2. The score of sequence y is computed as follows,

$$s(h, y) = \sum_{n=1}^{N} W_{n,y_n} + \sum_{n=2}^{N} T_{y_{n-1},y_n} \tag{1}$$

where W is the score matrix of each tag at each time step and T is the transition matrix between tags.

The probability of sequence y is calculated by softmax function, where $Y(h)$ represents all possible tag sequences.

$$p(y \mid h) = \frac{e^{s(h,y)}}{\sum_{\tilde{y} \in Y(h)} e^{s(h,\tilde{y})}} \tag{2}$$

The maximum likelihood loss function is used for training.

$$L_{\text{CRF}} = \log(p(y \mid h)) \tag{3}$$

During inference, the predicted tag sequence with the maximum score is obtained with Viterbi algorithm.

$$y^* = \arg \max_{\tilde{y} \in Y(h)} s(h, \tilde{y}) \tag{4}$$

Span Boundary Detection with Biaffine. As shown in Fig. 2, the hidden layer sequence after Conditional LayerNorm goes through a bidirectional LSTM and two seperate nonlinear layers to learn the representation of start and end of the span. Finally, the score of a span i is calculated by a Biaffine classifier as follows,

$$h_i^s = MLP_{\text{start}}\ (h_i) \tag{5}$$

$$h_i^e = MLP_{\text{end}}\ (h_i) \tag{6}$$

$$r(i) = h_i^{s^T} U h_i^e + W\ (h_i^s \oplus h_i^e) + b \tag{7}$$

where U is a $N * C * N$ tensor, W is a $2N * C$ matrix, b is the bias, N is the length of the sentence, C is the number of entity categories $+1$(non-entity).

We assign span i a NER category y_i:

$$y_i = \arg\max r(i) \tag{8}$$

The learning objective of our named entity recognizer is to assign a correct category to each valid span. Hence it is a multi-class classification problem and we optimise the model with softmax cross-entropy:

$$p(i_c) = \frac{\exp(r(i_c))}{\sum_{\hat{c}=1}^{C} \exp(r(i_{\hat{c}}))} \tag{9}$$

$$L_{\text{Biaffine}} = -\sum_{i=1}^{N}\sum_{c=1}^{C} y_{ic} \log p(i_c) \tag{10}$$

The Combined Loss. The final loss function of the model is weighted by the loss function of CRF and the loss function of Biaffine, as shown below:

$$L = \alpha^* L_{\text{CRF}} + \beta^* L_{\text{Biaffine}} \tag{11}$$

where α and β are positive real number and their sum equals 1. They can be learned and updated iteratively with the training and we initialize both of them as 0.5.

3.2   Multi-strategies (MS)

Three strategies are adopted to enhance the performance, including Adaptive Pre-training (AP), Adversarial Training (AT) and model stacking with Cross Validation (CV). In order to reduce distribution differences between the task data and data used by the pre-trained model, we use CMeEE data for task-adaptive pre-training [6] based on the pre-trained model NEZHA [19] with Whole Word Masking (WWM) strategy to get a new domain adaptive pre-trained model CME-NEZHA. In order to improve the robustness of the model, we employ adversarial training [9] with Fast Gradient Method (FGM) strategy. Lastly, 5-fold cross validation is adopted to prevent model overfitting and exploit advantages of multi-models. Five models are trained and contribute equally to the final decision.

4   Datasets

Two public datasets are used for experiments, CMeEE for nested NER and CCKS2019 for flat NER. Statistics of the two datasets are shown in Table 1, including sizes of the training, validate and test sets. As can be seen, the size of CMeEE is larger while the average text length of CCKS2019 is longer.

The texts of CMeEE are from textbooks of clinical pediatrics, which contain 9 types of entities, including Body (bod), Disease (dis), Symptom (sym), Medical procedure (pro), Medical equipment (equ), Drug (dru), Medical examination

Table 1. Statistics of datasets

Dataset	Training set	Validation set	Test set	Average sentence length
CMeEE	15000	5000	3000	>50 characters
CCKS2019	800	200	379	>390 characters

Table 2. Entity statistics of CMeEE and CCKS2019

Entity Type	Entity number	Percent	Average entity length
bod	26589	28%	3.37
dis	24077	26%	5.35
sym	18579	20%	6.70
pro	9610	10%	5.30
dru	6331	7%	4.74
ite	4091	4%	4.37
mic	3019	3%	4.31
equ	1392	1%	4.30
dep	494	1%	2.86
Total	94182	100%	4.91
Anatomy	11520	49%	2.48
Disease	5535	23%	6.98
Drug	2307	10%	3.71
Laboratory	1785	8%	4.00
Image	1317	5%	3.79
Operation	1191	5%	12.85
Total	23655	100%	4.36

item (ite), Department (dep) and microorganism (mic). The texts of CCKS2019 are from electronic medical records, which contain 6 types of entities, including Disease and diagnosis, Image examination, Laboratory examination, Operation, Drug and Anatomy. As show in Table 2, the distributions of entities are imbalanced in both corpora. The top 3 dominant types of entities in CMeEE are bod, dis, and sym, while the top 3 dominant types of entities in CCKS2019 are Anatomy, Disease and Drug. On average, entities of sym and Operation are the longest in the two corpora respectively.

Table 3. Nested entity statistics of CMeEE

Flat entity	Nested entity	Percent of nested	Percent of nested in sym
84119	10063	10.68%	30.21%

As shown in Table 3, 10.68% of all entities in CMeEE are nested entities and 30.21% entities of sym are nested entities. Entities nested in sym entities are

Table 4. Entities nested in sym

Entity type	Number	Percent	Example of nested entity
bod	4706	84.84%	{无色胶冻样 [痰]bod}sym {Colorless jelly like [sputum]bod}sym
ite	486	8.76%	{[胸片]ite 异常}sym {[Chest radiograph]ite Abnormal}sym
dis	229	4.13%	{逐步发生全身弛缓性 [瘫痪]dis}sym {Progressive generalized flaccid [paralysis]dis}sym
pro	59	1.06%	{[肺部听诊]pro 呼吸音减弱}sym {[Lung auscultation]pro respiratory sound is reduced}sym
dru	28	0.50%	{[维生素A]dru 摄入不足}sym {[vitamin A]dru Insufficient intake}sym
mic	26	0.47%	{气道分泌物[细菌]mic 培养阳性}sym {Airway secretion [bacteria]mic culture positive}sym
equ	13	0.23%	{长期[呼吸机]equ 依赖}sym {Long-term [respirator]equ dependence}sym

shown Table 4. All entity types except dep have entities nested in sym, where bod is the dominant type.

5   Experiments

5.1   Query Generation

As shown in Table 5, for CMeEE, we put example entities into the query, while for CCKS2019, we take the description of the entity type as the query.

5.2   Experimental Settings

We retrain the pre-trained model NEZHA based on the CMeEE corpus by 100 epochs. Then we fine-tune the model for NER by 4 epochs. We set the batch size to 16, dropout to 0.1, NEZHA learning rate to 2.5e-5, other learning rate to 2.5e-3, and maximum text length to 256. NVIDIA GTX2080Ti is used to run the program. Micro average F1 is chosen as the evaluation metric.

5.3   Comparison with Previous Models

Baselines on CMeEE Corpus. (1) MacBERT-large and Human are from [20]. MacBERT is variant of BERT, taking a MLM (Masked Language Model) as correction strategy. Human denotes the annotating result of human. (2) BERT-CRF, BERT-Biaffine and RICON are from [5]. BERT-CRF solves sequence labeling with CRF, BERT-Biaffine detects span boundary with Biaffine, and RICON learns regularity inside entities. (3) Lattice-LSTM, Lattice-LSTM+Med-BERT, FLAT-Lattice, Medical-NER, and Medical NER+Med-BERT are from

Table 5. Query for different entity types in CMeEE and CCKS2019

Entity type	Query
bod	在文本中找出身体部位，例如细胞、皮肤、抗体
	Find body parts in the text, for example, cells, skin and antibodies
dep	在文本中找出科室，例如科,室
	Find departments in the text, for example, department and room
dis	在文本中找出疾病，例如癌症、病变、炎症、增生、肿瘤
	Find diseases in the text, for example, cancer and pathological changes
dru	在文本中找出药物，例如胶囊、疫苗、剂
	Find drugs in the text, for example, capsule, vaccine and agent
equ	在文本中找出医疗设备，例如装置、器、导管
	Find medical devices in the text, for example, device and conduit
ite	在文本中找出医学检验项目，例如尿常规、血常规
	Find medical test items in the text, for example, urine routine and blood routine
mic	在文本中找出微生物，例如病毒、病原体、抗原、核糖
	Find micro organisms in the text, for example, virus and pathogen
pro	在文本中找出医疗程序，例如心电图、病理切片、检测
	Find medical procedures in the text, for example, electrocardiogram and pathological section
sym	在文本中找出临床表现，例如疼痛、痉挛、异常
	Find clinical manifestations in the text, for example, pain and spasm
Anatomy	找出疾病、症状和体征发生的人体解剖学部位
	Find where in the human anatomy the disease, symptoms and signs occur
Disease	找出医学上定义的疾病和医生在临床工作中对病因、病生理、分型分期等所作的判断
	Find medically defined diseases and physicians' judgments regarding etiology, pathophysiology, staging, etc., in clinical work-up
Drug	找出用于疾病治疗的具体化学物质
	Find specific chemicals for disease treatment
Image	找出影像检查（X线、CT、MR、PETCT等）+造影+超声+心电图
	Find imaging examinations (X-ray, CT, Mr, PETCT, etc.) + contrast + ultrasound + ECG
Laboratory	找出在实验室进行的物理或化学检查
	Find physical or chemical examinations performed in the laboratory
Operation	找出医生在患者身体局部进行的切除、缝合等治疗，是外科的主要治疗方法
	Find the main treatment in surgery that doctors perform locally on the patient's body, such as excision, suture, etc.

[15]. Lattice-LSTM, Lattice-LSTM+Med-BERT and FLAT-Lattice incorporate lexicon to decide entity boundary. Medical NER and Medical NER+Med-BERT introduce big dictionary and pre-trained domain model.

Table 6. Comparison with previous models on CMeEE

Model	Precision/%	Recall/%	F1 score/%
MacBERT-large [20]	–	–	62.40
Human [20]	–	–	67.00
BERT-CRF [5]	58.34	64.08	61.07
BERT-Biaffine [5]	64.17	61.29	62.29
RICON [5]	66.25	64.89	65.57
Lattice-LSTM [15]	57.10	43.60	49.44
Lattice-LSTM+Med-BERT [15]	56.84	47.58	51.80
FLAT-Lattice [15]	66.90	70.10	68.46
Medical NER [15]	66.41	70.73	68.50
Medical NER+Med-BERT [15]	**67.99**	70.81	69.37
MRC-MTL-MS(Ours)	67.21	**71.89**	**69.47**

Baselines on CCKS2019 Corpus. (1)BERT-BiLSTM-CRF is from [4], taking CRF for sequence labeling. (2)BBC+Lexicon+Glyph is from [24], introducing lexicon and glyph information. (3) WB-Transformer+SA is from [21], taking self-attention for semantic enrichment. (4) ELMo-lattice-LSTM-CRF is from [14], fusing ELMo and lexicon to improve sequence labeling performance. (5) ACNN is from [8], composed of hierarchical CNN and attention mechanism. (6) FS-TL is from [11], fusing stroke information with transfer learning.

Table 7. Comparison with previous models on CCKS2019

Model	Precision/%	Recall/%	F1 score/%
BERT-BiLSTM-CRF [4]	73.84	75.31	74.53
BBC+Lexicon+Glyph [24]	85.17	84.13	84.64
WB-Transformer+SA [21]	–	–	84.98
ACNN [8]	83.07	**87.29**	85.13
FS-TL [11]	–	–	85.16
ELMo-lattice-LSTM-CRF [14]	84.69	85.35	85.02
MRC-MTL-MS(Ours)	**85.29**	85.32	**85.31**

As shown in Table 6 and 7, our MRC-MTL-MS model outperforms all comparison models on both the nested NER corpus CMeEE and the flat NER corpus CCKS2019.

5.4   Ablation Experiments

The ablation experiments are shown in Table 8. MRC-Base is the same with [13], pointer network is used to detect span boundary. MRC-CRF only uses CRF for decoding. MRC-Biaffine only uses Biaffine for decoding. MRC-MTL integrates CRF and Biaffine with multi-task learning and use CRF as the final decoder. We can see that multi-task learning model outperforms single-task models. Adaptive Pre-training (AP), Adversarial Training (AT), and model stacking with Cross Validation (CV) strategies further improve the performance. Among which, CV contributes the most. Compared with MRC-Base, the improvement of F1 score on the nested NER corpus is 2.56%, which is higher than that of 1.63% on the flat NER corpus.

Table 8. Ablation experiments on CMeEE and CCKS2019

Model	CMeEE/%			CCKS2019/%		
	Precision	Recall	F1 score	Precision	Recall	F1 score
MRC-Base	67.98	65.87	66.91	82.63	84.76	83.68
MRC-CRF	67.17	67.25	67.21	84.40	84.91	84.65
MRC-Biaffine	**70.71**	64.09	67.24	83.22	83.77	83.49
MRC-MTL	64.58	71.76	67.98	84.42	84.97	84.70
+AP	66.28	70.34	68.25	84.23	85.24	84.73
+AP+AT	68.04	69.16	68.59	84.20	**85.39**	84.79
+AP+AT+CV	67.21	**71.89**	**69.47**	**85.29**	85.32	**85.31**

5.5   Experiments on Different Types of NEs

Experimental results of different types of NEs on the two corpora are shown in Table 9 respectively. As can be seen, on CMeEE, the entity type dru has the highest F1 score 81.17%, while the entity type ite has the lowest F1 score. The averagely longest and most nested entity type sym also has low F1 score and needs further study. The overall F1 scores on CCKS2019 are high and the entity type Drug also has the highest F1 score 95.25%, indicating that Drug entities are easier to recognize. For those entity types with low scores, like ite and Laboratory, constructing related lexicons maybe useful for improvement.

Table 9. Results of different types of NEs on CMeEE and CCKS2019

Entity type	Precision/%	Recall/%	F1 score/%
bod	62.92	71.33	66.86
dis	76.78	80.69	78.69
dru	75.38	87.93	81.17
dep	54.24	88.89	67.37
equ	74.48	81.20	77.70
ite	51.06	49.23	50.13
mic	76.64	82.16	79.30
pro	61.91	71.50	66.36
sym	58.49	54.68	56.52
Mac-Avg	65.77	74.18	69.72
Anatomy	85.25	87.07	86.15
Disease	85.63	85.56	85.60
Drug	95.45	95.05	95.25
Image	86.65	87.64	87.14
Laboratory	74.54	67.97	71.10
Operation	85.91	79.01	82.32
Mac-Avg	85.57	83.72	84.63

5.6   Case Study

Table 10 gives two examples from CMeEE. In the first example, the MRC-Base model does not correctly detect the boundary of the entity "郎飞结上的补体被激活" (Complement on Ranvier knot is activated), while the MRC-MTL-MS model correctly recognizes the boundary and the entity type. In the second example, the MRC-Base model correctly detects the boundary of the entity "高血压" (hypertension), but predicts a wrong label. The MRC-MTL-MS model correctly recognizes the polysemous entity, indicating its superiority in disambiguating polysemous entities.

Table 10. Two cases with labels BIES

Sentence	AMAN的一个早期表现就是郎飞结上的补体被激活。
	An early manifestation of AMAN is that complement on Ranvier knot is activated.
Entity	郎飞结上的补体被激活
	Complement on Ranvier knot is activated.
Golden Labels	B-SYM I-SYM I-SYM I-SYM I-SYM I-SYM I-SYM I-SYM I-SYM E-SYM
MRC	B-BOD I-BOD E-BOD O O O O O O O
MRC-MTL-MS	B-SYM I-SYM I-SYM I-SYM I-SYM I-SYM I-SYM I-SYM I-SYM E-SYM
Sentence	患儿情况好，只 1 例发生慢性排异及高血压。
	The condition of the child is good, and only one develops chronic rejection and hypertension.
Entity	高血压
	hypertension
Golden Labels	B-SYM I-SYM E-SYM
MRC	B-DIS I-DIS E-DIS
MRC-MTL-MS	B-SYM I-SYM I-SYM

6 Conclusion

This paper proposes a MRC-based multi-task model for Chinese medical NER, enhancing MRC-CRF with Biaffine to recognize the named entities more accurately. To further improve the model, we introduce multi-strategies, including adaptive pre-training, adversarial training and model stacking with cross validation. Our model can cope with both flat NER and nested NER. Experiments on the nested NER corpus CMeEE and the flat NER corpus CCKS2019 show the effectiveness of our model. In the future, we will incorporate domain knowledge to improve the recognition performance on hard named entities.

Acknowledgements. We would like to thank the anonymous reviewers for their insightful and valuable comments. This work was supported in part by Major Program of National Social Science Foundation of China (Grant No.17ZDA318, 18ZDA295), National Natural Science Foundation of China (Grant No.62006211), and China Postdoctoral Science Foundation (Grant No.2019TQ0286, 2020M682349).

References

1. Cao, J., et al.: Electronic medical record entity recognition via machine reading comprehension and biaffine. Discrete Dyn. Nat. Soc. **2021** (2021)

2. Chen, X., Ouyang, C., Liu, Y., Bu, Y.: Improving the named entity recognition of Chinese electronic medical records by combining domain dictionary and rules. Int. J. Environ. Res. Pub. Health **17**(8), 2687 (2020)
3. Chowdhury, S., et al.: A multitask bi-directional RNN model for named entity recognition on Chinese electronic medical records. BMC Bioinf. **19**(17), 75–84 (2018)
4. Dai, Z., Wang, X., Ni, P., Li, Y., Li, G., Bai, X.: Named entity recognition using BERT BiLSTM CRF for Chinese electronic health records. In: 2019 12th International Congress on Image and Signal Processing, Biomedical Engineering and Informatics (CISP-BMEI), pp. 1–5 (2019)
5. Gu, Y., Qu, X., Wang, Z., Zheng, Y., Huai, B., Yuan, N.J.: Delving deep into regularity: a simple but effective method for Chinese named entity recognition. arXiv preprint arXiv:2204.05544 (2022)
6. Gururangan, S., et al.: Don't stop pretraining: adapt language models to domains and tasks. In: Proceedings of the 58th Annual Meeting of the Association for Computational Linguistics, pp. 8342–8360 (2020)
7. Han, X., Wang, Z., Zhang, J., Wen, Q., Lin, Y.: Overview of the CCKS 2019 knowledge graph evaluation track: entity, relation, event and QA. arXiv preprint arXiv:2003.03875 (2020)
8. Kong, J., Zhang, L., Jiang, M., Liu, T.: Incorporating multi-level CNN and attention mechanism for Chinese clinical named entity recognition. J. Biomed. Inform. **116**, 103737 (2021)
9. Kurakin, A., Goodfellow, I., Bengio, S.: Adversarial machine learning at scale. arXiv preprint arXiv:1611.01236 (2016)
10. Lafferty, J.D., McCallum, A., Pereira, F.C.: Conditional random fields: probabilistic models for segmenting and labeling sequence data. In: Proceedings of the Eighteenth International Conference on Machine Learning, pp. 282–289 (2001)
11. Li, N., Luo, L., Ding, Z., Song, Y., Yang, Z., Lin, H.: DUTIR at the CCKS-2019 task1: improving Chinese clinical named entity recognition using stroke ELMo and transfer learning. In: Proceedings of the 4th China Conference on Knowledge Graph and Semantic Computing (CCKS 2019), pp. 24–27 (2019)
12. Li, X., Zhang, H., Zhou, X.H.: Chinese clinical named entity recognition with variant neural structures based on BERT methods. J. Biomed. Inform. **107**, 103422 (2020)
13. Li, X., Feng, J., Meng, Y., Han, Q., Wu, F., Li, J.: A unified MRC framework for named entity recognition. In: Proceedings of the 58th Annual Meeting of the Association for Computational Linguistics, pp. 5849–5859 (2020)
14. Li, Y.: Chinese clinical named entity recognition in electronic medical records: development of a lattice long short-term memory model with contextualized character representations. JMIR Med. Inform. **8**(9), e19848 (2020)
15. Liu, N., Hu, Q., Xu, H., Xu, X., Chen, M.: Med-BERT: A pre-training framework for medical records named entity recognition. IEEE Trans. Ind. Inf. **18**(8), 5600–5608 (2021)
16. Luo, L., Yang, Z., Song, Y., Li, N., Lin, H.: Chinese clinical named entity recognition based on stroke ELMo and multi-task learning. Chin. J. Comput. **43**(10), 1943–1957 (2020)
17. Qin, Q., Zhao, S., Liu, C.: A BERT-BIGRU-CRF model for entity recognition of Chinese electronic medical records. Complexity **2021** (2021)
18. Wan, Q., Liu, J., Wei, L., Ji, B.: A self-attention based neural architecture for Chinese medical named entity recognition. Math. Biosci. Eng. **17**(4), 3498–3511 (2020)

19. Wei, J., et al.: NEZHA: neural contextualized representation for Chinese language understanding. arXiv preprint arXiv:1909.00204 (2019)

20. Zhang, N., et al.: CBLUE: a Chinese biomedical language understanding evaluation benchmark. In: Proceedings of the 60th Annual Meeting of the Association for Computational Linguistics (Volume 1: Long Papers), pp. 7888–7915 (2022)

21. Zhang, Z., Qin, X., Qiu, Y., Liu, D.: Well-behaved transformer for Chinese medical NER. In: 2021 3rd International Conference on Natural Language Processing (ICNLP), pp. 162–167 (2021)

22. Zhao, S., Cai, Z., Chen, H., Wang, Y., Liu, F., Liu, A.: Adversarial training based lattice LSTM for Chinese clinical named entity recognition. J. Biomed. Inform. **99**, 103290 (2019)

23. Zheng, H., Qin, B., Xu, M.: Chinese medical named entity recognition using CRF-MT-adapt and NER-MRC. In: 2021 2nd International Conference on Computing and Data Science (CDS), pp. 362–365 (2021)

24. Zhong, S., Yu, Q.: Improving Chinese medical named entity recognition using glyph and lexicon. In: Proceedings of 2021 International Conference on Advanced Education and Information Management (AEIM 2021), pp. 75–80 (2021)

25. Zhu, Q., et al.: HITSZ-HLT at semEval-2021 task 5: ensemble sequence labeling and span boundary detection for toxic span detection. In: Proceedings of the 15th International Workshop on Semantic Evaluation (SemEval-2021), pp. 521–526 (2021)

A Multi-Gate Encoder for Joint Entity and Relation Extraction

Xiong Xiong[1,2], Yunfei Liu[1,2], Anqi Liu[1], Shuai Gong[1,2], and Shengyang Li[1,2(✉)]

[1] Key Laboratory of Space Utilization, Technology and Engineering Center
for Space Utilization, Chinese Academy of Sciences, Beijing, China
{xiongxiong20,liuyunfei,liuaq,gongshuai19,shyli}@csu.ac.cn
[2] University of Chinese Academy of Sciences, Beijing, China

Abstract. Named entity recognition and relation extraction are core sub-tasks of relational triple extraction. Recent studies have used parameter sharing or joint decoding to create interaction between these two tasks. However, ensuring the specificity of task-specific traits while the two tasks interact properly is a huge difficulty. We propose a multi-gate encoder that models bidirectional task interaction while keeping sufficient feature specificity based on gating mechanism in this paper. Precisely, we design two types of independent gates: task gates to generate task-specific features and interaction gates to generate instructive features to guide the opposite task. Our experiments show that our method increases the state-of-the-art (SOTA) relation F1 scores on ACE04, ACE05 and SciERC datasets to 63.8% (+1.3%), 68.2% (+1.4%), 39.4% (+1.0%), respectively, with higher inference speed over previous SOTA model.

Keywords: Joint entity and relation extraction · Gating mechanism · Transformer

1 Introduction

Extracting relational facts from unstructured texts is a fundamental task in information extraction. This task can be decomposed into two sub-tasks: Named Entity Recognition (NER) [11], which aims to recognize the boundaries and types of entities; and Relation Extraction (RE) [35], which aims to extract semantic relations between entities. The extracted relational triples in the form of (subject, relation, object) are basic elements of large-scale knowledge graphs [18].

Traditional approaches perform NER and RE in a pipelined fashion [5,13,40]. They first extract all the entities in a given text, and then identify pairwise relations between the extracted entities. However, because the two sub-tasks are modeled independently, pipelined methods are vulnerable to error propagation issue. Since the interaction between NER and RE is neglected, the errors accumulated in the previous NER stage cannot be corrected in the subsequent RE stage. To resolve this issue, some joint models have been proposed to model these two tasks simultaneously. Early feature-based joint models [23,34] rely on complicated feature engineering to build interaction between entities and relations. More recently, neural joint models have attracted increasing research interest and have demonstrated promising performance on joint entity and relation extraction.

In existing neural joint models, there are mainly two ways to build the interaction between NER and RE: parameter sharing and joint decoding. In parameter sharing methods [2, 8, 36], NER model and RE model are built on top of a shared encoding layer to achieve joint learning. However, approaches based on parameter sharing implicitly rather than explicitly model the inter-task interaction, leading to insufficient excavation of the inherent association between the two tasks. Moreover, these two tasks focus on different contextual information [33, 39], but methods of sharing representations cannot provide task-specific features with enough specificity for the two tasks. In terms of error propagation, parameter sharing methods alleviate the error propagation between tasks, but to a limited extent, because these models still perform pipelined decoding. Another family of approaches adopt unified tagging framework in the form of sequences [38], tables [24, 37], or graphs [12, 31] to integrate the information of entities and relations as a whole and perform joint decoding to extract relational triples. Although these methods enhance the inter-task interaction, the specificity of task features is not well considered since the entities and relations still share contextual representations in essence. Moreover, all these joint decoding methods require complex joint decoding algorithms, and it is challenging to balance the accuracy of joint decoding and the abundance of task-specific features.

Accordingly, the main challenge of joint entity and relation extraction is to construct proper interaction between NER and RE while ensuring the specificity of task-specific features. Wang and Lu et al. [27] adopt two types of representations to generate task-specific representations, sequence representations for NER and table representations for RE, separately. These two types of representations interact with each other to model inter-task interaction. Yan et al. [32] perform neuron partition in an autoregressive manner to generate task-specific features jointly in order to build inter-task interaction. They combine the task-specific features and global features as the final input to the task modules. Inspired by Yan et al. [32]'s work, we adopt the task modules they used that model each relation separately with tables [23], and we propose a simple but effective feature encoding approach for joint entity and relation extraction, achieving excellent results while being less computationally intensive. We will detail the differences and our advantages in Sect. 3.5.

In this work, we propose a **Multi-Gate Encoder (MGE)** that control the flow of feature information based on gating mechanism, so as to filter out undesired information and retain desired information. MGE has two types of gates: task gates and interaction gates. Task gates are used to generate task-specific features, and interaction gates control how much information flows out to guide the opposite task. The output of interaction gate is combined with the opposite task-specific features to generate the input of corresponding task module, resulting in a bidirectional interaction between NER and RE while maintaining sufficient specificity of task-specific features.

The main contributions of this work are summarized below:

1. A multi-gate encoder for joint entity and relation extraction is proposed, which effectively promotes interaction between NER and RE while ensuring the specificity of

task features. Experimental results show that our method establishes the new state-of-the-art on three standard benchmarks, namely ACE04, ACE05, and SciERC.
2. We conduct extensive analyses to investigate the superiority of our model and validate the effectiveness of each component of our model.
3. The effect of relation information on entity recognition is examined. Our additional experiments suggest that relation information contributes to predicting entities, which helps clarify the controversy on the effect of relation signals.

2   Related Work

The task of extracting relational triples from plain text can be decomposed into two sub-task: Named Entity Recognition and Relation Extraction. The two tasks can be performed in a pipelined manner [5, 13, 33, 39] or in a joint manner [23, 27, 32, 38].

Traditional pipelined methods [5, 13, 40] firstly train a model to extract entities and then train another model to classify the relation type between subject and object for each entity pair. Recent pipelined approaches [33, 39] still follow this pattern and adopt marker-based span representations to learn different contextual representations between entities and relations, and between entity pairs, which sheds some light on the importance of feature specificity. Although Zhong and Chen et al. [39] and Ye et al. [33] achieve better performance than previous pipelined methods and some joint methods, they still run the risk of error propagation and do not adequately account for interactions between tasks. To ease these issues, some joint models that extract entities and relations jointly has been proposed.

Joint entity and relation extraction is a typical multi-task scenario, and how to handle the interaction between tasks is a frequently discussed topic. Early joint models [23, 34] rely on feature engineering to build task interaction. More recently, many neural joint models have been proposed and show promising performance. Miwa and Bansal et al. [22] builds a sequence tagging model for NER and a dependency tree model for RE separately on top of a shared LSTM layer and performs joint learning, achieving task interaction through parameter sharing. Zeng et al. [36] uses sequence-to-sequence learning framework with copy mechanism to jointly extract entities and relations. Bekoulis et al. [3] builds a CRF layer for NER and a sigmoid layer for RE on a shared LSTM layer. Eberts and Ulges et al. [10] proposes a span-based joint model for entity and relation extraction. They performs span classification and span filtering to extract entity spans and then performs relation classification based on the contextual span representations from BERT [7] encoder. All these approaches construct the interaction between NER and RE through parameter sharing. Another class of methods adopts joint decoding to fuse the two tasks together. Li and Ji et al. [16] uses structured perceptron with beam search to extract entities and relations simultaneously. Wang et al. [28] proposes a transition system to convert the joint task into a directed graph. Wang et al. [30] introduces a novel handshaking tagging scheme to formulate joint extraction as a token pair linking problem. Zhang et al. [37] and Ren et al. [24] convert the task into a table-filling problem.

In addition to building interaction between tasks, another important issue is the specificity of task features. As recent studies [33, 39] have shown, generating specific contextual features for different tasks can achieve better results on the overall task than sharing input features. Zhong and Chen et al. [39] and Ye et al. [33] both use a pretrained language model (e.g., BERT) for NER and another for RE to obtain different contextual representations for specific task. However, fine-tuning distinct pre-trained encoders for the two task separately is computationally expensive. In our work, we adopts gating mechanism to balance the flow of feature information, taking into account both the interaction between tasks and the specificity of task features.

3 Method

In this section, we first formally define the problem of joint entity and relation extraction and then detail the structure of our model. Finally, we discuss how our model differs from the approach we follow and explain why our method performs better.

3.1 Problem Definition

The problem of joint entity and relation extraction can be decomposed into two subtasks: NER and RE. Let $\mathcal{E}$ denotes the set of predefined entity types and $\mathcal{R}$ denotes the set of predefined relation types. Given a sentence containing N words, $X = \{x_1, x_2, \ldots, x_N\}$, the goal of NER is to extract an entity type $e_{ij} \in \mathcal{E}$ for each span $s_{ij} \in S$ that starts with x_i and ends with x_j, where S is the set of all the possible spans in X. For RE, the goal is to extract a relation type $r_{i_1 i_2} \in \mathcal{R}$ for each span pair whose start words are x_{i_1} and x_{i_2} respectively. Combining the results of NER and RE, we get the final output of this problem $Y_r = \{(e_{i_1 j_1}, r_{i_1 i_2}, e_{i_2 j_2})\}$, where $e_{i_1 j_1}, e_{i_2 j_2} \in \mathcal{E}, r_{i_1 i_2} \in \mathcal{R}$.

3.2 Multi-gate Encoder

We adopt BERT [7] to encode the contextual information of input sentences. As shown in Fig. 1, our proposed MGE employs four gates to control the flow of feature information based on gating mechanism. The two task gates are designed to generate task-specific features for NER and RE, while the two interaction gates aim to generate interaction features that have a positive effect on the opposite task. The task-specific features and interaction features are combined to form the input of task modules, carrying out bidirectional task interaction through feature exchange.

Let $H_b \in \mathbb{R}^{N \times d}$ denotes the contextual feature matrix of sentence X extracted by BERT encoder, where d is the hidden size of BERT layer. In order to preliminarily build the specificity between entity recognition features and relation extraction features, we generate candidate entity features H_e^c and candidate relation features H_r^c based on BERT output representations as follows:

$$H_e^c = \tanh (H_b W_e + b_e)$$
$$H_r^c = \tanh (H_b W_r + b_r), \tag{1}$$

where $W_{(\cdot)} \in \mathbb{R}^{d \times h}$ and $b_{(\cdot)} \in \mathbb{R}^h$ denote trainable weights and bias and h is the hidden size in MGE. $\tanh(\cdot)$ means $tanh$ activation function. The candidate features will be

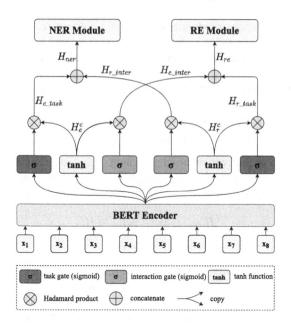

Fig. 1. The architecture of our proposed MGE. There are two types of gates in the encoder: task gates and interaction gates. H_e^c and H_r^c denote candidate entity features and candidate relation features respectively. H_{e_task} and H_{r_task} denote task-specific features generated by task gates. H_{e_inter} and H_{r_inter} denote interaction features generated by interaction gates to guide the opposite task. H_{ner} and H_{re} are the final input features to NER module and RE module.

input to the task gates and interaction gates of corresponding task for further feature filtering to generate task-specific features and interaction features.

The task gates decide what information in the candidate features is contributing to the corresponding specific task, which is implemented by a sigmoid layer. The sigmoid layer produces values in the range of zero to one, indicating how much information is to be transmitted. A value of zero means no information is allowed to pass, whereas a value of one means all the information is allowed to pass. We calculate entity task gate G_{e_task} and relation task gate G_{r_task} as below:

$$
\begin{aligned}
G_{e\_task} &= \sigma\left(H_b W_{e\_task} + b_{e\_task}\right) \\
G_{r\_task} &= \sigma\left(H_b W_{r\_task} + b_{r\_task}\right),
\end{aligned}
\tag{2}
$$

where $\sigma\left(\cdot\right)$ represents sigmoid activation function. $W_{(\cdot)} \in \mathbb{R}^{d \times h}$ and $b_{(\cdot)} \in \mathbb{R}^h$ denote weights and bias. The entity task gate G_{e_task} and relation task gate G_{r_task} work independently and are specialized in filtering information useful for specific task in candidate features to obtain task-specific features for entity recognition and relation extraction respectively. We calculate the Hadamard (element-wise) product between task gates and candidate features to generate task-specific features for NER and RE:

$$
\begin{aligned}
H_{e\_task} &= G_{e\_task} \odot H_e^c \\
H_{r\_task} &= G_{r\_task} \odot H_r^c,
\end{aligned}
\tag{3}
$$

where $\odot$ denotes Hadamard product operation. H_{e_task} and H_{r_task} represent entity task-specific features and relation task-specific features respectively.

Similarly, the interaction gates decide what information in entity candidate features H_e^c is helpful for guiding relation extraction and what information in H_r^c is helpful for guiding entity recognition. This is also implemented through sigmoid activation function:

$$G_{e\_inter} = \sigma\left(H_b W_{e\_inter} + b_{e\_inter}\right)$$
$$G_{r\_inter} = \sigma\left(H_b W_{r\_inter} + b_{r\_inter}\right), \tag{4}$$

where G_{e_inter} denotes entity interaction gate and G_{r_inter} denotes relation interaction gate. $W_{(\cdot)} \in \mathbb{R}^{d \times h}$ and $b_{(\cdot)} \in \mathbb{R}^h$ denote weights and bias. These two interaction gates are then applied to candidate features to generate interaction features:

$$H_{e\_inter} = G_{e\_inter} \odot H_e^c$$
$$H_{r\_inter} = G_{r\_inter} \odot H_r^c, \tag{5}$$

where H_{e_inter} denotes entity interaction features used to guide RE and H_{r_inter} denotes relation interaction features used to guide NER.

Finally, we perform feature exchange based on the task-specific features and interaction features to achieve bidirectional interaction between NER and RE. Specifically, we concatenate entity task-specific features H_{e_task} and relation interaction features H_{r_inter}, and relation task-specific features H_{r_task} is concatenated with entity interaction features H_{e_inter}:

$$H_{ner} = H_{e\_task} \oplus H_{r\_inter}$$
$$H_{re} = H_{r\_task} \oplus H_{e\_inter}, \tag{6}$$

where $\oplus$ means concatenation operation. $H_{ner} \in \mathbb{R}^{N \times 2h}$ and $H_{re} \in \mathbb{R}^{N \times 2h}$ are the final features to be input to NER and RE task modules respectively. Through exchanging features that are designed to guide the opposite task and combining task-specific features, H_{ner} and H_{re} balance the task interaction and feature specificity of NER and RE.

3.3   Table-Filling Modules

Following Yan et al. [32], we adopt table-filling framework to extract entities and relations, which treats both NER and RE as table filling problems. For NER, the goal is to predict all the entity spans and corresponding entity types. Specifically, we construct a $N \times N$ type-specific table for each entity type $k \in \mathcal{E}$, whose element at row i and column j represents the probability of span $s_{ij} \in S$ belonging to type k. We firstly concatenate the representations of every two tokens based on H_{ner} and connect a fully-connected layer to reduce the hidden size. Then we employ layer normalization [1] and ELU activation [6] to obtain table representations of spans. Formally, for span s_{ij} that starts with x_i and ends with x_j, we compute the table representation $T_{ner}^{i,j} \in \mathbb{R}^h$ as follows:

$$T_{ner}^{i,j} = \text{ELU}(\text{LayerNorm}([H_{ner}^i; H_{ner}^j]W_e^h + b_e^h)), \tag{7}$$

where $H_{ner}^i \in \mathbb{R}^{2h}$ and $H_{ner}^j \in \mathbb{R}^{2h}$ denote the vectors corresponding to words x_i and x_j in entity features $H_{ner} \in \mathbb{R}^{N \times 2h}$ that containing both entity task-specific information and relation interaction information. $W_e^h \in \mathbb{R}^{4h \times h}$ and $b_e^h \in \mathbb{R}^h$ are trainable parameters. To predict the probability of span s_{ij} belonging to entity type k, we project the hidden size to $|\mathcal{E}|$ with a fully-connected layer followed by a sigmoid activation function:

$$p(e_{ij} = k) = \sigma(T_{ner}^{i,j} W_e^{tag} + b_e^{tag}), \forall k \in \mathcal{E}, \tag{8}$$

where $W_e^{tag} \in \mathbb{R}^{h \times |\mathcal{E}|}$ and $b_e^{tag} \in \mathbb{R}^{|\mathcal{E}|}$ are trainable parameters and $|\mathcal{E}|$ represents the number of predefined entity types.

The goal of RE table-filling module is to predict the start word of each entity and classify the relations between them. The structure of RE module is formally analogous to the NER module. Similar to NER, we construct a $N \times N$ type-specific table for each relation type $l \in \mathcal{R}$. For the table corresponding to relation l, the element at row i and column j represents the probability that the i-th word x_i and the j-th word x_j in a sentence are respectively the start words of subject entity and object entity of relation type l. For x_i and x_j, we compute the table representations $T_{re}^{i,j} \in \mathbb{R}^h$ as follows:

$$T_{re}^{i,j} = \text{ELU}(\text{LayerNorm}([H_{re}^i; H_{re}^j]W_r^h + b_r^h)), \tag{9}$$

where $H_{re}^i \in \mathbb{R}^{2h}$ and $H_{re}^j \in \mathbb{R}^{2h}$ denote the vectors corresponding to words x_i and x_j in features $H_{re} \in \mathbb{R}^{N \times 2h}$ that containing both relation task-specific information and entity interaction information. $W_r^h \in \mathbb{R}^{4h \times h}$ and $b_r^h \in \mathbb{R}^h$ are trainable parameters. The probability that x_i and x_j are the start words of the subject and object of relation type l is calculated as follows:

$$p(r_{ij} = l) = \sigma(T_{re}^{i,j} W_r^{tag} + b_r^{tag}), \forall l \in \mathcal{R}, \tag{10}$$

where $W_r^{tag} \in \mathbb{R}^{h \times |\mathcal{R}|}$ and $b_r^{tag} \in \mathbb{R}^{|\mathcal{R}|}$ are trainable parameters and $|\mathcal{R}|$ represents the number of predefined relation types. We obtain the prediction results of NER module and RE module under the following conditions:

$$p(e_{i_1 j_1} = k_1) \geq 0.5; \ p(r_{i_1 i_2} = l) \geq 0.5; \ p(e_{i_2 j_2} = k_2) \geq 0.5 \tag{11}$$

where $k_1, k_2 \in \mathcal{E}, l \in \mathcal{R}$. For a fair comparison, the hyper-parameter threshold is set to be 0.5 without further fine-tuning as in previous works.

Combining the prediction results of NER and RE task modules, we can get the final relational triples in a given sentence:

$$Y_r = \{(e_{i_1 j_1}, r_{i_1 i_2}, e_{i_2 j_2})\}, e_{i_1 j_1}, e_{i_2 j_2} \in \mathcal{E}, r_{i_1 i_2} \in \mathcal{R}, \tag{12}$$

where $e_{i_1 j_1}$ and $e_{i_2 j_2}$ are entity spans predicted by NER task module, and $r_{i_1 i_2}$ denotes the relation between head-only entities predicted by RE task module.

3.4   Loss Function

During training, we adopt binary cross entropy loss for both NER and RE task modules. Given a sentence containing N words, we compute the NER loss and RE loss as follows:

$$\mathcal{L}_{\text{NER}} = -\sum_{i=1}^{N}\sum_{j=i}^{N}\sum_{k\in\mathcal{E}}\hat{p}(e_{ij}=k)\log p(e_{ij}=k) + (1-\hat{p}(e_{ij}=k))\log\left(1-p(e_{ij}=k)\right)$$

$$\mathcal{L}_{\text{RE}} = -\sum_{i=1}^{N}\sum_{j=1}^{N}\sum_{l\in\mathcal{R}}\hat{p}(r_{ij}=l)\log p(r_{ij}=l) + (1-\hat{p}(r_{ij}=l))\log\left(1-p(r_{ij}=l)\right), \tag{13}$$

where $\hat{p}(e_{ij}=k)$ and $\hat{p}(r_{ij}=l)$ represent ground truth labels. $p(e_{ij}=k)$ and $p(r_{ij}=l)$ are the probability predicted by NER and RE modules. The final training goal is to minimize the sum of these two losses:

$$\mathcal{L} = \mathcal{L}_{\text{NER}} + \mathcal{L}_{\text{RE}}. \tag{14}$$

3.5 Differences from PFN

Our method differs from PFN [32] in the following ways: (1) We generate interaction features using distinct interaction gates, which are independent of the process of generating task-specific features. (2) All feature operations in MGE are performed in a non-autoregressive manner, i.e., all tokens in the sentence are processed in a single pass, resulting in increased efficiency. As a result, our method is simpler while still ensuring proper NER-RE interaction. Furthermore, as demonstrated in Sect. 4, our model outperforms PFN on three public datasets and achieves faster inference speed while employing the same task modules and pre-trained encoders.

4 Experiments

4.1 Dataset

We evaluate our model on three popular English relation extraction datasets: ACE05 [26], ACE04 [9] and SciERC [19]. The ACE05 and ACE04 datasets are collected from various domains, such as news articles and online forums. Following Luan et al. [20], we split ACE04 into 5 folds and ACE05 into 10051 sentences for training, 2424 sentences for validation, and 2050 sentences for test[1]. And we follow Yan et al. [32] to construct the development set of ACE04 with 15% of the training set.

The SciERC dataset is collected from 500 AI paper abstracts, and includes annotations for scientific entities, their relations, and coreference clusters. It consists six predefined scientific entity types and seven predefined relation types. In our experiments, we only use the annotation information of entities and relations. We download the processed dataset from the project website[2] of Luan et al. [19], including 1861 sentences for training, 275 sentences for validation and 551 sentences for test. Table 1 shows the statistics of ACE04, ACE05 and SciERC datasets.

---

[1] We process the datasets with scripts provided by Luan et al. [20]: https://github.com/luanyi/DyGIE/tree/master/preprocessing.

[2] http://nlp.cs.washington.edu/sciIE/.

Table 1. Statistics of datasets. $|\mathcal{E}|$ and $|\mathcal{R}|$ are numbers of entity and relation types.

Dataset	$|\mathcal{E}|$	$|\mathcal{R}|$	#Entities	#Relations	#Sentences		
					Train	Dev	Test
ACE05	7	6	38,287	7,070	10,051	2,424	2,050
ACE04	7	6	22,708	4,084	8,683 (5-fold)		
SciERC	6	7	8,094	4,684	1,861	275	551

4.2 Evaluation

Following standard evaluation protocol, we use micro F1 score as an evaluation for both NER and RE. For NER task, an entity is considered as correct if its boundary and type are both predicted correctly. For RE task, a relational triple is correct only if its relation type and the boundaries and types of entities are correct.

4.3 Implementation Details

For fair comparison, we use *albert-xxlarge-v1* [15] as the base encoder for ACE04 and ACE05. And for SciERC, we use *scibert-scivocab-uncased* [4] as the base encoder. Regarding the use of cross-sentence context [20,21], that is, to extend each sentence by its context for better contextual representations, we don't adopt this experimental setting considering the fairness of experimental comparisons. Zhong and Chen et al. [39] extend each sentence to a fixed context window size of 300 words for entity model and 100 words for relation model. Ye et al. [33] set the context window size to be 512 words for entity model and 256/384 words for relation model. Although cross-sentence context may further enhance the performance of entity recognition and relation extraction, if the research focus is not on the cross-sentence context, the different cross-sentence context lengths will greatly affect the experimental results, making it difficult to conduct fair comparisons. All our experiments are carried out in single-sentence setting and we compare with the experimental results of other baselines under the single-sentence setting.

Our model is implemented with PyTorch and we train our models with Adam optimizer of a linear scheduler with a warmup ratio of 0.1. For all the experiments, the learning rate and training epoch are set to be $2e-5$ and 100 respectively. We set the batch size to be 4 for SciERC and 16 for ACE04 and ACE05. Following previous work [32], the max length of input sentence is set to be 128. All the models are trained with a single NVIDIA Titan RTX GPU. We select the model with the best average F1 score of NER and RE on the development set, and report the average F1 of 5 runs on the test set.

4.4 Baselines

We compare our model with the following baselines: (1) **BiLSTM** [14,22]: these models perform NER and RE based on shared Bi-directional LSTMs. Miwa and Bansal

Table 2. Overall F1 scores on the test set of ACE04, ACE05, and SciERC. Results of PURE are reported in single-sentence setting for fair comparison.

Model	Encoder	ACE05		ACE04		SciERC	
		NER	RE	NER	RE	NER	RE
SPTree [22]	LSTM	83.4	55.6	81.8	48.4	-	-
Katiyar and Cardie [14]	LSTM	82.6	53.6	79.6	45.7	-	-
Multi-turn QA [17]	BERT	84.8	60.2	83.6	49.4	-	-
Table-Sequence [27]	ALBERT	89.5	64.3	88.6	59.6	-	-
SPE [29]	SciBERT	-	-	-	-	68.0	34.6
PURE [39]	ALBERT	**89.7**	65.6	88.8	60.2	-	-
	SciBERT	-	-	-	-	66.6	35.6
PFN [32]	ALBERT	89.0	66.8	**89.3**	62.5	-	-
	SciBERT	-	-	-	-	66.8	38.4
MGE (Ours)	ALBERT	**89.7**	**68.2**	**89.3**	**63.8**	-	-
	SciBERT	-	-	-	-	**68.4**	**39.4**

et al. [22] treats entity recognition as a sequence tagging task and represents the relations between entities in dependency tree. Katiyar and Cardie et al. [14] formulates both entity recognition and relation detection as sequence tagging tasks. (2) **Multi-turn QA** [17]: it converts the task into a multi-turn question answering task: each entity type and relation type has its corresponding pre-designed question template, and entities and relations are extracted by answering template questions with standard machine reading comprehension (MRC) [25] framework. (3) **Table-Sequence** [27]: this work uses a sequence encoder and a table encoder to learn task-specific representations for NER and RE separately, and models task interaction through combining these two types of representations. (4) **SPE** [29]: this method proposes a span encoder and span pair encoder to add intra-span and inter-span information to the pre-trained model for entity and relation extraction task. (5) **PURE** [39]: this work builds two independent encoders for NER and RE separately and performs entity relation extraction in a pipelined fashion. PURE experimentally validates the importance of learning different contextual representations for entities and relations separately. (6) **PFN** [32]: this work proposes a partition filter network to generate task-specific features and shared features of the two tasks, and then combining global features to extract entities and relations with table-filling framework.

Among these baselines, the two BiLSTM based methods build task interaction through parameter sharing, Multi-turn QA is a paradigm shift based method, PURE is a pipelined method, and Table-Sequence, SPE and PFN are methods based on multiple representations interaction.

4.5   Main Results

Table 2 reports the results of our approach MGE compared with other baselines on ACE05, ACE04 and SciERC. As is shown, MGE achieves the best results in terms of

F1 score against all the comparison baselines. For NER, MGE achieves similar performance to PURE [39] on ACE05 but surpasses PURE by an absolute entity F1 of +0.5%, +1.8% on ACE04 and SciERC. And for RE, our method obtains a substantially +2.6%, +3.6%, +3.8% absolute relation F1 improvement over PURE on ACE05, ACE04, and SciERC respectively. This demonstrates the superiority of the bidirectional task interaction in our model compared to the unidirectional interaction in PURE.

In comparison to the previous state-of-the-art model PFN [32], we can see that our method achieves a similar entity F1 to PFN on ACE04, but an absolute relation F1 improvement of +1.3%. This suggests that, given the same NER performance, our method can obtain a better RE performance, implying that the entity knowledge in our method more effectively leads the RE task. Furthermore, on ACE05, MGE surpasses PFN by an absolute F1 improvement of +0.7% and +1.4% in NER and RE, respectively. On SciERC, we get a 1.6% higher entity F1 and a 1.0% higher relation F1 compared to PFN. Note that we use the same pre-trained encoders and task modules as PFN, and these improvements demonstrate the effectiveness of our proposed multi-gate encoder.

4.6   Inference Speed

As described in Sect. 3.5, our method employs a non-autoregressive way for feature encoding, which is simpler and faster than the autoregressive approach in PFN. In order to experimentally compare the model efficiency, we conduct experiments to evaluate these two models' inference speed on the test set of ACE05 and SciERC datasets. We perform inference experiments on a single NVIDIA Titan V GPU with a batch size of 32.

Table 3. We compare our MGE model with PFN model in both relation F1 and inference speed. We use $scibert - scivocab - uncased$ for SciERC and $albert - xxlarge - v1/bert - base - cased$ for ACE05. † marks the inference speed on ACE05 when using $bert - base - cased$ encoder.

Model	SciERC		ACE05	
	RE (F1)	Speed (sent/s)	RE (F1)	Speed (sent/s)
PFN	38.4	342.2	66.8/60.8†	34.2/387.2†
MGE (Ours)	**39.4**	**479.2**	**68.2/62.0†**	**36.0/567.6†**

Table 3 shows the relation F1 scores and the inference speed of PFN and MGE. We use $scibert-scivocab-uncased$ encoder for SciERC and $albert-xxlarge-v1/bert-base - cased$ [7] encoder for ACE05. As is shown, with the same pre-trained model, our method obtains +1.0% improvement in relation F1 score with +40% speedup on the test set of SciERC. On ACE05, our model achieves a relation F1 improvement of +1.4% compared to PFN, but only slightly accelerates the inference speed (34.2 vs 36.0) when using $albert - xxlarge - v1$ pre-trained model. This is because $albert - xxlarge - v1$ contains 223M parameters, which is much larger than the 110M parameters in $scibert-$

$scivocab - uncased$ and $bert - base - cased$, and most of the computational cost of the model is concentrated in the pre-trained model part. As a result, the speedup provided by MGE does not appear to be significant. Therefore, we also evaluate the inference speed on ACE05 using $bert - base - cased$. As Table 3 shows, our model achieves +47% speedup and an absolute relation F1 improvement of +1.2% on ACE05 when using $bert - base - cased$. This clearly demonstrates that our proposed MGE can improve the performance of joint entity and relation extraction while accelerating the model inference speed.

5   Analysis

In this section, we conduct ablation study on ACE05, ACE04 and SciERC to investigate how each component of MGE affects the final performance, where we apply $albert - xxlarge - v1$ encoder for ACE05 and ACE04, $scibert - scivocab - uncased$ encoder for SciERC. Specifically, we ablate the task gate or interaction gate to verify their effectiveness.

Table 4. F1 scores of ablation study on ACE05, ACE04 and SciERC. B denotes BERT encoder. G_{e_task}, G_{r_task}, G_{e_inter} and G_{r_inter} means entity task gate, relation task gate, entity interaction gate and relation interaction gate.

Encoder					ACE05		ACE04		SciERC	
B	G_{e_task}	G_{r_task}	G_{e_inter}	G_{r_inter}	NER	RE	NER	RE	NER	RE
✓	✓	✓	✓	✓	89.7	**68.2**	**89.3**	**63.8**	68.4	**39.4**
✓	-	✓	✓	✓	89.7	67.4	88.8	62.2	68.2	37.5
✓	✓	-	✓	✓	89.9	67.8	88.8	62.6	68.0	39.1
✓	✓	✓	-	✓	89.4	67.4	89.1	63.0	**68.5**	38.9
✓	✓	✓	✓	-	**90.0**	66.6	89.2	63.6	68.2	38.7
✓	✓	✓	-	-	**90.0**	66.1	88.4	62.8	67.9	37.8

5.1   Effect of Task Gates

We remove task gates from the complete MGE structure to explore whether they can generate effective task-specific features. As shown in Table 4, when we remove the entity task gate, the entity F1 scores on the ACE04 and SciERC datasets decrease by 0.5% and 0.2%, respectively. And when we remove the relation task gate, the relation F1 scores on ACE05, ACE04 and SciERC datasets decrease by 0.4%, 1.2% and 0.3%, respectively. This indicates that task gates can effectively generate task-specific features to improve the performance of NER and RE.

5.2   Effect of Interaction Gates

We also investigate the effect of the MGE entity interaction gate and relation interaction gate on task interaction. As there is no entity interaction gate, it is similar to weakening the guidance of entity information on the relation extraction task when compared to the unaffected MGE model. After deleting the entity interaction gate, the relation F1 scores on the ACE05, ACE04, and SciERC datasets decrease by 0.8%, 0.8%, and 0.5%, respectively, as shown in Table 4. In MGE, this highlights the effectiveness of the entity interaction gate.

Although it is widely accepted that entity information is necessary for relation extraction, previous research on the impact of relation information on entity recognition has been mixed. Zhong and Chen et al. [39] claims that relation information has no significant improvement on entity model. However, Yan et al. [32] discover that relation signals have a significant impact on entity prediction. Our research also sheds light on this contentious issue. In MGE, the guidance of relation information on entity recognition is cut off when the relation interaction gate is ablate. The entity F1 scores decrease on ACE04 and SciERC but increase on ACE05 when the relation interaction gate is removed. Our experimental results match the experimental analysis of Yan et al. [32]. They conclude that relation information is helpful for predicting entities that appear in relational triples, but not for entities outside relational triples. According to Yan et al. [32], there are fewer entities belonging to relational triples in ACE05, compared with ACE04 and SciERC. Consequently, the relation information is comparatively less helpful for entity recognition in ACE05 but has a positive effect on entity recognition in ACE04 and SciERC. To sum up, the relation interaction gate can effectively generate interaction features to facilitate the recognition of entities within triples.

Moreover, when we remove both the entity interaction gate and the relation interaction gate, the relation F1 scores on ACE05, ACE04 and SciERC datasets decrease by 2.1%, 1.0% and 1.6%, respectively. This shows the effectiveness of interaction gates in MGE for task interaction in joint entity relation extraction.

5.3 Bidirectional Interaction vs Unidirectional Interaction

From Table 4, we also observe that employing only an entity interaction gate or only a relation interaction gate in the encoder performs worse than adopting these two gates simultaneously. This means that the two tasks of entity recognition and relation extraction are mutually reinforcing, and bidirectional interaction between NER and RE is more effective than unidirectional interaction.

6   Conclusion

In this paper, we propose a multi-gate encoder for joint entity and relation extraction. Our model adopts gate mechanism to build bidirectional task interaction while ensuring the specificity of task features by controlling the flow of feature information. Experimental results on three standard benchmarks show that our model achieves state-of-the-art F1 scores for both NER and RE. We conduct extensive analyses on three datasets to investigate the superiority of our model and validate the effectiveness of each component of our model. Furthermore, our ablation study suggests that relation information contributes to entity recognition, which helps to clarify the controversy on the effect of relation information.

Acknowledgements. This work was supported by the National Defense Science and Technology Key Laboratory Fund Project of the Chinese Academy of Sciences: Space Science and Application of Big Data Knowledge Graph Construction and Intelligent Application Research and Manned Space Engineering Project: Research on Technology and Method of Engineering Big Data Knowledge Mining.

References

1. Ba, J.L., Kiros, J.R., Hinton, G.E.: Layer normalization. arXiv preprint arXiv:1607.06450 (2016)
2. Bekoulis, G., Deleu, J., Demeester, T., Develder, C.: Adversarial training for multi-context joint entity and relation extraction. In: Proceedings of the 2018 Conference on Empirical Methods in Natural Language Processing, Brussels, Belgium, October-November 2018, pp. 2830–2836. Association for Computational Linguistics (2018). https://doi.org/10.18653/v1/D18-1307. https://aclanthology.org/D18-1307
3. Bekoulis, G., Deleu, J., Demeester, T., Develder, C.: Joint entity recognition and relation extraction as a multi-head selection problem. CoRR abs/1804.07847 (2018)
4. Beltagy, I., Lo, K., Cohan, A.: SciBERT: a pretrained language model for scientific text. In: Proceedings of the 2019 Conference on Empirical Methods in Natural Language Processing and the 9th International Joint Conference on Natural Language Processing (EMNLP-IJCNLP), Hong Kong, China, November 2019, pp. 3615–3620. Association for Computational Linguistics (2019). https://doi.org/10.18653/v1/D19-1371. https://aclanthology.org/D19-1371
5. Chan, Y.S., Roth, D.: Exploiting syntactico-semantic structures for relation extraction. In: Proceedings of the 49th Annual Meeting of the Association for Computational Linguistics: Human Language Technologies, Portland, Oregon, USA, June 2011, pp. 551–560. Association for Computational Linguistics (2011). https://aclanthology.org/P11-1056
6. Clevert, D.A., Unterthiner, T., Hochreiter, S.: Fast and accurate deep network learning by exponential linear units (ELUs). arXiv preprint arXiv:1511.07289 (2015)
7. Devlin, J., Chang, M.W., Lee, K., Toutanova, K.: BERT: pre-training of deep bidirectional transformers for language understanding. In: Proceedings of the 2019 Conference of the North American Chapter of the Association for Computational Linguistics: Human Language Technologies, vol. 1 (Long and Short Papers), Minneapolis, Minnesota, June 2019, pp. 4171–4186. Association for Computational Linguistics (2019). https://doi.org/10.18653/v1/N19-1423. https://aclanthology.org/N19-1423
8. Dixit, K., Al-Onaizan, Y.: Span-level model for relation extraction. In: Proceedings of the 57th Annual Meeting of the Association for Computational Linguistics, Florence, Italy, July 2019, pp. 5308–5314. Association for Computational Linguistics (2019). https://doi.org/10.18653/v1/P19-1525. https://aclanthology.org/P19-1525
9. Doddington, G., Mitchell, A., Przybocki, M., Ramshaw, L., Strassel, S., Weischedel, R.: The automatic content extraction (ACE) program - tasks, data, and evaluation. In: Proceedings of the Fourth International Conference on Language Resources and Evaluation (LREC 2004), Lisbon, Portugal, May 2004. European Language Resources Association (ELRA) (2004). https://www.lrec-conf.org/proceedings/lrec2004/pdf/5.pdf
10. Eberts, M., Ulges, A.: Span-based joint entity and relation extraction with transformer pre-training. In: ECAI 2020, pp. 2006–2013. IOS Press (2020)
11. Florian, R., Ittycheriah, A., Jing, H., Zhang, T.: Named entity recognition through classifier combination. In: Proceedings of the Seventh Conference on Natural Language Learning at HLT-NAACL 2003, pp. 168–171 (2003). https://aclanthology.org/W03-0425

12. Fu, T.J., Li, P.H., Ma, W.Y.: GraphRel: modeling text as relational graphs for joint entity and relation extraction. In: Proceedings of the 57th Annual Meeting of the Association for Computational Linguistics, Florence, Italy, July 2019, pp. 1409–1418. Association for Computational Linguistics (2019). https://doi.org/10.18653/v1/P19-1136. https://aclanthology.org/P19-1136

13. Gormley, M.R., Yu, M., Dredze, M.: Improved relation extraction with feature-rich compositional embedding models. In: Proceedings of the 2015 Conference on Empirical Methods in Natural Language Processing, Lisbon, Portugal, September 2015, pp. 1774–1784. Association for Computational Linguistics (2015). https://doi.org/10.18653/v1/D15-1205. https://aclanthology.org/D15-1205

14. Katiyar, A., Cardie, C.: Going out on a limb: joint extraction of entity mentions and relations without dependency trees. In: Proceedings of the 55th Annual Meeting of the Association for Computational Linguistics (Volume 1: Long Papers), Vancouver, Canada, July 2017, pp. 917–928. Association for Computational Linguistics (2017). https://doi.org/10.18653/v1/P17-1085. https://aclanthology.org/P17-1085

15. Lan, Z., Chen, M., Goodman, S., Gimpel, K., Sharma, P., Soricut, R.: ALBERT: a lite BERT for self-supervised learning of language representations. In: ICLR (2020)

16. Li, Q., Ji, H.: Incremental joint extraction of entity mentions and relations. In: Proceedings of the 52nd Annual Meeting of the Association for Computational Linguistics (Volume 1: Long Papers), Baltimore, Maryland, June 2014, pp. 402–412. Association for Computational Linguistics (2014). https://doi.org/10.3115/v1/P14-1038. https://aclanthology.org/P14-1038

17. Li, X., et al.: Entity-relation extraction as multi-turn question answering. In: Proceedings of the 57th Annual Meeting of the Association for Computational Linguistics. pp. 1340–1350. Association for Computational Linguistics (2019). https://doi.org/10.18653/v1/P19-1129. https://aclanthology.org/P19-1129

18. Lin, Y., Liu, Z., Sun, M., Liu, Y., Zhu, X.: Learning entity and relation embeddings for knowledge graph completion. In: Twenty-Ninth AAAI Conference on Artificial Intelligence (2015)

19. Luan, Y., He, L., Ostendorf, M., Hajishirzi, H.: Multi-task identification of entities, relations, and coreference for scientific knowledge graph construction. In: Proceedings of the 2018 Conference on Empirical Methods in Natural Language Processing, pp. 3219–3232. Association for Computational Linguistics (2018). https://doi.org/10.18653/v1/D18-1360. https://aclanthology.org/D18-1360

20. Luan, Y., Wadden, D., He, L., Shah, A., Ostendorf, M., Hajishirzi, H.: A general framework for information extraction using dynamic span graphs. In: Proceedings of the 2019 Conference of the North American Chapter of the Association for Computational Linguistics: Human Language Technologies, vol. 1 (Long and Short Papers), Minneapolis, Minnesota, June 2019, pp. 3036–3046. Association for Computational Linguistics (2019). https://doi.org/10.18653/v1/N19-1308. https://aclanthology.org/N19-1308

21. Luoma, J., Pyysalo, S.: Exploring cross-sentence contexts for named entity recognition with BERT. In: Proceedings of the 28th International Conference on Computational Linguistics, Barcelona, Spain, December 2020, pp. 904–914. International Committee on Computational Linguistics (2020). https://doi.org/10.18653/v1/2020.coling-main.78. https://aclanthology.org/2020.coling-main.78

22. Miwa, M., Bansal, M.: End-to-end relation extraction using LSTMs on sequences and tree structures. In: Proceedings of the 54th Annual Meeting of the Association for Computational Linguistics (Volume 1: Long Papers), Berlin, Germany, August 2016, pp. 1105–1116. Association for Computational Linguistics (2016). https://doi.org/10.18653/v1/P16-1105. https://aclanthology.org/P16-1105

23. Miwa, M., Sasaki, Y.: Modeling joint entity and relation extraction with table representation. In: Proceedings of the 2014 Conference on Empirical Methods in Natural Language Processing (EMNLP), Doha, Qatar, October 2014, pp. 1858–1869. Association for Computational Linguistics (2014). https://doi.org/10.3115/v1/D14-1200. https://aclanthology.org/D14-1200

24. Ren, F., et al.: A novel global feature-oriented relational triple extraction model based on table filling. In: Proceedings of the 2021 Conference on Empirical Methods in Natural Language Processing, Online and Punta Cana, Dominican Republic, November 2021, pp. 2646–2656. Association for Computational Linguistics (2021). https://doi.org/10.18653/v1/2021.emnlp-main.208. https://aclanthology.org/2021.emnlp-main.208

25. Seo, M., Kembhavi, A., Farhadi, A., Hajishirzi, H.: Bidirectional attention flow for machine comprehension, June 2018. https://arxiv.org/abs/1611.01603. Number: arXiv:1611.01603 [cs]

26. Walker, C., Strassel, S., Medero, J., Maeda, K.: ACE 2005 multilingual training corpus. Linguist. Data Consort. Philadelphia **57**, 45 (2006)

27. Wang, J., Lu, W.: Two are better than one: joint entity and relation extraction with table-sequence encoders. In: Proceedings of the 2020 Conference on Empirical Methods in Natural Language Processing (EMNLP), pp. 1706–1721. Association for Computational Linguistics, November 2020. https://doi.org/10.18653/v1/2020.emnlp-main.133. https://aclanthology.org/2020.emnlp-main.133

28. Wang, S., Zhang, Y., Che, W., Liu, T.: Joint extraction of entities and relations based on a novel graph scheme. In: Proceedings of the 27th International Joint Conference on Artificial Intelligence, IJCAI 2018, pp. 4461–4467. AAAI Press (2018)

29. Wang, Y., Sun, C., Wu, Y., Yan, J., Gao, P., Xie, G.: Pre-training entity relation encoder with intra-span and inter-span information. In: Proceedings of the 2020 Conference on Empirical Methods in Natural Language Processing (EMNLP), pp. 1692–1705. Association for Computational Linguistics, November 2020. https://doi.org/10.18653/v1/2020.emnlp-main.132. https://aclanthology.org/2020.emnlp-main.132

30. Wang, Y., Yu, B., Zhang, Y., Liu, T., Zhu, H., Sun, L.: TPLinker: single-stage joint extraction of entities and relations through token pair linking. In: Proceedings of the 28th International Conference on Computational Linguistics, Barcelona, Spain, December 2020, pp. 1572–1582. International Committee on Computational Linguistics (2020). https://doi.org/10.18653/v1/2020.coling-main.138. https://aclanthology.org/2020.coling-main.138

31. Xue, F., Sun, A., Zhang, H., Chng, E.S.: GDPNet: refining latent multi-view graph for relation extraction. In: Thirty-Fifth AAAI Conference on Artificial Intelligence, AAAI, pp. 2–9 (2021)

32. Yan, Z., Zhang, C., Fu, J., Zhang, Q., Wei, Z.: A partition filter network for joint entity and relation extraction. In: Proceedings of the 2021 Conference on Empirical Methods in Natural Language Processing, Punta Cana, Dominican Republic, November 2021, pp. 185–197. Association for Computational Linguistics (2021). https://doi.org/10.18653/v1/2021.emnlp-main.17. https://aclanthology.org/2021.emnlp-main.17

33. Ye, D., Lin, Y., Li, P., Sun, M.: Pack together: entity and relation extraction with levitated marker. In: Proceedings of ACL 2022 (2022)

34. Yu, X., Lam, W.: Jointly identifying entities and extracting relations in encyclopedia text via a graphical model approach. In: Coling 2010: Posters, Beijing, China, August 2010, pp. 1399–1407. Coling 2010 Organizing Committee (2010). https://aclanthology.org/C10-2160

35. Zelenko, D., Aone, C., Richardella, A.: Kernel methods for relation extraction. In: Proceedings of the 2002 Conference on Empirical Methods in Natural Language Processing (EMNLP 2002), pp. 71–78. Association for Computational Linguistics, July 2002. https://doi.org/10.3115/1118693.1118703. https://aclanthology.org/W02-1010

36. Zeng, X., Zeng, D., He, S., Liu, K., Zhao, J.: Extracting relational facts by an end-to-end neural model with copy mechanism. In: Proceedings of the 56th Annual Meeting of the Association for Computational Linguistics (Volume 1: Long Papers), Melbourne, Australia, July 2018, pp. 506–514. Association for Computational Linguistics (2018). https://doi.org/10.18653/v1/P18-1047. https://aclanthology.org/P18-1047
37. Zhang, M., Zhang, Y., Fu, G.: End-to-end neural relation extraction with global optimization. In: Proceedings of the 2017 Conference on Empirical Methods in Natural Language Processing, Copenhagen, Denmark, September 2017, pp. 1730–1740. Association for Computational Linguistics (2017). https://doi.org/10.18653/v1/D17-1182. https://aclanthology.org/D17-1182
38. Zheng, S., Wang, F., Bao, H., Hao, Y., Zhou, P., Xu, B.: Joint extraction of entities and relations based on a novel tagging scheme. In: Proceedings of the 55th Annual Meeting of the Association for Computational Linguistics (Volume 1: Long Papers), Vancouver, Canada, July 2017, pp. 1227–1236. Association for Computational Linguistics (2017). https://doi.org/10.18653/v1/P17-1113. https://aclanthology.org/P17-1113
39. Zhong, Z., Chen, D.: A frustratingly easy approach for entity and relation extraction. In: Proceedings of the 2021 Conference of the North American Chapter of the Association for Computational Linguistics: Human Language Technologies, pp. 50–61. Association for Computational Linguistics, June 2021. https://doi.org/10.18653/v1/2021.naacl-main.5. https://aclanthology.org/2021.naacl-main.5
40. Zhou, G., Su, J., Zhang, J., Zhang, M.: Exploring various knowledge in relation extraction. In: Proceedings of the 43rd Annual Meeting of the Association for Computational Linguistics (ACL 2005), Ann Arbor, Michigan, June 2005, pp. 427–434. Association for Computational Linguistics (2005). https://doi.org/10.3115/1219840.1219893. https://aclanthology.org/P05-1053

Improving Event Temporal Relation Classification via Auxiliary Label-Aware Contrastive Learning

Tiesen Sun and Lishuang Li[(✉)]

School of Computer Science and Technology, Dalian University of Technology, Dalian, China
`lils@dlut.edu.cn`

Abstract. Event Temporal Relation Classification (ETRC) is crucial to natural language understanding. In recent years, the mainstream ETRC methods may not take advantage of lots of semantic information contained in golden temporal relation labels, which is lost by the discrete one-hot labels. To alleviate the loss of semantic information, we propose learning Temporal semantic information of the golden labels by Auxiliary Contrastive Learning (TempACL). Different from traditional contrastive learning methods, which further train the PreTrained Language Model (PTLM) with unsupervised settings before fine-tuning on target tasks, we design a supervised contrastive learning framework and make three improvements. Firstly, we design a new data augmentation method that generates augmentation data via matching templates established by us with golden labels. Secondly, we propose patient contrastive learning and design three patient strategies. Thirdly we design a label-aware contrastive learning loss function. Extensive experimental results show that our TempACL effectively adapts contrastive learning to supervised learning tasks which remain a challenge in practice. TempACL achieves new state-of-the-art results on TB-Dense and MATRES and outperforms the baseline model with up to $5.37\% F_1$ on TB-Dense and $1.81\% F_1$ on MATRES.

Keywords: Temporal relation classification · Contrastive learning

1 Introduction

The temporal relations of events are used to describe the occurring sequence of events in an article. Therefore understanding the temporal relations of events in articles is useful for many downstream tasks such as timeline creation [12], generating stories [4], forecasting social events [10], and reading comprehension [15]. Hence, the ETRC task is an important and popular natural language understanding research topic among NLP community.

The ETRC task is to determine the occurrence sequence of a given event pair. The context of the event pair is usually given to aid judgment. Ning et al. [14] first encoded the event pairs into embedded representations and then used

M. Sun et al. (Eds.): CCL 2022, LNAI 13603, pp. 180–193, 2022.
https://doi.org/10.1007/978-3-031-18315-7_12

fully connected layers as a classifier to generate confidence scores for each category of temporal relations. All related works of the NLP community since then have followed the classification view: classifying the embedded representations. Naturally, we can encode the context and events into a better embedding space in which the different relations are distinguished well, to get better classification results.

Traditionally, all recent works use one-hot vectors to represent golden temporal relation labels in the training stage. However, the one-hot vector reduces the label with practical semantics to the zero-one vector. It makes the embedded representations extracted by the ETRC models waiting for classifying be the similarities of the instances with the same label. But, the similarities are not equal to the label semantics, and lead to arbitrary prediction and poor model generalization, especially for confused instances. In brief, the one-hot vectors which represent temporal relation categories lose much semantic information.

To cope with the loss of semantic information in golden labels, we propose to learn the lost semantic information by contrastive learning, which is well confirmed and most competitive method for learning representations under unsupervised settings, so that the ETRC model can obtain better event representations. However, effectively adapting contrastive learning to supervised learning tasks remains a challenge in practice. General methods such as [3], which continue to train the PTLM model using unsupervised contrastive learning on the input texts (without labels) from the target task before fine-tuning, apply contrastive learning to supervised representation learning mechanically. They discard the category information in the process of further training. In the supervised ETRC task, we want the event pair representations with the same category to be as close as possible without collapsing. But direct application of the unsupervised contrastive learning loss function would prevent them from getting closer, because it discard the category information. It's an inherent problem of self-supervised contrastive learning. So the standard contrastive learning is not natural for the supervised ETRC task. To solve this problem we designed label-aware contrastive learning loss and design a new contrastive learning framework. Additionally, we argue that we can do contrastive learning in the intermediate layers of the PTLM as same as the last layer simultaneously. In a cascade structure, a change in previous layers affects the subsequent layers and continuous positive changes will make the learning process easier. Hence, we propose patient contrastive learning and design three patient strategies.

Overall, we propose TempACL: Firstly, we manually construct templates based on the semantics of labels and get augmentation sentences by matching the labels of instances. Secondly, we train the encoder of key samples which are necessary for contrastive learning by the augmentation datasets established by the ETRC datasets and the augmentation sentences. Thirdly, we jointly train the ETRC model with cross entropy loss and label-aware contrastive learning loss using a patient contrastive learning strategy.

The main contributions of this paper can be summarized as follows:

1. We propose learning the lost semantic information in golden labels by contrastive learning, and then design TempACL, a supervised contrastive learning framework based on a new data augmentation method designed by us. To our knowledge, we are the first to propose using contrastive learning on the ETRC task.
2. In order to make our TempACL achieve better performance, we design label-aware contrastive learning loss and patient contrastive learning strategy.
3. We demonstrate the effectiveness of our TempACL on TB-Dense and MATRES datasets. Our TempACL outperforms the current best models with up to $2.13\% F_1$ on TB-Dense and $1.26\% F_1$ on MATRES and outperforms the baseline model with up to $5.37\% F_1$ on TB-Dense and $1.81\% F_1$ on MATRES.

2   Related Work

2.1   Event Temporal Relation Classification

Since the birth of pre-trained language models, researchers have mainly used them to encode event representations and design many new methods based on them. Wang et al. [19] propose a JCL method that makes the classification model learn their designed logical constraints within and across multiple temporal and subevent relations by converting these constraints into differentiable learning objectives. Zhou et al. [24] propose the CTRL-PG method, which leverages the Probabilistic Soft Logic rules to model the temporal dependencies as a regularization term to jointly learn a relation classification model. Han et al. [8] propose the ECONET system, which further trains the PTLM with a self-supervised learning strategy with mask prediction and a large-scale temporal relation corpus. Zhang et al. [23] propose the TGT network that integrates both traditional multi-head self-attention and a new temporal-oriented attention mechanism and utilizes a syntactic graph that can explicitly find the connection between two events. Tan et al. [18] propose the Poincaré Event Embeddings method which encodes events into hyperbolic spaces. They argue that the embeddings in the hyperbolic space can capture richer asymmetric temporal relations than the embeddings in the Euclidean space. And they also proposed the HGRU method which additionally uses an end-to-end architecture composed of hyperbolic neural units, and introduces common sense knowledge [14].

All of the above methods use the one-hot vector and lose the semantic information of the golden label. To take advantage of the missing semantic information, we make the target ETRC model learn from them via contrastive learning.

2.2   Contrastvie Learning

Contrastive learning aims to learn efficient representations by pulling semantically close neighbors together and pushing non-neighbors away [7]. In recent years, self-supervised contrastive learning and supervised contrastive learning have attracted more and more researchers to study them.

Self-supervised Contrastvie Learning. In computer vision (CV), We et al. [21] propose MemoryBank, which maintain a large number of representations of negative samples during training and update negative sample representations without increasing batch size. He et al. [9] propose MoCo, which designs the momentum contrast learning with two encoders and employs a queue to save the recently encoded batches as negative samples. Chen et al. [2] proposed the SimCLR which learns representations for visual inputs by maximizing agreement between differently augmented views of the same sample via a contrastive loss. Grill et al. [5] propose BYOL, which uses asymmetric two networks and discards negative sampling in self-supervised learning. In Natural Language Processing (NLP), Yan et al. [22] propose ConSERT, which has a similar model structure to SimCLR, except that ResNet is replaced by Bert and the mapping header is removed. And they also propose multiple data augmentation strategies for contrastive learning, including adversarial attack, token shuffling, cutoff and dropout.

Supervised Contrastvie Learning. Khosla et al. [11] extend the self-supervised contrastive approach to the fully-supervised setting in the CV domain, and take many positives per anchor in addition to many negatives (as opposed to self-supervised contrastive learning which uses only a single positive). Gunel et al. [6] extends supervised contrastive learning to the NLP domain with PTLMs.

Different from ConSERT we design a new data augmentation method based on templates in our contrastive learning framework. And different from Khosla's work, we design a new supervised contrastive loss which still uses only a single positive but does not treat the sentence representations with the same label as negative examples.

3   Our Baseline Model

Our baseline model is comprised of an encoder and a classifier. We use RoBERTa [13] as our encoder and use two fully connected layers and a tanh activation function between them as our classifier. Recently, most of the related works use RoBERTa as an encoder, because RoBERTa can achieve better results on the ETRC task than BERT in practice.

Each instance is composed of an event temporal triplet t (i.e. ($< e_1 >$, $< e_2 >, r$), where $< e_1 >$ and $< e_2 >$ are event mentions and r is the temporal relation of the event pair.) and the context s of the events which may be a single sentence or two sentences.

We first tokenize the context and get a sequence of tokens $X_{[0,n)}$ with length n. Then we feed the $X_{[0,n)}$ into RoBERTa. One event mention may correspond to multiple tokens, so we send the token embeddings corresponding to these tokens to an average pooling layer to get the final event representation e_i. Next, we combine e_1 and e_2 into a classification vector $e_1 \oplus e_2$, where $\oplus$ is used to denote concatenation. Finally, we feed the classification vector into the classifier

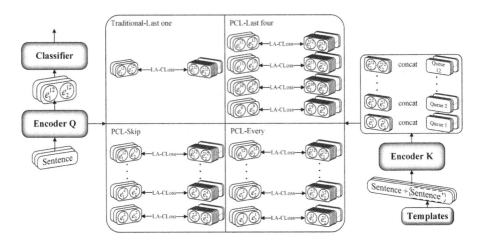

Fig. 1. Joint training with patient contrastive learning. We name the PLTM which encodes positive and negative key samples as Encoder K and the PLTM used for ETRC as Encoder Q.

followed by a soft-max function to get confidence scores for each category of temporal relations.

4   Self-supervised Contrastive Learning

Contrastive learning is learning by pulling similar instance pairs closer and pushing dissimilar instance pairs farther. The core of self-supervised contrastive learning is to generate augmented examples of original data examples, create a predictive task where the goal is to predict whether two augmented examples are from the same original data example or not, and learn the representation network by solving this task. He et al. [9] formulate contrastive learning as a dictionary look-up problem and propose an effective contrastive loss function L_{CL} with similarity measured by dot product:

$$L_{CL} = -\log \frac{\exp\left(q \cdot k^+ / \tau\right)}{\exp\left(q \cdot k^+ / \tau\right) + \sum_{\{K^-\}} \exp\left(q \cdot k^- / \tau\right)} \tag{1}$$

where q is a query representation, k^+ is a representation of the positive (similar) key sample, k^- are representations of the negative (dissimilar) key samples, K^- is a negative key samples set, and τ is a temperature hyper-parameter. He et al. [9] also propose maintaining the dictionary as a queue of data samples. It allows contrastive learning to reuse the previous batch of key samples so that we can increase the number of negative samples without increasing the batch size, thus improving the performance of the model. The dictionary size is a flexible hyper-parameter. The samples in the dictionary are progressively replaced. The current batch is enqueued to the dictionary, and the oldest batch in the queue

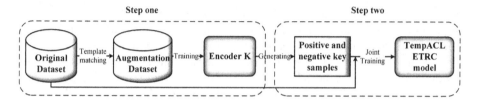

Fig. 2. Overall process of TempACL

Table 1. Templates. All the six temporal relation labels are in TB-Dense and * indicates the temporal relation label also exists in MATRES.

Temporal relation	Templates
AFTER*	the beginning of the event of $< e_1 >$ is after the end of the event of $< e_2 >$
BEFORE*	the end of the event of $< e_1 >$ is before the beginning of the event of $< e_2 >$
INCLUDES	the beginning of the event of $< e_1 >$ is before the beginning of the event of $< e_2 >$ and the end of event of $< e_1 >$ is after the end of the event of $< e_2 >$
IS_INCLUDED	the beginning of the event of $< e_1 >$ is after the beginning of the event of $< e_2 >$ and the end of event of $< e_1 >$ is before the end of the event of $< e_2 >$
VAGUE*	the temporal relation between the event of $< e_1 >$ and the event of $< e_2 >$ is vague
SIMULTANEOUS*	the event of $< e_1 >$ and the event of $< e_2 >$ have the same beginning and end time

is removed. In this paper, we follow this part of their work and transfer it to the supervised ETRC task.

5   TempACL Approach

In this section, we introduce our TempACL approach in details and draw the overall process of TempACL in Fig. 2. TempACL aims to encoder semantic information of golden temporal relation labels and uses contrastive learning to make the baseline model extract better event representations. Hence, we first train Encoder K used for encoding semantic information of golden temporal relation labels, and then jointly train the baseline model with auxiliary contrastive learning via the label-aware contrastive learning loss function and a patient strategy. Specially, we fix the parameters of the Encoder K in the joint training stage.

5.1   Training Encoder K

First of all, we need to establish templates. In order to make the positive key samples encoded by Encoder K contain as much and as detailed semantic information of golden temporal relation labels as possible, we need to create efficient templates that automatically convert each golden temporal relation label into a temporal information-enriched sentence s' to enrich the semantic information of golden temporal relation labels. We argue that the time span of events (i.e., the duration of the events) guides ETRC. So we use the start and end times of events and the temporal relation between events to describe the temporal relation of the event pair on a subtle level. We show the templates in Table 1.

Subsequently, we build the augmentation dataset. For each record (t, s) in original Dataset, we use r to match the templates and get s' by filling events into the corresponding positions in the template, then concatenate s and s' to get an augmentation sentence $s_{aug} = s + s'$, finally get a new record (t, s_{aug}). We combine all new records into an augmentation dataset.

Finally, we use the augmentation dataset to train the Encoder K with the help of the classifier which we propose in Sect. 3 under supervised setting. Encoder K is a RoBERTa model.

5.2   Joint Training with Patient Label-Aware Contrastive Loss

The trained Encoder K has been obtained, we can start joint training in Fig. 1. We send s in the original dataset to Encoder Q, and then get event pair representations $\{e_{1j} \oplus e_{2j}\}_{j=1}^{12}$ in different layers of Encoder Q. e_{ij} is the hidden state corresponding to the event i from the j-th RoBERTa Layer. We simultaneously send s_{aug} in the augmentation dataset to Encoder K, and then get event pair representations $\{\hat{e}_{1j} \oplus \hat{e}_{2j}\}_{j=1}^{12}$ in different layers of Encoder K. $\hat{e}_{ij}$ is the hidden state corresponding to the event i from the j-th RoBERTa Layer, and $\hat{}$ is used to denote the hidden state from the Encoder K. We normalized $e_{1j} \oplus e_{2j}$ as the query q and $\hat{e}_{1j} \oplus \hat{e}_{2j}$ as key k with L2 Norm. According to different patient strategies, queries and keys of different layers were selected for comparative learning.

We should not mechanically apply the loss function of self-supervised contrastive learning in Eq. 1 to the supervised ETRC directly. In the supervised ETRC task, we want the event pair representations with the same category to be as close as possible without collapsing. But L_{CL} treat the key samples in the queue, whose event pair have the same temporal relation with the event pair of the query sample, as negative key samples. Therefore, in the process of minimizing the L_{CL}, the event pair representations with the same category are mutually exclusive, which confuse the ETRC model. So we propose label-aware contrastive loss function L_{LACL}:

$$L_{LACL} = -\sum_{i=1}^{N} \left(\log \frac{\exp\left(q \cdot k^+/\tau\right)}{\exp\left(q \cdot k^+/\tau\right) + \sum_{\{K'^-\}} \exp\left(q \cdot k'^-/\tau\right)} \right)_i \quad (2)$$

where $\bar{K}^-$ is negative key samples set which except the key samples with the same label as q, and N is the number of training samples. In practice, we convert $q \cdot k$ where $k \in \{k : k \in K^-, k \notin K'^-\}$ to -10^6 by matrix operations.

Inspired by Sun et al. [17], we argue that using the event pair representations of the intermediate layers of the Encoder Q and the event pair representations of the intermediate layers of the Encoder Q for additional contrastive learning can enhance the learning of semantics of the Encoder Q, and improve the performance of the baseline model. Hence we propose patient label-aware contrastive learning loss L_{PCL} based on Eq. 2:

$$L_{PCL} = -\sum_{j \in J} \sum_{i=1}^{N} \frac{1}{\|J\|} \left(\log \frac{\exp\left(q \cdot k^+/\tau\right)}{\exp\left(q \cdot k^+/\tau\right) + \sum_{\{K'^-\}} \exp\left(q \cdot k'^-/\tau\right)} \right)_{i,j} \quad (3)$$

where J is the set of intermediate layers involved in contrastive learning. Specifically, we propose three patient contrastive learning strategies: (1) PCL-Last four: we contrast the last four layers of the Encoder Q and Encoder K (Fig. 1 upper right). (2) PCL-Skip: we contrast every two layers of the Encoder Q and Encoder K (Fig. 1 lower left). (3) PCL-Every: we contrast every layers of the Encoder Q and Encoder K (Fig. 1 lower right).

Finally, we jointly train ETRC task and auxiliary label-aware contrastive learning task with the final loss function L_{final}:

$$L_{finall} = \alpha L_{CE} + \beta L_{PCL} \quad (4)$$

where L_{CE} is cross-entropy loss function, α and β are hyper-parameters which weight the importances of ETRC task and auxiliary label-aware contrastive learning task.

6 Experiments and Results

In this section, we perform experiments on TB-Dense and MATERS and prove our TempACL performs better than previous state-of-the-art methods. Details on the datasets, experimental setup, and experimental results are provided in the following subsections.

TB-Dense TB-Dense [1] is a densely annotated dataset for the ETRC and annotated based on TimeBank. It also annotates the temporal relations of pairs of events across sentences, different from TimeBank which only annotates events in the same sentence. It annotates a total of 6 temporal relations (AFTER, BEFORE, INCLUDE, IS INCLUDED, VAGUE, SIMULTANEOUS). We follow the split strategy of Han et al. [8] and Zhange et al. [23] which uses 22 documents as train set, 5 documents as dev set and 9 documents as test set.

MATERS MATERS [16] is refined from 275 documents in TimeBank and TempEval (containing AQUAINT and Platinum). Ning et al. [16] design a novel multi-axis (i.e., main, intention, opinion and hypothetical axes) annotation scheme to further annotate the 275 documents. There are only 4 temporal

Table 2. Data statistics for TB-Dense and MATRES

	TB-Dense		MATRES	
	Documents	Triplets	Documents	Triplets
Train	22	4032	204	10097
Dev	5	629	51	2643
Test	9	1427	20	837

relations (BEFORE, AFTER, EQUAL and VAGUE) different from TB-Dense and the EQUAL is the same as SIMULTANEOUS. We follow the official split strategy that uses TimeBank and AQUAINT for training and Platinum for testing. We also follow the previous works [14,18] that randomly select 20 percents of the official train documents as dev set.

We briefly summarize the data statistics for TB-Dense and MATRES in Table 2.

6.1 Dataset

6.2 Experimental Setup

In the process of training Encoder K, we add a dropout layer between the Encoder K and the Classifier and set the drop probability to 0.5, in order to make the key samples contain more useful temporal information. We train Encoder K 10 and 20 epochs respectively on TB-Dense and MATRES. We set the batch size to 24, the τ to 0.1, the learning rate of the Classifier to 5e−4 and the learning rate of RoBERTa to 5e−6. We use grid search strategy to select the best $\alpha \in [0.7: 1.4]$ and $\beta \in [0.01: 0.001]$. As for the dimension of the hidden states between two fully connected layers in the Classifier, we set it to 36. We set the size of the queue to 3840 and 9600 respectively on TB-Dense and MATRES.

6.3 Main Results

As shown in Table 3, we compare our approach with other state-of-the-art methods in recent years on TB-Dense and MATRES. We report the best F_1 value for each method. The compared methods have been introduced in Sect. 2. And the results of compared methods are directly taken from the cited papers except CERT[1]. We reproduce CERT and record the results.

We observe that our baseline model achieves $63.56\%F_1$ on TB-Dense and $79.95\%F_1$ on MATRES. It demonstrates that our baseline model can effectively classify temporal relation, and even achieves a competitive performance that is close to the current best $80.5\%F_1$ on MATRES. Furthermore, our TempACL outperforms previous state-of-the-art methods on ETRC with up to $2.13\%F_1$ on TB-Dense and $1.26\%F_1$ on MATRES. Compared with CERT, the traditional

---

[1] https://github.com/UCSD-AI4H/CERT.

Table 3. Comparison of various approaches on ETRC on TB-Dense and MATRES. Bold denotes the best performing model. F_1-score (%)

Method		TB-Dense	MATRES
JCL [19]	RoBERTa base	-	78.8
ECONET [8]	RoBERTa Large	66.8	79.3
TGT [23]	BERT Large	66.7	80.3
Poincaré event embeddings [18]	RoBERTa base	–	78.9
HGRU+knowledge [18]	RoBERTa base	–	80.5
CERT [3]	RoBERTa base	64.92	80.46
Baseline (ours)	RoBERTa base	63.56	79.95
TempACL (ours)	RoBERTa base	**68.93**	**81.76**

self-supervised contrastive learning method, our TempACL achieves $4.01\%F_1$ and $1.30\%F_1$ improvement respectively. These experimental results prove the effectiveness of learning semantic information of golden temporal relation labels via patient label-aware contrastive learning. There are three possible reasons for the effectiveness: (1) The difference between the query representation and the key representation comes from the semantic information of the golden temporal relation label, because the input of Encoder Q doesn't have the label information but the input of Encoder K input does. The L_{LACL} forces q closer to K to reduce the difference. So that in the process of minimizing L_{LACL} Encoder Q learns the label semantic information and forces itself to extract more useful information related to golden temporal relation labels from the sentences that do not contain any golden temporal relation label information. (2) The supervised contrastive learning framework and L_{LACL} designed by us is more suitable for the ETRC task than the traditional self-supervised contrastive learning method. (3) The data augmentation method proposed by us not only utilizes the semantic information of labels but also enriches the semantic information of labels.

Different from JCL and HGRU, which use external commonsense knowledge to enrich the information contained in event representations, TempACL enables the model to better mine the information contained in original sentences. Compared to ECONET and TGT, which use a larger pre-trained language model, or TGT and HGRU, which use networks with complex structures followed RoBERTa base or BERT Large, TempACL enables a smaller and simpler model which only contains a RoBERTa base and two fully connected layers to achieve the state-of-the-art performance.

6.4 Ablation Study and Qualitative Analysis

We observe that, TempACL make improvements of $5.37\%F_1$ and $1.81\%F_1$ on TB-Dense and MATRES respectively compared with the baseline model. In this section, we first qualitatively analyze key samples, and then we do the ablation experiments to further study the effects of patient strategies and label-aware

Table 4. Results of TempACL with different strategies. F_1-score (%)

Method	TB-Dense	MATRES
Traditional-last one	66.17	80.95
PCL-Last four	68.93	81.76
PCL-Skip	67.73	80.46
PCL-Every	65.23	80.37

Table 5. Results of TempACL with different contrastive learning loss. F_1-score (%)

Method	TB-Dense	MATRES
TempACL-LACL	68.93	81.76
TempACL-TCL	66.03	80.89
Baseline	63.56	79.95

contrastive learning loss. We ensure that all ablation results are optimal by using optimal strategies under the given conditions.

Qualitative Analysis. Wang et al. [20] propose to justify the effectiveness of contrastive learning in terms of simultaneously achieving both alignment and uniformity. Hence we reduce the dimension of key samples in each layer through PCA and represent it in Fig. 3 on TB-Dense. All four contrastive strategies we used to utilize the key samples of the last layer, so we take Fig. 3(l) to analyze the alignment and uniformity of TempACL. On the one hand, we can see that there are 6 clusters of representations that are well-differentiated even in two dimensions. Our method maps key samples with the same category to a relatively dense region. These well demonstrate that our embedded knowledge has a strong alignment. On the other hand, we also can see that the 5 clusters, which represent temporal categories in Fig. 3(l) right, are farther from the VAGUE cluster than each other. It means that our embedded knowledge retains as much category information as possible. The farther away different clusters are, the more category information and differences are retained. Moreover, different key samples with the same category distribute evenly within the dense region, which means that our key samples retain as much instance information as possible. Furthermore, the more evenly distributed they are, the more information they retain. These well demonstrate that our embedded knowledge has a strong uniformity. We find that the key samples encoded by the last four layers of the Encoder K have strong alignment and uniformity.

Last One Strategy vs Patient Strategy. In Sect. 5.2 we propose three patient strategies. In this section, we do experiments to study which strategy is optimal and report the experimental results in Table 4. PCL-Last four achieves the best results on both TB-Dense and MATRES. On the one hand, PCL-Last

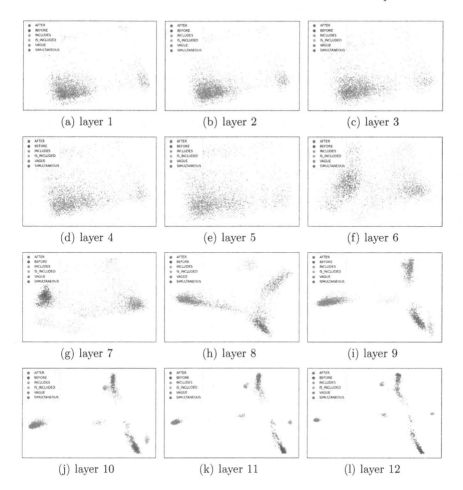

Fig. 3. The distributions of key samples of each RoBERTa layers on TB-Dense.

four provides more positive and negative samples. In Fig. 3, the distribution of key samples in the last four layers also indicates that these positive and negative samples have great value in learning. On the other hand, this layer-by-layer approach greatly reduces the difficulty of learning. In the PTLM, different sublayers are cascade, and the changes in the output in the front layers influence the latter layers. PCL-every performs poorly and worse than Traditional-Last one, because the first eight layers do not provide good positive and negative key samples, and learning them confuses the model. However PCL-Skip performs better than Traditional-Last one. This is because the number of bad key samples in PCL-Skip is relatively small, which makes the negative impact of these bad key samples much smaller. The layer-by-layer approach reduces the difficulty of learning and the benefits outweigh the negative impact.

Label-Aware Contrastive Loss vs Traditional Contrastive Loss. In order to determine whether our proposed label-aware contrastive loss has a positive effect, we conduct a comparative experiment and record the experimental results in Table 5. We compare the TempACL with label-aware contrastive learning loss (TempACL-LACL) and the TempACL with traditional contrastive learning loss (TempACL-TCL) on TB-Dense and MATRES respectively. We can see that the TempACL-LACL achieves $2.90\%F_1$ and $0.87\%F_1$ performance improvement over the TempACL-TCL respectively. It shows the benefit of eliminating key samples with the same label as the query from the negative samples set. The reason is that using key samples, which have the same label as the query, as negative samples prevent instances of the same label from learning similar event representations to some extent, which runs counter to the ETRC's aims. And the label-aware contrastive learning loss can avoid such a situation.

7   Conclusion

In recent years, the mainstream ETRC methods focus on using discrete values to represent temporal relation categories and lose too much semantic information contained in golden labels. So we propose TempACL, which makes the ETRC model learn the lost semantic information in golden labels via contrastive learning. Extensive experiments prove the contrastive learning framework in TempACL is more suitable for the supervised ETRC task than traditional self-supervised contrastive learning. The patient contrastive learning strategy designed by us provides more useful positive and negative key samples and reduces the difficulty of contrastive learning. The label-aware contrastive learning loss designed by us avoids the negative interactions between different queries and keys in the same category, which is an inherent problem of self-supervised contrastive learning.

Acknowledgments. This work is supported by grant from the National Natural Science Foundation of China (No. 62076048), the Science and Technology Innovation Foundation of Dalian (2020JJ26GX035).

References

1. Cassidy, T., McDowell, B., Chambers, N., Bethard, S.: An annotation framework for dense event ordering. In: ACL (Volume 2: Short Papers), pp. 501–506 (2014)
2. Chen, T., Kornblith, S., Norouzi, M., Hinton, G.: A simple framework for contrastive learning of visual representations. In: International conference on machine learning, pp. 1597–1607. PMLR (2020)
3. Fang, H., Wang, S., Zhou, M., Ding, J., Xie, P.: Cert: contrastive self-supervised learning for language understanding. arXiv e-prints pp. arXiv-2005 (2020)
4. Goldfarb-Tarrant, S., Chakrabarty, T., Weischedel, R., Peng, N.: Content planning for neural story generation with aristotelian rescoring. In: EMNLP, pp. 4319–4338 (2020)

5. Grill, J.B., et al.: Bootstrap your own latent - a new approach to self-supervised learning. In: Advances in Neural Information Processing Systems, vol. 33, pp. 21271–21284 (2020)

6. Gunel, B., Du, J., Conneau, A., Stoyanov, V.: Supervised contrastive learning for pre-trained language model fine-tuning. arXiv preprint arXiv:2011.01403 (2020)

7. Hadsell, R., Chopra, S., LeCun, Y.: Dimensionality reduction by learning an invariant mapping. In: 2006 IEEE Computer Society Conference on Computer Vision and Pattern Recognition (CVPR 2006), vol. 2, pp. 1735–1742 (2006)

8. Han, R., Ren, X., Peng, N.: ECONET: effective continual pretraining of language models for event temporal reasoning. In: EMNLP, pp. 5367–5380 (2021)

9. He, K., Fan, H., Wu, Y., Xie, S., Girshick, R.: Momentum contrast for unsupervised visual representation learning. In: 2020 IEEE/CVF Conference on Computer Vision and Pattern Recognition (CVPR), pp. 9726–9735. IEEE (2020)

10. Jin, W., et al.: Forecastqa: a question answering challenge for event forecasting with temporal text data, pp. 4636–4650 (2021)

11. Khosla, P., et al.: Supervised contrastive learning. Adv. Neural. Inf. Process. Syst. **33**, 18661–18673 (2020)

12. Leeuwenberg, A., Moens, M.F.: Temporal information extraction by predicting relative time-lines. In: Proceedings of the 2018 Conference on Empirical Methods in Natural Language Processing (2018)

13. Liu, Y., et al: A robustly optimized BERT pretraining approach. arXiv preprint arXiv:1907.11692 (2019)

14. Ning, Q., Subramanian, S., Roth, D.: An improved neural baseline for temporal relation extraction. In: EMNLP-IJCNLP, pp. 6203–6209 (2019)

15. Ning, Q., Wu, H., Han, R., Peng, N., Gardner, M., Roth, D.: TORQUE: a reading comprehension dataset of temporal ordering questions. In: EMNLP, pp. 1158–1172 (2020)

16. Ning, Q., Wu, H., Roth, D.: A multi-axis annotation scheme for event temporal relations. In: ACL (Volume 1: Long Papers), pp. 1318–1328 (2018)

17. Sun, S., Cheng, Y., Gan, Z., Liu, J.: Patient knowledge distillation for BERT model compression. In: EMNLP-IJCNLP, pp. 4323–4332 (2019)

18. Tan, X., Pergola, G., He, Y.: Extracting event temporal relations via hyperbolic geometry. In: EMNLP, pp. 8065–8077 (2021)

19. Wang, H., Chen, M., Zhang, H., Roth, D.: Joint constrained learning for event-event relation extraction. In: EMNLP, pp. 696–706 (2020)

20. Wang, T., Isola, P.: Understanding contrastive representation learning through alignment and uniformity on the hypersphere. In: International Conference on Machine Learning, pp. 9929–9939. PMLR (2020)

21. Wu, Z., Xiong, Y., Yu, S., Lin, D.: Unsupervised feature learning via non-parametric instance-level discrimination. arXiv preprint arXiv:1805.01978 (2018)

22. Yan, Y., Li, R., Wang, S., Zhang, F., Wu, W., Xu, W.: Consert: a contrastive framework for self-supervised sentence representation transfer. arXiv e-prints pp. arXiv-2105 (2021)

23. Zhang, S., Huang, L., Ning, Q.: Extracting temporal event relation with syntactic-guided temporal graph transformer. arXiv preprint arXiv:2104.09570 (2021)

24. Zhou, Y.,et al.: Clinical temporal relation extraction with probabilistic soft logic regularization and global inference. In: AAAI, vol. 35, pp. 14647–14655 (2021)

Machine Translation and Multilingual
Information Processing

Towards Making the Most of Pre-trained Translation Model for Quality Estimation

Chunyou Li[1], Hui Di[2], Hui Huang[1], Kazushige Ouchi[2], Yufeng Chen[1], Jian Liu[1], and Jinan Xu[1(✉)]

[1] Beijing Key Lab of Traffic Data Analysis and Mining, Beijing Jiaotong University, Beijing 100044, China
{21120368,chenyf,jianliu,jaxu}@bjtu.edu.cn
[2] Toshiba (China) Co., Ltd., Beijing, China
dihui@toshiba.com.cn, kazushige.ouchi@toshiba.co.jp

Abstract. Machine translation quality estimation (QE) aims to evaluate the quality of machine translation automatically without relying on any reference. One common practice is applying the translation model as a feature extractor. However, there exist several discrepancies between the translation model and the QE model. The translation model is trained in an autoregressive manner, while the QE model is performed in a non-autoregressive manner. Besides, the translation model only learns to model human-crafted parallel data, while the QE model needs to model machine-translated noisy data. In order to bridge these discrepancies, we propose two strategies to post-train the translation model, namely Conditional Masked Language Modeling (CMLM) and Denoising Restoration (DR). Specifically, CMLM learns to predict masked tokens at the target side conditioned on the source sentence. DR firstly introduces noise to the target side of parallel data, and the model is trained to detect and recover the introduced noise. Both strategies can adapt the pre-trained translation model to the QE-style prediction task. Experimental results show that our model achieves impressive results, significantly outperforming the baseline model, verifying the effectiveness of our proposed methods.

Keywords: Quality estimation · Machine translation · Denoising restoration

1 Introduction

Machine translation has always been the hotspot and focus of research. Compared with traditional methods, neural machine translation (NMT) has achieved great success. However, current translation systems are still not perfect to meet the real-world applications without human post-editing. Therefore, to carry out risk assessment and quality control for machine translation, how to evaluate the quality of machine translation is also an important problem.

© The Author(s), under exclusive license to Springer Nature Switzerland AG 2022
M. Sun et al. (Eds.): CCL 2022, LNAI 13603, pp. 197–211, 2022.
https://doi.org/10.1007/978-3-031-18315-7_13

Quality Estimation (QE) aims to predict the quality of machine translation automatically without relying on reference. Compared with commonly used machine translation metrics such as BLEU [18] and METEOR [13], QE can be applicable to the case where reference translations are unavailable. It has a wide range of applications in post-editing and quality control for machine translation. The biggest challenge for QE is data scarcity. Since QE data is often limited in size, it is natural to transfer bilingual knowledge from parallel data to the QE task.

One well-known framework for this knowledge transfer is the predictor-estimator framework, in which the predictor is trained on large parallel data and used to extract features, and the estimator will make quality estimation based on features provided by the predictor. The predictor is usually a machine translation model, which can hopefully capture the alignment or semantic information of the source and the target in a pair. Kim et al. [11] first proposed to use an RNN-based machine translation model as the feature extractor, to leverage massive parallel data to alleviate the sparsity of annotated QE data. Wang et al. [23] employed a pre-trained translation model as the predictor and added pseudo-PE information to predict translation quality.

However, there are two discrepancies between machine translation and quality prediction, which impedes the NMT model to be directly adopted for feature extraction. i) Translation task is usually a language generation task trained in an autoregressive manner, where each token is only conditioned on previous tokens unidirectionally. But QE is a language understanding task performed in a non-autoregressive manner, therefore each token could attend to the whole context bidirectionally. ii) The predictor is trained on human-crafted parallel data and only learns to model the alignment between correct translation pairs. However, the QE task needs to model machine-translated, imperfect translation pairs. Both discrepancies may hinder the adaptation of the pre-trained NMT model to the downstream QE task, leading a degradation of model performance [25].

In this paper, we propose two strategies to alleviate the discrepancies, named as Conditional Mask Language Modeling (CMLM) and Denoising Restoration (DR). Both strategies are applied to the pre-trained NMT model and can be deemed as a post-training phase. The CMLM is to train the NMT model to recover the masked tokens at the target side in a non-autoregressive manner, where each token can attend to the whole target sequence bidirectionally. Furthermore, the DR first generates erroneous translation by performing conditionally masked language modeling, and then trains the NMT model to detect the introduced noise and recover the target sequence, which is also performed in a non-autoregressive manner. Both methods can adapt the autoregressive NMT model to non-autoregressive QE prediction. Moreover, compared with CMLM, DR removes the introduction of [MASK] token (which may also cause the discrepancy between pre-training and QE prediction). Besides, adversarially using another model with knowledge distillation to generate noise could provide more natural and harder training samples, thereby pushing the translation model better model the semantic alignment between the imperfect translation and source sequence. After the post-training phase, the NMT model is better adapted to the quality prediction task, and can serve as a better feature extractor.

Our contributions can be summarized as follows:

- We propose two strategies for post-training the NMT model to bridge the gaps between machine translation and quality estimation, which can make the NMT model more suitable to act as the feature extractor for the QE task.
- We conduct experiments on the WMT21 QE tasks for En-Zh and En-De directions, and our methods outperform the baseline model by a large margin, proving its effectiveness. We also perform in-depth analysis to dig into the discrepancies between translation and quality prediction.

2 Background

2.1 Task Description

Quality Estimation aims to predict the translation quality of an MT system without relying on any reference. In this task, the dataset is expressed in the format of triplet (s, m, q), where s represents the source sentence, m is the translation output from a machine translation system, and q is the quality score of machine translation.

Generally, Quality Estimation task includes both word-level and sentence-level tasks. In word-level task, the prediction is done both on source side (to detect which words caused errors) and target side (to detect mistranslated or missing words). In sentence-level task, it will mark each sentence with a score, which can be calculated based on different standards, consists of Human-targeted Translation Edit Rate (HTER) [21], Direct Assessment (DA) [8], Multidimensional Quality Metrics (MQM) [15], etc. In this work, we mainly focus on sentence level post-editing effort prediction, which is measured by:

$$HTER = (I + D + R)/L, \tag{1}$$

where I, D and R are the number of Insertions, Deletions and Replacement operations required for post-editing, and L is the reference length. However, labeling the data requires post-editing for the machine translations by experts, leading the label of QE data too expensive to obtain, which makes QE highly data-sparse.

2.2 Previous Work

Generally, sentence-level QE is fomulated as a regression task. Early approaches were based on features fed into a traditional machine learning method, such as QuEst++ [22] and MARMOT [14] system. These model usually has two modules: the feature extraction module and the classification module. But they relied on heuristic artificial feature designing, which limits their development and application [10]. With the increasing popularity of deep learning methods, researchers resort to distributed representations and recurrent networks to encode translation pairs. However, the limited size of training samples impedes the learning of deep networks [16]. To solve this problem, a lot of research has been done to use additional resource (both bilingual and monolingual) to strengthen the representation [11]. After the emergence of BERT [5], some work attempts to use the pre-trained language model as a predictor directly and add a simple linear on top of the model to obtain the predictions [1,2], which has led to significant improvements.

Among all the deep learning-based methods, one commonly used framework for QE is the predictor-estimator framework, where the predictor is used as a feature extractor and the estimator uses the features to make predictions. The predictor is usually a translation model, which can alleviate the problem of data sparsity by transferring bilingual knowledge from parallel data. Kim et al. [11] firstly proposed the predictor-estimator framework to leverage massive parallel data to improve QE results, they applied an RNN-based machine translation model as the predictor and added a bidirectional RNN as estimator to predict QE scores, which achieved excellent performance especially in sentence-level QE. Fan et al. [6] used Transformer-based NMT model as the predictor to extract high-quality features, and used 4-dimensional mis-matching features from this model to improve performance. Wang et al. [24] pre-trained left-to-right and right-to-left deep Transformer models as the predictor and introduced a multi-layer bidirectional Gated Recurrent Unit (Bi-GRU) as the estimator to make prediction. Wu et al. [26] reformed Transformer-based predictor-estimator by using multidecoding during the machine translation module, then implemented LSTM-based and Transformer-based estimator with top-K and multi-head attention strategy to enhance the sentence feature representation. Wang et al. [23] employed a pre-trained translation model as the predictor and added pseudo-PE information to predict translation quality, which obtained the best result in the English-German direction of WMT20. However, despite various of improvement has been made on the predictor-estimator framework, the discrepancy problem between machine translation and quality estimation is not systematically investigated.

3   Approach

In this section, we first describe the NMT-based QE architecture, and then describe our proposed post-training strategies.

3.1   QE Architecture

The QE architecture is shown in Fig. 1. Our work follows the predictor-estimator framework. The predictor is a translation model trained with the transformer architecture on parallel data, which has learned the feature extraction ability of

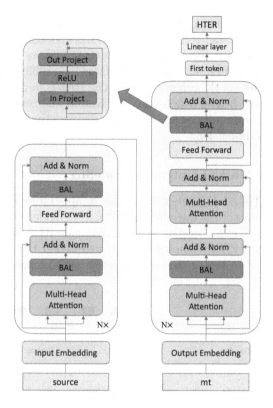

Fig. 1. The illustration of the QE model. The *source* and *mt* sentence are fed into encoder and decoder respectively. The BAL is integrated after the self-attention layer and the FFN layer, respectively. In order to better adapt to QE task, the causal mask in decoder is removed.

bilingual inputs after a long-term and large-scale pre-training. Therefore, adding only a linear layer on the top of translation model and fine-tuning with a small amount of QE data can achieve promising results.

As shown in Fig. 1, the final hidden vector of the neural machine translation model corresponding to the first input token is fed into a simple linear layer to make quality prediction, which is given by:

$$HTER_{pred} = W_s^T h^{(0)} + b_0, \tag{2}$$

where $h^{(0)} \in \mathbb{R}^H$ is the hidden vector of the first input token, $W_s \in \mathbb{R}^H$ represents a weight matrix, H is the dimension of hidden states, $b_0 \in \mathbb{R}^1$ is the bias. The loss function is the mean squared error between $HTER_{pred}$ and $HTER_{true}$, which can be written as:

$$L_{QE} = MSE(HTER_{pred}, HTER_{true}) \tag{3}$$

Since the size of training dataset is relatively small, the model is easy to be over-fitted when all parameters are updated. Incorporating the insights from Wang et al. [23], the Bottleneck Adapter Layers (BAL) [9] are integrated into the neural machine translation model, which alleviates the problem of overfitting by freezing the parameters of the original model. The BAL is implemented with two simple fully-connected layers, a non-linear activation and residual connections, where the hidden representations are first expanded two times and then reduced back to the original dimension.

3.2 Conditional Masked Language Modeling

The Conditional Masked Language Modeling is illustrated in Fig. 2. Despite using the same architecture as the machine translation model, the CMLM utilizes a mask language modeling objective at the target side [7]. The source sentence is sent to the encoder, while some tokens are corrupted at the target side. Then the CMLM is trained to recover the corrupted target sentence.

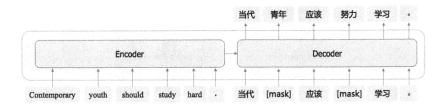

Fig. 2. The illustration of the CMLM. At the target side, some tokens are replaced with [mask] symbol or random token. Note that it also needs to remove the casual mask in decoder.

In terms of implementation, given a parallel sentence pair $<x, y>$, we generate a corrupted sentence y' with a 25% mask ratio. When the i-th token is chosen to be masked, it may be replaced with the [MASK] token 20% of the time or a random token 80% of the time. The training objective for CMLM is to maximize: $P(y_i|x, y')$, where y_i is the i-th token, x and y' represent the source sentence and the corrupted target sentence, respectively. More specifically, we reuse the parameters of the neural machine translation model instead of training the model from scratch, and the model is trained with data in the same domain as the QE data.

Translation model is a natural language generation model trained in an autoregressive manner, where each token can only pay attention to the tokens before it, and the tokens after it are masked out. On the contrary, QE task is a natural language understanding task in which each token needs to be concerned with the whole context. Through this mask-prediction task focusing on bidirectional information, the model can learn the context-based representation of the token at the target side, thereby adapting the unidirectional NMT decoder to the bidirectional prediction task.

3.3 Denoising Restoration

Inspired by Electra [3], to further mitigate the discrepancy of data quality, we apply the Denoising Restoration strategy to post-train the neural machine translation model. The model architecture is illustrated in Fig. 3, which can be divided into the Noiser and the Restorer. The Noiser is used to create noisy samples, and the restorer is used to recover the noisy samples. After that, only the Restorer would be used as the predictor and the Noiser would be dropped.

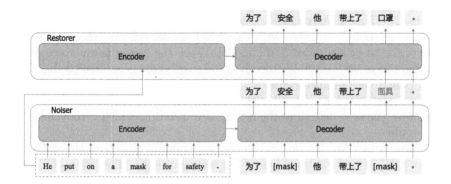

Fig. 3. The Noiser-Restorer architecture.

The Noiser is first trained to introduce noise at the target side. It has the same architecture as the CMLM, the difference is that we utilize the decoding results of the to-be-evaluated NMT model as the training objective of the Noiser, where the to-be-evaluate NMT model is used to generate QE data. Specifically, given a parallel sentence pair $<x, y>$, we use the to-be-evaluted NMT model to generate the translation $\tilde{y}$ of x. Then the Noiser is trained with the new parallel sentence pair $<x, \tilde{y}>$. After the training of the Noiser, we put the Noiser and the Restorer together for training with parallel data$<x, y>$. Moreover, it is performed by dynamic mask strategy with the masked positions decided on-the-fly, where the mask ratio is same as that of the CMLM. The loss function is defined as follows:

$$L_{DR} = -\sum_{i=1}^{L} log P(l = l_i | x, \hat{y}), l_i \in \{1, 2, ..., V\}, \tag{4}$$

where L is the length of sentence, $\hat{y}$ is the sentence generated by the Noiser, V is the size of vocabulary.

The reason for introducing Noiser is that in the CMLM strategy, there is a large deviation between the sentences generated by randomly adding noise and real machine translation, which is easily detected and may limit the performance. Limited by the performance of the Noiser, it is certain that not all tokens can be recovered completely and correctly. Therefore, the target sequence generated by the Noiser is noisy compared with reference translation. Meanwhile, since the Noiser utilizes a decoder with language modeling capabilities for generation, the generated sentences are more natural without obvious lexical and syntactic errors. Similarly, real machine translation noise is also natural and does not have significant lexical and syntactic errors, so the noise generated by the Noiser is closer to the real noise distribution than the noise generated by random replacement. A possible example is shown in the Fig. 3.

In addition, we utilize knowledge distillation technique [12] in the Noiser, which is used to transfer specific patterns and knowledge among different sequence generation models. In our scenario, the decoding process of the to-be-evaluated NMT model has a fixed pattern, so the translation results obtained by decoding the source sentences with this NMT model contains the noise distribution of the to-be-evaluated NMT model. When the Noiser learns to recover a corrupted token, both training objectives and context are generated by this NMT model. Hence, the obtained Noiser would have a similar decoding space with the to-be-evaluated NMT model. Note that the Noiser could produce pseudo translations with the same length as the reference translation, which is convenient for later training.

Despite both adopting non-autoregressive training objective, the difference between CMLM and Restorer lies in the source of noise. The noise of CMLM comes from random masking, while the noise of Restorer comes from language model generation. On the one hand, the noise generated by the Noiser is more consistent with the noise distribution of the to-be-evaluated NMT model, so during the training, the Restorer can learn the modeling ability for noise data with specific distribution. On the other hand, since the noise generated by the Noiser is more natural and more difficult to identify, the obtained Restorer would have a better feature extraction ability and can identify trivial translation errors. In cases where QE needs to model machine-translated noisy data, the Restorer is more suitable for QE task.

4   Experiments

4.1   Settings

Dataset. Our experiments focus on the WMT21 QE tasks for English-to-Chinese (En-Zh) and English -to-German (En-De) directions. The QE data in each direction contains a training set of 7000, a validation set of 1000, and a test set of 1000. Besides, we also use the test set of WMT20. To train our own NMT model, we use the En-Zh and En-De parallel data released by the organizers[1], which contains roughly 20M sentence pairs for each direction after cleaning. For the CMLM and DR, We first trained a BERT-based domain classifier and

---

[1] https://www.statmt.org/wmt21/quality-estimation-task.html.

then screened 200K in-domain data from WikiMatrix for each direction[2]. The validation set we use is the training set of the QE task.

Implementation Details. All our programs are implemented with Fairseq [17]. For the NMT model, we use Transformer-base architecture. We apply byte-pair-encoding (BPE) [20] tokenization to reduce the number of unknown tokens and set BPE steps to 32000. The learning rate is set to 5e−4. This setting is adopted in both En-Zh and En-De directions.

For the CMLM, the casual mask is removed and learning rate is set to 5e-5. For the Noiser-Restorer model, the parameters of the Noiser are frozen and the learning rate for the Restorer is 5e−5. For the Noiser, we use the decoding results of the to-be-evaluated NMT model as the training objective. We use inverse-square-root scheduler in above three models. For the QE model, it trained for 30 epochs and the hyperparameter patience is set to 5. The activation function in the BAL is ReLU. We batch sentence pairs with 4096 tokens and use the Adam optimizer with $\beta_1 = 0.9$, $\beta_2 = 0.98$ and $\epsilon = 10^{-8}$. The learning rate is 1e-4 without any scheduler.

The training data for all models is preprocessed by Fairseq based on the vocabulary and BPE vocabulary of the NMT model. For fair comparison, we tune all the hyper-parameters of our model on the validation data, and report the corresponding results for the testing set. The main metric we use is Pearson's Correlation Coefficient. We also calculate Spearman Coefficient, but it is not a ranking reference in the QE task.

4.2   Main Results

We compare our models with the following methods:

PLM-Baseline: Pre-training language models (PLM) are directly used as the predictor without integrating the BAL layer. In our experiments, DistilBert [19] and XLM-RoBERTa [4] were selected, and the baseline of organisers is also implemented by XLM-RoBERTa.

NMT-Baseline: An NMT model pre-trained on parallel data is used as the predictor, where NMT(finetune) is obtained by continuing to finetune on the in-domain data used by CMLM and DR.

The experimental results in both En-Zh and En-De directions are reported in Table 1. The Test20 is officially corrected, so there are no up-to-date results. As can be seen, the performance of the baseline model is relatively poor. By leveraging MLM training strategies, the CMLM can better focus on contextual information and achieves much better performance than NMT model. Moreover, the denoising restoration strategy further enhances the feature extraction ability of Restorer by introducing noise that is consistent with the distribution of NMT and outperforms the CMLM in two language pairs. This illustrates that our approaches alleviate the discrepancy between the NMT model and the QE model,

---

[2] http://data.statmt.org/wmt21/translation-task/WikiMatrix.

206   C. Li et al.

Table 1. Experiment results on both En-Zh and En-De directions. 'XLM-R' and 'DistilBERT' are implemented by us based on XLM-RoBERTa and DistilBERT. 'Avg' represents the average value of the pearson over two datasets. '-' indicates missing results.

Direction	System	Test21		Test20		Avg
		Pearson↑	Spearman↑	Pearson↑	Spearman↑	
En-Zh	XLM-R (WMT-baseline)	0.282	–	–	–	0.282
	DistilBert	0.257	0.223	0.340	0.334	0.299
	XLM-R	0.265	0.219	0.323	0.318	0.294
	NMT	0.286	0.242	0.322	0.312	0.304
	NMT (finetune)	0.294	0.243	0.322	0.311	0.308
	CMLM	0.334	0.273	0.355	0.345	0.345
	DR	**0.342**	**0.275**	**0.362**	**0.353**	**0.352**
En-De	XLM-R (WMT-baseline)	0.529	–	–	–	0.529
	DistilBert	0.466	0.433	0.432	0.427	0.449
	XLM-R	0.537	0.492	**0.469**	**0.464**	0.503
	NMT	0.528	0.491	0.427	0.424	0.478
	NMT (finetune)	0.532	0.491	0.438	0.430	0.485
	CMLM	0.569	0.518	0.450	0.437	0.509
	DR	**0.577**	**0.521**	0.460	0.424	**0.519**

thereby making the NMT model better adapted to the QE task. Combined with the official ranking, in En-Zh direction, our single model outperforms other systems except the first place (which adapt multiple ensemble techniques and data-augmentation).

The CMLM and DR also perform better than the fine-tuned NMT model, which indicates the performance gains of them are not due to the introduction of additional datasets. Besides, the NMT-based models are more effective than PLM-Baseline in most of the comparisons, we consider that the NMT model is naturally fit for machine translation related tasks, benefiting from the knowledge of bilingual alignment.

5 Analysis

5.1 The Impact of Mask Ratio and [MASK] Symbol

During the training stage, the number of corrupted tokens may affect the performance of the model, which is related to the mask ratio. We conduct experiments to study the impact of different mask ratio and the results are illustrated in Fig. 4.

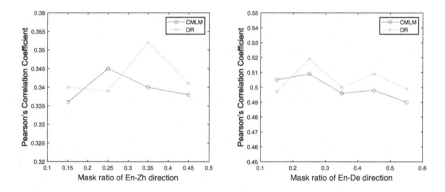

Fig. 4. The illustration of the CMLM. At the target side, some tokens are replaced with [mask] symbol or random token. Note that it also needs to remove the casual mask in decoder.

We find that the two diagrams exhibit roughly the same pattern. The QE performance first improves, but when the mask ratio is too high, the results start to decline. This is because as the mask ratio increases, the quality of the pseudo data is gradually approaching the real machine translation, therefore the model can better model semantic alignment between the imperfect translation and source. However, when the mask ratio is too high, most of the input sentence is covered and it is too difficult for the model to restore them, thus the model can barely learn anything useful and the performance is degraded. We also observe that the performance peak of the Noiser-Restorer model in En-Zh direction comes later than that in the En-De direction. One possible reason is that the Noiser in the En-Zh direction performs better than that in the En-De direction, we will explain this in the next subsection.

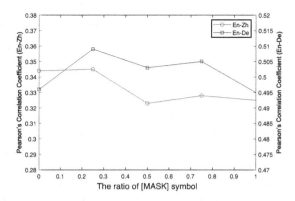

Fig. 5. The impact of the [MASK] symbol.

In the CMLM strategy, among the corrupted tokens, some will be replaced with [MASK] symbol, and the others will be replaced with random tokens. We fix the mask ratio and then gradually increase the proportion of corrupted tokens replaced with [MASK] symbol to study the impact of introducing [MASK] symbol. The results are presented in Fig. 5. We can observe that performance get worse as the introduced [MASK] symbol increases. It may be caused by the mismatch between pre-training and fine-tuning when too many [MASK] tokens are introduced, as they never appear during the fine-tuning stage. Furthermore, using only random replacement does not give the best results, which proves that the performance improvement brought by DR is not only due to the removal of [MASK] symbol but also benefits from the introduction of natural noise close to the real machine translation.

5.2   The Impact of Knowledge Distillation

In the implementation of the Noiser, we use the decoding results of the to-be-evaluated NMT model as the training objective of the Noiser. Our motivation is to make the Noiser learn the knowledge implied by to-be-evaluated model, so as to generate sentences that is closer to the noise of real machine translation. We conduct experiments to verify the effective of this scheme, and the results are shown in Table 2.

Table 2. The comparison results of Noiser-Restorer under two strategies. '$w/$ kd' and 'w/o kd' denote with or without knowledge distillation, respectively. The 'MAE' is the Mean Absolute Error.

Direction	System	Test21		Test20		Avg
		Pearson↑	MAE↓	Pearson↑	MAE↓	
En-Zh	Noiser-Restorer w/o kd	0.328	0.240	0.346	**0.226**	0.337
	Noiser-Restorer $w/$ kd	**0.334**	**0.202**	**0.360**	0.233	**0.347**
En-De	Noiser-Restorer w/o kd	0.546	**0.125**	**0.449**	0.144	**0.498**
	Noiser-Restorer $w/$ kd	**0.549**	0.128	0.436	**0.133**	0.493

For a fair comparison, we extracted another dataset from WikiMatrix instead of the one used to train the Noiser for experiments. According to the experimental results, we find that the scheme plays an obvious role in the En-Zh direction, which shows that the Noiser generates pseudo data consistent with the noise distribution of the to-be-evaluated NMT model, thereby improving the performance. However, the situation is different for the En-De direction, where the results are not improved or even slightly decreased as a whole. We speculate that it may be affected by the performance of the to-be-evaluated neural machine translation model. We studied the QE dataset and came up with the results shown in the Table 3.

Table 3. The statistical results of translation quality for QE dataset in En-Zh and En-De directions. The values in the table represent the average value of hter label.

Direction	train	valid	test21	test20
En-Zh	0.4412	0.2839	0.2283	0.3329
En-De	0.1784	0.1830	0.1754	0.1667

HTER indicates human-targeted translation edit rate, and the higher HTER is, the worse the translation quality is. As can be seen in Table 3, the average value of HTER in the En-Zh direction is generally higher than that in the En-De direction. This shows that the to-be-evaluated NMT model has a better translation effect in the En-De direction, thus the machine translation is not much different from the reference translation. It is difficult for Noiser to learn the pattern contained in the NMT model, so the knowledge distillation does not play a significant role.

5.3 Different Loss Calculation Methods

Base on previous researches, there are two ways to calculate the loss:

i. Following BERT, calculating the loss only on the small subset that was masked out.
ii. Calculating the loss over all input tokens at the target side.

Table 4. Experimental results of different loss calculation methods in En-Zh and En-De directions. 'Only-Corrupted' and 'All-Tokens' mean the loss is calculated on the corrupted tokens and all input tokens, respectively.

Direction	System	Test21		Test20		Avg
		Pearson↑	MAE↓	Pearson↑	MAE↓	
En-Zh	Only-Corrupted	0.328	0.217	0.348	**0.227**	0.338
	All-Tokens	**0.334**	**0.202**	**0.355**	0.233	**0.345**
En-De	Only-Corrupted	**0.574**	**0.125**	0.445	0.136	**0.510**
	All-Tokens	0.568	0.126	**0.450**	**0.132**	0.509

We compare these two methods on the CMLM strategy and the results are shown in Table 4. In the En-Zh direction, the method of calculating the loss on all tokens is better than that only on the corrupted tokens. However, the situation is a little different in the En-De direction. We speculate that English and German belong to the same family of languages, and the prediction is relatively simple, so adding this additional information has little effect. Overall, the performance of the two methods is roughly equivalent.

6   Conclusion

When applying the pre-trained machine translation model to feature extraction for QE, there are two discrepancies between the NMT model and the QE model. One is the difference in data quality, the other is the regressive behavior of the decoder. In this paper, we propose two strategies to adapt the neural machine translation model to QE task, namely Conditional Masked Language Modeling and Denoising Restoration. The CMLM adopts a mask-prediction task at the target side, which allows the model to learn context-based representations. Moreover, the DR employs a Noiser-Restorer architecture, where the Noiser is used to generate sentences with the same noise distribution as machine translation, then the Restorer will detect and recover the introduced noise. Compared with the original NMT model, our methods bridge the gaps between the NMT model and the QE model, making it more suitable for the QE task. The experimental results verify the effectiveness of our methods.

The main work in this paper focuses on sentence-level task. Intuitively, the discrepancy also exists on word-level quality estimation when applying the pre-trained NMT model, and our strategies could function without any adaptation. Besides, enhancing the estimator can also improve QE performance, and we will leave this as our future work.

Acknowledgements. The research work descried in this paper has been supported by the National Key R&D Program of China (2020AAA0108001) and the National Nature Science Foundation of China (No. 61976015, 61976016, 61876198 and 61370130). The authors would like to thank the anonymous reviewers for their valuable comments and suggestions to improve this paper.

References

1. Chen, Y., et al.: HW-TSC's participation at WMT 2021 quality estimation shared task. In: Proceedings of the Sixth Conference on Machine Translation, pp. 890–896 (2021)
2. Chowdhury, S., Baili, N., Vannah, B.: Ensemble fine-tuned mBERT for translation quality estimation. arXiv preprint arXiv:2109.03914 (2021)
3. Clark, K., Luong, M.T., Le, Q.V., Manning, C.D.: Electra: pre-training text encoders as discriminators rather than generators. arXiv preprint arXiv:2003.10555 (2020)
4. Conneau, A., et al.: Unsupervised cross-lingual representation learning at scale. arXiv preprint arXiv:1911.02116 (2019)
5. Devlin, J., Chang, M.W., Lee, K., Toutanova, K.: BERT: pre-training of deep bidirectional transformers for language understanding. arXiv preprint arXiv:1810.04805 (2018)
6. Fan, K., Wang, J., Li, B., Zhou, F., Chen, B., Si, L.: "Bilingual expert" can find translation errors. In: Proceedings of the AAAI Conference on Artificial Intelligence, vol. 33, pp. 6367–6374 (2019)
7. Ghazvininejad, M., Levy, O., Liu, Y., Zettlemoyer, L.: Mask-predict: parallel decoding of conditional masked language models. arXiv preprint arXiv:1904.09324 (2019)

8. Graham, Y., Baldwin, T., Moffat, A., Zobel, J.: Can machine translation systems be evaluated by the crowd alone. Nat. Lang. Eng. **23**(1), 3–30 (2017)
9. Houlsby, N., et al.: Parameter-efficient transfer learning for NLP. In: International Conference on Machine Learning, pp. 2790–2799. PMLR (2019)
10. Huang, H., Di, H., Xu, J., Ouchi, K., Chen, Y.: Unsupervised machine translation quality estimation in black-box setting. In: Li, J., Way, A. (eds.) CCMT 2020. CCIS, vol. 1328, pp. 24–36. Springer, Singapore (2020). https://doi.org/10.1007/978-981-33-6162-1_3
11. Kim, H., Lee, J.H.: Recurrent neural network based translation quality estimation. In: Proceedings of the First Conference on Machine Translation: Volume 2, Shared Task Papers, pp. 787–792 (2016)
12. Kim, Y., Rush, A.M.: Sequence-level knowledge distillation. arXiv preprint arXiv:1606.07947 (2016)
13. Lavie, A., Denkowski, M.J.: The meteor metric for automatic evaluation of machine translation. Mach. Transl. **23**(2), 105–115 (2009)
14. Logacheva, V., Hokamp, C., Specia, L.: Marmot: a toolkit for translation quality estimation at the word level. In: Proceedings of the Tenth International Conference on Language Resources and Evaluation (LREC 2016), pp. 3671–3674 (2016)
15. Lommel, A., Uszkoreit, H., Burchardt, A.: Multidimensional quality metrics (MQM): a framework for declaring and describing translation quality metrics. Rev. Tradumàtica: Tecnol. Traducció **12**, 455–463 (2014)
16. Martins, A.F., Junczys-Dowmunt, M., Kepler, F.N., Astudillo, R., Hokamp, C., Grundkiewicz, R.: Pushing the limits of translation quality estimation. Trans. Assoc. Comput. Linguist. **5**, 205–218 (2017)
17. Ott, M., et al.: fairseq: a fast, extensible toolkit for sequence modeling. arXiv preprint arXiv:1904.01038 (2019)
18. Papineni, K., Roukos, S., Ward, T., Zhu, W.J.: BLEU: a method for automatic evaluation of machine translation. In: Proceedings of the 40th Annual Meeting of the Association for Computational Linguistics, pp. 311–318 (2002)
19. Sanh, V., Debut, L., Chaumond, J., Wolf, T.: Distilbert, a distilled version of BERT: smaller, faster, cheaper and lighter. arXiv preprint arXiv:1910.01108 (2019)
20. Sennrich, R., Haddow, B., Birch, A.: Neural machine translation of rare words with subword units. arXiv preprint arXiv:1508.07909 (2015)
21. Snover, M., Dorr, B., Schwartz, R., Micciulla, L., Makhoul, J.: A study of translation edit rate with targeted human annotation. In: Proceedings of the 7th Conference of the Association for Machine Translation in the Americas: Technical Papers, pp. 223–231 (2006)
22. Specia, L., Paetzold, G., Scarton, C.: Multi-level translation quality prediction with quest++. In: Proceedings of ACL-IJCNLP 2015 system demonstrations, pp. 115–120 (2015)
23. Wang, M., et al.: HW-TSC's participation at WMT 2020 quality estimation shared task. In: Proceedings of the Fifth Conference on Machine Translation, pp. 1056–1061 (2020)
24. Wang, Z., et al.: Niutrans submission for CCMT19 quality estimation task. In: China Conference on Machine Translation, pp. 82–92. Springer (2019)
25. Weiss, K., Khoshgoftaar, T.M., Wang, D.D.: A survey of transfer learning. J. Big Data **3**(1), 1–40 (2016). https://doi.org/10.1186/s40537-016-0043-6
26. Wu, H., et al.: Tencent submission for WMT20 quality estimation shared task. In: Proceedings of the Fifth Conference on Machine Translation, pp. 1062–1067 (2020)

Supervised Contrastive Learning
for Cross-Lingual Transfer Learning

Shuaibo Wang[1], Hui Di[2], Hui Huang[3], Siyu Lai[1], Kazushige Ouchi[2],

Yufeng Chen[1(✉)], and Jinan Xu[1]

[1] School of Computer and Information Technology, Beijing Jiaotong University,
Beijing 100044, China
{wangshuaibo,20120374,chenyf,jaxu}@bjtu.edu.cn
[2] Toshiba (China) Co., Ltd., Beijing, China
dihui@toshiba.com.cn, kazushige.ouchi@toshiba.co.jp
[3] Harbin Institute of Technology, Harbin, China

Abstract. Multilingual pre-trained representations are not well-aligned by nature, which harms their performance on cross-lingual tasks. Previous methods propose to post-align the multilingual pre-trained representations by multi-view alignment or contrastive learning. However, we argue that both methods are not suitable for the cross-lingual classification objective, and in this paper we propose a simple yet effective method to better align the pre-trained representations. On the basis of cross-lingual data augmentations, we make a minor modification to the canonical contrastive loss, to remove false-negative examples which should not be contrasted. Augmentations with the same class are brought close to the anchor sample, and augmentations with different class are pushed apart. Experiment results on three cross-lingual tasks from XTREME benchmark show our method could improve the transfer performance by a large margin with no additional resource needed. We also provide in-detail analysis and comparison between different post-alignment strategies.

Keywords: Multilingual pre-trained representations · Contrastive learning · Cross-lingual

1 Introduction

Cross-lingual transfer learning aims to transfer the learned knowledge from a resource-rich language to a resource-lean language. The main idea of crosss-lingual transfer is to learn a shared language-invariant feature space for both languages, so that a model trained on the source language could be applied to the target language directly. Such generalization ability greatly reduces the required annotation efforts, and has urgent demand in real-world applications.

Recent multilingual pre-trained models, such as XLM-RoBERTa (XLM-R) [5], have been demonstrated surprisingly effective in the cross-lingual scenario. By fine-tuning on labeled data in a source language, such models can generalize to other target

© The Author(s), under exclusive license to Springer Nature Switzerland AG 2022
M. Sun et al. (Eds.): CCL 2022, LNAI 13603, pp. 212–225, 2022.
https://doi.org/10.1007/978-3-031-18315-7_14

languages even without any additional training. This has become a de-facto paradigm for cross-lingual language understanding tasks.

Despite their success in cross-lingual transfer tasks, multilingual pre-training commonly lacks explicit cross-lingual supervision, and the representations for different languages are not inherently aligned. To further improve the transferability of multilingual pre-trained representations, previous works propose different methods for cross-lingual alignment. Zheng et al. [28] and Lai et al. [14] propose to augment the training set with different views, and align the pre-trained representations of different languages by dragging two views closer. However, simply bringing different views closer would easily lead to representation collapse and performance degradation [22]. Meanwhile, Pan et al. [19] and Wei et al. [25] propose to incorporate additional parallel data, and align the pre-trained representations by contrasting positive and negative samples. However, monotonously treating all random samples equally negative is inconsistent with the classification objective.

In this work, we propose a simple yet effective method to better post-align the multilingual representations on downstream tasks, which can both avoid representation collapse and meanwhile induce classification bias. With only training data for the source language available, our method performs cross-lingual fine-tuning by two steps. 1) Firstly, the original training data is augmented with different views, including code-switching, full-translation and partial-translation. All views could provide cross-lingual supervision for post-alignment. 2) Given one training sentence as the anchor point, the corresponding augmented view serves as the positive sample, and other augmented views with different labels serve as the negative samples, contrastive learning is performed by pulling positive samples together and pushing apart negative samples. This is called Supervised Contrastive Learning (SCL), and can be deemed as a cross-lingual regularizer to be combined with conventional fine-tuning.

We perform experiments on two cross-lingual classification tasks, namely XNLI (cross-lingual inference) and PAWS-X (cross-lingual paraphrase identification) [6,26]. We compare different alignment methods, and our proposed method outperforms previous methods by a large margin, proving its effectiveness. Besides, we also apply our method on the cross-lingual retrieval task of BUCC[1] and tatoeba [1]. We use the data from PAWS-X as supervision, and fine-tune the pretrained model by contrasting samples with their machine translation. Our proposed method again outperforms other methods by a large margin.

Detailed analysis and discussion are provided to compare different post-alignment methods for pre-trained representations, and to prove the necessity of label-supervision when performing cross-lingual contrastive learning.

2 Background

2.1 Contrastive Learning

Contrastive learning aims at maximizing the similarity between the encoded query q and its matched positive samples k^+ while keeping randomly sampled keys $\{k_0, k_1, k_2, ...\}$

---

[1] https://comparable.limsi.fr/bucc2017/.

far away from it. With similarity measured by a score function $s(q, k)$, InfoNCE [18] loss is commonly used to this end:

$$L_{ctl} = \frac{\exp(s(q, k^+))}{\exp(s(q, k^+)) + \sum_{i=1}^{n} \exp(s(q, k_i^-))}$$

Contrastive learning has led to significant improvements in various domains [9, 10]. Recently, Khosla et al. [12] propose to incorporate label-supervision to the fine-tuning of pre-trained models, and obtain improvement on multiple datasets of the GLUE benchmark, and our work is inspired by them. However, their method is only targeted at monolingual tasks.

2.2 Cross-Lingual Transfer

Cross-lingual transfer learning aims to transfer the learned knowledge from a resource-rich language to a resource-lean language. Despite recent success in large-scale language models, how to adapt models trained in high-resource languages (e.g., English) to low-resource ones still remains challenging. Several benchmarks are proposed to facilitate the progress of cross-lingual transfer learning [11, 17], where models are fine-tuned on English training set and directly evaluated on other languages.

Recently, several pre-trained multilingual language models are proposed for cross-lingual transfer, including multilingual BERT [7], XLM [15], and XLM-R [5]. The models work by pre-training multilingual representations using some form of language modeling, and have made outstanding progress in cross-lingual tasks. However, most existing models use only single-language input for language model finetuning, without leveraging the intrinsic cross-lingual alignment. Therefore, several methods have been proposed to post-align the pre-trained representations, by introducing some form of cross-lingual supervision. Cao et al. [2] and Dou et al. [8] propose to generate word alignment information from parallel data, and push the aligned words in parallel data to have similar representations. Pan et al. [19], Wang et al. [23] and Wei et al. [25] propose to utilize contrastive learning for post-alignment by contrasting positive and negative samples, where positive samples are parallel to each other while negative samples are randomly picked. Zheng et al. [28] and Lai et al. [14] propose to augment the training set with different views, and align the representations by dragging two views close to each other. In a nutshell, despite all variations of supervision in both sentence or word-level, from both parallel data or automatically crafted data, the alignment must be performed by inter-lingual comparing, either by bringing two representations closer or contrasting a representation with random sampled representations. However, we argue that both methods are in contradiction with the cross-lingual classification objective, for which we will give detailed analysis in Sect. 3.2 (Fig. 1).

3   Approach

In this section, we first introduce the three cross-lingual data augmentation methods. Based on that, we propose three paradigms to post-align the multilingual representations, and provide theoretical analysis and comparison for them.

3.1 Cross-Lingual Data Augmentation

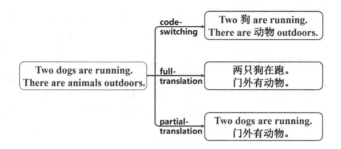

Fig. 1. Different cross-lingual data-augmentation methods. Here we use sentence-pair classification as an example, therefore each sample contains two sentences.

In this work, we do not want to incorporate any parallel data (which is inaccessible in a lot of scenarios, especially for a resource-lean language that we want to transfer to). Therefore, to provide cross-lingual supervision for post-alignment, we propose three data augmentation methods:

1. Code-switching: Following Qin et al. [20], we randomly select words in the original text in the source language and replace them with target language words in the bilingual dictionaries, to generate code-switched data. The intuition is to help the model automatically and implicitly align the replaced word vectors in the source and all target languages by mixing their context information, and the switched words can serve as anchor point for aligning two representation space.
2. Full-translation: Machine translation has been proved to be an effective data augmentation strategy under the cross-lingual scenario. It can provide translations almost in-line-with human performance, and therefore serves as a strong baseline for cross-lingual tasks.
3. Partial-translation: This method simply takes a portion of input and replace it with its translation in another language. According to Singh et al. [21], partial-translation could provide inter-language information, where the non-translated portion serves as the anchor point. This is somehow akin to code-switching, and can be deemed as code-switching in segment-level.

The three methods can provide cross-lingual supervision in a coarse-to-fine manner (sentence-level, segment-level, word-level). We perform all the three methods to the whole training set. Each training sample could be code-switched multiple times with different results, and each task contains translation into multiple languages, leading to multiple views from a cross-lingual perspective.

3.2 Cross-Lingual Alignment: What Do We Want?

Many experiments [2, 13] suggest that to achieve reasonable performance in the cross-lingual setup, the source and the target languages need to share similar representations.

However, current multilingual pre-trained models are commonly pre-trained without explicit cross-lingual supervision. Therefore, the cross-lingual transfer performance can be further improved by additional cross-lingual alignment.

Given the training sample in source language and its cross-lingual augmentations, previous methods perform cross-lingual alignment in two different trends: Multi-view Alignment [14,28] or Contrastive Learning [19,25]. The multi-view alignment is to bring the sample and the corresponding augmentation together, while the contrastive learning is to bring these two together while pushing apart other random sampled augmentations. Suppose we are working with a batch of training examples of size N, $\{x_i, y_i\}, i = 1, ...N$, x_i denotes the training sample, while y_i is the label, the two different objectives can be denoted as follows:

$$L_{MVA} = -s(\Phi(x_i), \Phi(\hat{x}_i))$$

$$L_{CL} = -\log \frac{s(\Phi(x_i), \Phi(\hat{x}_i))}{s(\Phi(x_i), \Phi(\hat{x}_i)) + \sum_{j=1}^{N} \mathbb{I}_{j \neq i} s(\Phi(x_i), \Phi(\hat{x}_j))}$$

where $\Phi(\cdot) \in R_d$ denotes the $L2$-normalized embedding of the final encoder hidden layer before the softmax projection, and $\hat{x}_i$ denotes the augmented view (code-switching, full-translation, partial-translation, etc.), and s(q, k) denotes the similarity measure (cosine similarity, KL divergence, etc.). MVA is short for multi-view alignment, and CL is short for contrastive learning.

Since in vanilla contrastive learning, the similarity function is normally in the form of exponential, therefore L_{CL} can be detached into two terms:

$$L_{CL} = \underbrace{-s(\Phi(x_i), \Phi(\hat{x}_i)))}_{alignment} + \underbrace{\log(e^{s(\Phi(x_i), \Phi(\hat{x}_i))} + e^{\sum_{j=1}^{N} \mathbb{I}_{j \neq i} s(\Phi(x_i), \Phi(\hat{x}_j))})}_{uniformity}$$

where the first term optimize the alignment of representation space, and the second term optimize the uniformity, as discussed in Wang et al. [24]. According to Gao et al. [9], let W be the sentence embedding matrix corresponding to x_i, i.e., the i-th row of W is $\Phi(x_i)$, optimizing the *uniformity* term essentially minimizes an upper bound of the summation of all elements in $WW^\top$, and inherently "flatten" the singular spectrum of the embedding space.

However, the *uniformity* term in L_{CL} is in contradiction with the classification objective. In classification task, we want the representations to be clustered in several bunches, each bunch corresponds to a class. Or else to say, we want the representations to be inductively biased, rather than uniformly distributed.

On the other hand, it is obvious that the multi-view alignment objective L_{MVA} is to solely maximize the alignment. This would easily lead to representation collapse, since simply projecting all representations to one data point could easily reduce the *alignment* term to zero. Contrast between samples is necessary to avoid collapse, and simply removing the *uniformity* term is also not what we want. (Fig. 2).

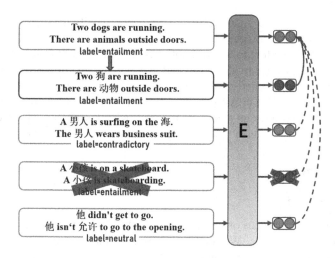

Fig. 2. Our proposed supervised contrastive learning. Solid line connects positive pairs while dashed line connects negative pairs. Notice the false negative sample is removed.

3.3 Better Alignment with SCL

To better perform cross-lingual alignment, we propose to introduce label information to the vanilla contrastive learning, named as Supervised Contrastive Learning (SCL):

$$L_{SCL} = -\log \frac{s(\Phi(x_i), \Phi(\hat{x}_i))}{s(\Phi(x_i), \Phi(\hat{x}_i)) + \sum_{j=1}^{N} \mathbb{I}_{y_j \neq y_i} s(\Phi(x_i), \Phi(\hat{x}_j))}$$

More concretely, our modification is based on InfoNCE loss [18], therefore the similarity function is written as:

$$s(\Phi(x_i), \Phi(\hat{x}_i)) = e^{cos(\Phi(x_i), \Phi(\hat{x}_i))/\tau}$$

where $\tau > 0$ is an adjustable scalar temperature parameter that controls the separation of classes. Empirical observations show that both $L2$-normalization of the encoded embedding representations (which is incorporated in the calculation of cosine similarity) and an adjustable scalar temperature parameter τ improve performance. This can serve as a cross-lingual regularization term and be combined with the canonical classification loss:

$$L_{CE} = y_i \cdot \log(1 - \hat{y}_i) + \hat{y}_i \cdot \log(1 - y_i)$$

$$L_{total} = L_{CE} + \lambda L_{SCL}$$

where λ is a scalar weighting hyperparameter that we tune for each downstream task.

The core idea is simple, just to remove the negative samples which belong to the same class with the anchor point. Therefore, only samples from different classes would be pulled apart. The modified $uniformity$ term is not to unify the representations any more, but to push the multilingual decision clusters apart from each other.

This loss can be applied to a variety of encoders, not just limited to multilingual pre-trained transformer-like models. The loss is meant to capture similarities between examples of the same class and contrast them with examples from other classes. This is in line with the objective of cross-lingual alignment. When we are doing cross-lingual alignment, what we really want to do is to transfer the representation for a certain class to another language, rather than to learn a unified multilingual representation space.

4 Experiments

4.1 Data Preparation

In this work, we mainly focus on sentence-level tasks, for which the aggregated representation is easily accessible. We conduct experiments on two cross-lingual sentence-pair classification tasks: natural language inference and paraphrase identification. The Cross-lingual Natural Language Inference corpus (XNLI) [6] asks whether a premise sentence entails, contradicts, or is neutral toward a hypothesis sentence. The Cross-lingual Paraphrase Adversaries from Word Scrambling (PAWS-X) [26] dataset requires to determine whether two sentences are paraphrases. Both tasks are from XTREME benchmark [11]. Despite their intrinsic different objective, both tasks can be formalized as sentence-pair classification tasks. For both tasks, the training set is in English, while human annotated development and test sets are available for a bunch of different languages. The model is evaluated on the test data of the task in the target languages.

For cross-lingual data augmentation, we first randomly sample a target language and then adapt the generating method for each data augmentation method. Since XNLI covers more target languages than PAWS-X, we set $t_f = 2, t_p = 2, t_c = 1$ in XNLI, and $t_f = 1, t_p = 1, t_c = 1$ in PAWS-X, where t_f, t_p and t_c respectively represent the number of samples generated by full-translation, partial translation and code-switching for each training data. Therefore, each training batch contains $6 \times batch\_size$ sentence pairs in XNLI and $4 \times batch\_size$ sentence pairs in PAWS-X. The code-switching ratio r_c is set as 0.75 in XNLI and 0.5 in PAWS-X. For cross-lingual retrieval tasks mentioned below, each training pair from PAWS-X is detached into two sentences when feeding to the model, and we do not incorporate code-switching as data augmentation.

4.2 Setup

For sentence pair classification tasks of XNLI and PAWS-X, we concatenate the input as the formation defined by XLM-R:

```
[s] input1 [\s] input2 [\s]
```

and we use the final hidden layer corresponding to [s] as aggregated representation. For retrieval tasks of BUCC and tatoeba, we perform alignment on the same aggregated representation, but the retrieval is performed on the averaged pooled eighth layer, following the related works [3,4]. Adam optimizer is applied with a learning rate of 5e−6. Batch size is set as 24 for XNLI, 36 for PAWS-X and 48 for retrieval.

Table 1. Experiment results on XNLI. Results with † are reimplemented by us with their released codes. InfoXLM [3] and HITCL [25] use contrastive learning while xTune [28] uses multi-view alignment. Notice xTune uses more augmentation data and model ensemble compared to us.

Method	en	ar	bg	de	el	es	fr	hi	ru	sw	th	tr	ur	vi	zh	Avg
cross-lingual transfer (Models are fine-tuned on English training data only.)																
InfoXLM	86.4	74.2	79.3	79.3	77.8	79.3	80.3	72.2	77.6	67.5	74.6	75.6	67.3	77.1	77.0	76.5
HITCL	86.3	74.8	80.6	79.5	78.9	81.3	80.5	73.1	79.0	69.9	75.7	75.4	69.7	77.4	77.6	77.3
xTune†	84.7	76.7	81.0	79.9	79.4	81.6	80.5	75.6	77.9	68.4	75.4	77.2	72.2	78.1	77.4	77.7
XLMR-base	84.8	72.7	78.8	77.9	76.5	79.8	78.9	72.2	76.5	66.8	73.9	73.7	68.0	76.8	75.4	75.5
MVA	85.0	75.0	79.1	78.2	78.1	79.7	79.1	72.5	76.8	68.9	75.5	74.5	70.0	76.9	77.4	76.5
CL	84.4	75.5	80.0	79.3	78.7	80.4	79.8	74.1	78.3	71.5	76.1	76.0	71.0	78.2	77.8	77.4
SCL	**86.3**	**77.8**	**81.7**	**81.3**	**80.6**	**82.7**	**81.8**	**76.3**	**80.4**	**73.8**	**78.9**	**78.1**	**73.1**	**80.5**	**80.2**	**79.6**
translate-train (Models are fine-tuned on both English data and its translations.)																
InfoXLM	86.5	78.9	82.4	82.3	81.3	83.0	82.6	77.8	80.6	73.3	78.9	79.5	71.6	81.0	80.7	80.0
HITCL	86.5	78.1	82.2	80.8	81.6	83.2	82.3	76.7	81.3	73.8	78.6	80.5	73.9	80.4	80.7	80.0
xTune†	86.6	79.7	82.7	82.2	81.9	83.1	82.3	78.9	80.9	75.7	78.4	79.8	75.3	80.5	80.0	80.5
XLMR-base	84.3	76.9	80.3	79.8	79.1	81.5	80.3	75.3	78.1	72.9	77.1	77.4	70.8	79.8	79.7	78.2
MVA	85.4	78.5	81.5	81.8	**80.6**	82.3	81.0	77.3	79.9	74.1	**78.8**	78.2	73.5	80.2	80.2	79.6
CL	85.9	77.2	81.6	80.5	80.0	81.7	81.5	76.5	80.3	73.5	77.8	78.2	72.5	79.9	79.9	79.1
SCL	**86.4**	78.8	82.0	82.0	80.5	**82.9**	82.3	77.3	80.5	74.5	78.6	**79.7**	74.2	**80.9**	80.3	80.1

We evaluate a number of strong baselines and the three post-align strategies discussed in the former section. The baseline is trained with cross-entropy loss with no alignment term serving as cross-lingual regularizer. Then we create cross-lingual augmentations with different methods, and apply different alignment strategies. Three groups of augmentations (full-translation, partial translation, code-switching) are mixed together. The bilingual dictionaries we used for code-switch substitution are from MUSE [16]. For languages that cannot be found in MUSE, we ignore these languages since other bilingual dictionaries might be of poorer quality. The machine translated training set is taken from the XTREME repository, which is obtained by an in-house translation model from Google.

We mainly compare with models that learn multilingual contextual representations as they have achieved state-of-the-art results on cross-lingual tasks. All cross-lingual alignment strategies are applied to pre-trained XLM-R-base. Following the trend of Hu et al. [11], we mainly consider the following two scenarios:

Cross-Lingual Transfer: The models are fine-tuned on English training data, and directly evaluated on different target languages.

Translate-Train: The models are fine-tuned on the concatenation of English training data and its translation to all target languages. Translate-train is normally a strong baseline for cross-lingual transfer tasks. For classification tasks, it is straightforward that the translation should be assigned with the same label.

In both settings, the alignment term is combined with the canonical cross-entropy loss to be back-propagated together. We use KL Divergence as the similarity measure for multi-view alignment. For contrastive learning, we only consider in-batch negative samples, leaving more complicated methods (e.g. to maintain a memory bank for negative samples [10]) to the future.

Table 2. Experiment results on PAWS-X. Results with † are reimplemented by us with their released codes.

Method	en	de	es	fr	ja	ko	zh	avg
cross-lingual transfer (Models are fine-tuned on English training data only.)								
InfoXLM†	94.7	89.7	90.1	90.4	78.7	79.0	82.3	86.4
xTune†	93.7	90.2	89.9	90.4	82.6	81.9	84.3	87.6
XLMR-base	94.5	88.4	89.4	89.3	76.0	77.2	82.6	85.3
MVA	95.0	89.1	90.9	90.6	79.5	81.1	83.7	87.1
CL	94.6	89.8	91.3	90.9	78.9	80.0	82.8	86.9
SCL	**95.3**	**91.3**	**91.8**	**91.7**	**83.2**	**84.5**	**85.7**	**89.0**
translate-train (Models are fine-tuned on both English data and its translations.)								
InfoXLM†	94.5	90.5	91.6	91.7	84.4	83.9	85.8	88.9
xTune†	93.9	90.4	90.9	91.7	85.6	86.8	86.6	89.4
XLMR-base	95.0	89.8	91.8	91.6	81.2	84.3	84.4	88.3
MVA	95.3	90.9	92.0	91.8	83.1	83.6	85.3	88.8
CL	95.4	90.2	92.1	91.4	81.7	84.0	85.3	88.6
SCL	**95.5**	**91.4**	**92.3**	**92.3**	**83.2**	**85.0**	**87.2**	**89.5**

4.3 Main Results

As shown in Table 1 and Table 2, we can see that our proposed method could improve the cross-lingual transfer results of pre-trained XLM-R by a large margin. Our method is especially effective in zero-shot setting, where the accuracy is improved by 4.1 points on XNLI and 3.7 points on PAWS-X. Our method can also achieve significant improvement in translate-train setting, where the accuracy is improved by 1.9 points on XNLI and 1.2 points on PAWS-X. Results are consistently improved among all languages, despite their relation with English close or not.

The results of multi-view alignment and vanilla contrastive learning, despite using the same augmentation data, underperform our method on both datasets. This proves the pre-trained representations are better aligned according to the label information after SCL. Different representations, despite belonging to different languages, are projected to the same cluster if they belong to the same class.

SCL is a simple yet effective framework to align the pre-trained multilingual representations on downstream tasks. Cross-lingual signals can be obtained by machine translation or bilingual dictionary, therefore no extra human annotation is needed. While previous works also propose other methods to align the pre-trained representations, the results in Table 1 and 2 prove the superiority of our method.

5 Analysis and Discussion

5.1 Different Augmentations

In this section, we want to explore the influence of different cross-lingual augmentations. We apply different groups of augmentations under the zero-shot setting, and compare the results on different tasks.

Table 3. Experiment results on XNLI and PAWS-X based on different cross-lingual data augmentations, including full-translation, partial translation, and code-switching. For each group of data, we apply all three post-align methods.

AugData	Method	XNLI		PAWS-X	
		en	avg	en	avg
None	XLMR	84.9	75.5	94.5	85.3
Full-trans	MVA	85.2	76.6	94.9	87.1
	CL	85.0	77.9	94.9	87.2
	SCL	85.6	**79.2**	95.3	**88.7**
Partial-trans	MVA	83.7	75.7	95.2	86.5
	CL	84.5	76.9	94.9	86.6
	SCL	85.3	78.4	95.3	88.1
Code-switch	MVA	85.3	76.4	94.7	86.1
	CL	84.5	76.1	95.2	86.5
	SCL	84.8	76.2	95.1	87.2

As shown in Table 3, we can see that the results of full translation and partial translation are better than code-switching. We think it is because the information provided by code-switching is comparably sparse, only a few anchor words covered by the bilingual dictionary. On the other side, well-trained machine translation system can provide fluent and accurate translation, therefore the multilingual representation can be better aligned. We can also tell that the results of our proposed method outperform the counterparts again on both datasets, proving its superiority.

5.2 Similarity Measure

Table 4. Experiment results of different similarity measures and loss weight λ on XNLI. Here we only use the augmentation of full-translation, and the results is in cross-lingual setting. We do not experiment on PAWS-X due to resource limitation.

Similarity measure	Lambda	XNLI	
		en	avg
KLDiv	1	85.19	76.64
	10	85.05	76.71
Symmetric KLDiv	1	84.67	76.17
	10	83.85	76.20
Cosine similarity	1	83.03	75.16
	10	84.05	76.38
Mean-square error	1	83.95	75.37
	10	84.35	76.58

The similarity measure in L_{MVA} has many alternatives. Previous studies on multi-view learning propose all kinds of measures [27], such as Cosine-Similarity, Mean-Square

Error, Kullback-Leibler Divergence and Symmetric Kullback-Leibler Divergence. Suppose we are dealing with an input x and its augmentation $\hat{x}$, different similarity measures can be denoted as:

$$L_{KLDiv} = \Phi(x) log \frac{\Phi(\hat{x})}{\Phi(x)}$$

$$L_{SymKLdiv} = \Phi(x) log \frac{\Phi(\hat{x})}{\Phi(x)} + \Phi(\hat{x}) log \frac{\Phi(x)}{\Phi(\hat{x})}$$

$$L_{cosine} = \frac{\Phi(x) \cdot \Phi(\hat{x})}{||\Phi(x)|| \, ||\Phi(\hat{x})||}$$

$$L_{MSE} = ||\Phi(x) - \Phi(\hat{x})||^2$$

where $\Phi(\cdot)$ denotes the $L2$-normalized aggregated representation. We experiment different similarity measures on the multi-view alignment objective, in combination with different loss weight λ, and the results are shown in Table 4. Surprisingly, we do not see a clear difference between different measures, and in the end we decide to use cosine similarity with $\lambda = 10$ in all experiments. On the other hand, λ is set as 1 for contrastive learning.

5.3   Contrast Temperature

Table 5. Experiment results of different contrast temperatures on XNLI and PAWS-X. Here we only use the augmentation of full-translation, and the results are based on supervised contrastive learning.

setting	temp	XNLI		PAWS-X	
		en	avg	en	avg
Cross-transfer	1.0	85.6	79.2	95.3	88.7
	0.3	85.2	79.1	94.8	88.7
	0.1	85.8	79.2	95.3	88.2
Translate-train	1.0	86.4	79.8	95.4	89.0
	0.3	85.8	79.8	95.4	89.1
	0.1	85.9	79.5	95.3	89.2

Previous empirical observations show that an adjustable scalar temperature parameter τ can improve the performance of contrastive learning [10,24]. Lower temperature increases the influence of examples that are harder to separate, effectively creating harder negatives. However, we do not find such a pattern in our experiments, as shown in Table 5, and finally we decide to set the temperature τ as 1.0 in all experiments.

5.4   SCL for Cross-Lingual Retrieval

To further prove the importance of label information in cross-lingual fine-tuning, we also apply the alignment methods on cross-lingual sentence retrieval tasks. We experiment on two datasets, BUCC[2] and tatoeba [1]. Both datasets aim at extracting parallel

---

[2] https://comparable.limsi.fr/bucc2017.

sentences from a comparable corpus between English and other languages, with BUCC covering 4 languages and tatoeba covering more than 100 languages. To compare with previous works, we only use a subset of tatoeba (33 languages) in this work.

The pre-trained multilingual models are able to provide language-deterministic representations by nature. Previous works directly calculate the similarity of different sentences by representations from the pre-trained model, to determine whether two sentences are parallel or not [3,4,11]. In this work, we propose to use the data of paraphrase identification, including the original training sentence pairs and their translations to six languages, to post-align the pre-trained representations.

We compare the previously proposed three strategies to post-align the pre-trained representations. Since we are dealing with retrieval task, the sentence pair from two different languages are encoded separately by the pre-trained XLM-R. We apply the alignment training methods on the aggregated representation. For multi-view alignment, only two translation pairs are pulled closer to each other. For vanilla contrastive learning, we treat all translation pairs as positive while the others as negative. For our proposed SCL, both translation pairs and translation with paraphrasing pairs are deemed as positive, while the others are deemed as negative, as denoted by the following formula:

$$L_{SCL} = -\sum_{j=1}^{N} \mathbb{I}_{y_{ij}=1} \log \frac{s(\Phi(x_i), \Phi(\hat{x}_j))}{s(\Phi(x_i), \Phi(\hat{x}_j)) + \sum_{k=1}^{N} \mathbb{I}_{y_{ik}\neq 1} s(\Phi(x_i), \Phi(\hat{x}_k))}$$

where x_i is a training sample and $\hat{x}_i$ is its translation, and $y_{ij} = 1$ denotes x_i and x_j are a paraphrase pair. After the fine-tuning stage, following previous work, we utilize the average pooled hidden representation of the eighth layer of the pre-trained model as the sentence representation.

As shown in Table 6 and Table 7, paraphrase identification dataset with translated augmentation, despite containing noise generated by the MT model, can provide cross-lingual signal to post-align the multilingual representations. Vanilla contrastive learning can perform alignment space by pulling translation pairs together and pushing translation pairs apart, but paraphrase pairs also possess the same semantics, and should not be contrasted as negative samples. After introducing label information into contrast, the

Table 6. Experiment results on BUCC2018 test set. Results with * are released by XTREME [11]. We apply different post-align strategies on pre-trained XLM-RoBERTa-base model using the training set of PAWS-X with translation augmentation.

Method	en-de	en-fr	en-ru	en-zh	avg
mBERT*	62.5	62.6	51.8	50.0	56.7
XLM*	56.3	63.9	60.6	46.6	56.8
XLMR-large*	67.6	66.5	73.5	56.7	66.0
XLMR-base	82.68	74.85	82.08	64.09	75.93
MVA	43.92	26.24	38.71	7.58	29.11
CL	87.22	79.93	86.88	78.83	83.21
SCL	**88.82**	**81.88**	**88.01**	**82.47**	**85.29**

Table 7. Experiment results on tatoeba. Result with ∗ is released by [4]. xx denotes the 33 languages as experimented in [3] and [4], and we release the averaged accuracy in both directions.

Method	en-xx	xx-en
XLMR-base∗	55.50	53.40
XLM-E [4]	65.00	62.30
InfoXLM [3]	68.62	67.29
XLMR-base	55.60	53.49
MVA	28.00	27.79
CL	78.80	77.87
SCL	**80.41**	**80.84**

retrieval accuracy is further improved by 2–3 points. On the contrary, multi-view alignment would lead to representation collapse and cannot converge at all. This is in line with our previous analysis.

6 Conclusion

In this paper, we propose to improve cross-lingual fine-tuning with supervised contrastive learning. Cross-lingual supervision is created by augmenting the training set, and different methods to post-align the multilingual pre-trained representation are compared. We propose to incorporate label-information when performing cross-lingual contrastive fine-tuning, and outperforms previous methods by a large margin on four cross-lingual transfer benchmark datasets.

Canonical cross-entropy has many intrinsic problems, especial when performing transfer learning tasks, and contrastive learning can be a decent supplementary. By alleviating the commonality and differences between different examples, representations are efficiently transferred from one domain or language to another. In the future, we would explore the application of supervised contrastive learning on other transfer learning tasks, including token-level classification, language generation, cross-domain transfer, etc.

Acknowledgement. This research work is supported by the National Key R&D Program of China (2020AAA0108001), the National Nature Science Foundation of China (No. 61976016, 61976015 and 61876198) and Toshiba (China) Co., Ltd. The authors would like to thank the anonymous reviewers for their valuable comments and suggestions to improve this paper.

References

1. Artetxe, M., Schwenk, H.: Massively multilingual sentence embeddings for zero-shot cross-lingual transfer and beyond. Trans. Assoc. Comput. Linguist. **7**, 597–610 (2019)
2. Cao, S., Kitaev, N., Klein, D.: Multilingual alignment of contextual word representations. In: Proceedings of ICLR (2020)

3. Chi, Z., et al.: InfoXLM: an information-theoretic framework for cross-lingual language model pre-training. In: Proceedings of ACL (2021)
4. Chi, Z., et al.: XLM-E: cross-lingual language model pre-training via ELECTRA. CoRR (2021)
5. Conneau, A., et al.: Unsupervised cross-lingual representation learning at scale. In: Proceedings of ACL (2020)
6. Conneau, A., et al.: Xnli: Evaluating cross-lingual sentence representations. In: Proceedings of EMNLP (2018)
7. Devlin, J., Chang, M.W., Lee, K., Toutanova, K.: BERT: pre-training of deep bidirectional transformers for language understanding. In: Proceedings of ACL (2019)
8. Dou, Z., Neubig, G.: Word alignment by fine-tuning embeddings on parallel corpora. In: Proceedings of ACL (2021)
9. Gao, T., Yao, X., Chen, D.: SimCSE: simple contrastive learning of sentence embeddings. In: Proceedings of EMNLP (2021)
10. He, K., Fan, H., Wu, Y., Xie, S., Girshick, R.: Momentum contrast for unsupervised visual representation learning. In: Proceedings of CVPR (2020)
11. Hu, J., Ruder, S., Siddhant, A., Neubig, G., Firat, O., Johnson, M.: Xtreme: a massively multilingual multi-task benchmark for evaluating cross-lingual generalization. CoRR abs/2003.11080 (2020)
12. Khosla, P., et al.: Supervised contrastive learning. In: Proceedings of NeurIPS (2020)
13. Kulshreshtha, S., Redondo Garcia, J.L., Chang, C.Y.: Cross-lingual alignment methods for multilingual BERT: a comparative study. In: Proceedings of ACL (2020)
14. Lai, S., Huang, H., Jing, D., Chen, Y., Xu, J., Liu, J.: Saliency-based multi-view mixed language training for zero-shot cross-lingual classification. In: Proceedings of ACL (2021)
15. Lample, G., Conneau, A.: Cross-lingual language model pretraining. Adv. Neural Inf. Process. Syst. (NeurIPS) (2019)
16. Lample, G., Conneau, A., Denoyer, L., Ranzato, M.: Unsupervised machine translation using monolingual corpora only. In: Proceedings of ICLR (2018)
17. Liang, Y., et al.: Xglue: a new benchmark dataset for cross-lingual pre-training, understanding and generation. arXiv (2020)
18. van den Oord, A., Li, Y., Vinyals, O.: Representation learning with contrastive predictive coding. CoRR (2018)
19. Pan, L., Hang, C.W., Qi, H., Shah, A., Potdar, S., Yu, M.: Multilingual BERT post-pretraining alignment. In: Proceedings of ACL (2021)
20. Qin, L., Ni, M., Zhang, Y., Che, W.: CoSDA-ML: multi-lingual code-switching data augmentation for zero-shot cross-lingual NLP. In: Proceedings of IJCAI (2020)
21. Singh, J., McCann, B., Keskar, N.S., Xiong, C., Socher, R.: XLDA: cross-lingual data augmentation for natural language inference and question answering. CoRR (2019)
22. Tao, C., et al.: Exploring the equivalence of siamese self-supervised learning via a unified gradient framework. CoRR (2021)
23. Wang, L., Zhao, W., Liu, J.: Aligning cross-lingual sentence representations with dual momentum contrast. In: Proceedings of EMNLP (2021)
24. Wang, T., Isola, P.: Understanding contrastive representation learning through alignment and uniformity on the hypersphere. In: Proceedings of ICML (2020)
25. Wei, X., Weng, R., Hu, Y., Xing, L., Yu, H., Luo, W.: On learning universal representations across languages. In: Proceedings of ICLR (2021)
26. Yang, Y., Zhang, Y., Tar, C., Baldridge, J.: PAWS-X: a cross-lingual adversarial dataset for paraphrase identification. In: Proceedings of EMNLP (2019)
27. Yang, Z., Cheng, Y., Liu, Y., Sun, M.: Reducing word omission errors in neural machine translation: a contrastive learning approach. In: Proceedings of ACL (2019)
28. Zheng, B., et al.: Consistency regularization for cross-lingual fine-tuning. In: Proceedings of ACL (2021)

Minority Language Information Processing

Interactive Mongolian Question Answer Matching Model Based on Attention Mechanism in the Law Domain

Yutao Peng[1,2,3], Weihua Wang[1,2,3(✉)], and Feilong Bao[1,2,3]

[1] College of Computer Science, Inner Mongolia University, Hohhot, China
yutao.peng@mail.imu.edu.cn, {wangwh,csfeilong}@imu.edu.cn
[2] National & Local Joint Engineering Research Center of Intelligent Information Processing Technology for Mongolian, Hohhot, China
[3] Inner Mongolia Key Laboratory of Mongolian Information Processing Technology, Hohhot, China

Abstract. Mongolian question answer matching task is challenging, since Mongolian is a kind of low-resource language and its complex morphological structures lead to data sparsity. In this work, we propose an Interactive Mongolian Question Answer Matching Model (IMQAMM) based on attention mechanism for Mongolian question answering system. The key parts of the model are interactive information enhancement and max-mean pooling matching. Interactive information enhancement contains sequence enhancement and multi-cast attention. Sequence enhancement aims to provide a subsequent encoder with an enhanced sequence representation, and multi-cast attention is designed to generate scalar features through multiple attention mechanisms. Max-Mean pooling matching is to obtain the matching vectors for aggregation. Moreover, we introduce Mongolian morpheme representation to better learn the semantic feature. The model experimented on the Mongolian corpus, which contains question-answer pairs of various categories in the law domain. Experimental results demonstrate that our proposed Mongolian question answer matching model significantly outperforms baseline models.

Keywords: Mongolian · Question answer matching · Interactive information enhancement · Law domain

1 Introduction

Question answer matching is used to identify the relationship between the question-answer pairs, and it is one of the application scenarios of text matching. Text matching is an important fundamental technology in Natural Language Processing (NLP) and can be applied to a large number of NLP tasks, such as Information Retrieval (IR), Natural Language Inference (NLI), question answering (QA) system, dialogue system, etc. For the tasks of Information Retrieval,

M. Sun et al. (Eds.): CCL 2022, LNAI 13603, pp. 229–244, 2022.
https://doi.org/10.1007/978-3-031-18315-7_15

text matching is utilized to compute the relevance between queries and documents to select the relevant documents [4]. For the tasks of Natural Language Inference, text matching is employed to judge whether the premise can infer the hypothesis [1]. And for the question answering tasks, text matching is applied to pick the answers that are most relevant to a given question [16].

With the development of deep learning, text matching methods with neural network are increasingly emerging. These methods can be divided into two types-representation-based match and interaction-based match. The first type is representation-based match [4,11,14], which is focused on modeling the representations of the two sentences, so that they are encoded into semantic vectors in the same embedding space. The second type is interaction-based match [2,17,21], which is targeted at interacting with each information between sentence pairs to improve the process of representation learning. Interaction-based match performs better than representation-based match, because representation-based match lacks a comparison of lexical and syntactic information between sentence pairs, while interaction-based match can take advantage of the interactive information across sentence pairs to enhance their own representations. Therefore, interactive matching methods are currently the mainstreaming methods of text matching.

However, the development of Mongolian question answering system is relatively slow, and there are few studies about it. The first reason for the slow development is that Mongolian is a kind of low-resource language. It lacks public labeled corpus. The second reason is the data-sparse problem caused by complex Mongolian morphological structures. Mongolian is an agglutinative language and its root can be followed by different suffixes, which is different from Chinese and English.

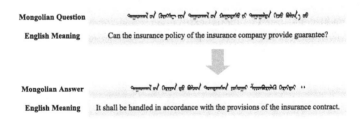

Fig. 1. A Mongolian question-answer pair example.

In this paper, we construct a Mongolian question answering data set in the law domain. An example is shown in Fig. 1, there are two Mongolian sentences, including the question and its corresponding answer. Our task is to judge whether the answer corresponds to the question. In order to solve the problem of insufficient information enhancement of previous interaction-based matching methods, we propose an Interactive Mongolian Question Answer Matching Model (IMQAMM), which combines interactive information enhancement and max-mean pooling matching. Interactive information enhancement concatenates a series of feature vectors to get the enhanced sequence representation and adopts a compression function to reduce feature vectors to scalars based on multiple attention mechanisms for the issue of data-sparse. Max-Mean pooling matching is to compute the maximum and average cosine similarities corresponding to each morpheme representation.

The paper is organized as follows: Sect. 2 introduces the related work. Section 3 presents the details of our Mongolian question answer matching model. Section 4 shows our experimental setup and results. Section 5 gives the conclusion and the future work.

2   Related Work

Text semantic matching is the core of retrieval question answering system. In recent years, there has been a lot of research on text semantic matching, which has driven the development of question answering systems. Early work on text semantic matching was based on relatively simple models to compare the sentence pairs. Most of these work was based on sentence encoding methods. Huang et al. (2013) proposed Deep Structured Semantic Models (DSSM), which projected queries and documents into a common low-dimensional space to get similarities between them. Since the CNN has the characteristics of local perception and parameter sharing, Shen et al. (2014) improved the DSSM model and proposed the Convolutional Latent Semantic Model (CLSM). To tackle the limitations of RNN in capturing contextual dependencies, Palangi et al. (2014) presented the Long Short Term Memory DSSM (LSTM-DSSM). Mueller and Thyagarajan (2016) proposed the Manhattan LSTM (MaLSTM) model, which utilized the siamese LSTM to compute the Manhattan distance between sentence pairs. Shen et al. (2018) proposed Directional Self-Attention Network (DiSAN) without any RNN or CNN for sentence encoding. Yang and Kao (2020) proposed a Siamese sentence encoder that would not propagate any interactive information between sentence pairs. The matching methods based on attention networks have gradually developed [5,16,24]. Tan et al. (2016) used the attentive LSTM to match questions and passage answers with question information. Yin et al. (2016) explored computing the attention matrix before and after convolution to select correct answers for a question. Kim et al. (2019) used densely-connected recurrent neural network and concatenated the co-attentive features in multiple layers for semantic sentence matching.

Compare-Aggregate networks are very popular in different tasks [2,17,18, 20,21]. Wang and Jiang (2017) presented a compare-aggregate model that performed word-level matching by element-wise multiplication or subtraction and aggregated by CNN. Wang et al. (2017) proposed a bilateral multi-perspective matching (BiMPM) model, which used multi-perspective cosine matching strategy between encoded sentence pairs. Chen et al. (2017) improved the approach proposed by Parikh et al. (2016) and achieved sequential inference model using chain LSTMs. Tay et al. (2017) presented ComProp Alignment-Factorized Encoders (CAFE) that used factorization machines to compress the alignment vectors into scalar features, which can effectively augment the word representations. Tay et al. (2018) explored using Multi-Cast Attention Networks (MCAN) to improve learning process by adopting several attention variants and performing multiple comparison operators.

These text semantic matching models laid the foundation for later IR models and QA systems. Although these models have achieved state-of-the-art performance on various datasets, they may not be suitable for low-resource agglutinative languages. In this paper, we introduce Mongolian morpheme representation, then use interactive information enhancement to take full advantage of the information across Mongolian question-answer pairs and apply max-mean pooling matching to capture the maximum influence and the overall influence between Mongolian question-answer pairs.

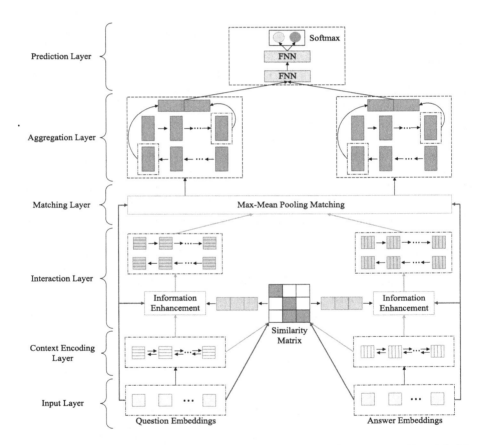

Fig. 2. Architecture for Interactive Mongolian Question Answer Matching Model (IMQAMM), where the initial morpheme representations and the contextual representations are respectively applied to compute the similarity matrix for interactive information enhancement.

3 Model Architecture

In this section, we will describe our model architecture layer by layer. Figure 2 shows a high-level view of the architecture, and then the details of our model are given as follows.

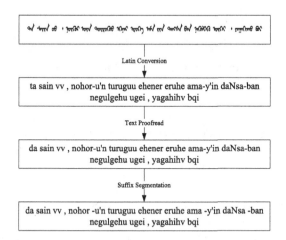

Fig. 3. An example of traditional Mongolian transformation steps.

3.1 Input Layer

Mongolian is a kind of agglutinative language with complex morphological structures [19]. Although there are natural spaces between Mongolian words, morphological segmentation is still needed for us. Mongolian word-formation is achieved by appending different suffixes to the stem, and they can also be concatenated layer by layer, which can lead to data sparsity. In this paper, we use Latin to deal with Mongolian and segment the suffixes to get the morpheme representations [22].

Before getting the morpheme representations of Mongolian question-answer pairs, we need to make some transformations to the traditional Mongolian language. As shown in Fig. 3, the steps of transformation are divided into three steps. First of all, we convert the traditional Mongolian alphabet to the corresponding Latin alphabet. Next, because a Mongolian glyph can map to different letters, it is necessary to proofread the text [8]. Finally, the suffixes connect to the stem through a Narrow No-Break Space (NNBS) (U+202F, Latin:"-"), so we can segment the suffixes to get the independent training units.

To obtain the morpheme embeddings of Mongolian question-answer pairs, we adopt Word2Vec [9], which contains CBOW (Continuous Bag of Word) and Skip-gram. And we choose the Skip-gram model to train the morpheme vectors.

3.2   Context Encoding Layer

LSTM is a variant of RNN, which can capture contextual dependencies effectively. In order to better represent the semantic information, we utilize the bi-directional LSTM (BiLSTM) to extract contextual features from question embeddings q and answer embeddings a.

$$\bar{q}_i = BiLSTM(q,\ i)\ ,\ \forall i\ \in\ [1,\ \ldots,\ m] \tag{1}$$

$$\bar{a}_j = BiLSTM(a,\ j)\ ,\ \forall j\ \in\ [1,\ \ldots,\ n] \tag{2}$$

where m is the length of question sentence, and n is the length of answer sentence.

3.3   Interaction Layer

In this layer, we introduce the interactive information enhancement, which contains sequence enhancement based on LSTMs and multi-cast attention using four variants of attention mechanism.

Sequence Enhancement. Inspired by the ESIM proposed by Chen et al. (2017), we also adopt the non-parameterized comparison strategy for sequence enhancement. Firstly, we calculate the similarity matrix between a question-answer pair encoded by BiLSTM.

$$e_{ij} = \bar{q}_i^T \bar{a}_j \tag{3}$$

Then the key of the strategy is soft alignment attention, which can get an attentive vector of a weighted summation of the other hidden states ($\bar{a}_j$ or $\bar{q}_i$). This process is shown in the following formulas:

$$\tilde{q}_i = \sum_{j=1}^{n} \frac{\exp\left(e_{ij}\right)}{\sum_{k=1}^{n} \exp\left(e_{ik}\right)} \bar{a}_j\ ,\ \forall i \in [1,\ldots,m] \tag{4}$$

$$\tilde{a}_j = \sum_{i=1}^{m} \frac{\exp\left(e_{ij}\right)}{\sum_{k=1}^{m} \exp\left(e_{kj}\right)} \bar{q}_i\ ,\ \forall j \in [1,\ldots,n] \tag{5}$$

where $\tilde{q}_i$ is a weighted summation of $\{\bar{a}_j\}_{j=1}^{n}$, $\tilde{a}_j$ is a weighted summation of $\{\bar{q}_i\}_{i=1}^{m}$.

Finally, we use the original hidden states and the attentive vectors to compute the difference and the element-wise product, which are then concatenated with the original hidden states and the attentive vectors.

$$T_i^q = [\bar{q}_i; \tilde{q}_i; \bar{q}_i - \tilde{q}_i; \bar{q}_i \odot \tilde{q}_i]\ ,\ \forall i \in [1,\ldots,m] \tag{6}$$

$$T_j^a = [\bar{a}_j; \tilde{a}_j; \bar{a}_j - \tilde{a}_j; \bar{a}_j \odot \tilde{a}_j]\ ,\ \forall j \in [1,\ldots,n] \tag{7}$$

Co-attention. Co-attention is a pair-wise attention mechanism, which has a natural symmetry between sentence pairs or other pairs [7]. Co-attention is a kind of variant of attention mechanism, and in this work, we decide to adopt four variants of attention mechanism: (1) **max-pooling co-attention**, (2) **mean-pooling co-attention**, (3) **alignment-pooling co-attention**, and (4) **self attention**.

The first step is to connect question and answer by calculating the similarity matrix between the initial morpheme embeddings of question-answer pairs.

$$s_{ij} = q_i^T M a_j \tag{8}$$

where M is a trainable parameter matrix.

Extractive pooling includes max-pooling and mean-pooling. **Max-pooling co-attention** aims to attend each morpheme of the sequence based on the maximum effect on each morpheme of the other sequence, while **mean-pooling co-attention** is focused on the average effect. The formulas are as following:

$$q_1' = Softmax(\max_{col}(s))^\top q \qquad a_1' = Softmax(\max_{row}(s))^\top a \tag{9}$$

$$q_2' = Softmax(\underset{col}{mean}(s))^\top q \qquad a_2' = Softmax(\underset{col}{mean}(s))^\top a \tag{10}$$

where q_1', q_2', a_1' and a_2' are the co-attentive representations of q or a.
Similar to the sequence enhancement mentioned above, **alignment-pooling co-attention** is computed individually to softly align each morpheme to the other sequence. The process is shown in the following formulas:

$$\tilde{q}_i' = \sum_{j=1}^{n} \frac{\exp(s_{ij})}{\sum_{k=1}^{n} \exp(s_{ik})} a_j \ , \ \forall i \in [1,\dots,m] \tag{11}$$

$$\tilde{a}_j' = \sum_{i=1}^{m} \frac{\exp(s_{ij})}{\sum_{k=1}^{m} \exp(s_{kj})} q_i \ , \ \forall j \in [1,\dots,n] \tag{12}$$

where $\tilde{q}_i'$ is a weighted summation of $\{a_j\}_{j=1}^{n}$, $\tilde{a}_j'$ is a weighted summation of $\{q_i\}_{i=1}^{m}$.

Self attention is applied to both question and answer independently. The sentence representation is denoted by x instead of q or a. The self attention function is computed as:

$$x_i' = \sum_{j=1}^{l} \frac{\exp(s_{ij})}{\sum_{k=1}^{l} \exp(s_{ik})} x_j \tag{13}$$

where x_i' is the self-attentional representation of x_j, l is the length of the sentence.

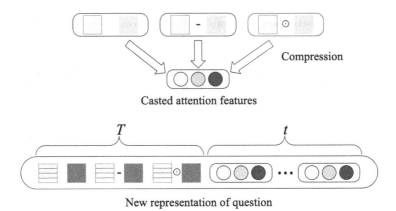

Fig. 4. Information enhancement of question.

Multi-cast Attention. Multi-cast attention can get a multi-casted feature vector from multiple attention mechanisms. Each attention mechanism performs concatenation, subtractive and multiplicative operations respectively, and uses a compression function to get three scalars. The initial morpheme embeddings of a question-answer pair q and a are replaced by x, and $\tilde{x}$ is the attentive vector. The casted attention features for each attention mechanism are shown in the following formulas:

$$f_{con} = F_c([\tilde{x}; x]) \tag{14}$$

$$f_{sub} = F_c(\tilde{x} - x) \tag{15}$$

$$f_{mul} = F_c(\tilde{x} \odot x) \tag{16}$$

where F_c is a compression function, $[.;.]$ is the concatenation operator and $\odot$ is the element-wise product.

Factorization Machines (FM) can make predictions on any real-valued feature vector [13]. Therefore, we adopt FM as a compression function to get casted scalars. The function is as follows:

$$F(x) = w_0 + \sum_{i=1}^{n} w_i x_i + \sum_{i=1}^{n} \sum_{j=i+1}^{n} <v_i, v_j> x_i x_j \tag{17}$$

where $w_0 \in \mathbb{R}$, $w_i \in \mathbb{R}^n$, $v_1, \ldots, v_n \in \mathbb{R}^{n \times k}$, and k is the number of latent factors of the FM model.

For each Mongolian question-answer pair, we apply four variants of attention mechanism mentioned above: (1) Max-pooling co-attention (2) Mean-pooling co-attention (3) Alignment-pooling co-attention and (4) Self-attention. Take the question sentence as an example, as shown in the Fig. 4, three scalars are generated from each attention mechanism, so the final multi-casted feature vector is $t \in \mathbb{R}^{12}$. As such, for each morpheme, we concatenate the enhanced sequence representation T and the multi-casted feature vector t to get the new representation O^q. And O^a can be obtained in the same way.

$$O_i^q = [T_i^q; t_i^q] \ , \ \forall i \in [1, \ldots, m] \tag{18}$$

$$O_j^a = [T_j^a; t_j^a] \ , \ \forall j \in [1, \ldots, n] \tag{19}$$

We use BiLSTM to encode interaction information at each time-step of O^q and O^a.

$$\overrightarrow{h_i^q} = \overrightarrow{LSTM}(h_{i-1}^q, O_i^q) \quad i = 1, \ldots, m \qquad \overleftarrow{h_i^q} = \overleftarrow{LSTM}(h_{i+1}^q, O_i^q) \quad i = m, \ldots, 1 \tag{20}$$

$$\overrightarrow{h_j^a} = \overrightarrow{LSTM}(h_{j-1}^a, O_j^a) \quad j = 1, \ldots, n \qquad \overleftarrow{h_j^a} = \overleftarrow{LSTM}(h_{j+1}^a, O_j^a) \quad j = n, \ldots, 1 \tag{21}$$

3.4 Matching Layer

To match question-answer pairs, we adopt the max-mean pooling matching strategy. Firstly, the cosine function is defined as follows:

$$sim = f_s(v_1, v_2; W) \tag{22}$$

where v_1 and v_2 are the d-dimensional vectors to be matched, $W \in \mathbb{R}^{l \times d}$ is the trainable parameter matrix, and l is the number of perspectives. For each dimension of the dimension space, it can be assigned different weights. Thus, the matching value from the k-th perspective is calculated by the formula as follows:

$$sim_k = cosine(W_k \circ v_1, W_k \circ v_2) \tag{23}$$

where $\circ$ represents the element-wise product, W_k is the k-th low of W.

Then we compare each time-step of question (or answer) representation against all time-steps of answer (or question) representation. For convenience, we only define the matching direction $q \to a$.

Morpheme Matching: For the initial morpheme embeddings of question-answer pairs, we define the max-mean pooling matching strategy. The formulas are as following:

$$\overline{sim_i^q}{}^{-max} = \max_{j \in (1 \ldots n)} f_s(q, a; W^1) \tag{24}$$

$$\overline{sim_i^q}{}^{-mean} = \underset{j \in (1 \ldots n)}{mean} \ f_s(q, a; W^1) \tag{25}$$

Interaction Matching: And for the representations of question-answer pairs after interaction, we also define the max-mean pooling matching strategy in forward direction and backward direction. Figure 5 shows the max-mean pooling matching in forward direction. The formulas are as following:

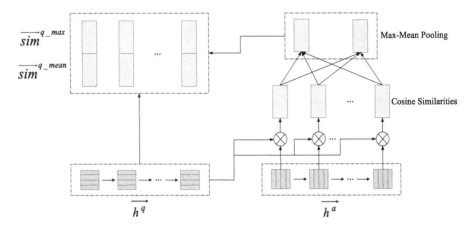

Fig. 5. The max-mean pooling matching in forward direction of matching direction $q \rightarrow a$.

$$\overrightarrow{sim}_i^{q\_max} = \max_{j \in (1...n)} f_s\left(\overrightarrow{h_i^q}, \overrightarrow{h_j^a}; W^2\right) \qquad \overleftarrow{sim}_i^{q\_max} = \max_{j \in (1...n)} f_s\left(\overleftarrow{h_i^q}, \overleftarrow{h_j^a}; W^3\right) \tag{26}$$

$$\overrightarrow{sim}_i^{q\_mean} = \underset{j \in (1...n)}{mean} f_s\left(\overrightarrow{h_i^q}, \overrightarrow{h_j^a}; W^2\right) \qquad \overleftarrow{sim}_i^{q\_mean} = \underset{j \in (1...n)}{mean} f_s\left(\overleftarrow{h_i^q}, \overleftarrow{h_j^a}; W^3\right) \tag{27}$$

At last, we concatenate all the results of the max-mean pooling matching.

$$sim_i^q = [\overline{sim}_i^{q\_max}; \overline{sim}_i^{q\_mean}; \overrightarrow{sim}_i^{q\_max}; \overrightarrow{sim}_i^{q\_mean}; \overleftarrow{sim}_i^{q\_max}; \overleftarrow{sim}_i^{q\_mean}] \tag{28}$$

where $i \in [1, \ldots, m]$, max is element-wise maximum and $mean$ is element-wise mean. The calculation process of sim_j^a is similar to that of sim_i^q.

3.5 Aggregation Layer

We utilize BiLSTM to aggregate the matching vectors sim_i^q and sim_j^a, which are calculated from two matching directions $q \rightarrow a$ and $a \rightarrow q$.

$$\overrightarrow{v_i^q} = \overrightarrow{LSTM}(v_{i-1}^q, sim_i^q) \quad i = 1, \ldots, m \qquad \overleftarrow{v_i^q} = \overleftarrow{LSTM}(v_{i+1}^q, sim_i^q) \quad i = m, \ldots, 1 \tag{29}$$

$$\overrightarrow{v_j^a} = \overrightarrow{LSTM}(v_{j-1}^a, sim_j^a) \quad j = 1, \ldots, n \qquad \overleftarrow{v_j^a} = \overleftarrow{LSTM}(v_{j+1}^a, sim_j^a) \quad j = n, \ldots, 1 \tag{30}$$

Then we concatenate the last hidden states of BiLSTM models used in two matching directions.

$$y_{out} = [\overrightarrow{v_m^q}; \overleftarrow{v_1^q}; \overrightarrow{v_n^a}; \overleftarrow{v_1^a}] \tag{31}$$

3.6   Prediction Layer

Mongolian question answer matching in this paper is a binary classification problem. We then pass the output of aggregation y_{out} into a two-layer feed-forward neural network and a softmax layer.

$$y_{pred} = softmax(W_2^F \cdot tanh(W_1^F \cdot y_{out} + b_1^F) + b_2^F) \tag{32}$$

where $W_1^F \in \mathbb{R}^{h_1 \times h_2}$, $b_1^F \in \mathbb{R}^{h_2}$, $W_2^F \in \mathbb{R}^{h_2 \times 2}$, $b_2^F \in \mathbb{R}^2$.

3.7   Model Training

To train our model, we minimize the binary cross-entropy loss.

$$\mathcal{L} = -\frac{1}{N} \sum_{i=1}^{N} [y_i \log P_i + (1 - y_i) \log(1 - P_i)] \tag{33}$$

where N is the number of labels, $y_i \in \{0,1\}$ and P_i is the predicted probability.

4   Experiments

In this section, we describe our experimental setup and give our experimental results.

4.1   Data Set and Evaluation Metrics

Our Mongolian question answering data set is translated from the Chinese question answering corpus and crawled from the Mongolian web sites. In order to improve the generalization ability of the model, we extend the original data set and construct negative samples. The ratio of positive and negative samples is 1 : 1. The data set contains 265194 question-answer pairs and each category is randomly divided into train, dev and test with the percent 80%, 10% and 10%, respectively.

We adopt Precision (P), Recall (R), F1-score (F1) and Accuracy (Acc) as the evaluation metrics of our experiments.

4.2   Model Configuration

We implement our model in TensorFlow. The batch size is set to 128, the epoch is set to 20, the max sentence length is set to 50 and the number of perspectives is set to 5. We use pre-trained 300-dimensional Mongolian Word2Vec embeddings. The size of hidden layers of all BiLSTM layers is set to 100. We use dropout with a rate of 0.1, which is applied to every layer. For training, we use the Adam optimizer [6] with an initial learning rate of 0.0005 to update parameters.

4.3   Baselines

In this subsection, we compare our model with several matching models on the Mongolian question answering data set. The first two models are based on sentence encoding methods, the next two models are based on attentive networks, while the others are based on compare-aggregate networks.

1) **SINN:** Yang and Kao (2020) proposed the model that applied self-attention based on RNN and CNN for sentence encoding.
2) **DiSAN:** Shen et al. (2018) proposed the model that used directional self-attention for encoding, and compressed features with multi-dimensional self-attention.
3) **ABCNN:** Yin et al. (2016) proposed the model that computed the attention matrix before and after convolution for modeling sentence pairs.
4) **DRCN:** Kim et al. (2019) proposed the model that used stacked RNN and co-attentive features to enhance representation.
5) **MULT:** Wang and Jiang (2017) presented the model that performed word-level matching by element-wise multiplication and aggregated by CNN.
6) **CAFE:** Tay et al. (2017) presented the model that adopted factorization machines to compress the alignment vectors into scalar features for augmenting the word representations.
7) **MCAN:** Tay et al. (2018) presented the model that adopted several attention variants and performed multiple comparison operators.
8) **ESIM:** Chen et al. (2017) presented the sequential inference model using chain LSTMs.

4.4 Results

Table 1 and Table 2 report the overall performance of the different models and the performance comparison of each category.

Table 1 presents that our Interactive Mongolian Question Answer Matching Model (IMQAMM) achieves an accuracy of 83.02%, which has already outperformed all the baseline models. Notably, IMQAMM has an improvement of about 1.23% compared to the highest ESIM in the baseline models. It shows that the introduction of multi-cast attention is helpful. IMQAMM outperforms

Table 1. Test accuracy on Mongolian question answering data set.

Model	Acc(%)
SINN	75.21
DiSAN	81.69
ABCNN	73.78
DRCN	75.31
MULT	81.19
CAFE	81.27
MCAN	81.63
ESIM	81.79
IMQAMM	**83.02**

Table 2. Performance comparison of different methods on test set.

Model	Matched			Mismatched		
	P(%)	R(%)	F1(%)	P(%)	R(%)	F1(%)
SINN	72.53	81.17	76.60	78.62	69.25	73.64
DiSAN	82.73	80.11	81.40	80.72	83.27	81.98
ABCNN	71.10	80.11	75.34	77.23	67.44	72.00
DRCN	77.53	71.29	74.28	73.43	79.33	76.27
MULT	82.80	78.74	80.72	79.73	83.64	81.64
CAFE	80.97	81.74	81.35	81.57	80.79	81.18
MCAN	80.78	83.01	81.88	82.53	80.25	81.37
ESIM	82.23	81.10	81.66	81.36	82.47	81.91
IMQAMM	83.68	82.04	**82.85**	82.39	84.00	**83.18**

MCAN and CAFE by 1.39% and 1.75%, which proves the significance of sequence enhancement. Compared with DRCN and ABCNN, the five models at the bottom of Table 1 have significant improvements, thus compare-aggregate networks can provide more interactive information than attentive networks in this task. And the performance of our model is higher than SINN and DiSAN, which indicates that our interactive model is better than the sentence encoding based methods on Mongolian question answering data set.

Table 2 presents the performance comparison of different methods. The improvements of IMQAMM over the highest ESIM on the matched F1 score and mismatched F1 score are 1.19% and 1.27%. Compared with all the baseline methods, our IMQAMM is competitive in each category.

4.5   Ablation Study

As shown in Table 3, we conduct an ablation study to analyze the influence of each component. We remove three parts from IMQAMM to examine the influence: 1) Multi-Cast Attention. 2) Morpheme Matching. 3) Interaction Matching.

According to the results of ablation experiments in Table 3, we can see the key components of our model. Firstly, when removing Multi-Cast Attention, the accuracy decreases by 0.38%, which proves that Multi-Cast Attention is helpful for our model. Secondly, we find that Morpheme Matching is necessary for our model. When we remove it, the accuracy is reduced by 0.6%. Finally, when removing Interaction Matching, we can observe that the performance of our model drops dramatically. The accuracy drops from 83.02% to 80.52%. This result shows that Interaction Matching is crucial for our model.

Table 3. Ablation study on Mongolian question answering data set.

Model	Acc(%)
IMQAMM	**83.02**
w/o Multi-cast attention	82.64
w/o Morpheme matching	82.42
w/o Interaction matching	80.52

5   Conclusion

In this paper, we propose an Interactive Mongolian Question Answer Matching Model (IMQAMM), which mainly combines interactive information enhancement and max-mean pooling matching. First of all, we make some transformations to traditional Mongolian language and introduce the morpheme vectors. Second, we enhance the sequence representation by concatenating a series of feature vectors. Third, the multi-cast attention is introduced to alleviate the data-sparse problem caused by complex Mongolian morphological structures. Finally, the max-mean pooling matching strategy is applied to match question-answer pairs in two directions. Experimental results show that our model performed well on the Mongolian question answering data set.

However, there is still a lot of room for improvement. In the future work, we will consider using the pre-trained language model BERT to get a better initialization, which may help improve the performance of our model.

Acknowledgements. This work is supported by National Key R&D Program (Nos. 2018YFE0122900); National Natural Science Foundation of China (Nos. 62066033, 61773224); Inner Mongolia Applied Technology Research and Development Fund Project (Nos. 2019GG372, 2020GG0046, 2021GG0158, 2020PT0002); Inner Mongolia Achievement Transformation Project (Nos. 2019CG028); Inner Mongolia Natural Science Foundation (2020BS06001); Inner Mongolia Autonomous Region Higher Education Science and Technology Research Project (NJZY20008); Inner Mongolia Autonomous Region Overseas Students Innovation and Entrepreneurship Startup Program; Inner Mongolia Discipline Inspection and Supervision Big Data Laboratory Open Project. We are grateful for the useful suggestions from the anonymous reviewers.

References

1. Bowman, S., Angeli, G., Potts, C., Manning, C.: A large annotated corpus for learning natural language inference. arXiv preprint arXiv:1508.05326 (2015)
2. Chen, Q., Zhu, X., Ling, Z., Wei, S., Jiang, H., Inkpen, D.: Enhanced LSTM for natural language inference. arXiv preprint arXiv:1609.06038 (2016)
3. Mirakyan, M., Hambardzumyan, K., Khachatrian, H.: Natural language inference over interaction space. arXiv preprint arXiv:1709.04348 (2018)
4. Huang, P., He, X., Gao, J., Deng, L., Acero, A., Heck, L.: Learning deep structured semantic models for web search using clickthrough data. In: Proceedings of the

22nd ACM International Conference on Information & Knowledge Management, pp. 2333–2338 (2013)

5. Kim, S., Kang, I., Kwak, N.: Semantic sentence matching with densely-connected recurrent and co-attentive information. In: Proceedings of the AAAI Conference on Artificial Intelligence, vol. 33, no. 01, pp. 6586–6593 (2019)

6. Kingma, D., Ba, J.: Adam: a method for stochastic optimization. arXiv preprint arXiv:1412.6980 (2014)

7. Lu, J., Yang, J., Batra, D., Parikh, D.: Hierarchical question-image co-attention for visual question answering. arXiv preprint arXiv:1606.00061 (2016)

8. Lu, M., Bao, F., Gao, G., Wang, W., Zhang, H.: An automatic spelling correction method for classical Mongolian. In: Douligeris, C., Karagiannis, D., Apostolou, D. (eds.) KSEM 2019. LNCS (LNAI), vol. 11776, pp. 201–214. Springer, Cham (2019). https://doi.org/10.1007/978-3-030-29563-9_19

9. Mikolov, T., Sutskever, I., Chen, K., Corrado, G., Dean, J.: Distributed representations of words and phrases and their compositionality. In: Advances in Neural Information Processing Systems, pp. 3111–3119 (2013)

10. Mueller, J., Thyagarajan, A.: Siamese recurrent architectures for learning sentence similarity, vol. 30, no. 1 (2015)

11. Palangi, H., et al.: Semantic modelling with long-short-term memory for information retrieval. arXiv preprint arXiv:1412.6629 (2014)

12. Parikh, A., Täckström, O., Das, D., Uszkoreit, J.: A decomposable attention model for natural language inference. arXiv preprint arXiv:1606.01933 (2016)

13. Rendle, S.: Factorization machines. In: IEEE International Conference on Data Mining, pp. 995–1000 (2010)

14. Shen, Y., He, X., Gao, J., Deng, L., Mesnil, G.: A latent semantic model with convolutional-pooling structure for information retrieval. In: Proceedings of the 23rd ACM International Conference on Conference on Information and Knowledge Management, pp. 101–110 (2014)

15. Shen, T., Zhou, T., Long, G., Jiang, J., Pan, S., Zhang, C.: DiSAN: directional self-attention network for RNN/CNN-free language understanding. In: Thirty-Second AAAI Conference on Artificial Intelligence, vol. 32, no. 1 (2018)

16. Tan, M., Dos Santos, C., Xiang, B., Zhou, B.: Improved representation learning for question answer matching. In: Proceedings of the 54th Annual Meeting of the Association for Computational Linguistics (Volume 1: Long Papers), pp. 464–473 (2016)

17. Tay, Y., Tuan, L., Hui, S.: Compare, compress and propagate: enhancing neural architectures with alignment factorization for natural language inference. arXiv preprint arXiv:1801.00102 (2017)

18. Tay, Y., Tuan, L., Hui, S.: Multi-cast attention networks for retrieval-based question answering and response prediction. arXiv preprint arXiv:1806.00778 (2018)

19. Wang, W., Bao, F., Gao, G.: Mongolian named entity recognition using suffixes segmentation. In: 2015 International Conference on Asian Language Processing (IALP), pp. 169–172 (2015)

20. Wang, S., Jiang, J.: A compare-aggregate model for matching text sequences. In: Proceedings of 5th International Conference on Learning Representations (2017)

21. Wang, Z., Hamza W., Florian, R.: Bilateral multi-perspective matching for natural language sentences. arXiv preprint arXiv:1702.03814 (2017)

22. Wang, W., Bao, F., Gao, G.: Learning morpheme representation for Mongolian named entity recognition. Neural Process. Lett. **50**(3), 2647–2664 (2019). https://doi.org/10.1007/s11063-019-10044-6

23. Yang, K., Kao, H.: Generalize sentence representation with self-inference. In: Proceedings of the AAAI Conference on Artificial Intelligence, vol. 34, pp. 9394–9401 (2020)
24. Yin, W., Schütze, H., Xiang, B., Zhou, B.: ABCNN: attention-based convolutional neural network for modeling sentence pairs. In: Transactions of the Association for Computational Linguistics, vol. 4, pp. 259–272 (2016)

Language Resource and Evaluation

TCM-SD: A Benchmark for Probing Syndrome Differentiation via Natural Language Processing

Mucheng Ren[1] , Heyan Huang[1](✉) , Yuxiang Zhou[1] , Qianwen Cao[1] ,
Yuan Bu[2], and Yang Gao[1]

[1] School of Computer Science and Technology, Beijing Institute of Technology,
Beijing, China
{renm,hhy63,yxzhou,qwcao,gyang}@bit.edu.cn
[2] Xuzhou City Hospital of Traditional Chinese Medicine, Xuzhou, China

Abstract. Traditional Chinese Medicine (TCM) is a natural, safe, and effective therapy that has spread and been applied worldwide. The unique TCM diagnosis and treatment system requires a comprehensive analysis of a patient's symptoms hidden in the clinical record written in free text. Prior studies have shown that this system can be informationized and intelligentized with the aid of artificial intelligence (AI) technology, such as natural language processing (NLP). However, existing datasets are not of sufficient quality nor quantity to support the further development of data-driven AI technology in TCM. Therefore, in this paper, we focus on the core task of the TCM diagnosis and treatment system—syndrome differentiation (SD)—and we introduce the first public large-scale benchmark for SD, called TCM-SD. Our benchmark contains 54,152 real-world clinical records covering 148 syndromes. Furthermore, we collect a large-scale unlabelled textual corpus in the field of TCM and propose a domain-specific pre-trained language model, called ZY-BERT. We conducted experiments using deep neural networks to establish a strong performance baseline, reveal various challenges in SD, and prove the potential of domain-specific pre-trained language model. Our study and analysis reveal opportunities for incorporating computer science and linguistics knowledge to explore the empirical validity of TCM theories.

Keywords: Natural language processing · Bioinformatics · Traditional chinese medicine

1 Introduction

As an essential application domain of natural language processing (NLP), medicine has received remarkable attention in recent years. Many studies have explored the integration of a variety of NLP tasks with medicine, including question answering [21,29], machine reading comprehension [17,37], dialogue [38],

---

This work is supported by funds from the National Natural Science Foundation of China (No.U21B2009).

M. Sun et al. (Eds.): CCL 2022, LNAI 13603, pp. 247–263, 2022.
https://doi.org/10.1007/978-3-031-18315-7_16

named entity recognition [11,12], and information retrieval [20]. Meanwhile, numerous datasets in the medical domain with different task formats have also been proposed [17,21,29]. These have greatly promoted the development of the field. Finally, breakthroughs in such tasks have led to advances in various medical-related applications, such as decision support [9,23] and International Classification of Disease (ICD) coding [4,36].

However, most existing datasets and previous studies are related to modern medicine, while traditional medicine has rarely been explored. Compared to modern medicine, traditional medicine is often faced with a lack of standards and scientific explanations, making it more challenging. Therefore, it is more urgent to adopt methods of modern science, especially NLP, to explore the principles of traditional medicine, since unstructured texts are ubiquitous in this field.

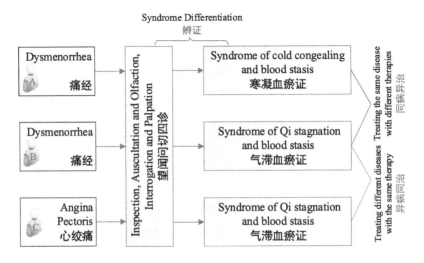

Fig. 1. Concept of Traditional Chinese Medicine (TCM) syndrome differentiation.

TCM, as the representative of traditional medicine, is a medical system with a unique and complete theoretical basis formed by long-term medical practice under the influence and guidance of classical Chinese materialism and dialectics. Unlike modern medicine, in which medical professionals assign treatments according to disease type, TCM practitioners conduct in-depth analyses based on evidence collected from four diagnostics methods—inspection, auscultation and olfaction, interrogation, and palpation—to determine which type of **syndrome (zheng, 证)** the patient experiencing. Different treatment methods are then adopted according to the type of syndrome. Therefore, patients with the same disease may have different syndromes and thus receive different treatments, while patients with different diseases may have the same syndrome and thus undergo the same treatment. These concepts are called "treating the same disease with different therapies (同病异治) " and "treating different diseases with the same therapy (异病同治) ," respectively, which are the core methods upheld by TCM.

For the example shown in Fig. 1, patients A and B have the same disease—dysmenorrhea—but one is influenced by cold while the other is driven by Qi stagnation (which is a specific concept in TCM). Thus, different therapies would be assigned. However, patient C suffered from angina pectoris but shared the same syndrome as patient B. Therefore, they would be treated with similar therapies. Thus, the **syndrome**, instead of the disease, can be regarded as the primary operating unit in the TCM medical system, which not only effectively summarizes the patients' symptoms but also determines the subsequent treatment. In this process, known as **syndrome differentiation**, *the inferencing task of deciding which syndrome is associated with a patient based on clinical information*, is a vital pivot of the TCM medical system.

In recent years, with the discovery of artemisinin [30] and the beneficial clinical manifestations of TCM to treat COVID-19 [34,41], TCM has increasingly attracted attention. There have been some studies in which NLP techniques were used to explore SD tasks [19,22,33,39,40], but the development has been significantly hindered by the lack of large-scale, carefully designed, public datasets.

Therefore, this paper aims to further integrate traditional medicine and artificial intelligence (AI). In particular, we focus on the core task of TCM—syndrome differentiation (SD)—to propose a high-quality, public SD benchmark that includes 54,152 samples from real-world clinical records. To our best knowledge, this is the first time that a textual benchmark has been constructed in the TCM domain. Furthermore, we crawled data from the websites to construct a TCM domain text corpus and used this to pre-train a domain-specific language model called as ZY-BERT (where ZY came from the Chinese initials of TCM). The experiments and analysis of this dataset not only explored the characteristics of SD but also verified the effectiveness of domain-specific language model.

Our contributions are summarized as follows:

1. We have systematically constructed the first public large-scale SD benchmark in a format that conforms to NLP, and established the strong baselines. This can encourage researchers use NLP techniques to explore the principles of TCM that are not sufficiently explained in other fields.
2. We proposed two novel methods, pruning and merging, which could normalize the syndrome type, improve the quality of the dataset, and also provide a reference for the construction of similar TCM datasets in the future.
3. We proposed a domain-specific language model named as ZY-BERT pre-trained with a large-scale unlabeled TCM domain corpus, which produces the best performances so far.

2   Preliminaries

To facilitate the comprehension of this paper and its motivation and significance, we will briefly define several basic concepts in TCM and analyze the differences between TCM and modern medicine.

2.1   Characteristics of Traditional Chinese Medicine (TCM) Diagnosis

The most apparent characteristic of TCM is that it has a unique and complete diagnostic system that differs from modern medicine. In modern medicine, with the assistance of medical instruments, the type of disease can be diagnosed according to the explicit digital indicators, such as blood pressure levels. However, TCM adopts abstract indicators, such as Yin and Yang, Exterior and Interior, Hot and Cold, and Excess and Deficiency.

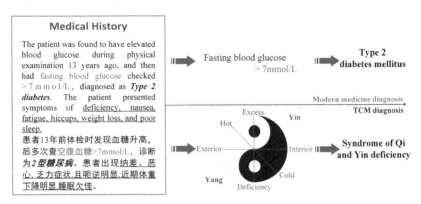

Fig. 2. Different diagnostic processes of TCM and modern medicine for the same medical history.

As shown in Fig. 2, given a medical history, modern medicine diagnoses the disease based on the level of fasting blood glucose, while TCM would map the various symptoms into a specific space with a unique coordinate system, analyze the latent causes, and combine them to determine a certain syndrome. Compared with the apparent numerical indicators of modern medicine, the concept of TCM is far more abstract and challenging to explain with modern medical theories.

However, TCM's difficult-to-describe nature does not mean that it has no value or rationality. In contrast, TCM has various complete and self-contained SD theories. Therefore, to explore TCM, we should not confine ourselves to the biomedical field. We may adopt NLP to explore TCM, which mainly consists of unstructured text. The linguistic characteristics may offer a scientific way to explain TCM theories. Therefore, in this paper, we present an SD dataset for further development.

2.2   Differences Between ICD Coding and Syndrome Differentiation

Automatic ICD coding is defined as assigning disease codes to Electronic Medical Records (EMR) , which is similar to TCM syndrome differentiation. Yet the two tasks are worlds apart in difficulty. Generally, the name of a patient's disease is directly recorded in EMR, and the task of the ICD coding is simply to normalize the names of these diseases in the manner of the ICD standard, without requiring

Table 1. Comparison of medical datasets in traditional and modern medicine. This table only includes textual data. The abbreviations in the table are defined as follows: classification (Class.), machine reading comprehension (MRC), de-identification (De-ID.), disease name recognition (DNR), natural language inference (NLI), recognizing question entailment (RQE), and question answering (QA).

	Medical system	Domain	# of syndromes	# of samples	Task Type	Is available?	Language
This Work	Traditional Medicine	General	148	54,152	Class.,MRC	Yes	Chinese
Wang [32]	Traditional Medicine	Liver Cirrhosis	3	406	Class	No	Chinese
Zhang [39]	Traditional Medicine	Stroke	3	654	Class	No	Chinese
Wang [33]	Traditional Medicine	Diabetes	12	1,180	Class	No	Chinese
Pang [22]	Traditional Medicine	AIDS	7	12,000	Class	No	Chinese
Johnson [13]	Modern Medicine	Critical Care	-	53,423	-	Yes	English
Stubbs [28]	Modern Medicine	General	-	1,304	De-ID	Yes	English
Dougan [8]	Modern Medicine	General	-	6,892	DNR	Yes	English
Abacha [1]	Modern Medicine	General	-	405;203;383	NLI;RQE;QA	Yes	English
Tian [29]	Modern Medicine	General	-	46,731	MRC	Yes	Chinese

a deep understanding of the context. For the example shown in Fig. 2, **Type 2 diabetes** has already described in the medical history so that ICD coding can be easily completed. While the syndrome differentiation not only requires collecting scattering evidence from the context through deep understanding, but also need to execute reliable and feasible inference, which brings a huge challenge to the model.

3   Related Works

There are three main streams of work related to this manuscript: medical dataset, natural language processing in syndrome differentiation and domain specific pretrained language model.

3.1   Medical Datasets

In recent years, health record systems in hospitals have been moving towards digitalization and electronization, and a large amount of clinical data has been accumulated. To make more effective use of these data and provide better medical services, some studies led by MIMIC-III [13] have shared these valuable data with medical researchers around the world [8,28]. Subsequently, with the development of AI, the domain characteristics of various studies have been combined to design various task-oriented datasets [17,21,29]. These datasets have greatly promoted the development of AI in the medical field and have had a profound impact on society in terms of health and well-being.

However, as shown in Table 1, most of these publicly available datasets focus on modern medicine, there are far fewer datasets on traditional medicine. This is because, compared with traditional medicine, modern medicine has a rigorous, scientific, and standardized medical system, which can efficiently collect high-quality data. Furthermore, the standardization of traditional medicine is still in

Table 2. Summary of pre-training details for the various BERT models.

Model	Corpus	Domain	Language	Corpus Size
BERT [7]	Wiki+Books	General	EN	3.3B tokens
RoBERTa-wwm [5]	Web Crawl	General	CN	5.4B tokens
MacBERT [6]	Web Crawl	General	CN	5.4B tokens
SciBERT [3]	Web Crawl	Science	EN	3.2B tokens
BioBERT [16]	PubMed	Medical	EN	4.5B tokens
ClinicalBERT [2]	MIMIC	Medical	EN	0.5B tokens
BlueBERT [24]	PubMed+MIMIC	Medical	EN	4.5B tokens
PubMedBERT [10]	PubMed	Medical	EN	3.1B tokens
TCM-BERT [35]	Web Crawl	Medical (TCM)	CN	0.02B tokens
ZY-BERT (Ours)	Web Crawl	Medical (TCM)	CN	0.4B tokens

the development stage, which makes the collection and construction of relevant datasets extremely challenging. Thus the scarce TCM SD datasets has hindered the development of AI in this field. To alleviate this issue, we constructed the first large-scale, publicly available dataset for TCM SD.

3.2 Natural Language Processing (NLP) in Syndrome Differentiation

At present, most existing studies have treated SD as a multi-class classification task (i.e., taking the medical records as the input and output the predicted one from numerous candidate syndrome labels). Zhang [39] used support vector machines to classify three types of syndromes for stroke patients. Zhang [40] also introduced an ensemble model consisting of four methods, a back-propagation neural network, the random forest algorithm, a support vector classifier, and the extreme gradient boosting method, to classify common diseases and syndromes simultaneously. Wang [33] proposed a multi-instance, multi-task convolutional neural network (CNN) framework to classify 12 types of syndromes in 1,915 samples. Pang [22] proposed a multilayer perceptron (MLP) model with an attention mechanism to predict the syndrome types of acquired immunodeficiency syndrome (AIDS). Similarly, Liu [19] proposed a text-hierarchical attention network for 1,296 clinical records with 12 kinds of syndromes. However, these approaches only worked well for small-scale datasets. Our work established a series of strong baseline models and conducted comparisons on a larger-scale datasets.

3.3 Domain Specific Pre-trained Language Model

Large-scale neural language models pre-trained on unlabelled text has proved to be a successful approach for various downstream NLP tasks. A representative example is Bidirectional Encoder Representations from Transformers

(BERT) [7], which has become a foundation block for building task-specific NLP models. However, most works typically focus on pre-training in the general domain, while domain-specific pre-training has not received much attention. Table 2 summarizes common language models pre-trained in either general domain or specific domain. In general, biomedical and science are mainstream fields of pre-training language model, but in the filed of TCM, there is no much work that has been conducted as for as we know.

The reasons may be two-fold. On the one hand, TCM lacks large-scale public text corpus, like Wikipedia and PubMed. We deal with this issue by presenting a corpus in TCM domain via crawling and collecting related documents from the websites and books. On the other hand, there is also a lack of downstream tasks that can verify the performance of the pre-training language model, thus we propose the syndrome differentiation task to measure its effectiveness.

To be noticed, an existing work already proposed a language model in the filed of TCM, named as TCM-BERT [35], but it did not undergo pre-training of large-scale corpus, but was only finetuned on small-scale nonpublic corpus (0.02B tokens). While, our work provide a more completed TCM-domain corpus (over 20 times larger) and verify its effectiveness during pre-training stage.

4   Benchmark and Methods

The TCM-SD benchmark that we collected contains over 65,000 real-world Chinese clinical notes. Table 3 presents an example. Specifically, each clinical note contains the following five components: **Medical history** is the critical information for completing SD. It mainly describes a patient's condition at admission; **Chief complaint** is a concise statement describing the main symptoms that appeared in the medical history; **Four diagnostic methods record (FDMR)** is a template statement consisting of four main TCM diagnostic methods: inspection, auscultation and olfaction, interrogation, and palpation; **ICD-10 index number and name** represents the name and corresponding unique ID of the patient's disease; **Syndrome name** is the syndrome of the current patient. However, the raw data could not be used directly for the SD task due to the lack of quality control. Therefore, a careful normalization was further conducted to preprocess the data.

4.1   Syndrome Normalization

Like ICD, TCM already has national standards for the classification of TCM diseases, named *Classification and Codes of Diseases and Zheng of Traditional Chinese Medicine* (GB/T15657-1995), which stipulates the coding methods of diseases and the zheng of TCM. However, TCM standardization is still in its early phase of development and faces inadequate publicizing and implementation [31]. Some TCM practitioners still have low awareness and different attitudes toward TCM standardization, resulting in inconsistent naming methods for the same syndrome.

Table 3. A sample clinical record from the TCM-SD dataset with related external knowledge. An explicit match between the medical history and external knowledge is marked in blue, while the text in orange is an example of an implicit match that required temporal reasoning.

Medical History
The patient began to suffer from repeated dizziness more than eight years ago, and the blood pressure measured in a resting-state was higher than normal many times. The highest blood pressure was 180/100 mmHg, and the patient was clearly diagnosed with hypertension. The patient usually took Nifedipine Sustained Release Tablets (20 mg), and the blood pressure was generally controlled, and dizziness occasionally occurred. Four days before the admission, the patient's dizziness worsened after catching a cold, accompanied by asthma, which worsened with activity. Furthermore, the patient coughed yellow and thick sputum. The symptoms were not significantly relieved after taking antihypertensive drugs and antibiotics, and the blood pressure fluctuated wildly. On admission, the patient still experienced dizziness, coughing with yellow mucous phlegm, chills, no fever, no conscious activity disorder, no palpitations, no chest tightness, no chest pain, no sweating, a weak waist and knees, less sleep and more dreams, forgetfulness, dry eyes, vision loss, red hectic cheeks, and dry pharynx, five upset hot, no nausea and vomiting, general eating and sleeping, and normal defecation. 患者8年余前开始反复出现头晕，多次于静息状态下测血压高于正常，最高血压180/100 mmHg，明确诊断为高血压，平素服用硝苯地平缓释片20 mg，血压控制一般，头晕时有发作。此次入院前4天受凉后头晕再发加重，伴憋喘，动则加剧，咳嗽、咳黄浓痰，自服降压药、抗生素症状缓解不明显，血压波动大。入院时：仍有头晕，咳嗽、咳黄粘痰，畏寒，无发热，无意识活动障碍，无心慌、胸闷，无胸痛、汗出，腰酸膝软，少寐多梦，健忘，两目干涩，视力减退，颧红咽干，五心烦热，无恶心呕吐，饮食睡眠一般，二便正常。
Chief Complaint
Repeated dizziness for more than eight years, aggravated with asthma for four days. 反复头晕8年余，加重伴喘憋4天。
Four Diagnostic Methods Record
Mind: clear; spirit: weak; body shape: moderate; speech: clear,..., tongue: red with little coating; pulse: small and wiry. 神志清晰，精神欠佳，形体适中，语言清晰，...，舌红少苔，脉弦细。
ICD-10 Name and ID: Vertigo (眩晕病) BNG070
Syndrome Name: Syndrome of Yin deficiency and Yang hyperactivity 阴虚阳亢证
External Knowledge Corpus:
A syndrome with Yin deficiency and Yang hyperactivity is a type of TCM syndrome. It refers to Yin liquid deficiency and Yang loss restriction and hyperactivity. Common symptoms include dizziness, hot flashes, night sweats, tinnitus, irritability, insomnia, red tongue, less saliva, and wiry pulse. It is mainly caused by old age, exposure to exogenous heat for a long period, the presence of a serious disease for a long period, emotional disorders, and unrestrained sexual behavior. Common diseases include insomnia, vertigo, headache, stroke, deafness, tinnitus, premature ejaculation, and other diseases. 阴虚阳亢证，中医病证名。是指阴液亏虚，阳失制约而偏亢，以头晕目眩，潮热盗汗，头晕耳鸣，烦躁失眠，舌红少津，脉细数为常见证的证候，多因年老体衰，外感热邪日久，或大病久病迁延日久，情志失调，房事不节等所致。常见于不寐、眩晕、头痛、中风、耳聋耳鸣、早泄等疾病中。

Therefore, based on the above issues, we accomplish syndrome normalization in two stages: merging and pruning.

Merging operation is mainly used in two cases. The first is cases in which the current syndrome has multiple names, and all appear in the dataset. For example, *syndrome of wind and heat* (风热证) and *syndrome of wind and heat attacking the external* (风热外袭证) belong to the same syndrome, and we would merge them into one unified name. In this case, we used the national standards for screening. Another is that the current syndrome name does not exist in a standardized form. Therefore, we recruited experts to conduct syndrome differentiation according to the specific case clinical records and finally merge the invalid syndromes into standard syndromes. For example, *syndrome of spleen and kidney yang failure* (脾肾阳衰证) would be merged into *syndrome of spleen and kidney yang deficiency* (脾肾阳虚证) .

Pruning operation is mainly applied to syndromes with non-standard names that experts fail to differentiate due to vague features. In addition, since syndrome names are hierarchically graded, we pruned out syndromes with higher grades to ensure that the syndromes that appear in the current dataset are the most basic grade, that is the most specific ones that determine the subsequent treatment. For example, *syndrome of wind and cold* (风寒证) is a high-grade syndrome, and its clinical manifestations can be a *syndrome of exterior tightened by wind-cold* (风寒束表证) or *syndrome of wind-cold attacking lung* (风寒袭肺证) ; each has different symptoms and treatment methods.

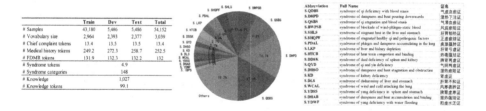

Fig. 3. The characteristics and syndrome distribution in the dataset.

4.2 Dataset Statistics

After normalization, the number of syndromes in the dataset was reduced from the original 548 categories to 244. Considering that some syndromes are infrequent, we further filtered out syndrome categories containing fewer than 10 samples when partitioning the dataset. Then, the processed dataset with 148 syndrome categories and 54,152 samples was divided into a training set, a development (Dev) set, and a test set with a ratio of 8:1:1. The dataset characteristics and syndrome distribution shown in Fig. 3.

Since the data were collected from real-world scenarios, the distribution of syndromes was inevitably unbalanced, leading to a significant gap between the number of rare syndromes and the number of the common ones. The subsequent experiments demonstrate the challenges brought by long-tail distribution issues, and we show that this issue can be mitigated by introducing external knowledge and domain-specific pre-training.

4.3 External Knowledge

Current clinical records do not contain any relevant knowledge about the target syndromes, which causes models to have to rely on remembering patterns to complete the task. Therefore, we constructed an external unstructured knowledge corpus encompassing 1,027 types of TCM syndromes by web crawling for information on all the TCM syndromes on the online[1]. Specifically, the knowledge of each syndrome consisted of three parts: the cause of the syndrome, the main manifestations, and common related diseases. Table 3 shows an example. We demonstrate the effectiveness of this knowledge in the experimental section.

4.4 ZY-BERT

In general, ZY-BERT differs with TCM-BERT in two main parts: data and pre-training task.

First, the scale and quality of unlabelled text corpus directly affect the performance of pre-trained language models. Previous work TCM-BERT [35] directly used clinical records as pre-training corpus, resulting in monotonic data type and limited corpus size, which could not meet the needs of large-scale pre-training language model. To deal with this issue, we collected unlabelled data varies in different types from the TCM related websites, including books, articles from websites and academic papers from China National Knowledge Infrastructure (CNKI), counting over 400 million tokens.

Furthermore, the previous work TCM-BERT adopts char masking (CM) and next sentence prediction (NSP) as the pre-training tasks. However, Chinese words usually consist of multiple characters and masking single character might destroy the meaning of the whole word. For example, the word phrase *Yang Deficiency(阳虚)* consists of two characters. Thus, we borrowed the idea of Whole Word Masking from Cui [5] and replace NSP with it, which could add challenges to the model training process and allow the model to learn more complex linguistic features.

Finally, the pre-trained language model consists of 24 Transformer layers, with input dimensionality of 1024. Each transformer contains 16 attention heads. Then we trained the model 300K steps with a maximum learning rate 5e-5 and a batch size of 256. Other hyperparameters and pre-training details are kept same as the ones used in Liu [18].

5 Experiments

We selected the multi-class classification task as the primary form of SD to directly compare the performances of the existing models against the TCM-SD dataset, and used the accuracy and Macro-F1 as evaluation metrics. Specifically, the chief complaint and medical history were concatenated as the inputs, i.e. *[CLS] Chief Complaint [SEP] Medical History [SEP]*, where [CLS] and [SEP]

---

[1] www.dayi.org.cn.

are special tokens used for classification and separation. Then the model predicts the target syndromes from 148 candidate labels based on the representation of [CLS] token.

5.1 Baseline

The baseline methods we used consisted of four types: statistical methods, classical neural-network-based (NN-based) methods, language-model-based (LM-based) methods and domain-specific LM-based methods.

Statistical Methods. These methods were the decision tree (DT) and support vector machine (SVM) methods. These two statistical methods have been widely used in previous studies on SD.

Classical NN-Based Methods. These methods included a Bi-LSTM [27], a Bi-GRU [25], and a two-layer CNN [14]. Word embeddings were retrieved from the Chinese version of BERT [5].

LM-Based Methods. These methods included several popular LMs, such as BERT [7], RoBERTa [18], distillBERT [26], and ALBERT [15]. These models concatenate multiple pieces of text with special tokens as inputs, make classifications based on the hidden states of the first token, or determine the start and end of the answer by training two classifiers.

Domain-Specific LM-Based Methods. These methods are similar with LM-based ones but usually pre-trained on domain-specific corpus rather than general domain corpus. TCM-BERT [35] and our proposed ZY-BERT are the two LM used in this manuscripts.

5.2 Main Results

Table 4 presents the performances of all the methods for the classification task. Generally, all the methods had good accuracy, which demonstrated that the models were effective at fitting when enough examples were supplied. However, each syndrome in the TCM-SD dataset should have the same importance. Thus, the Macro-F1 is a more accurate metric to evaluate the performances of the models. The Macro-F1 scores achieved by the models were much lower than the accuracy, which demonstrated the challenges of the imbalanced TMC-SD datasets.

Moreover, the statistical methods achieved better scores than the classical NN-based methods. This is because the structures designed for focusing on contextualized representations, such as the Bi-LSTM and Bi-GRU networks, were not good at capturing features, and the performances were worse. In contrast, the SVM and CNN methods were good at extracting local features and obtained better scores. Nonetheless, the language models still achieved the highest scores, demonstrating the effectiveness of the large-scale corpus pre-training.

Table 4. Performance for the classification task. The marker [†] refers to *p*-value <0.01.

Method	Dev				Test			
	Acc.	Macro-F1	Macro-R	Macro-P	Acc.	Macro-F1	Macro-R	Macro-P
DT	59.42%	20.68%	21.33%	21.52%	59.10%	21.67%	22.38%	22.20%
SVM	77.63%	32.13%	29.56%	43.10%	78.53%	36.37%	32.98%	49.35%
BiLSTM	69.30%	17.53%	15.08%	14.76%	69.65%	15.15%	15.65%	17.08%
BiGRU	73.57%	19.53%	20.12%	21.81%	74.43%	20.93%	21.90%	23.76%
CNN	77.56%	31.79%	30.39%	37.99%	78.58%	32.83%	31.29%	39.19%
BERT	79.44%	34.18%	34.12%	38.00%	80.17%	35.45%	34.99%	42.00%
distilBERT	79.09%	36.07%	36.62%	38.13%	80.46%	40.24%	39.99%	45.84%
ALBERT	79.62%	37.88%	37.65%	41.94%	80.51%	40.50%	39.57%	46.54%
RoBERTa	80.81%	43.18%	42.55%	47.68%	**82.26%**	47.55%	45.72%	54.15%
TCM-BERT	79.48%	37.84%	37.60%	42.00%	80.55%	41.58%	40.91%	48.47%
ZY-BERT(ours)	**81.43%**[†]	**49.47%**[†]	**48.89%**[†]	**54.08%**[†]	82.19%[†]	**51.01%**[†]	**49.42%**[†]	**57.70%** [†]

6   Discussion

6.1   Effect of Domain-Specific Pre-training

The last two rows in Table 4 indicates the effects of domain-specific pre-training. To be noticed, our proposed ZY-BERT achieved the astonishing performance improvement and mitigated long-tail distribution issue greatly. On the one hand, Macro-F1 score achieved by ZY-BERT is over 4% larger than that achieved by RoBERTa, demonstrating the effectiveness of large-scale domain-specific corpus for domain-specific tasks. On the other hand, ZY-BERT also achieves over 10% Macro-F1 scores higher than the previous domain-specific model TCM-BERT, which proves the quality and reliability of the TCM domain corpus constructed by us.

6.2   Effect of Knowledge

To testify the effectiveness of the external knowledge corpus, we leveraged knowledge into the model by concatenating the relevant syndrome knowledge with the medical history. However, due to the length limits of the language models, feeding knowledge of all syndromes into the model is infeasible under classification setting. Thus we converted the task from classification to extractive MRC, and designed the following three settings shown in Table 5 to evaluate the significance of the knowledge.

Firstly, we concatenated the original inputs with all syndrome names, and asked the model to extract the target syndrome spans from the context. The competitive results shown between MRC and classification tasks demonstrated that the model had a consistent ability among different task formats without external knowledge. Then we further conducted two groups of experiments. In the first group, instead of concatenating all syndrome names, we only included

Table 5. Performance with the machine reading comprehension (MRC) task.

Method	Dev				Test			
	EM	Macro-F1	Macro-R	Macro-P	EM	Macro-F1	Macro-R	Macro-P
Medical History + All Syndromes								
BERT	77.27%	40.71%	41.10%	43.26%	78.20%	45.60%	45.32%	50.15%
RoBERTa	78.71%	45.09%	44.30%	49.38%	80.42%	47.57%	46.42%	51.89%
Medical History + Five Syndromes								
BERT	95.59%	77.12%	76.32%	81.04%	95.83%	82.33%	81.35%	86.34%
RoBERTa	95.75%	79.16%	78.74%	82.79%	95.86%	84.42%	84.92%	86.74%
Medical History + Five Syndromes + Knowledge								
BERT	95.24%	81.21%	81.33%	84.61%	96.06%	85.15%	84.48%	87.92%
RoBERTa	**95.33%**	**81.53%**	**81.76%**	**84.49%**	**96.26%**	**85.88%**	**85.59%**	**89.09%**

five syndromes, where one was the target syndrome and the other four were randomly selected. In the second group, we appended the corresponding knowledge for each syndrome selected in the first group. The superior results achieved by the latter group demonstrate the importance of knowledge.

However, the outstanding performance, either with knowledge or without knowledge, was mainly due to the fact that we manually narrowed down the search range to five syndromes. We used the term frequency–inverse document frequency (TFIDF) to search for relevant knowledge from the knowledge corpus based on medical history, and P@5 was only 3.94%. Thus, knowledge is essential, but finding it is difficult.

6.3 Ablation Study

Table 6 shows the results of the ablation study on the TCD-SD dataset. Removing either the medical history or the chief complaint resulted in lower performances, especially if only the chief complaint was taken into account. This was because the chief complaint was typically too short to include sufficient features for classification. However, the chief complaint and medical history complemented each other in a coarse-to-fine fashion.

6.4 Error Analysis

By analyzing the error cases, we found that the vast majority of errors occurred in the category with few samples, and fitting only according to the data distribution was still the most significant issue. Except for algorithmic problems, we concluded that there were three main error types:

Complex Reasoning. As shown in Table 3, besides the explicit match marked in blue, there was an implicit match marked in orange that required temporal reasoning. Additionally, the task also included complex reasoning, such as numerical reasoning, spatial reasoning and negative reasoning.

Table 6. Ablation study on the TCM-SD dataset.

Method	Dev				Test			
	Acc.	Macro-F1	Macro-R	Macro-P	Acc.	Macro-F1	Macro-R	Macro-P
Only Chief Complaint								
BERT	70.56%	23.15%	26.34%	26.34%	71.58%	24.08%	25.38%	24.08%
RoBERTa	71.36%	28.55%	28.85%	33.13%	72.91%	30.78%	34.54%	34.54%
Only Medical History								
BERT	79.40%	33.50%	33.46%	37.90%	79.62%	35.57%	35.13%	42.18%
RoBERTa	79.80%	41.40%	40.12%	45.38%	81.83%	45.19%	43.03%	53.78%
Chief Complaint + Medical History								
BERT	79.44%	34.18%	34.12%	38.00%	80.17%	35.45%	34.99%	42.00%
RoBERTa	**80.81%**	**43.18%**	**42.55%**	**47.68%**	**82.26%**	**47.55%**	**45.72%**	**54.15%**

Incomplete Knowledge. The current models do not take into account the concepts that arise from the SD task, such as Yin and Yang. Therefore, the models do not know how to map the symptoms into the special coordinate system of the TCM diagnostics system.

Out-of-Vocabulary. In the clinical records, there exists not only academic medical-related terms but also various rare traditional characters in TCM, which impeded the understanding of the context.

7   Conclusions

This paper introduced a meaningful task, SD, in TCM and its connection with NLP and presented the first public large-scale benchmark of SD: TCM-SD. Furthermore, a knowledge corpus supporting the model understanding and the large-scale TCM domain corpus for pre-training were constructed. Moreover, one domain-specific pre-training language model named as ZY-BERT was proposed. The experiments on this dataset demonstrated the challenges, the inadequacy of existing models, the importance of knowledge and the effectiveness of domain-specific pre-training. This work can greatly promote the internationalization and modernization of TCM, the proposed benchmark and associated baseline models provide a basis for subsequent research.

Acknowledgements. The data used in this paper were only routine diagnosis and treatment data of patients, excluding any personal information of the patients (such as name, age, and telephone number). This study did not interfere with normal medical procedures or create an additional burden to medical staff, and no experiments were conducted on patients. **All the data have been desensitized**. Therefore, this paper does not involve ethical issues and waives the requirement of individual patient consent. We public TCM-SD dataset, TCM-domain corpus and ZY-BERT model at https://github.com/Borororo/ZY-BERT. We thank the reviewers for their helpful and constructive comments. And we thank M.D. Yonglan Zhou for her insightful and professional suggestions.

References

1. Abacha, A.B., Shivade, C., Demner-Fushman, D.: Overview of the MEDIQA 2019 shared task on textual inference, question entailment and question answering. In: Proceedings of the 18th BioNLP Workshop and Shared Task, pp. 370–379 (2019)
2. Alsentzer, E., Murphy, J., Boag, W., et al.: Publicly available clinical BERT embeddings. In: Proceedings of the 2nd Clinical Natural Language Processing Workshop, pp. 72–78. Association for Computational Linguistics, Minneapolis, Minnesota, USA (2019). https://doi.org/10.18653/v1/W19-1909. https://aclanthology.org/W19-1909
3. Beltagy, I., Lo, K., Cohan, A.: SciBERT: a pretrained language model for scientific text. In: Proceedings of the 2019 Conference on Empirical Methods in Natural Language Processing and the 9th International Joint Conference on Natural Language Processing (EMNLP-IJCNLP), pp. 3615–3620 (2019)
4. Cao, P., Yan, C., Fu, X., et al.: Clinical-coder: assigning interpretable ICD-10 codes to Chinese clinical notes. In: Proceedings of the 58th Annual Meeting of the Association for Computational Linguistics: System Demonstrations, pp. 294–301. Association for Computational Linguistics, Online (Jul 2020). https://doi.org/10.18653/v1/2020.acl-demos.33. https://www.aclweb.org/anthology/2020.acl-demos.33
5. Cui, Y., Che, W., Liu, T., Qin, B., Yang, Z.: Pre-training with whole word masking for Chinese BERT. IEEE/ACM Trans. Audio, Speech, Lang. Process. **29**, 3504–3514 (2021)
6. Cui, Y., Che, W., Liu, T., et al.: Revisiting pre-trained models for Chinese natural language processing. In: Findings of the Association for Computational Linguistics: EMNLP 2020, pp. 657–668. Association for Computational Linguistics, Online (2020). https://doi.org/10.18653/v1/2020.findings-emnlp.58. https://aclanthology.org/2020.findings-emnlp.58
7. Devlin, J., Chang, M.W., Lee, K., Toutanova, K.: BERT: pre-training of deep bidirectional transformers for language understanding. arXiv preprint arXiv:1810.04805 (2018)
8. Doğan, R.I., Leaman, R., Lu, Z.: NCBI disease corpus: a resource for disease name recognition and concept normalization. J. Biomed. Inform. **47**, 1–10 (2014)
9. Feng, J., Shaib, C., Rudzicz, F.: Explainable clinical decision support from text. In: Proceedings of the 2020 Conference on Empirical Methods in Natural Language Processing (EMNLP), pp. 1478–1489. Association for Computational Linguistics, Online (2020). https://doi.org/10.18653/v1/2020.emnlp-main.115. https://www.aclweb.org/anthology/2020.emnlp-main.115
10. Gu, Y., Tinn, R., Cheng, H., et al.: Domain-specific language model pretraining for biomedical natural language processing. ACM Trans. Comput. Healthc. (HEALTH) **3**(1), 1–23 (2021)
11. He, Y., Zhu, Z., Zhang, Y., et al.: Infusing disease knowledge into BERT for health question answering, medical inference and disease name recognition. In: Proceedings of the 2020 Conference on Empirical Methods in Natural Language Processing (EMNLP), pp. 4604–4614. Association for Computational Linguistics, Online (2020). https://doi.org/10.18653/v1/2020.emnlp-main.372. https://www.aclweb.org/anthology/2020.emnlp-main.372
12. Jochim, C., Deleris, L.: Named entity recognition in the medical domain with constrained CRF models. In: Proceedings of the 15th Conference of the European Chapter of the Association for Computational Linguistics: Volume 1, Long Papers,

pp. 839–849. Association for Computational Linguistics, Valencia, Spain (2017). https://www.aclweb.org/anthology/E17-1079

13. Johnson, A.E., Pollard, T.J., Shen, L., et al.: Mimic-iii, a freely accessible critical care database. Sci. data **3**(1), 1–9 (2016)

14. Kim, Y.: Convolutional neural networks for sentence classification. In: Proceedings of the 2014 Conference on Empirical Methods in Natural Language Processing (EMNLP), pp. 1746–1751. Association for Computational Linguistics, Doha, Qatar (2014). https://doi.org/10.3115/v1/D14-1181. https://aclanthology.org/D14-1181

15. Lan, Z., Chen, M., Goodman, S., et al.: ALBERT: A lite BERT for self-supervised learning of language representations. arXiv preprint arXiv:1909.11942 (2019)

16. Lee, J., Yoon, W., Kim, S., et al.: BioBERT: a pre-trained biomedical language representation model for biomedical text mining. Bioinformatics **36**(4), 1234–1240 (2020)

17. Li, D., Hu, B., Chen, Q., et al.: Towards medical machine reading comprehension with structural knowledge and plain text. In: Proceedings of the 2020 Conference on Empirical Methods in Natural Language Processing (EMNLP), pp. 1427–1438. Association for Computational Linguistics, Online (2020). https://doi.org/10.18653/v1/2020.emnlp-main.111. https://www.aclweb.org/anthology/2020.emnlp-main.111

18. Liu, Y., Ott, M., Goyal, N., et al.: RoBERTa: a robustly optimized BERT pre-training approach. arXiv preprint arXiv:1907.11692 (2019)

19. Liu, Z., He, H., Yan, S., et al.: End-to-end models to imitate traditional Chinese medicine syndrome differentiation in lung cancer diagnosis: model development and validation. JMIR Med. Inform. **8**(6), e17821 (2020)

20. Liu, Z., Peng, E., Yan, S., et al.: T-know: a knowledge graph-based question answering and infor-mation retrieval system for traditional Chinese medicine. In: Proceedings of the 27th International Conference on Computational Linguistics: System Demonstrations, pp. 15–19. Association for Computational Linguistics, Santa Fe, New Mexico (2018). https://www.aclweb.org/anthology/C18-2004

21. Pampari, A., Raghavan, P., Liang, J., et al.: emrQA: a large corpus for question answering on electronic medical records. In: Proceedings of the 2018 Conference on Empirical Methods in Natural Language Processing, pp. 2357–2368. Association for Computational Linguistics, Brussels, Belgium (2018). https://doi.org/10.18653/v1/D18-1258. https://www.aclweb.org/anthology/D18-1258

22. Pang, H., Wei, S., Zhao, Y., et al.: Effective attention-based network for syndrome differentiation of AIDS. BMC Med. Inform. Decis. Mak. **20**(1), 1–10 (2020)

23. Panigutti, C., Perotti, A., Panisson, A., et al.: Fairlens: auditing black-box clinical decision support systems. Inf. Process. Manag. **58**(5), 102657 (2021)

24. Peng, Y., Yan, S., Lu, Z.: Transfer learning in biomedical natural language processing: an evaluation of BERT and ELMo on ten benchmarking datasets. In: Proceedings of the 18th BioNLP Workshop and Shared Task, pp. 58–65. Association for Computational Linguistics, Florence, Italy (2019). https://doi.org/10.18653/v1/W19-5006. https://aclanthology.org/W19-5006

25. Qing, L., Linhong, W., Xuehai, D.: A novel neural network-based method for medical text classification. Future Internet **11**(12), 255 (2019)

26. Sanh, V., Debut, L., Chaumond, J., Wolf, T.: DistilBERT, a distilled version of BERT: smaller, faster, cheaper and lighter. arXiv preprint arXiv:1910.01108 (2019)

27. Schuster, M., Paliwal, K.K.: Bidirectional recurrent neural networks. IEEE Trans. Signal Process. **45**(11), 2673–2681 (1997)

28. Stubbs, A., Kotfila, C., Uzuner, Ö.: Automated systems for the de-identification of longitudinal clinical narratives: overview of 2014 i2b2/uthealth shared task track 1. J. Biomed. Inform. **58**, S11–S19 (2015)

29. Tian, Y., Ma, W., Xia, F., et al.: ChiMed: a Chinese medical corpus for question answering. In: Proceedings of the 18th BioNLP Workshop and Shared Task, pp. 250–260. Association for Computational Linguistics, Florence, Italy (2019). https://doi.org/10.18653/v1/W19-5027. https://www.aclweb.org/anthology/W19-5027

30. Tu, Y.: Artemisinin–a gift from traditional Chinese medicine to the world (Nobel lecture). Angew. Chem. Int. Ed. **55**(35), 10210–10226 (2016)

31. Wang, J., Guo, Y., Li, G.L.: Current status of standardization of traditional Chinese medicine in China. Evid.-Based Complement. Altern. Med. **2016** (2016)

32. Wang, Y., Ma, L., Liu, P.: Feature selection and syndrome prediction for liver cirrhosis in traditional Chinese medicine. Comput. Methods Programs Biomed. **95**(3), 249–257 (2009)

33. Wang, Z., Sun, S., Poon, J., et al.: CNN based multi-instance multi-task learning for syndrome differentiation of diabetic patients. In: 2018 IEEE International Conference on Bioinformatics and Biomedicine (BIBM), pp. 1905–1911. IEEE (2018)

34. Yang, Y., Islam, M.S., Wang, J., et al.: Traditional Chinese medicine in the treatment of patients infected with 2019-new coronavirus (SARS-CoV-2): A review and perspective. Int. J. Biol. Sci. **16**(10), 1708 (2020)

35. Yao, L., Jin, Z., Mao, C., et al.: Traditional Chinese medicine clinical records classification with BERT and domain specific corpora. J. Am. Med. Inform. Assoc. **26**(12), 1632–1636 (2019)

36. Yuan, Z., Tan, C., Huang, S.: Code synonyms do matter: multiple synonyms matching network for automatic ICD coding. arXiv preprint arXiv:2203.01515 (2022)

37. Yue, X., Jimenez Gutierrez, B., Sun, H.: Clinical reading comprehension: a thorough analysis of the emrQA dataset. In: Proceedings of the 58th Annual Meeting of the Association for Computational Linguistics, pp. 4474–4486. Association for Computational Linguistics, Online (2020). https://doi.org/10.18653/v1/2020.acl-main.410. https://www.aclweb.org/anthology/2020.acl-main.410

38. Zeng, G., Yang, W., Ju, Z., et al.: MedDialog: large-scale medical dialogue datasets. In: Proceedings of the 2020 Conference on Empirical Methods in Natural Language Processing (EMNLP), pp. 9241–9250. Association for Computational Linguistics, Online (2020). https://doi.org/10.18653/v1/2020.emnlp-main.743. https://www.aclweb.org/anthology/2020.emnlp-main.743

39. Zhang, D., Gan, Z., Huang, Z.: Study on classification model of traditional Chinese medicine syndrome types of stroke patients in convalescent stage based on support vector machine. In: 2019 10th International Conference on Information Technology in Medicine and Education (ITME), pp. 205–209. IEEE (2019)

40. Zhang, H., Ni, W., Li, J., et al.: Artificial intelligence-based traditional Chinese medicine assistive diagnostic system: validation study. JMIR Med. Inform. **8**(6), e17608 (2020)

41. Zhang, L., Yu, J., Zhou, Y., et al.: Becoming a faithful defender: traditional Chinese medicine against coronavirus disease 2019 (COVID-19). Am. J. Chin. Med. **48**(04), 763–777 (2020)

COMPILING: A Benchmark Dataset for Chinese Complexity Controllable Definition Generation

Jiaxin Yuan[1,2], Cunliang Kong[1,2,3], Chenhui Xie[1,2,3], Liner Yang[1,2,3(✉)], and Erhong Yang[1,3]

[1] National Language Resources Monitoring and Research Center Print Media Language Branch, Beijing Language and Culture University, Beijing, China
lineryang@gmail.com
[2] School of Information Science, Beijing Language and Culture University, Beijing, China
[3] Beijing Advanced Innovation Center for Language Resources, Beijing Language and Culture University, Beijing, China

Abstract. The definition generation task aims to generate a word's definition within a specific context automatically. However, owing to the lack of datasets for different complexities, the definitions produced by models tend to keep the same complexity level. This paper proposes a novel task of generating definitions for a word with controllable complexity levels. Correspondingly, we introduce **COMPILING**, a dataset given detailed information about Chinese definitions, and each definition is labeled with its complexity levels. The COMPILING dataset includes 74,303 words and 106,882 definitions. To the best of our knowledge, it is the largest dataset of the Chinese definition generation task. We select various representative generation methods as baselines for this task and conduct evaluations, which illustrates that our dataset plays an outstanding role in assisting models in generating different complexity-level definitions. We believe that the COMPILING dataset will benefit further research in complexity controllable definition generation.

Keywords: Definition generation · Controllable generation · Prompt learning

1 Introduction

Definition Generation (DG) is the task of describing the meaning that a word takes in a specific context. This task can help language learners by providing explanations for unfamiliar words. Recent researches [17,32] attempted to apply the task to the field of Intelligent Computer-Assisted Language Learning (ICALL), and have made a significant progress.

Previous studies on DG mainly concentrate on generating different definitions for polysemous words [8,22,25], or generating definitions with appropriate specificity [14]. In these studies, researchers have faced various issues, such as the high complexity

---

J. Yuan and C. Kong—Equal contribution.

problem. High complexity definitions contain words that are more difficult than the defined word, and hence are labored for language learners to read and understand. Nevertheless, there have been few focuses on complexity controllable generation of definitions. A possible reason is that the complexities of definitions are not provided in currently existed datasets, which leads to the difficulty of automatic training and evaluation.

Actually, the problems mentioned above are especially prominent in the language environment of Chinese. Definitions with suitable complexity are in urgent practical needs for Chinese as Foreign Language (CFL) learners. According to the Ministry of Education of China, by the end of 2020, more than 20 million foreign students are learning Chinese. But as [30] pointed out, since the difficulty of definitions is not considered, most existing dictionaries cannot meet CFL learner's requirements. Besides, the existing Chinese learner dictionaries contain only a small number of words. For instance, the Contemporary Chinese Learner Dictionary (CCLD) only has about 6,400 words. In contrast, the Modern Chinese Dictionary (MCD), which is designed for native speakers, has about 69,000 words.

Therefore, in this work, we focus on the task of generating definitions for CFL learners with appropriate complexities. At present, there are two datasets used for the Chinese definition generation task, but neither of them can meet the needs of this task. The most widely used CWN dataset [6,20,28] was built from the Chinese WordNet [13], which is a knowledge base of sense distinction[1]. This dataset is limited in size with 8,221 words. [32] constructed a dataset from the 5th edition of MCD. But it only collects disyllabic nouns and verbs, and additional annotation of formation rules is required. Besides, both datasets didn't provide the complexity of definitions, which is essential information in the controllable generation.

To enhance the study of this task, we propose to build a novel benchmark dataset named **COMPILING** (Chinese c**OMP**lex**I**ty contro**L**lable def**IN**ition **G**eneration). The dataset is large and of high quality, which contains 127,757 entries in total. Each entry consists of a word, an example, a definition, and two complexity measurements of this definition. More specifically, we build the dataset by using two Chinese dictionaries, namely the CCLD and the 7th edition of MCD. The former collects fewer words, but the definitions are simpler. The latter is the opposite. By combining these two dictionaries, we obtain a large amount of definitions that vary in different complexities.

In order to quantitatively measure the *complexity* of definitions, we refer to the graded vocabularies formulated by HSK (Chinese Proficiency Test). HSK is set up to test the proficiency of non-native speakers. It has nine levels from easy to hard, and each level corresponds to a vocabulary. The COMPILING dataset contains an average level and a maximum level of each definition.

We find that both dictionaries tend to use phrases rather than complete sentences as examples in some cases. For instance, the word "规模" (scale) has two example phrases in MCD (Modern Chinese Dictionary), which are "规模宏大" (large scale) and "初具规模" (begin to take shape). We think that short phrases might be helpful for language learners to understand, but complete sentences can provide more context in

---

[1] http://lope.linguistics.ntu.edu.tw/cwn2.

the automatic definition generation. Thus, we design an algorithm to expand the phrases into sentences (Sect. 4.2).

We believe that this dataset can further enhance the research on Chinese complexity controllable definition generation, which could not only benefit the language learners, but also low literacy readers, as well as people with aphasia or dyslexia. We also provide baselines of mainstream generation methods as references (Sect. 6).

In summary, our contributions are listed below:

– We propose a novel task of generating definitions for a word with appropriate complexity. The task is of great use in helping CFL learners to learn the vocabulary.
– We propose the **COMPILING** dataset that is of large scale and high quality. This dataset could serve as the benchmark of the task we proposed.
– We perform several experiments on the COMPILING dataset and the results demonstrate it could assist models to achieve effective complexity controllable generations.

2   Related Work

2.1   Definition Generation

[23] first proposed the definition modeling task and use word embeddings to generate definitions of the corresponding words. Referencing on the problem of word sense disambiguation, [17] and [8] incorporated word contexts into definition modeling and demonstrated its effectiveness of distinguishing different meanings. Recent work [15] reformulates the task as generating descriptions using extracted knowledge. Research on Chinese definition modeling was first proposed by [28], they adapted a transformer-based model and incorporated sememes into the model to provide more external semantic knowledge. [6] redefined the Chinese definition modeling as generating the corresponding definition for a target word and its context. [32] utilized the characteristics of Chinese by adding formation features to enhance definition modeling. Besides, there are also studies on multilingual definition generation [20] and combining extraction and generation for this task [16].

Notably, [19] proposed to generate simple definitions employing a multitasking framework. Since the lack of a definition dataset with different complexities, they managed to generate both complex and simple definitions in an unsupervised way.

Differently, we focus on building the benchmark dataset for different Chinese definition generation tasks and hope it could be beneficial for further research.

2.2   Controllable Generation

Controllable generation is widely adapted in kinds of language modeling tasks. For instance, data augmentation [1], dialog generation [7], storytelling [10], and so on. And the objects controlled in different studies vary from each other. Specifically, considering the significance of sentiment in poetry definition, [2] proposed a model to generate poetry with controllable emotions. [9] first presented a framework to develop questions about specific answers that meet target difficulty levels. To attract more readers, [18] introduced a headline generation model to produce enticing titles with target three styles. Likewise, in order to explore and release the practical value of definition gener-ation, we propose the complexity controllable definition generation task committed to producing definitions satisfying users of all levels.

Currently, the most controllable generation tasks are achieved based on pre-trained learning models. And [29] summarized the common methods as Finetuning, Retrain PLMs, and Post-Process and we utilize the first method to control the complexity of the definition more efficiently.

2.3 Prompt Learning

In recent years, the pre-trained model with fine-tuning has gradually become the main-stream of natural language processing tasks. Due to the complex training objectives and large hyperparameter groups, large-scale pre-training models can effectively extract features from a large amount of supervised and unsupervised data. By storing the learned knowledge in parameters and fine-tuning the model for specific tasks, the same model can be applied to a series of downstream natural language processing tasks [11].

Prompt learning is a method of fully learning knowledge by adding additional text to the model's input. Prompt can be divided into artificial and automatic construction according to the text attached to the input [11]. Among them, automatically constructed prompts are divided into discrete and continuous ones. A discrete prompt refers to the fact that the constructed prompt is composed of actual text symbols, and applicable tasks include text classification [12], text generation [31], etc.

Although the combination of pre-training and fine-tuning methods can be adapted to most NLP tasks, when it comes to each specific task, the number of parameters that need to be adjusted for are vast. By adopting prompt learning, the pre-training model can be applied to the required tasks by only modifying the part of the prompt for different downstream tasks. Therefore, the training process will become more efficient.

3   Problem Formulation

In this work, we aim to generate a definition d^c with appropriate complexity c, for a given word and example sentence (w^*, e). This task is feasible because the word and it's corresponding definition should be assumed to have the same semantics. A common solution is to predict tokens in the definition one by one, depending on the previous words and the other conditions, which can be formulated as:

$$P(d^c|w^*, e, c) = \prod_{t=1}^{T} P(d_t^c|d_{<t}^c, w^*, e, c), \tag{1}$$

where d_t^c is the t-th token in the definition, and T is the total length of definition. Each probability distribution can be approximated by the following equation:

$$P(d_t^c|d_{<t}^c, w^*, e, c) \propto \exp(W h_t/\tau), \tag{2}$$

where W is a matrix collecting word vectors, h_t is a vector summarizing inputs at current time-step, and τ is a hyper-parameter for temperature, set to 1 in default.

4   Dataset Construction

The source corpora are extracted from the MCD and CCLD, both published by the Commercial Press. For corpus from MCD and CCLD, we process them separately with the same construction methods and finally put them together.

The construction of the COMPILING dataset is divided into three stages: data structured annotation, example sentences expansion, and post-processing. First, we propose a strategy for building structured datasets due to the high complexity and compact construction of automatically extracted data. In this phase, we set up a platform. It not only helps annotators proofread and audit corpus data more efficiently but is also conducive for us to check and collect data. Besides, since the context of a targeted word in the dictionary is always a collocation instead of a complete sentence, we then conduct expanding context to enhance the overall abundance of language for our proposed datasets. Furthermore, to divide definitions into different complexity levels, we calculate the HSK level of each description.

4.1   Data Structured Annotation

In the beginning, we collect initial data and find they are disorganized and complex in structure, which is problematic to conduct automatic processing. Hence, we start up data structured annotation. To better manage and boost the whole process, we build up a platform before the formal annotation and deploy it on two servers, one for corpus from MCD, and the other for corpus from CCLD. This platform could not only serve specifically for this task, but it is also appropriate for the construction of any resource by replacing the data.

Concentrating on tackling the problem of disorganized data, we suggest a series of rules for annotation. For a particular word, its attached contents include its spell, definition, example sentences of the usage of a specific definition, and so on. Hence, we propose to add labels before corresponding contents to distinguish different types of data, which is conducive for computers to extract this information based on their labels automatically. Both dictionaries have instructions illustrating the meta-information, such as the organization of entries, the style of definitions and examples, and basic usages. We invite a student who majors in linguistics to formulate the annotation guidelines based on the instructions, which will be the reference for annotators. By doing so, we hope annotators could restore that language information and the relationships between them to a large extent. Then, we invite 20 students majoring in linguistics to annotate the corpora on our platform regarding the guidelines. This phase lasted for two months.

4.2   Example Sentences Expansion

While the information extracted from dictionaries is large and abundant, the context attached to the targeted words given in dictionaries is too short to provide enough knowledge for the model to learn and generate descriptions. In the second stage of construction, considering the significance of sentences, we start up example sentence expansion. For contexts without sufficient length in the original corpus, we tend to find sentences with a longer length and higher quality in the new canon for replacement,

---

Algorithm 1. Example Sentences Expansion

Input: phrase p, corpus C
Output: examples E
1: $D \leftarrow \{\}, E \leftarrow []$
2: **for** $sentence$ **in** C **do**
3:     **if** p **in** $sentence$ **then**
4:         $score \leftarrow pplScore(sentence)$ ▷ Compute the PPL score for each sentence.
5:         $D[sentence] \leftarrow score$
6:     **end if**
7: **end for**
8: $sortedExamples \leftarrow descSortByValue(D)$ ▷ Descendant sort by the scores.
9: **for** $i = 0 \rightarrow topN$ **do**   ▷ $topN$ is set to 5 in practice.
10:     $E.add(sortedExamples[i])$
11: **end for**

---

and the specific process is as follows. We first screened each example sentence in the annotated texts. We set the length threshold to six, and if the length of the initial context is longer than the threshold, we will retain the sentences; otherwise, we will find longer sentences with more abundant information in the new corpus to cover the original ones. It is worth noting that if a term contains more than one sentence (collocation), for each sentence (collocation), we will replace it with new matching contexts.

We design Algorithm 1 to match and gain new high-quality sentences. Given the ambiguity of most words, we utilize an allocation as the input of Algorithm 1 instead of a phrase to ensure the found sentences contain the corresponding usage of a specific definition. As shown in Algorithm 1, we collect all the sentences that fit the requirements and grade them by utilizing Perplexity (PPL)[2], which is one of the most common metrics for evaluating language fluency. Eventually, the top five sentences in the rankings are designated to replace those original short contexts.

4.3 Post Processing

Difficulty Classification. The most crucial step of constructing a complexity-controlled dataset is integrating the difficulty level of definition into the dataset. We utilize the HSK metric to represent the complexity degree. HSK[3], called the Chinese Proficiency Test, set to evaluate the Chinese proficiency and application of non-native speakers. It is divided into nine levels, and the difficulty increases progressively from low to high. For convenience, we regard the seventh, eighth, and ninth levels as a whole. Finally, we set seven complexity levels of HSK, and each level corresponds to a vocabulary. For words that are not included in the first seven-level, we classify them as the highest level.

Entry Construction. Besides, For each definition, we first conduct word segmentation, then calculate the average and highest HSK level, and combine the HSK level into the dataset. Eventually, each entry of the COMPILING dataset consists of a target word,

---

[2] https://huggingface.co/docs/transformers/perplexity.
[3] http://www.chinesetest.cn.

its definition, the average and highest HSK level, and the contexts of the corresponding usage of this description.

Table 1. The main statistics of the COMPILING dataset.

Datasets	Count		Average length	
	Words	Entries	Definition	Context
MCD	67,801	101,314	13.8	27.5
CCLD	6,502	26,443	13.4	20.4

5   Dataset Analysis

As mentioned before, the smallest unit of the COMPILING dataset consists of five parts. In particular, if a word is polysemous or has numerous contexts, they are regarded as distinct entries. For instance, as shown in Table 2, the word "收拾" (clear up) has four different definitions, and each of them follows an example sentence. Hence there are four entries of "收拾" (clear up) in total.

As shown in Table 1, we analyze statistics of data extracted from MCD and CCLD, respectively. Table 3 shows the basic statistics of the COMPILING dataset and another dataset of Chinese definition modeling. For training, the given definitions of each entry are seen as the ground truth.

Table 2. Example entries of COMPILING dataset.

Word	Definition	Average	Maximum	Sentence	Source
收拾 clear up	使变干净整齐；整理 To make clean and tidy	2	3	东西都收拾好了，可以出门了。 With everything packed up, we're ready to go.	CCLD
收拾 repair	使有毛病的东西功能正常；修理 To make something defective function properly	2	4	我的手机坏了，得找厂家收拾一下。 My phone is out of order so I have to ask manufacturer for help.	CCLD
收拾 settle	整理；整顿 Put in order	4	6	冬储夏衣，夏藏冬衣，收拾屋子，还要照看外孙女。 Store summer clothes in the winter, hide winter clothes in the summer, clean the house, and look after her granddaughter.	MCD
收拾 kill	消灭；杀死 Eliminate	8	10	据点的敌人，全叫我们收拾了。 All the enemies in the stronghold have been eliminated.	MCD

To better highlight the complexity degree of the dataset, we set levels 1–3 in HSK as the simple grade, levels 3–7 as the medium grade, and levels 7–9 and 9+ as hard quality. We count the HSK level distribution of definitions of COMPILING, as shown in Fig. 1.

Table 3. Statistics of Chinese definition modeling datasets.

Datasets	Count		Average length	
	Words	Entries	Definition	Context
CWN	8,221	84,542	9.07	21.57
COMPILING	74,303	127,757	13.60	23.95

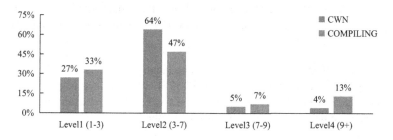

Fig. 1. The distribution of average HSK level in CWN and COMPILING.

The distribution of definitions in the COMPILING dataset in the three levels is closer than CWN. Given the particularity of the Complexity Controllable definition generation task, it is necessary to construct a dataset including entries covering all difficulty levels. In this way, the model can learn and distinguish the complexity of descriptions, hence generating a new definition of a word with a target complexity level.

Hence, the COMPILING dataset could be applied to both general definition generation tasks and those which incorporate the complexity of definitions, demonstrating its value in being as a benchmark dataset.

6   Experiments

6.1   Baselines

This section introduces several methods for common generation tasks, which can serve as baselines for our proposed task.

LOG-CaD. LOG-CaD [17] is a model for generating descriptions for words and phrases. This model summarizes clues from the static, contextualized, as well as character-level embeddings of the given word, and then employs an LSTM-decoder for the generation. A gated attention mechanism is employed to capture and filter information from the embeddings during decoding.

Transformser. We treat the task as a special type of single language translation and directly use the original transformer model proposed by [26]. We concatenate the word and example sentence as the input sequence and train the model to generate the definition. We use the same approach to deal with the input and output in BERT and BART models. All hyper-parameters are set according to the original paper for a fair comparison.

BERT. Pretrained language models have been widely used in various NLP tasks in recent years. By obtaining prior knowledge during pretraining, the PLMs can encode the input sentence more effectively. Thus, we use the Chinese-bert-base [4] model to initialize all the parameters in a transformer encoder and employ a transformer decoder for the generation. Note that the decoder is trained from scratch without initialization.

BART. Unlike BERT, BART [21] is a pretrained encoder-decoder language model, which is more suitable for generation tasks. Since the monolingual BART only support English, we use the multilingual version of BART and set both source and target language as Chinese for this task.

MT5. T5 is one of the representative pre-training language models. It considers all NLP tasks as a uniform text-to-text paradigm. mT5 [27] is a multi-language variant of T5, and its performance on various benchmark tasks is generally outstanding. Therefore, we choose mT5 to perform the prompt learning method.

Table 4. Datasets divided by HSK level.

Complexity	HSK	Entries
Easy	1–3	48,458
Medium	4–7	53,945
Hard	7+	25,354

6.2   Settings

As a benchmark dataset introduced to enhance the Chinese definition generation task, we set up the experiments to verify the effectiveness of the COMPILING dataset.

Regardless of Complexity Levels. We first design the experiment to evaluate the overall performance of the baseline models on our dataset. In this setting, we train the models using the entire training set, despite of the different complexity levels. And the purpose of this setting is to provide a comparison standard for other experiments. We divide the dataset into training, development, and test sets according to 8:1:1. The training data are fine-tuned according to the input formats of different models.

Complexity Specific Models. To evaluate the significant role of the COMPILING dataset in generating definitions across various difficulties, we set up an experiment to train the model on different complexity-level sub-datasets. First of all, we split the dataset into three subsets on basis of the average HSK level. As shown in Table 4, the HSK levels of definitions in Easy Set are between 1 to 3, Medium Set corresponding to level 4–6, and Hard Set corresponding to level 7+. Then we split each subset into training, development, and test sets according to the ratio of 8:1:1. Finally, we fine-tune the BART model utilizing these three training sets, and hence getting three models. Each one could generate definitions with its corresponding complexity level.

Unified Model Based on Prompt Learning. To assist the model to generate descriptions with different complexity of demand, we adopt the method of prompt learning. It allows the model to learn by adding tokens that represent difficulty information to the inputs, such as <extra_id_1> for level 1 (lowest), <extra_id_2> for level 2, and so on. The training set is formed by prefacing each definition of the COMPILING dataset with the corresponding special tokens. Each entry of the final dataset includes: <extra_id_x>, target word, its corresponding definitions and context. During the training phase, the model encodes both complexity and definition information. In the analysis stage, aiming to verify the effectiveness of this method, we select 10 entries from the test set of the COMPILING dataset. For each entry, only its difficulty token is modified with the other information keep remaining, so as to construct two copies of the entry. It is worth noting that the principle of constructing the new complexity tokens is, that the two new entries and the original one(a group of data) differ by at least 2 levels or more, which means they can represent easy, medium, and hard complexity respectively. For example, if the definition of the source entry is specified with the difficulty as 3, the complexities of the two copies of it need to be constructed as at least 1 and 5. Finally, a total of 30 entries are included in the new test set. Then, we perform the model on this new test set to observe whether the generated definitions are differentiated in line with their specified complexity.

6.3   Evaluation Metrics

In order to better analyze and quantify the experimental results, we select three evaluation metrics: BLEU [24], NIST [5] and HSK, which are used to comprehensively evaluate the quality and complexity level of generated definitions.

BLEU. BLEU (Bilingual Evaluation Understudy) [24] was originally proposed for the evaluation of machine translation research. The core of BLEU is to separately calculate the N-gram in the generated and the reference sentence, and then compare them one by one to count the times that can be matched. The higher times illustrate higher accuracy. However, the shorter reference segment always leads to more co-occurrence times, which means the shorter generated definitions tend to get a higher BLEU score.

NIST. On the basis of BLEU, NIST (National Institute of Standards and Technology) [5] adds the calculation of the information weight of N-gram. While the BLEU simply sums up the number of N-grams, the NIST sums up the information weights and then divides it by the number of N-gram segments in the whole sentence. In this way, the weightage of those N-grams which appear less frequently will be heavier.

HSK. As mentioned in Sect. 4.3, HSK is a test set to evaluate the Chinese proficiency and application ability of non-native Chinese speakers. Based on the purpose of assisting CFL learners to understand Chinese well, we select HSK to measure the complexity level of definitions. Besides, we set seven difficulty levels (scores) of HSK and each of them corresponds to a vocabulary. The final level of a definition is determined by the average score of its segments.

Table 5. Experiment results on the COMPILING dataset.

Models	Dev			Test		
	BLEU	NIST	HSK	BLEU	NIST	HSK
LOG-CaD	27.66	25.55	3.74	27.71	27.88	3.85
Transformer	28.61	25.85	3.92	28.58	31.00	3.96
BERT	**32.95**	29.66	4.05	**32.03**	30.56	4.08
BART	29.49	**36.90**	**4.76**	30.63	**42.79**	**4.80**

6.4 Results and Analysis

Regardless of Complexity Levels. We report the experimental results on the entire COMPILING dataset in Table 5. The results show that PLMs outperforms the other two methods in terms of the BLEU and NIST scores apparently. However, the results of BERT and BART models diverged on these two metrics. Since NIST assigns different weights to tokens, we believe it better reflects the model's performance. We confirmed this by reading the generated samples. We also notice that as the model performance improves, so does the average HSK level of the generated definitions. This phenomenon is because simpler words are used more frequently, and hence are more easily learned by models. As the modeling ability improves, the better-performing models learn to use more complex words. This can be challenging for future complexity controllable definition generation works, i.e., improving the performance and reducing the generation complexity at the same time.

Complexity Specific Models. Table 6 illustrates experiment results on three different subsets. As listed in the table, we not only test on the subset in which the model is trained, but also on other subsets. Generally, all the models perform best on the subset it was trained, and poorly on other subsets. Moreover, the performance decays as the complexity level between the model and data increases. Definitions with different complexity have different lexical and syntax, resulting in poor cross-complexity generalization. Besides, we found that even on different test sets, definitions generated by the same model have similar complexity.

Table 6. Experiment results in terms of complexity controllable generation on three test sets.

Models	Easy set			Medium set			Hard set		
	BLEU	NIST	HSK	BLEU	NIST	HSK	BLEU	NIST	HSK
BART-Easy	**32.44**	**64.40**	2.40	21.56	27.61	2.73	25.89	7.95	2.74
BART-Medium	22.92	24.59	4.70	**27.69**	**40.68**	4.86	29.37	16.09	5.01
BART-Hard	22.49	3.55	**8.46**	23.70	7.04	**8.45**	**46.57**	**18.22**	**8.76**

Unified Model Based on Prompt Learning. MT5-base [27] was selected as the bench-mark model in this experiment. The best PPL obtained from the definitions generated on the validation set is 38.44. The BLEU and NIST of the model on the test set are 27.42 and 4.66, respectively. The model generates interpretations based on the new test mentioned in Sect. 6.2. Table 7 lists two examples where it is fairly obvious that the resulting definitions are differentiated and conform to the expectations for their specified complexity levels. To evaluate the complexity of generating definitions more accurately, we adopt automatic evaluation, ranking the difficulty of each group[4]. The automatic evaluation is based on the Chinese Text Complexity Analysis Platform (CTAP)[5] [3]. We selected the features of word diversity and word density that reflect the difficulty of paraphrases and calculated the scores of definitions in each group based on the above features. Finally, the scatter distribution diagram is shown in Fig. 2. It can be seen that the complexity score of the Hard Group is mainly above 5, and the number of definitions with the highest score is the largest. The definition in the Easy Group scored the lowest overall score. This means the difficulty level of the model-generated interpretations obtained by automatic evaluation is roughly in line with expectations. The result proves the effectiveness of prompt learning on complexity controllable task, but since the difference in the overall distribution of scattered points in each group in the figure is not particularly obvious, it also reflects that there is room for exploration and improvement of this task in the future.

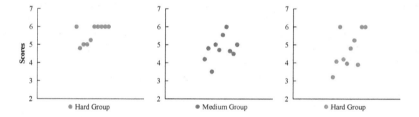

Fig. 2. The automatic evaluation results. For example, the scatters of the Hard Group represent those definitions that are specified as the hardest, and the ordinate corresponds to the scores obtained by the automatic rating.

7   Conclusion

In this work, we propose a novel task of generating Chinese complexity controllable definitions for a given word and example sentence. This task is of great use in helping CFL learners and low literacy readers. Meanwhile, we introduce the COMPILING dataset, which is a benchmark adapting to kinds of definition generation tasks. We also

---

[4] Each group of data refers to one original entry and its two copies, their specified complexity of definition is different and other information keep the same.

[5] http://ctap.wenmind.net.

provide several baselines for this task, among which the prompt learning method better assist models in generating definitions with specified complexity. Nevertheless, the experimental results also show that this task is challenging, and the performance needs further improvement.

Acknowledgements. This work was supported by the funds of Research Project of the National Language Commission (No. ZDI135-131, No. ZDI145-24) and Fundamental Research Funds for the Central Universities in BLCU (No. 21PT04). We would like to thank all anonymous reviewers for their valuable comments and suggestions on this work.

References

1. Amin-Nejad, A., Ive, J., Velupillai, S.: Exploring transformer text generation for medical dataset augmentation. In: Proceedings of LREC (2020)
2. Chen, H., Yi, X., Sun, M., Li, W., Yang, C., Guo, Z.: Sentiment-controllable Chinese poetry generation. In: Proceedings of IJCAI (2019)
3. Cui, Y., et al.: CTAP for Chinese: a linguistic complexity feature automatic calculation platform. In: Proceedings of LREC (2022)
4. Devlin, J., Chang, M.W., Lee, K., Toutanova, K.: BERT: pre-training of deep bidirectional transformers for language understanding. In: Proceedings of NAACL-HLT (2019)
5. Doddington, G.R.: Automatic evaluation of machine translation quality using n-gram co-occurrence statistics. In: Proceedings of HLT (2002)
6. Fan, Q., Kong, C., Yang, L., Yang, E.: Chinese definition modeling based on BERT and beam search. In: Proceedings of CCL (2020)
7. Firdaus, M., Chauhan, H., Ekbal, A., Bhattacharyya, P.: EmoSen: generating sentiment and emotion controlled responses in a multimodal dialogue system. In: IEEE Transactions on Affective Computing (2020)
8. Gadetsky, A., Yakubovskiy, I., Vetrov, D.P.: Conditional generators of words definitions. In: Proceedings of ACL (2018)
9. Gao, Y., Bing, L., Chen, W., Wang, J., King, I.: Difficulty controllable generation of reading comprehension questions. In: Proceedings of IJCAI (2019)
10. Goldfarb-Tarrant, S., Chakrabarty, T., Weischedel, R.M., Peng, N.: Content planning for neural story generation with Aristotelian rescoring. In: Proceedings of EMNLP (2020)
11. Han, X., et al.: Pre-trained models: past, present and future. AI Open 2 (2021)
12. Han, X., Zhao, W., Ding, N., Liu, Z., Sun, M.: PTR: prompt tuning with rules for text classification. ArXiv abs/2105.11259 (2021)
13. Huang, C.R., et al.: Chinese wordnet?: design, implementation, and application of an infrastructure for cross-lingual knowledge processing. J. Chin. Inf. Process. **24**, 14–23 (2010)
14. Huang, H., Kajiwara, T., Arase, Y.: Definition modelling for appropriate specificity. In: Proceedings of EMNLP (2021)
15. Huang, J., Shao, H., Chang, K.C.C.: CDM: combining extraction and generation for definition modeling. ArXiv abs/2111.07267 (2021)
16. Huang, J., Shao, H., Chang, K.C.: CDM: combining extraction and generation for definition modeling. CoRR abs/2111.07267 (2021)
17. Ishiwatari, S., et al.: Learning to describe unknown phrases with local and global contexts. In: Proceedings of NAACL (2019)
18. Jin, D., Jin, Z., Zhou, J.T., Orii, L., Szolovits, P.: Hooks in the headline: learning to generate headlines with controlled styles. In: Proceedings of ACL (2020)

19. Kong, C., Chen, Y., Zhang, H., Yang, L., Yang, E.: Multitasking framework for unsupervised simple definition generation. In: Proceedings of ACL (2022)
20. Kong, C., et al.: Toward cross-lingual definition generation for language learners. CoRR abs/2010.05533 (2020). https://arxiv.org/abs/2010.05533
21. Lewis, M., et al.: BART: denoising sequence-to-sequence pre-training for natural language generation, translation, and comprehension. arXiv preprint arXiv:1910.13461 (2019)
22. Mickus, T., Paperno, D., Constant, M.: Mark my word: a sequence-to-sequence approach to definition modeling. In: Proceedings of the First NLPL Workshop on DLNLP (2019)
23. Noraset, T., Liang, C., Birnbaum, L., Downey, D.: Definition modeling: learning to define word embeddings in natural language. In: Proceedings of AAAI (2017)
24. Papineni, K., Roukos, S., Ward, T., Zhu, W.J.: Bleu: a method for automatic evaluation of machine translation. In: Proceedings of ACL (2002)
25. Reid, M., Marrese-Taylor, E., Matsuo, Y.: VCDM: leveraging variational bi-encoding and deep contextualized word representations for improved definition modeling. In: Proceedings of EMNLP (2020)
26. Vaswani, A., et al.: Attention is all you need. In: Proceedings of NIPS (2017)
27. Xue, L., et al.: mT5: a massively multilingual pre-trained text-to-text transformer. In: Proceedings of NAACL (2021)
28. Yang, L., Kong, C., Chen, Y., Liu, Y., Fan, Q., Yang, E.: Incorporating sememes into Chinese definition modeling. In: IEEE/ACM Transactions on Audio, Speech and Language Processing, vol. 28 (2020)
29. Zhang, H., Song, H., Li, S., Zhou, M., Song, D.: A survey of controllable text generation using transformer-based pre-trained language models. ArXiv abs/2201.05337 (2022)
30. Zhang, Y.: Discussion on the Definitions in Chinese Learner's Dictionaries: Comparative Study of Domestic and Foreign Learner Dictionaries (Translated from Chinese). Chinese Teaching in the World (2011). https://www.cnki.com.cn/Article/CJFDTotal-SJHY201101017.htm
31. Zheng, C., Huang, M.: Exploring prompt-based few-shot learning for grounded dialog generation. ArXiv abs/2109.06513 (2021)
32. Zheng, H., et al.: Decompose, fuse and generate: a formation-informed method for Chinese definition generation. In: Proceedings of NAACL (2021)

NLP Applications

Can We Really Trust Explanations? Evaluating the Stability of Feature Attribution Explanation Methods via Adversarial Attack

Zhao Yang[1,2], Yuanzhe Zhang[1,2], Zhongtao Jiang[1,2], Yiming Ju[1,2], Jun Zhao[1,2], and Kang Liu[1,2,3(✉)]

[1] School of Artificial Intelligence, University of Chinese Academy of Sciences, Beijing 100049, China
{zhao.yang,yzzhang,zhongtao.jiang,yiming.ju,jzhao,kliu}@nlpr.ia.ac.cn
[2] National Laboratory of Pattern Recognition, Institute of Automation, Chinese Academy of Sciences, Beijing 100190, China
[3] Beijing Academy of Artificial Intelligence, Beijing 100084, China

Abstract. Explanations can increase the transparency of neural networks and make them more trustworthy. However, can we really trust explanations generated by the existing explanation methods? If the explanation methods are not stable enough, the credibility of the explanation will be greatly reduced. Previous studies seldom considered such an important issue. To this end, this paper proposes a new evaluation frame to evaluate the *stability* of current typical feature attribution explanation methods via textual adversarial attack. Our frame could generate adversarial examples with similar textual semantics. Such adversarial examples will make the original models have the same outputs, but make most current explanation methods deduce completely different explanations. Under this frame, we test five classical explanation methods and show their performance on several stability-related metrics. Experimental results show our evaluation is effective and could reveal the *stability* performance of existing explanation methods.

Keywords: Feature attribution · Explanation method · Adversarial attack

1 Introduction

Fueled by recent rapid development in deep learning, NLP systems have obtained promising results in several fields, such as medical, law and commerce [6,28]. However, besides the predicted results, users concern more on how these results are generated [18]. To this end, lots of emphases have been set upon the explanation methods for neural networks [4,17,26,30].

Although the current explanation methods have increased the transparency of the neural networks and provided explanations as supports for predicted

M. Sun et al. (Eds.): CCL 2022, LNAI 13603, pp. 281–297, 2022.
https://doi.org/10.1007/978-3-031-18315-7_18

results, most of them ignored important questions: *are these methods reliable and the generated explanations really trustful?* Besides the widely used focused properties of explanation methods, such as faithfulness, plausibility [1,3,14], readableness [4] and compactness [16,21], we believe *stability* is an important but often overlooked property [27]. When we put a small perturbation on the input, which would not change the input semantic and the output of the original model, we believe that the explanation method is not stable enough when we obtain the same outputs with quite different explanations. For example, Fig. 1 shows all results of major explanation methods would change when we just replace `fine` by `refined`, including LIME [26], Leave-one-out [17], Vanilla Gradient [30], Smooth Gradient [32], Integrated Gradient [35].

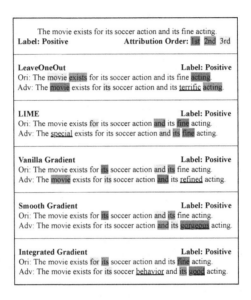

Fig. 1. An example of the result of our adversarial attack. We select a sentence from SST-2 and show the adversarial examples for explanation method **Vanilla Gradient** [30]. `Ori` and `Adv` stand for original sentence and corresponding adversarial example respectively. We show the three most important tokens and sign them in different colors. (Color figure online)

To fulfill the *stability* testing, we intuitively consider existing word-substitution based textual adversarial attack methods[1] [25,38], since it is under

---

[1] Feature attribution based explanation methods show the importance of each token to the prediction. Therefore, paraphrase-based attack methods do not fit because they would modify too many parts of inputs at once.

the black-box[2] settings and no need for the transparency of the model framework. However, we could not directly extend the current adversarial attack on the explanation methods. In our explanation stability test setting, the attack method should ensure the original prediction model has unchanged outputs for the adversarial examples, but the explanations vary, which is obviously different from the target of the common textual adversarial attacks. Thus, the main challenge is, for such adversarial examples, how to ensure the explanations are different but the outputs of the original model are the same. To this end, we modified the target of the standard textual adversarial attack to keep the prediction label of the adversarial examples unchanged. At the same time, we define two criteria to measure the difference between two explanations and add them respectively to the score function. Such explanation difference measurements are used to help the judgment of the adversarial examples' qualities in the attacking procedure.

Finally, we put the attack on five typical feature attribution explanation methods. Experimental results show their performance on *stability*. We find perturbation-based explanation methods perform better on *stability* than gradient-based methods. All of the source code and data will be available soon.

2   Related Work

2.1   Feature Attribution Explanation Method

Feature attribution explanation methods score each token of the input based on its contribution to the prediction label. We can easily find the key tokens according to the attribution value. These explanation methods can be simply classified as below two categories: perturbation-based methods and gradient-based methods.

Perturbation-based get the attribution score by perturbing the input sequence: **LIME** [26] sampled enough new sequences from the neighbor of the input sequence and fit the output logits of these sampled sequences by a linear function, the coefficients of the fitted function are the attribution score for each token. **Leave-one-out** [17] observed the probability change on the predicted class when erasing some certain word and the value of probability change is the attribution score for the removed word. Gradient-based methods compute the attribution score according to the gradient of the input: **Vanilla Gradient** [30] simply computed the gradient of the loss with respect to each token. **Smooth Gradient** [32] added small Gaussian noise to every embedding and take the average gradient value as the final attribution score for each token. **Integrated Gradient** [35] integrated the gradient along the path from a sequence of all-zero embeddings to the original input and take the integral value as the attribution score.

---

[2] Black-box refers to we can only utilize the outputs of the model during the attack. However, some explanation methods are not black-box such as gradient-based methods. Whether the explanation method is black-box has nothing to do with our black box attack method.

2.2   Evaluation of Explanation Methods

Recently, a collection of explanation methods has emerged exploring to interpret neural networks. To compare these explanation methods, various explanation metrics have been proposed. Faithfulness refers to how accurately the explanation reflects the true reasoning process of the model [13,14,37]. Plausibility refers to how convincing the explanation is to humans by comparing explanations that generated by explanation methods and human annotated explanations [3,9]. Besides, readableness measures whether human could understand the explanations [22] and compactness requires a explanation should be short or selective [16,21]. However, these evaluation metrics ignore whether the explanation method is reliable.

To evaluate the reliability of existing explanation methods, *consistency* and *stability* have been proposed. However, *consistency* is quite different from *stability* actually. To evaluate *consistency*, existing studies usually modified original model to generate different explanations when the inputs and outputs keep unchanged. [15] modified the attention value and maintain the output unchanged to illustrate attention is not explanation. [12] applied adversarial model manipulation to generate different explanations. [31] aims to sample based explanation methods. They modified the original classifier into two parts: original classifier for original instances and another model for instances in neighbor. [36] construct a new model which has similar outputs with original model but definitely different gradient. They added this model on original model and the added model shows similar prediction but totally different gradient-based explanations. Indeed, they all try to modified the original model to generate different explanations. However, for *stability*, we just put perturbation on inputs not on model, which is extremely different with *consistency*.

For *stability*, though existing works defined its specific meanings, only a few work design corresponding experiments to evaluate the performance of *stability*. [11] applied pixel-level perturbations to evaluate the stability. However, pixel-level perturbations can not be easily transferred in NLP. In NLP only [10] evaluated this property by manually constructing similar instances, which is much time-consuming and expensive. Therefore, in this paper, we automatically construct similar instances by learning from textual adversarial attack.

3   Formulation

In this section, we first introduce the basic information of the common textual adversarial attack in Sect. 3.1. Then we introduce how to formulate explanation adversarial attack in Sect. 3.2.

3.1   Textual Adversarial Attack

Formally, suppose that a sentence $x_k = \omega_1\omega_2\cdots\omega_n$, where ω_i is the i-th word in x_k. For a given classifier $P(y|x)$ and label set $Y = (y_1, y_2, ..., y_m)$, the model prediction y_k for x_k can be formulated as $y_k = arg\max_{y \in Y} P(y|x_k)$. The target is to find x_k', which can be formulated as:

$$x_k'$$
$$s.t. \quad y_k \neq y_k', \left\| x_k' - x_k \right\| < \epsilon \tag{1}$$

where x_k' is the adversarial example of x_k. The core constraint is to ensure the difference between x_k and x_k' is small enough. In this paper, we ensure the semantics of x_k and x_k' to be as similar as possible, which has been shown more imperceptible for human [39].

3.2 Explanation Adversarial Attack

Feature attribution explanation method can generate an explanation $e_k = (s_1, s_2, \cdots, s_n)$ according to x_k and its prediction y_k, where s_i is the attribution score of ω_i. Therefore, the target is to find x_k', which can be formulated as follow:

$$x_k'$$
$$s.t. \quad e_k \neq e_k', y_k' = y_k, \left\| x_k' - x_k \right\| < \epsilon \tag{2}$$

We also follow the common textual adversarial attack to keep the semantics of x_k and x_k' to be similar. And the most important difference is an extra constraint $y_k' = y_k$, we must ensure this constraint should be satisfied because of the definition of *stability*. Obviously, the constraint is contrary to the target of common textual attack, where $y_k' \neq y_k$. By contrast, our target is to ensure the explanations are different. Therefore, we will define how to measure explanation difference in the following section.

4   Attack Method

According to Sect. 3.2, we need to measure the explanation difference. Therefore, we propose two metrics in Sect. 4.1. Then we present our detailed attack strategies to attack existing explanation methods in Sect. 4.2.

4.1   Measuring the Explanation Difference

For feature attribution methods, people usually do not care the specific attribution score of each token but the relative importance ranks of these tokens. Therefore, we consider the rank differences between explanations. We can easily get the corresponding rank sequence R_k for explanation E_k in descending order, where $R_k = (r_1^k, r_2^k, ..., r_n^k)$, r_i^k stands for the descending rank of the i-th token in x_k. We can also get the corresponding position sequence $P_k = (p_1^k, p_2^k, ..., p_n^k)$ via `argsort`, p_i^k stands for the index of the i-largest attribution score in x_k. Based on this, we design two quantitative criteria to measure the difference between explanations.

Rank-count: In this setting, we compute the number of positions whose rank has changed:

$$d_{count}(E_i, E_j) = \sum_{k=1}^{n} ||r_k^i - r_k^j||_0 \qquad (3)$$

where $|| \cdot ||_0$ refers to the L0 norm.

Rank-topk: In this setting, we compute the size of intersection set of two position set of the top-k rank. The top-k set for e_i is the first k elements of position sequence r_i: $E_{topk}^i = \{p_1^i, p_2^i, ..., p_k^i\}$.

$$d_{topk}(E_i, E_j) = |E_{topk}^i \cap E_{topk}^j| \qquad (4)$$

where $| \cdot |$ refers to the size of a set.

For example, given $E_1 = \{0.1, 0.5, 0.3, 0.2\}$ and $E_2 = \{0.6, 0.3, 0.4, 0.2\}$. We get the rank sequence $R_1 = \{3, 0, 1, 2\}$ and $R_2 = \{0, 2, 1, 3\}$, then we can get the position sequence $P_1 = \{1, 2, 3, 0\}$ and $P_2 = \{0, 2, 1, 3\}$. Accordingly, we compute $d_{count}(E_1, E_2) = 3$ and $d_{topk}(E_1, E_2) = 2$ when $k = 3$.

4.2 Attack Strategies

Word-substitution based textual adversarial attack methods usually consist of two main steps: determining substitution order and selecting substitution words. In different steps, we employ different strategies. To determine the substitution order, we modify [29] as an example. To select substitution words, we utilize OpenHowNet [24] as the substitution resource [38]. Notably, other word-substitution based adversarial attack methods [2,25,38] are also applicable.

Determining Substitution Order. Formally, for a sentence $x = \omega_1\omega_2\cdots$ $\omega_i\cdots\omega_n$, to determine the substitution order, we compute the word saliency WS_i for token ω_i first. To compute WS_i , we should get $\hat{x}_i = \omega_1\omega_2\cdots \mathbf{0} \cdots\omega_n$ by replacing ω_i with $\mathbf{0}$.

$$WS_i = P(y_{ori}|x) - P(y_{ori}|\hat{x}_i) \qquad (5)$$

where y_{ori} refers to the original output label. We calculate the word saliency WS_i for all $\omega_i \in x$ and then we sort all of the tokens in descending order based on their saliency value. Then we substitute the words in this order [29].

Selecting Substitution Words. We construct candidate substitution set via sememes and utilize OpenHowNet [24] as the resource. Sememe is the minimum semantic unit of language [5] and the sememes of one word can composite the meaning of this word. Therefore, words that have the same sememe can substitute for each other [38]. As shown in Fig. 2, when we want to find substitution words for the original word **writer**. We utilize OpenHowNet to get its sememes

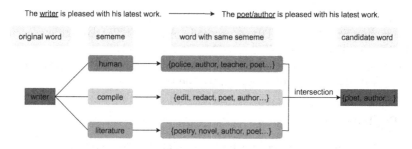

Fig. 2. An example of how to construct candidate substitution word set for the word writer by its sememes human, compile and literature.

human, compile and literature. Then we get three word sets that has these three sememes respectively. Finally, we compute the intersection of these three word sets and get the substitution word **poet** and **author** for the original word **writer**. According to [24] and [38], when we replace the word with the obtained substitution word, the semantic of the original sentence would not change.

After getting substitution set for the original word by above method, we still have to choose which word to substitute the original word. Therefore, we also need a quantitative criterion to help us to find the most suitable substitution word from the whole substitution set. Specifically, we define our score function as follow:

$$score(x_1, x_2) = d(e_1, e_2) \times (1 - ||y_1 - y_2||_0) \tag{6}$$

where $d(e_1, e_2)$ represent the explanation difference for x_1, x_2 and we directly employ the Eq. (3) and Eq. (4). y_1, y_2 are the prediction label for x_1, x_2. We directly force the labels must be same, otherwise the score would be zero.

With this score function, we can get the substitution word ω_i^* for ω_i in $x_i = \omega_1\omega_2\cdots\omega_i\omega_n$. This process can be formulate as follow:

$$\omega_i^* = \arg \max_{\omega_i \in L_{\omega_i}} score(x, x_i^{'}) \tag{7}$$

where $x_i^{'} = \omega_1\omega_2\cdots\omega_i^{'}\cdots\omega_n$ and L_{ω_i} is the candidate set for the word ω_i. Finally, ω_i^* is the substitution word for ω_i is x.

5 Experiments

5.1 Datasets and Models

Following previous explanation studies [3,9], we also select sentiment analysis as the target task. In specific, we choose SST-2 [33] and IMDB [19] as the test benchmark dataset and select the base version of BERT [8] and BiLSTM [7] as the target model.

For BERT, we utilize the base version of BERT. For BiLSTM, the hidden states are 256-dimensional and we utilize the 300-dimensional pre-trained Glove

[23] word embeddings. Our reproduced BERT can achieve accuracy of 91.28% and 91.36% on SST-2 and IMDB respectively. And BiLSTM can achieve accuracy of 85.50% and 90.38% on SST-2 and IMDB respectively.

To improve evaluation efficiency, we randomly sample 500 correctly classified instances with the length of 10–100 from the test set.

5.2   Explanation Methods

We select five classical feature attribution explanation methods in the two mainstream types to conduct our experiments:

A.   Perturbation-Based Explanation Method:

LIME [26] sampled enough sentences from the neighbor of the input and fit the output logits of these samples by a linear function. The coefficients of the obtained linear function is the corresponding attribution scores.

LeaveOneOut (LOO) [17] observed the probability change on the predicted class when erasing each word one by one and take this change value as the attribution score.

B.   Gradient-Based Explanation Method:

VanillaGradient (VG) [30] simply computed the gradient of the model loss with respect to the token and multiply with its embedding as its corresponding attribution score.

$$a_i = x_i \cdot \frac{\partial f(x_i)}{\partial x_i} \tag{8}$$

SmoothGradient (SG) [32] added small Gaussian noise to every embedding N times and average these N VanillaGradient value as the final attribution score.

$$a_i = \frac{1}{N} \sum_{i=1}^{N} (x_i + \mathcal{N}(0,1)) \cdot \frac{\partial f(x_i + \mathcal{N}(0,1))}{\partial (x_i + \mathcal{N}(0,1))} \tag{9}$$

where $\mathcal{N}(0,1)$ refers to the Gaussian noise.

IntegratedGradient (IG) [35] integrated the gradient along the path from a basic sequence x_i' to the original input x_i and take the integral value a_i as the attribution.

$$a_i = (x_i - x_i') \int_{\alpha=0}^{1} \frac{\partial f(x_i' + \alpha \times (x_i - x_i'))}{\partial \alpha} d\alpha \tag{10}$$

Specifically, it is time-consuming to compute integral value. To improve computation efficiency, we divide the integral area into K parts and obtain the approximate value of a_i [35].

$$a_i = (x_i - x_i') \sum_{m=1}^{K} \frac{\partial f(x_i' + \frac{m}{K} \times (x_i - x_i'))}{\partial x_i} \times \frac{1}{K} \tag{11}$$

5.3 Experimental Settings and Results

Explanation Similarity. Firstly, we fix m modified words to generate corresponding adversarial examples whose explanations are the most different. Then we use explanation similarity to evaluate the stability of explanation methods. More stable explanation methods could get higher explanation similarity. In specific, we employ three specific criteria including *change*, *spearman* and *inte*. *change* refers to the percentage of positions whose corresponding rank has changed, *spearman* refers to the spearman's rank order correlation efficient between the ranks of two explanations [34], and *inte* refers to the size of the intersection of the 5 most important tokens before and after perturbation [11]. Table 1 presents the experimental results of the five explanation methods that conduted on BERT and BiLSTM on the two datasets SST-2 and IMDB.

Table 1. Results of similarity of explanations between original instances and their adversarial examples by replacing m words for BERT and BiLSTM. *change* is defined as the percentage of positions whose corresponding ranks have changed. *spearman* is the spearman's rank order correlation between two explanations. *inte* is defined as the size of the intersection of the 5 most important tokens before and after perturbation.

Model	Dataset	Explanations	m=1			m=2			m=3		
			change↓	*spearman*↑	*inte*↑	*change*↓	*spearman*↑	*inte*↑	*change*↓	*spearman*↑	*inte*↑
BERT	SST-2	LIME	**79.87**	**0.80**	**3.87**	**84.03**	**0.78**	**3.81**	**86.52**	**0.76**	**3.75**
		LOO	89.13	0.64	3.14	92.62	0.62	3.09	94.12	0.61	3.03
		VG	92.99	0.48	2.83	95.65	0.45	2.71	97.11	0.42	2.64
		SG	92.86	0.55	2.92	95.71	0.53	2.87	96.70	0.52	2.83
		IG	86.79	0.71	3.45	90.01	0.69	3.38	91.69	0.67	3.37
	IMDB	LIME	**84.60**	**0.92**	**4.23**	**88.65**	**0.90**	**4.08**	**90.04**	**0.88**	**3.87**
		LOO	90.10	0.84	3.48	93.47	0.79	3.12	95.22	0.76	2.91
		VG	92.75	0.79	3.23	95.44	0.73	2.88	96.65	0.69	2.66
		SG	92.48	0.82	3.29	95.26	0.76	2.89	96.60	0.73	2.67
		IG	85.49	0.91	4.07	89.58	0.89	3.90	91.37	0.87	3.81
BiLSTM	SST-2	LIME	**71.18**	**0.81**	**4.02**	**80.38**	**0.74**	**3.78**	**84.22**	**0.68**	**3.63**
		LOO	75.76	0.77	3.89	84.07	0.71	3.70	86.96	0.67	3.60
		VG	78.20	0.75	3.78	85.04	0.62	3.52	88.50	0.56	3.36
		SG	77.83	0.77	3.85	84.49	0.68	3.55	87.21	0.64	3.40
		IG	73.55	0.79	3.99	81.73	0.72	3.75	85.39	0.67	3.61
	IMDB	LIME	**81.44**	**0.90**	**4.24**	**86.36**	**0.86**	**4.07**	**88.25**	**0.84**	**3.92**
		LOO	84.96	0.86	4.11	89.48	0.82	3.91	90.78	0.81	3.85
		VG	86.25	0.85	3.72	90.42	0.80	3.41	91.88	0.77	3.27
		SG	86.22	0.86	4.08	90.00	0.81	3.89	91.45	0.79	3.80
		IG	82.80	0.88	4.21	87.41	0.84	4.02	89.19	0.83	3.89

To evaluate *stability*, following its definition, we should ensure the same output and keep semantics of adversarial examples unchanged. For output consistency, we test the consistency of predictions between all test instances and their adversarial examples, which can achieve 100%. It means our methods satisfy the requirement of the same outputs. As for input semantic consistency, we perform human evaluation to check the semantic similarity between the adversarial example and the original example. Specifically, We invite 4 postgraduates score ranges 1 to 3 according to the semantic similarity between original instances and their adversarial examples. Scores of 1,2 and 3 indicate low, medium and high semantic similarity, respectively. Higher scores mean better consistency. Table 2 shows the results of human evaluation. These results show that our generated examples could keep semantics unchanged. Therefore, our experiment satisfies the definition of *stability* and the experimental results in Table 1 are convincing.

Table 2. Results of human evaluation. The human evaluation score is not an objective metric and the higher score does not stand for the better method. We list it here just to show the adversarial examples in Table 1 keep the semantic unchanged.

Model	Dataset	Explanation	m=1	m=2	m=3
BERT	SST-2	LIME	2.75	2.48	2.23
		LOO	2.74	2.46	2.18
		VG	2.73	2.42	2.12
		SG	2.74	2.44	2.14
		IG	2.75	2.47	2.21
	IMDB	LIME	2.82	2.67	2.41
		LOO	2.79	2.63	2.36
		VG	2.77	2.60	2.34
		SG	2.77	2.61	2.33
		IG	2.80	2.65	2.39
BiLSTM	SST-2	LIME	2.76	2.48	2.25
		LOO	2.73	2.44	2.19
		VG	2.72	2.41	2.13
		SG	2.72	2.44	2.16
		IG	2.75	2.46	2.23
	IMDB	LIME	2.81	2.67	2.37
		LOO	2.75	2.47	2.18
		VG	2.74	2.44	2.15
		SG	2.74	2.46	2.16
		IG	2.75	2.50	2.22

From the experimental results in Table 1, we find the *stability* performance of the five typical explanation methods keep same on different models and different datasets. And the *stability* performance (from good to bad) of these explanation methods is as follow: **LIME, Integrated Gradient, LeaveOneOut, Smooth Gradient, Vanilla Gradient**.

According to the results for different m in Table 1, when we replace more words, explanation difference obviously increases. However, from the human evaluation results in Table 2, we find the semantic consistency also decreases as m

increases. Therefore, one thing must be pointed out, to satisfy the semantic consistency of input, we should control the modification rate when we evaluate the *stability* of explanation methods.

Attack Success Rate. Secondly, following the common textual adversarial attack, We design a series of success conditions to check the attack success rate for different explanation methods. Combining with the finding in Sect. 5.3 that we should control the modification rate when evaluating *stability*, we set the maximum modification rate 20%. And existing textual adversarial attack also usually control the modification rate less than 20% [2,25,38].

Then we illustrate our formulated success conditions. We utilize the quantitative criteria introduced in Sect. 4.1 and then define the success conditions as $d_{count} > \alpha * length$ and $d_{topk} < \beta$ for different α, β. $d_{count} > \alpha * length$ refers to the proportion of positions whose ranks have changed in should bigger than α and we select α from $\{0.5, 0.6, 0.7, 0.8, 0.9, 0.95\}$. $d_{topk} < \beta$ refers to the size of intersection of the top-5 important tokens should smaller than β and we choose β from $\{1, 2, 3, 4, 5\}$. Obviously, bigger α and smaller β mean more difficult success conditions, and a smaller attack success rate on the same condition means a more stable explanation method. Given a sentence, if achieving the success condition with the modification rate less than 20% , we define this is a successful attack. Otherwise, when the success condition can not be achieved even on the maximum modification rate, we define this is a unsuccessful attack. Then we calculate the corresponding attack success rate on all examples.

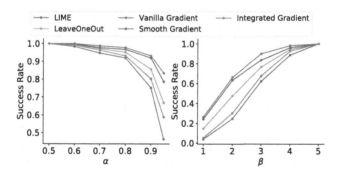

Fig. 3. Success rate for different success conditions. Left part shows the condition $d_{count} > \alpha * length$ for $\alpha \in \{0.5, 0.6, 0.7, 0.8, 0.9, 0.95\}$. Right part shows the condition $d_{topk} < \beta$ for $\beta \in \{1, 2, 3, 4, 5\}$. Success rate is the percentage of instances whose explanation difference could satisfy the condition. Bigger α and smaller β indicate more different explanations. A smaller success rate on the same success condition indicates a more stable method.

Figure 3 shows the results of BERT on SST-2. Under the two type of success conditions, we find the relative rank of the five explanation methods appears the same. And more difficult success condition would cause lower attack success rate. The *stability* performance (from good to bad) is the same as the results in Sect. 5.3: **LIME, Integrated Gradient, LeaveOneOut, Smooth Gradient, Vanilla Gradient.**

In summary, in our different experiment settings (Table 1 and Fig. 3), all experimental results consistently show that the *stability* performance (from good to bad) of the five methods is as follows: **LIME, Integrated Gradient, LeaveOneOut, Smooth Gradient, Vanilla Gradient.** Besides, we also observe perturbation-based methods have better performance on *stability* than gradient-based methods.

6 Discussion

Beyond the above experiments, our discussions would address the following research questions:

- **RQ1** How do the evaluation results change when replacing the two steps in the proposed attack strategy with othe existing methods?
- **RQ2** How can we improve the stability of explanation methods?

6.1 Correlation Analysis Between the Two Attack Steps and the Evaluation Results

To address **RQ1**, we modify the two steps in Sect. 4.2 to conduct experiments in the following parts:

Table 3. Results of explanation similarity for BERT on SST-2. ori refers to the results based on the word substitution order in Sect. 4.2 and rand refers to the results based on the random substitution order.

	m = 1						m = 2					
	change↓		*spearman*↑		*inte*↑		*change*↓		*spearman*↑		*inte*↑	
	ori	rand	ori	rand	ori	rand	ori	rand	ori	rand	ori	rand
LIME	**79.87**	**76.00**	**0.80**	**0.84**	**3.87**	**4.03**	**84.03**	**82.71**	**0.78**	**0.79**	**3.81**	**3.89**
LOO	89.13	84.25	0.64	0.76	3.14	3.48	92.62	90.40	0.62	0.69	3.09	3.25
VG	92.99	89.82	0.48	0.62	2.83	3.20	95.65	94.58	0.45	0.55	2.71	2.99
SG	92.86	89.13	0.55	0.65	2,92	3.23	95.71	94.20	0.53	0.55	2.87	2.99
IG	86.79	79.39	0.71	0.80	3.45	3.89	90.01	86.12	0.69	0.75	3.38	3.69

Effect of Substitution Order. To verify whether the other substitution order is effective to evaluate the *stability* of explanation methods, we utilize a random order to replace the substituion order in Sect. 4.2. Specifically, following experiments settings in Sect. 5.3, we select SST-2 and conduct experiments on BERT model. To improve efficiency, we only choose $m = 1$ and $m = 2$.

Table 3 shows the corresponding results. Compare to results in Table 1, all of the attack performance have dropped. In specific, for same explanation method on same setting, the *change* metric decreases and the *spearman* and *inte* metrics both increases, which stands for the higher explanation similarity. And this is consistent with the common textual adversarial attack, which has been shown the random order would much decrease the attack performance [25]. Besides, we find the *stability* performance of these five explanation methods still keep same as the previous findings.

Effect of Substitution Set. To verify whether the other substitution set is effective, we utilize WordNet [20] to construct substitution word set. We can easily find synonyms for a given word via WordNet. Following experiments settings in Sect. 5.3, we select IMDB and conduct experiments on BiLSTM model. To improve efficiency, we also only choose $m = 1$ and $m = 2$.

Similar to replacing the substitution order with random order, the attack performance also drop. And the *stability* performance of these five explanation methods also keep same.

In summary, our evaluation frame is independent to the specific substitution order and how to construct substitution set. These specific steps only influence the attack performance and could get the similar results of existing explanation methods when evaluating *stability* Table 4.

Table 4. Results of explanation similarity for BiLSTM on IMDB. `ori` refers to utilizing OpenHowNet to construct substitution set and `WN` refers to utilizing WordNet to construct substitution set.

	m = 1						m = 2					
	change↓		*spearman*↑		*inte*↑		*change*↓		*spearman*↑		*inte*↑	
	ori	WN	ori	WN	ori	WN	ori	WN	ori	WN	ori	WN
LIME	**81.44**	**78.89**	**0.90**	**0.92**	**4.24**	**4.41**	**86.36**	**83.21**	**0.86**	**0.89**	**4.07**	**4.09**
LOO	84.96	82.18	0.86	0.89	4.11	4.18	89.48	86.32	0.82	0.85	3.91	3.98
VG	86.25	83.79	0.85	0.87	3.72	4.02	90.42	88.14	0.80	0.83	3.41	3.85
SG	86.22	83.72	0.86	0.87	4.08	4.14	90.00	87.97	0.81	0.84	3.89	3.95
IG	82.80	79.97	0.88	0.90	4.21	4.27	87.41	84.56	0.84	0.87	4.02	4.05

6.2   Simply Improving Stability of Explanation Method

To address **RQ2**, we try to explore how to improve the *stability* of two explanation methods.

Adding More Noise. We explore the influence of the number of the added noise N (Eq. (9)) in Smooth Gradient. We select Spearman's rank order correlation as the evaluation metric. Figure 4 (left) shows the results. We find adding appropriate noises is useful and adding more noises is not meaningful.

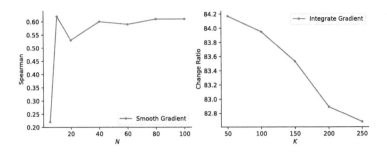

Fig. 4. The left figure shows the relation between Spearman's rank order correlation and the number of the added noise M in **Smooth Gradient**. The right figure shows the relation between change ratio and the number of the divided parts K in **Integrated Gradient**.

More Robust Mechanism. Integrated Gradient is a more robust mechanism compared to Simple Gradient and Smooth Gradient, because it satisfy *sensitivity* and *implementation invariance* these two important axiom [35]. We explore the influence of the divided parts K in Eq. (11). Figure 4 (right) shows the results of change rate. We find adding the number of the divided parts K is useful. The bigger K is, the more accurate the integral value is, which means more robust mechanism. Therefore, more robust mechanism could improve the *stability* of explanation methods.

Therefore, we can try to add appropriate noises and seek more robust mechanisms to make explanation methods more stable. And we take the further exploration of improving *stability* as our future work.

7   Conclusion

This paper proposes a new evaluation frame to evaluate the *stability* of typical feature attribution explanation methods via adversarial attack. Various experimental results on different experimental settings reveal their performance on *stability*, which also show the effectiveness of our proposed evaluation frame. We also conduct experiments to show the proposed frame is dependent of specific step. Therefore, we hope the proposed evaluation frame could be applied to evaluating the *stability* of feature attribution explanation methods in the future and attract more research on this important but often overlooked property.

8   Limitations

The proposed evaluation frame only focus on the rank of the feature attribution explanation methods. These explanation methods also provide specific attribution scores and these scores may further refine the proposed frame.

Acknowledgements. This work was supported by the National Natural Science Foundation of China (No. 61922085, 61831022, 61906196), the Key Research Program of the Chinese Academy of Sciences (Grant NO. ZDBS-SSW-JSC006) and the Youth Innovation Promotion Association CAS. This work was also supported by Yunnan provincial major science and technology special plan projects, under Grant:202103AA080015.

References

1. Adebayo, J., Gilmer, J., Muelly, M., Goodfellow, I., Hardt, M., Kim, B.: Sanity checks for saliency maps. arXiv preprint arXiv:1810.03292 (2018)
2. Alzantot, M., Sharma, Y., Elgohary, A., Ho, B.J., Srivastava, M., Chang, K.W.: Generating natural language adversarial examples. arXiv preprint arXiv:1804.07998 (2018)
3. Atanasova, P., Simonsen, J.G., Lioma, C., Augenstein, I.: A diagnostic study of explainability techniques for text classification. arXiv preprint arXiv:2009.13295 (2020)
4. Bastings, J., Aziz, W., Titov, I.: Interpretable neural predictions with differentiable binary variables. arXiv preprint arXiv:1905.08160 (2019)
5. Bloomfield, L.: A set of postulates for the science of language. Language **2**(3), 153–164 (1926)
6. Bommasani, R., et al.: On the opportunities and risks of foundation models. arXiv preprint arXiv:2108.07258 (2021)
7. Conneau, A., Kiela, D., Schwenk, H., Barrault, L., Bordes, A.: Supervised learning of universal sentence representations from natural language inference data. In: Proceedings of the 2017 Conference on Empirical Methods in Natural Language Processing, pp. 670–680. Association for Computational Linguistics, Copenhagen, Denmark (2017). https://doi.org/10.18653/v1/D17-1070. https://aclanthology.org/D17-1070
8. Devlin, J., Chang, M.W., Lee, K., Toutanova, K.: BERT: pre-training of deep bidirectional transformers for language understanding. arXiv preprint arXiv:1810.04805 (2018)
9. DeYoung, J., et al.: ERASER: a benchmark to evaluate rationalized NLP models. arXiv preprint arXiv:1911.03429 (2019)
10. Ding, S., Koehn, P.: Evaluating saliency methods for neural language models. arXiv preprint arXiv:2104.05824 (2021)
11. Ghorbani, A., Abid, A., Zou, J.: Interpretation of neural networks is fragile. In: Proceedings of the AAAI Conference on Artificial Intelligence, vol. 33, pp. 3681–3688 (2019)
12. Heo, J., Joo, S., Moon, T.: Fooling neural network interpretations via adversarial model manipulation. In: Advances in Neural Information Processing Systems, pp. 2925–2936 (2019)
13. Herman, B.: The promise and peril of human evaluation for model interpretability. arXiv preprint arXiv:1711.07414 (2017)
14. Jacovi, A., Goldberg, Y.: Towards faithfully interpretable NLP systems: how should we define and evaluate faithfulness? arXiv preprint arXiv:2004.03685 (2020)
15. Jain, S., Wallace, B.C.: Attention is not explanation. arXiv preprint arXiv:1902.10186 (2019)

16. Jiang, Z., Zhang, Y., Yang, Z., Zhao, J., Liu, K.: Alignment rationale for natural language inference. In: Proceedings of the 59th Annual Meeting of the Association for Computational Linguistics and the 11th International Joint Conference on Natural Language Processing (Volume 1: Long Papers), pp. 5372–5387. Association for Computational Linguistics, Online (2021). https://doi.org/10.18653/v1/2021.acl-long.417. https://aclanthology.org/2021.acl-long.417

17. Li, J., Monroe, W., Jurafsky, D.: Understanding neural networks through representation erasure. arXiv preprint arXiv:1612.08220 (2016)

18. Lipton, Z.C.: The mythos of model interpretability: in machine learning, the concept of interpretability is both important and slippery. Queue **16**(3), 31–57 (2018)

19. Maas, A.L., Daly, R.E., Pham, P.T., Huang, D., Ng, A.Y., Potts, C.: Learning word vectors for sentiment analysis. In: Proceedings of the 49th Annual Meeting of the Association for Computational Linguistics: Human Language Technologies, pp. 142–150. Association for Computational Linguistics, Portland, Oregon, USA (2011). https://aclanthology.org/P11-1015

20. Miller, G.A.: Wordnet: a lexical database for English. Commun. ACM **38**(11), 39–41 (1995)

21. Miller, T.: Explanation in artificial intelligence: insights from the social sciences. Artif. Intell. **267**, 1–38 (2019)

22. Molnar, C.: Interpretable Machine Learning. Lulu. com (2020)

23. Pennington, J., Socher, R., Manning, C.D.: Glove: global vectors for word representation. In: Proceedings of the 2014 conference on empirical methods in natural language processing (EMNLP), pp. 1532–1543 (2014)

24. Qi, F., Yang, C., Liu, Z., Dong, Q., Sun, M., Dong, Z.: OpenHowNet: an open sememe-based lexical knowledge base. arXiv preprint arXiv:1901.09957 (2019)

25. Ren, S., Deng, Y., He, K., Che, W.: Generating natural language adversarial examples through probability weighted word saliency. In: Proceedings of the 57th Annual Meeting of the Association for Computational Linguistics, pp. 1085–1097 (2019)

26. Ribeiro, M.T., Singh, S., Guestrin, C.: Why should i trust you? explaining the predictions of any classifier. In: Proceedings of the 22nd ACM SIGKDD International Conference on Knowledge Discovery and Data Mining, pp. 1135–1144 (2016)

27. Robnik-Šikonja, M., Bohanec, M.: Perturbation-based explanations of prediction models. In: Zhou, J., Chen, F. (eds.) Human and Machine Learning. HIS, pp. 159–175. Springer, Cham (2018). https://doi.org/10.1007/978-3-319-90403-0_9

28. Rudin, C.: Stop explaining black box machine learning models for high stakes decisions and use interpretable models instead. Nat. Mach. Intell. **1**(5), 206–215 (2019)

29. Samanta, S., Mehta, S.: Towards crafting text adversarial samples. arXiv preprint arXiv:1707.02812 (2017)

30. Simonyan, K., Vedaldi, A., Zisserman, A.: Deep inside convolutional networks: visualising image classification models and saliency maps. arXiv preprint arXiv:1312.6034 (2013)

31. Slack, D., Hilgard, S., Jia, E., Singh, S., Lakkaraju, H.: Fooling lime and SHAP: adversarial attacks on post hoc explanation methods. In: Proceedings of the AAAI/ACM Conference on AI, Ethics, and Society, pp. 180–186 (2020)

32. Smilkov, D., Thorat, N., Kim, B., Viégas, F., Wattenberg, M.: SmoothGrad: removing noise by adding noise. arXiv preprint arXiv:1706.03825 (2017)

33. Socher, R., et al.: Recursive deep models for semantic compositionality over a sentiment treebank. In: Proceedings of the 2013 Conference on Empirical Methods in Natural Language Processing, pp. 1631–1642 (2013)

34. Spearman, C.: The proof and measurement of association between two things. (1961)
35. Sundararajan, M., Taly, A., Yan, Q.: Axiomatic attribution for deep networks. arXiv preprint arXiv:1703.01365 (2017)
36. Wang, J., Tuyls, J., Wallace, E., Singh, S.: Gradient-based analysis of NLP models is manipulable. arXiv preprint arXiv:2010.05419 (2020)
37. Wiegreffe, S., Pinter, Y.: Attention is not not explanation. arXiv preprint arXiv:1908.04626 (2019)
38. Zang, Y., et al.: Word-level textual adversarial attacking as combinatorial optimization. In: Proceedings of the 58th Annual Meeting of the Association for Computational Linguistics, pp. 6066–6080 (2020)
39. Zhang, W.E., Sheng, Q.Z., Alhazmi, A., Li, C.: Adversarial attacks on deep-learning models in natural language processing: a survey. ACM Trans. Intell. Syst. Technol. (TIST) 11(3), 1–41 (2020)

Dynamic Negative Example Construction for Grammatical Error Correction Using Contrastive Learning

Junyi He, Junbin Zhuang, and Xia Li[✉]

Guangzhou Key Laboratory of Multilingual Intelligent Processing,
School of Information Science and Technology,
Guangdong University of Foreign Studies, Guangzhou, China
{junyihe,junbinzhuang,xiali}@gdufs.edu.cn

Abstract. Grammatical error correction (GEC) aims at correcting texts with different types of grammatical errors into natural and correct forms. Due to the difference of error type distribution and error density, current grammatical error correction systems may over-correct writings and produce a low precision. To address this issue, in this paper, we propose a dynamic negative example construction method for grammatical error correction using contrastive learning. The proposed method can construct sufficient negative examples with diverse grammatical errors, and can be dynamically used during model training. The constructed negative examples are beneficial for the GEC model to correct sentences precisely and suppress the model from over-correction. Experimental results show that our proposed method enhances model precision, proving the effectiveness of our method.

Keywords: Grammatical error correction · Contrastive learning · Negative example construction

1 Introduction

Grammatical error correction (GEC) [8,15,17] aims at correcting texts with different types of grammatical errors into natural and correct forms. It is an important research topic for both natural language processing and language education.

Most of the current GEC systems are developed for correcting writings by learners of English as a second language [2,5,8,15,17]. However, GEC for native writings is also worth exploring, as texts written by native speakers may also contain grammatical errors that should be corrected for enhancement of writing quality. Currently, it is not feasible to train a GEC model specifically for correcting native writings because GEC data containing native writings are not sufficient. Therefore, native writings are often corrected by GEC models that are trained on GEC data consisting of writings by non-native speakers such as the

M. Sun et al. (Eds.): CCL 2022, LNAI 13603, pp. 298–313, 2022.
https://doi.org/10.1007/978-3-031-18315-7_19

Lang-8 [21] and NUCLE [9] datasets. However, the error type distribution, error density and fluency are inconsistent between the writings by non-native and native speakers. Therefore, those GEC models may over correct sentences and produce a low precision of error correction [12]. In terms of this issue, contrastive learning (CL) [6,7,13,19] can be incorporated to help alleviate the over correction behaviour of the GEC models. The core idea is to take the over-corrected sentences as negative examples, and to effectively avoid or alleviate the problem of over correction by increasing the distance between the anchor sentence and the negative examples. So the focus is on how to construct effective negative examples for training the GEC models effectively. Previous studies about GEC models mainly focus on data augmentation for generating pseudo parallel training pairs as complement for the current insufficient GEC training data [27,30], or focus on improving the correction performance with a variety of model architectures [1,25,26], few of them focus on improving the performance of the GEC models with contrastive learning. To the best of our knowledge, Cao et al. [4] is the only recent work for that. In their work, they propose two approaches for constructing negative examples. First, they treat the beam search candidates produced by an off-the-shelf GEC model as negative examples. They find that many output candidates generated by beam search contain erroneous edits, and the constructed negative examples help suppress the trained GEC model from producing erroneous edits. Second, the source sentence is treated directly as a negative example if it contains grammatical errors. Their intuition is that there should be differences between the corrected output sentence and the source sentence, otherwise the GEC model fails to detect any grammatical errors in the source sentence. The negative examples constructed in this way suppress the trained GEC model from outputting the erroneous source sentences as they are without any modifications.

Although the aforementioned study produces good performance, we believe that there are still two points that can be improved: (1) The negative examples constructed with beam search may not be sufficient. Many beam search output candidates are the same as the target sentence and cannot be used as negative examples. That leads to a small number of the generated negative examples. In addition, the beam search candidates may contain unrealistic grammatical errors with a small number of error types, limiting the diversity of grammatical errors in the generated negative examples. As a result, the low diversity of the negative examples makes the GEC model less easier to learn to distinguish the negative examples from the anchor, which limits the improvement of error correction performance brought by contrastive learning. (2) They construct the negative examples with their negative example construction methods before model training. As a result, the GEC model can only be able to see a fixed set of negative examples in each iteration during training, which may reduce the generalization ability of the GEC model.

To this end, we propose a dynamic negative example construction method for grammatical error correction using contrastive learning. The proposed method contains a negative example construction strategy that makes use of realistic grammatical error patterns produced by humans to generate sufficient negative examples with more diverse grammatical errors. With the constructed negative examples, the GEC model can learn to correct sentences precisely and be suppressed from over-correction. Moreover, the proposed strategy is simple and lightweight, enabling it to be applied dynamically during the training process. In this manner, our method enhances the generalization ability of the GEC model.

The main contributions of this work are as follows:

(1) We propose a dynamic negative example construction method for grammatical error correction using contrastive learning. The proposed method can construct sufficient negative examples with diverse grammatical errors, and can be dynamically applied during model training. The constructed negative examples are beneficial for the model to correct sentences precisely and suppress it from over-correction.
(2) We conduct extensive experiments on the public CWEB dataset that contains native writings, and compare our proposed method with existing GEC studies focusing on negative example construction. Experimental results show that our proposed method indeed enhances model precision and suppresses the GEC model from over-correction.

2 Related Work

In this section, we briefly review different GEC methods, including the early rule-based methods, the widely used methods based on machine translation or BERT, and the recently proposed GEC methods using contrastive learning.

GEC Methods Based on Rules. Early GEC models are mostly rule-based pattern recognizers or dictionary-based linguistic analysis engines [20,22–24]. These rule-based methods require a set of pre-defined error recognition rules to detect grammatical errors in the input sentences. Once a certain span in the input sentence is matched by a certain rule, the error correction system provides a correction for the matched error.

GEC Methods Based on Machine Translation. GEC models based on machine translation have been proposed to "translate" wrong sentences into correct sentences. Brockett et al. [2] use a noisy channel model in conjunction with a statistical machine translation model for error correction. Felice et al. [11] propose a hybrid GEC model that integrates grammatical rules and a statistical machine translation model. They also adopt some techniques such as type filtering. Zheng and Ted [29] apply a neural machine translation model with the attention mechanism to GEC. In addition, they also introduce a method that uses a combination of an unsupervised alignment model and a word-level translation model to solve the problem of sparse and unrecognized words. Chollampatt et al. [8] integrate four convolutional neural translation models combined with a re-scoring mechanism. Kiyono et al. [17] construct the GEC model with Transformer and use many data augmentation techniques.

GEC Methods Based on BERT. Many studies have introduced the Transformer-based deep bidirectional language model BERT [10] into GEC, hoping that the correction performance can be improved with the help of its rich language knowledge and deep textual understanding ability. Awasthi et al. [1] modify the BERT structure to predict the edit operation of each word in the source sentence by sequence tagging. Then they apply the edit operations to the source sentence to construct its correct form. Chen et al. [5] use BERT to predict and annotate error spans in the input sentence, and subsequently rewrite the annotated error spans with a sequence model. Kaneko et al. [15] first fine-tune BERT with GEC data, then feed the output representations of the fine-tuned BERT to the GEC model as additional information for error correction.

GEC Methods Based on Contrastive Learning. Contrastive learning [6, 7,13,19] is a discriminative self-supervised learning method used to enhance the feature representation ability of deep learning models. For any training example, contrastive learning requires automatic construction of examples that are similar (positive examples) and dissimilar (negative examples) to an anchor. And during training, the model needs to reduce the distance between the anchor and the positive examples in the representation space, while to increase the distance between the anchor and the negative examples.

Cao et al. [4] try to use contrastive learning to improve the error correction ability of the GEC model. Since constructing positive examples is difficult for GEC, they propose a margin-based contrastive loss, which only requires to construct negative examples and does not require to construct positive examples. Their work is the most similar to ours. In view of the limitations of their negative example construction method, we propose a dynamic negative example construction method to better address the over correction problem of the GEC model in low error density native writings.

3   Our Method

3.1   Overall Architecture

As mentioned above, the purpose of this work is to incorporate contrastive learning into the GEC model to effectively alleviate the problem of over correction by increasing the distance between the anchor sentence and the negative examples. We illustrate our method in Fig. 1, which consists of two components: the negative example construction component and the contrastive learning component.

Given a training pair $(\boldsymbol{x}, \boldsymbol{y})$, where $\boldsymbol{x} = (x_1, x_2, \cdots, x_m)$ indicates the source sentence that may contain grammatical errors, x_i is the ith word, m is the source sentence length, and $\boldsymbol{y} = (y_1, y_2, \cdots, y_n)$ indicates the target sentence that is grammatically correct, y_j is the jth word, n is the target sentence length. The goal of the GEC task is to correct sentence $\boldsymbol{x}$ into sentence $\boldsymbol{y}$.

For the negative example construction component, we use the proposed negative example construction strategy to construct K negative examples $\tilde{\boldsymbol{Y}} = \{\tilde{\boldsymbol{y}}_1, \tilde{\boldsymbol{y}}_2, \cdots, \tilde{\boldsymbol{y}}_K\}$ for the training pair $(\boldsymbol{x}, \boldsymbol{y})$. Each negative example $\tilde{\boldsymbol{y}}_k$ is constructed as follows. First, several words in the target sentence $\boldsymbol{y}$ are randomly selected by a noising probability p. For each selected word y_j, a noised word y'_j is generated by the negative example construction strategy. The generated noised word y'_j is used to replace the selected word y_j. After replacing all selected words, the modified target sentence is treated as a constructed negative example $\tilde{y}_k$.

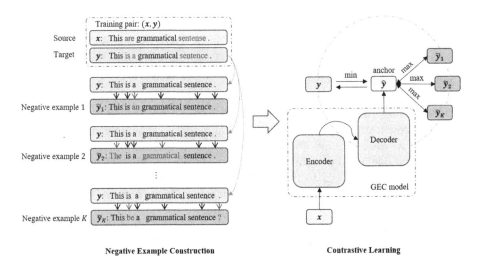

Negative Example Construction   **Contrastive Learning**

Fig. 1. Overall architecture of our proposed method. Our method consists of two components: the negative example construction component and the contrastive learning component. For the negative example construction component, we use the proposed negative example construction strategy to construct K negative examples $\tilde{Y} = \{\tilde{y}_1, \tilde{y}_2, \cdots, \tilde{y}_K\}$ for the training pair (x, y). For the contrastive learning component, we first input the source sentence x into the GEC model and obtain the decoder output $\hat{y}$. Then, we treat the decoder output $\hat{y}$ as an anchor, and maximize the distance between the anchor $\hat{y}$ and the negative examples $\tilde{y}_1, \tilde{y}_2, \cdots, \tilde{y}_K$ constructed by our proposed negative example construction strategy.

For the contrastive learning component, we first input the source sentence x into the GEC model and obtain the decoder output $\hat{y}$. Then, we treat the decoder output $\hat{y}$ as an anchor, and maximize the distance between the anchor $\hat{y}$ and the negative examples $\tilde{y}_1, \tilde{y}_2, \cdots, \tilde{y}_K$ constructed by our proposed negative example construction strategy.

3.2   Negative Example Construction Strategy

In this section, we detail the proposed negative example construction strategy. It contains three schemes: realistic scheme, random scheme and linguistic scheme. In most cases, we use the realistic scheme for constructing negative examples. When the realistic scheme is not applicable, we use the random scheme or the linguistic scheme instead. We demonstrate examples using our proposed strategy in Table 1.

Table 1. Demonstration of our proposed negative example construction strategy, which contains three schemes. Note that each linguistic transformation in the linguistic scheme is demonstrated separately for clarity. In practice, one of the linguistic transformations will be randomly selected.

Target sentence y	We are exploring negative example construction strategies.
Realistic Scheme	We is exploring negative example construction strategy.
Random Scheme	We are exploring Title example fill strategies.
Linguistic Scheme	
-synonym	We are exploring passive example building strategies.
-inflection	We are explored negative example constructed strategies.
-function word	They are exploring negative example construction strategies.
-case	we are exploring Negative example construction strategies.
-misspelling	We air exploding negative example construction strategies.

The realistic scheme makes use of the realistic grammatical error patterns produced by human beings for constructing negative examples. Realistic grammatical error patterns are effective for introducing realistic grammatical errors into error-free text and have been used in previous GEC studies for data augmentation [18] and error-aware BERT fine-tuning [14]. In this study, we utilize them for generating sufficient negative examples with more diverse grammatical errors. Specifically, we first extract all realistic grammatical error patterns {WRONG: CORRECT} from the training data, where WRONG indicates an erroneous word in a sentence and CORRECT indicates its correction. Then, we reverse their key-value pairs into the form of {CORRECT:WRONG} for negative example construction. When constructing a negative example, for each word y_j selected from the target sentence y, we randomly choose one of the {CORRECT:WRONG} patterns whose key CORRECT is y_j, and use the value WRONG as the noised word of y_j for replacement. The intuition is that we replace a correct word with a wrong word.

In practice, however, a word y_j randomly selected from the target sentence may not be one of the keys in the available {CORRECT:WRONG} pairs, such as an out-of-vocabulary word. To handle this case, we propose two additional schemes as compromise:

1) Random Scheme. Such a particular word is replaced by another word sampled from the vocabulary of the dataset in a uniform distribution.

2) Linguistic Scheme. Such a particular word is replaced by one of the five linguistic transformations described below. These linguistic transformations are used by some GEC studies to mimic realistic grammatical errors [14,18,27].

○ *Synonym Transformation.* Replacing y_j with one of its synonyms. It is helpful for generating word misuse errors (noun errors, verb errors, adjective errors, etc.) commonly appeared in writings, such as misusing *"situation"* as *"condition"*.

○ *Inflection Transformation.* Replacing y_j with one of its inflections. It imitates inflection misuse in the writings, such as misusing noun declension and verb conjugation. E.g., using the present tense of *"is"* where the past tense *"was"* is required.

○ *Function Word Transformation.* Replacing y_j with another function word that belongs to the same function word category of y_j. It imitates the improper function word uses in writings, such as misusing *"at"* as *"in"* and misusing *"to"* as *"towards"*.

○ *Case Transformation.* Replacing y_j with one of the three case patterns: lowercase, uppercase, and capitalize. It mimics the case errors made frequently by native English speakers due to their carelessness, such as lower-casing country names, city names and abbreviations.

○ *Misspelling Transformation.* Replacing y_j with one of its 10 most similar words. It mimics the misspelling errors commonly appeared in writings by the native English speakers due to carelessness or rapid typing with keyboards.

3.3 Dynamic Construction

Many contrastive learning studies [6,7,13] have proved that the variety of negative examples is beneficial for improving the performance of the trained model. In our method, the proposed negative example construction strategy is based on rules, and the operations required for constructing negative examples are merely random sampling and replacement. Therefore, they are lightweight and consume little time, enabling them to be dynamically applied during the training process.

As shown in Fig. 2, we depict the proposed dynamic negative example construction, and compare it with the static negative example construction. In the figure, (x, y) denotes a training pair, where x denotes the source sentence and y denotes the target sentence. $\tilde{Y}$ denotes the constructed negative examples. f_{static} denotes the static negative example construction strategy and f_{dynamic} denotes our proposed dynamic negative example construction strategy.

With static construction (the higher part of the figure), the negative examples $\tilde{Y}$ (blue) for the training pair (x, y) are constructed before the training process. And during training, the same set of negative examples constructed ($\tilde{Y}$) is used in each iteration. On the contrary, with dynamic construction (the lower part of the figure), different sets of negative examples are constructed dynamically for the training pair (x, y) in each iteration during training. Specifically, in iteration 1, a set of negative examples $\tilde{Y}_1$ (orange) are constructed with the negative example construction strategy f_{dynamic}. Similarly, another set of negative examples $\tilde{Y}_2$ (yellow) are constructed in iteration 2. In this manner, for the same training pair, dynamic construction enables the model to see different sets of negative examples in different iterations during training, and significantly increases the variety of the negative examples.

3.4 Model Training

Following Cao et al. [4], we use the weighted sum of the negative log likelihood loss L^{NLL} and a margin-based contrastive loss L^{CL} as the training loss L for each

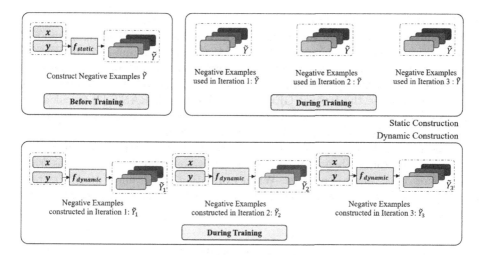

Fig. 2. Demonstration of the proposed dynamic negative example construction and its comparison with the static negative example construction.

training pair $(\boldsymbol{x}, \boldsymbol{y})$ to optimize model parameters, as in Eq. 1. α is a weighting parameter that controls the relative importance of the two losses. During training, the negative log likelihood loss L^{NLL} (Eq. 2) increases the similarity between the model output $\hat{\boldsymbol{y}}$ and the target sentence $\boldsymbol{y}$. And the contrastive loss L^{CL} (Eq. 3) discourages the model from generating each negative example $\tilde{\boldsymbol{y}}_k$ that contains grammatical errors. K is the number of constructed negative examples, and γ is the margin.

$$L = \alpha \cdot L^{\mathrm{NLL}} + (1 - \alpha) \cdot L^{\mathrm{CL}} \tag{1}$$

$$L^{\mathrm{NLL}} = -\boldsymbol{y} \log \hat{\boldsymbol{y}} \tag{2}$$

$$L^{\mathrm{CL}} = \frac{1}{K} \sum_{k=1}^{K} \max(-\boldsymbol{y} \log \hat{\boldsymbol{y}} + \tilde{\boldsymbol{y}}_k \log \hat{\boldsymbol{y}} + \gamma, 0) \tag{3}$$

4 Experiments

4.1 Datasets

We use the CWEB dataset [12] for experiments. It contains low error density writings from native English speakers and includes two domains. The G domain (CWEB-G) contains writings with a higher number of grammatical errors, and the S domain (CWEB-S) contains more professional writings with fewer grammatical errors.

The CWEB dataset only contains development data and test data but no training data. Following previous studies [4, 12], we extract the first 1,000 samples of CWEB-G and the first 1,000 of CWEB-S from the original development data and combine them to form the training data, which are used for training models and extracting realistic grammatical error patterns. The remaining of the original development data are taken as new development data for obtaining the best model during training. The original test data of CWEB are left unchanged, with which we evaluate the trained GEC models. We use ERRANT [3] to calculate precision, recall and $F_{0.5}$ for evaluating the correction performance of the GEC models. Statistics of the dataset are shown in Table 2.

The grammatical errors and their corresponding corrections are annotated by two annotators. When training the model, we only use the corrections from annotator 1 as target sentences. When evaluating the trained model on test data, we calculate the scoring performance against each annotator and take the average for report.

Table 2. Statistics of the CWEB dataset. **Original** is the statistics of the original dataset and **Derived** is the statistics after splitting the development set into training and development data.

Splits	Original		Derived	
Train	–	–	2,867	1,862
Dev	3,867	2,862	1,000	1,000
Test	3,981	2,864	3,981	2,864

4.2   Experiment Settings

We use Transformer-big [28] as the model architecture. Following Cao et al. [4], we use the pre-trained weights of GEC-PD [17] to initialize the GEC model. We use the Adam [16] optimizer with the learning rate set to 3e−5. We train the model for 10 epochs and validate it after each epoch on the development set. Model weights of the smallest validation loss is used as the best model for evaluation on the test set. We construct $K = 4$ negative examples for each training pair and set the noising probability p to 0.15. We run 3 times with different seeds for each experiment and take the average of the 3 runs for report to reduce randomness.

4.3   Compared Models

We compare our method with several strong baselines to prove the effectiveness of the proposed method:

Direct Inference. Making predictions on CWEB test data directly with an off-the-shelf GEC model developed for correcting writings by learners of English as a second language, without further training on CWEB training data. In experiments, we use GEC-PD [17] for this purpose.

NLL. The model is first initialized with the weights of the GEC-PD model. Then, it is trained on the training data merely with negative log-likelihood (i.e., without contrastive learning) and evaluated on the test data.

CL$_{2021}$. The model propsoed by Cao et al. [4]. They first initialize the model with the weights of GEC-PD. Then, they train the model on the training data with their contrastive learning method, and evaluate the trained model on the test data.

4.4 Overall Results and Analysis

The overall experimental results are shown in Table 3. **Direct Inference** are the results by the GEC-PD [17] model without further training on the training set. **NLL** are the results of the GEC model initialized with the weights of GEC-PD and trained merely using the negative log-likelihood loss without contrastive learning. **CL$_{2021}$** are the results reported in the paper of Cao et al. [4]. **Ours (Realistic+Rand)** are the results of our proposed method with realistic scheme & random scheme, and **Ours (Realistic+Ling)** are the results of our proposed method with realistic scheme & linguistic scheme. **Average** are the average results of CWEB-G and CWEB-S. The best scores of each column are shown in bold.

Table 3. Overall experiment results. **Direct Inference** are the results by the GEC-PD [17] model without further training on the training set. **NLL** are the results of the GEC model initialized with the weights of GEC-PD and trained merely using the negative log-likelihood loss without contrastive learning. **CL$_{2021}$** are the results reported in the paper of Cao et al. [4]. **Ours (Realistic+Rand)** are the results of our proposed method with realistic scheme & random scheme, and **Ours (Realistic+Ling)** are the results of our proposed method with realistic scheme & linguistic scheme. **Average** are the average results of CWEB-G and CWEB-S. The best scores of each column are shown in bold.

Model	CWEB-G			CWEB-S			Average		
	P	R	$F_{0.5}$	P	R	$F_{0.5}$	P	R	$F_{0.5}$
Direct Inference	21.18	23.01	21.45	17.27	15.76	16.92	19.22	19.38	19.18
NLL	40.46	18.93	32.76	36.78	16.66	29.51	38.62	17.79	31.14
CL$_{2021}$	37.21	**23.15**	33.03	36.30	**20.40**	**31.34**	36.76	**21.78**	32.19
Ours (Realistic+Rand)	41.37	19.80	33.80	38.06	17.08	30.48	39.71	18.44	32.14
Ours (Realistic+Ling)	**42.42**	19.06	**33.89**	**39.10**	16.80	30.82	**40.76**	17.93	**32.36**

First, it is shown that the results of **Direct Inference** with GEC-PD are low. It's average $F_{0.5}$ is 19.18. And its average precision is only 19.22, which is lower than other results by a large margin. That supports the finding that the GEC model developed for correcting writings by learners of English as a second language indeed produces low performance on the writings by native English speakers due to the low error density [12].

Second, we find that after training GEC-PD on the CWEB training data with our proposed method, the results are improved. Specifically, the average $F_{0.5}$ of our proposed **Realistic+Ling** (32.36) is higher than **NLL** (31.14) by 1.22, and higher than **CL$_{2021}$** (32.19) by 0.17.

Third, we can also see that our method significantly boosts the precision of the GEC model. For example, the precision of **Realistic+Ling** in CWEB-G and CWEB-S are 42.42 and 39.10, which are 1.96 and 2.32 higher than **NLL**, 5.21 and 2.80 higher than **CL$_{2021}$**. At the same time, it also produces the highest average precision (40.76). The higher precision of our GEC model illustrates that the grammatical errors detected by the model indeed are erroneous, rather than accurate. In the task of grammatical error correction, a GEC model with an ability to **accurately** correct the detected grammatical errors (higher precision) is more preferred than one with an ability to detect many grammatical errors but fail to correct them (higher recall). This is also reflected by the evaluation metric $F_{0.5}$ of GEC, which values the precision twice as the recall. Therefore, our proposed method is beneficial for enhancing the correction performance of the GEC model, as it indeed makes the model correct the detected grammatical errors precisely and suppresses the model from over-correction.

Finally, the results also show that **Realistic+Ling** produces higher average precision (40.76) and average $F_{0.5}$ (32.36) than **Realistic+Rand** (39.71 and 32.14). It proves that the pseudo grammatical errors generated by the linguistic transformations are beneficial and effective for the construction of negative examples, which leads to a better GEC model.

5   Discussion and Analysis

5.1   Case Study

In order to demonstrate that our proposed negative example construction strategy can indeed generate sufficient negative examples with realistic and diverse grammatical errors, we extracted one training pair from the CWEB dataset accompanied by their corresponding negative examples constructed by Cao et al. [4]'s method and those constructed with our proposed method, as shown in Table 4. In the training pair, there is a case error (*"allow"* → *"Allow"*), which is coloured red. In the negative examples, noises introduced by the negative example construction methods are coloured blue.

We can see that the first, third and fourth negative examples constructed by Cao et al. [4]'s method are the same as the source sentence. The second example contains an insertion error (*"pick"* → *"pick up"*). Obviously, these negative examples do not contain diverse and realistic grammatical errors, which is not helpful for the model to learn to correct properly from contrastive learning. On the other hand, the negative examples constructed using our proposed method contain a large number of diverse and realistic grammatical errors. For instance, the first example contains a preposition error (*"for"* → *"with"*). The second example

Table 4. Case study. We extracted one training pair from the CWEB dataset accompanied by their corresponding negative examples constructed by Cao et al. [4]'s method and those constructed with our proposed method. Grammatical errors in the training pair are coloured red. Noises in the negative examples introduced by the negative example construction methods are coloured blue. The negative examples constructed with our proposed method are more sufficient with more diverse grammatical errors.

Source sent	Allow them to pick some coloring sheets that you can print for them.
Target sent	Allow them to pick some coloring sheets that you can print for them.
Cao et al. [4]	allow them to pick some coloring sheets you can print for them.
	Allow them to pick up some coloring sheets you can print for them.
	allow them to pick some coloring sheets you can print for them.
	allow them to pick some coloring sheets you can print for them.
Ours	Allow them to pick some coloring sheets you can print with them.
	Allow them to pick some coloring piece you can prunt for them.
	Allow them to pick sum coloring sheets you can print for them.
	allow them to pick some coloring sheets you can print in them.

contains a synonym error (*"sheets"* → *"piece"*) and a misspelling error (*"print"* → *"prunt"*). From the negative examples with diverse and realistic errors, the GEC model can better learn to correct sentences precisely through contrastive learning.

5.2 Effect of Dynamic Construction

As mentioned above, our proposed dynamic negative example construction can increase the variety of the negative examples during model training. In this section, we investigate the effect of dynamic construction by comparing the scoring performance of the proposed Realistic+Rand and Realistic+Ling methods with static and dynamic construction respectively.

The experimental results are shown in Table 5. The left half shows the results of static construction, while the right half shows the results of dynamic construction. The results of each negative example construction method are the average of CWEB-G and CWEB-S. The higher results between the static and dynamic construction of each method are bolded.

As shown in the table, the dynamic results are generally higher than the static results. Specifically, the $F_{0.5}$ of static Realistic+Rand is 31.78, while that of the dynamic one is 32.14, with a performance gap of 0.36. The $F_{0.5}$ of static Realistic+Ling is 31.77, while the dynamic one is 32.36, with a large performance gap of 0.59. It proves that by increasing the variety of the negative examples during training, dynamic construction indeed increases the variety of the negative examples, thereby avoiding overfitting and enhancing the generalization ability of the GEC model.

Table 5. Scoring performance comparison of the proposed Realistic+Rand and Realistic+Ling methods with static and dynamic construction respectively.

Method	Static			Dynamic		
	P	R	$F_{0.5}$	P	R	$F_{0.5}$
Realistic+Rand	39.90	17.74	31.78	39.71	18.44	**32.14**
Realistic+Ling	38.75	18.73	31.77	40.76	17.93	**32.36**

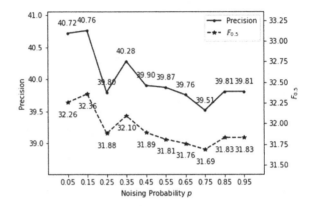

Fig. 3. Scoring performance of the GEC model at different values of p, from 0.05 to 0.95 at a 0.1 interval. The dynamic Realistic+Ling strategy is used for constructing negative examples in the experiment. The experiment results are obtained from averaging the results of CWEB-G and CWEB-S. When p is set to 0.15, the score reaches the highest (precision $= 40.76$, $F_{0.5} = 32.36$). As p gradually increases, the precision and $F_{0.5}$ drop gradually.

5.3   Effect of the Noising Probability

When constructing a negative example with our proposed negative example construction strategy, a noising probability p should be determined to randomly select words from the target sentence for replacement. In this section, we analyze the impact of different values of p on the correction performance. Specifically, we construct negative examples with the proposed dynamic Realistic+Ling strategy according to different values of p, from 0.05 to 0.95 at a 0.1 interval. The precision and $F_{0.5}$ at each probability are shown in Fig. 3, which are obtained from averaging the results of CWEB-G and CWEB-S.

The results show that when p is set to 0.15, the score reaches the highest (precision $= 40.76$, $F_{0.5} = 32.36$). As p gradually increases, the precision and $F_{0.5}$ drop gradually. The reason may be that as p increases, more words are selected from the target sentence for replacement. Therefore, the negative examples constructed are more different from the target sentence. The greater the difference between the target sentence and the negative example, the easier it is for the

GEC model to compare their differences, and the smaller the improvement in the error correction ability of the model obtained from contrastive learning.

6 Conclusion

In this paper, a dynamic negative example construction method for grammatical error correction using contrastive learning is proposed. The proposed method constructs sufficient negative examples with diverse grammatical errors dynamically during model training. The constructed negative examples are beneficial for the GEC model to correct sentences precisely and suppress the model from over-correction. Experimental results show that our proposed method enhances the correction precision significantly. In this study, positive example construction strategy is not proposed for grammatical error correction using contrastive learning, as it is hard to construct sentences that are morphologically different from but semantically identical to the target sentence. One possible solution for that may be utilizing data augmentation. In future work, we will investigate this topic in depth.

Acknowledgements. This work is supported by National Natural Science Foundation of China (No. 61976062).

References

1. Awasthi, A., Sarawagi, S., Goyal, R., Ghosh, S., Piratla, V.: Parallel iterative edit models for local sequence transduction. In: Proceedings of the 2019 Conference on Empirical Methods in Natural Language Processing and the 9th International Joint Conference on Natural Language Processing (EMNLP-IJCNLP), pp. 4260–4270. Association for Computational Linguistics (2019)
2. Brockett, C., Dolan, W.B., Gamon, M.: Correcting ESL errors using phrasal SMT techniques. In: Proceedings of the 21st International Conference on Computational Linguistics and 44th Annual Meeting of the Association for Computational Linguistics, pp. 249–256. Association for Computational Linguistics (2006)
3. Bryant, C., Felice, M., Briscoe, T.: Automatic annotation and evaluation of error types for grammatical error correction. In: Proceedings of the 55th Annual Meeting of the Association for Computational Linguistics (Volume 1: Long Papers), pp. 793–805. Association for Computational Linguistics (2017)
4. Cao, H., Yang, W., Ng, H.T.: Grammatical error correction with contrastive learning in low error density domains. In: Findings of the Association for Computational Linguistics: EMNLP 2021, pp. 4867–4874. Association for Computational Linguistics (2021)
5. Chen, M., Ge, T., Zhang, X., Wei, F., Zhou, M.: Improving the efficiency of grammatical error correction with erroneous span detection and correction. In: Proceedings of the 2020 Conference on Empirical Methods in Natural Language Processing (EMNLP), pp. 7162–7169. Association for Computational Linguistics (2020)
6. Chen, T., Kornblith, S., Norouzi, M., Hinton, G.: A simple framework for contrastive learning of visual representations. In: International Conference on Machine Learning, pp. 1597–1607 (2020)

7. Chen, X., Fan, H., Girshick, R., He, K.: Improved baselines with momentum contrastive learning. arXiv preprint arXiv:2003.04297 (2020)
8. Chollampatt, S., Ng, H.T.: A multilayer convolutional encoder-decoder neural network for grammatical error correction. In: Proceedings of the AAAI Conference on Artificial Intelligence (2018)
9. Dahlmeier, D., Ng, H.T., Wu, S.M.: Building a large annotated corpus of learner English: the NUS corpus of learner English. In: Proceedings of the Eighth Workshop on Innovative Use of NLP for Building Educational Applications, pp. 22–31. Association for Computational Linguistics (2013)
10. Devlin, J., Chang, M.W., Lee, K., Toutanova, K.: BERT: pre-training of deep bidirectional transformers for language understanding. In: Proceedings of the 2019 Conference of the North American Chapter of the Association for Computational Linguistics: Human Language Technologies, Volume 1 (Long and Short Papers), pp. 4171–4186. Association for Computational Linguistics (2019)
11. Felice, M., Yuan, Z., Andersen, Ø.E., Yannakoudakis, H., Kochmar, E.: Grammatical error correction using hybrid systems and type filtering. In: Proceedings of the Eighteenth Conference on Computational Natural Language Learning: Shared Task, pp. 15–24. Association for Computational Linguistics (2014)
12. Flachs, S., Lacroix, O., Yannakoudakis, H., Rei, M., Søgaard, A.: Grammatical error correction in low error density domains: a new benchmark and analyses. In: Proceedings of the 2020 Conference on Empirical Methods in Natural Language Processing (EMNLP), pp. 8467–8478. Association for Computational Linguistics (2020)
13. Gao, T., Yao, X., Chen, D.: SimCSE: simple contrastive learning of sentence embeddings. In: Proceedings of the 2021 Conference on Empirical Methods in Natural Language Processing, pp. 6894–6910. Association for Computational Linguistics (2021)
14. He, J., Li, X., Su, H., Chen, X., Yang, H., Chen, M.: EA-MLM: error-aware masked language modeling for grammatical error correction. In: 2021 International Conference on Asian Language Processing (IALP), pp. 363–368 (2021)
15. Kaneko, M., Mita, M., Kiyono, S., Suzuki, J., Inui, K.: Encoder-decoder models can benefit from pre-trained masked language models in grammatical error correction. In: Proceedings of the 58th Annual Meeting of the Association for Computational Linguistics, pp. 4248–4254. Association for Computational Linguistics (2020)
16. Kingma, D.P., Ba, J.: Adam: a method for stochastic optimization. arXiv preprint arXiv:1412.6980 (2014)
17. Kiyono, S., Suzuki, J., Mita, M., Mizumoto, T., Inui, K.: An empirical study of incorporating pseudo data into grammatical error correction. In: Proceedings of the 2019 Conference on Empirical Methods in Natural Language Processing and the 9th International Joint Conference on Natural Language Processing (EMNLP-IJCNLP), pp. 1236–1242. Association for Computational Linguistics (2019)
18. Li, X., He, J.: Data augmentation of incorporating real error patterns and linguistic knowledge for grammatical error correction. In: Proceedings of the 25th Conference on Computational Natural Language Learning, pp. 223–233. Association for Computational Linguistics (2021)
19. Liu, Y., Liu, P.: SimCLS: a simple framework for contrastive learning of abstractive summarization. In: Proceedings of the 59th Annual Meeting of the Association for Computational Linguistics and the 11th International Joint Conference on Natural Language Processing (Volume 2: Short Papers), pp. 1065–1072. Association for Computational Linguistics (2021)

20. Macdonald, N.H.: Human factors and behavioral science: the unix^{TM} writer's work-bench software: rationale and design. Bell Syst. Tech. J. **62**(6), 1891–1908 (1983)
21. Mizumoto, T., Komachi, M., Nagata, M., Matsumoto, Y.: Mining revision log of language learning SNS for automated Japanese error correction of second language learners. In: Proceedings of 5th International Joint Conference on Natural Language Processing, pp. 147–155. Asian Federation of Natural Language Processing (2011)
22. Richardson, S.D., Braden-Harder, L.C.: The experience of developing a large-scale natural language text processing system: critique. In: Second Conference on Applied Natural Language Processing, pp. 195–202. Association for Computational Linguistics (1988)
23. Sidorov, G.: Syntactic dependency based n-grams in rule based automatic English as second language grammar correction. Int. J. Comput. Linguist. Appl. **4**(2), 169–188 (2013)
24. Sidorov, G., Gupta, A., Tozer, M., Catala, D., Catena, A., Fuentes, S.: Rule-based system for automatic grammar correction using syntactic n-grams for English language learning (L2). In: Proceedings of the Seventeenth Conference on Computational Natural Language Learning: Shared Task, pp. 96–101. Association for Computational Linguistics (2013)
25. Stahlberg, F., Kumar, S.: Seq2Edits: sequence transduction using span-level edit operations. In: Proceedings of the 2020 Conference on Empirical Methods in Natural Language Processing (EMNLP), pp. 5147–5159. Association for Computational Linguistics (2020)
26. Sun, X., Wang, H.: Adjusting the precision-recall trade-off with align-and-predict decoding for grammatical error correction. In: Proceedings of the 60th Annual Meeting of the Association for Computational Linguistics (Volume 2: Short Papers), pp. 686–693. Association for Computational Linguistics (2022)
27. Takahashi, Y., Katsumata, S., Komachi, M.: Grammatical error correction using pseudo learner corpus considering learner's error tendency. In: Proceedings of the 58th Annual Meeting of the Association for Computational Linguistics: Student Research Workshop, pp. 27–32. Association for Computational Linguistics (2020)
28. Vaswani, A., et al.: Attention is all you need. In: Advances in Neural Information Processing Systems, vol. 30 (2017)
29. Yuan, Z., Briscoe, T.: Grammatical error correction using neural machine translation. In: Proceedings of the 2016 Conference of the North American Chapter of the Association for Computational Linguistics: Human Language Technologies, pp. 380–386. Association for Computational Linguistics (2016)
30. Zhao, W., Wang, L., Shen, K., Jia, R., Liu, J.: Improving grammatical error correction via pre-training a copy-augmented architecture with unlabeled data. In: Proceedings of the 2019 Conference of the North American Chapter of the Association for Computational Linguistics: Human Language Technologies, Volume 1 (Long and Short Papers), pp. 156–165. Association for Computational Linguistics (2019)

SPACL: Shared-Private Architecture Based on Contrastive Learning for Multi-domain Text Classification

Guoding Xiong[1], Yongmei Zhou[1,2][✉], Deheng Wang[1], and Zhouhao Ouyang[3]

[1] School of Cyber Security, Guangdong University of Foreign Studies, Guangzhou 510006, China
[2] Guangzhou Key Laboratory of Multilingual Intelligent Processing, Guangdong University of Foreign Studies, Guangzhou 510006, China
yongmeizhou@gdufs.edu.cn
[3] School of Computing, University of Leeds, Wood-house Lane, Leeds, West Yorkshire LS2 9JT, UK

Abstract. With the development of deep learning in recent years, text classification research has achieved remarkable results. However, text classification task often requires a large amount of annotated data, and data in different fields often force the model to learn different knowledge. It is often difficult for models to distinguish data labeled in different domains. Sometimes data from different domains can even damage the classification ability of the model and reduce the overall performance of the model. To address these issues, we propose a shared-private architecture based on contrastive learning for multi-domain text classification which can improve both the accuracy and robustness of classifiers. Extensive experiments are conducted on two public datasets. The results of experiments show that the our approach achieves the state-of-the-art performance in multi-domain text classification.

Keywords: Contrastive learning · Multi-domain · Text classification

1 Introduction

Text classification is one of the most basic tasks among the many tasks of Natural Langugae Processing (NLP). In recent years, the research work of text classification has produced a large number of applications and achieved remarkable results. With the continuous release of a large number of pretrained language models in recent years, such as BERT [5], ALBERT [11], RoBERTa [16] and other pretrained models, text classification problems have been able to achieve good results on the basis of neural network and pretrained models. However, most text classification problems are highly domain-dependent in that the meaning of the same word may transform in different domains. For example, the word apple expresses the fruit in kitchen review (e.g., I have shifted to an apple for lunch), while in electronics review, it means a brand of electronic products (e.g., I can't understand how apple sell so much ipod video). A common strategy, training multiple classifiers for different domains, is used to solve above problems. However, text data in reality often have characteristics of multiple domains and the cost of labeling a large number of multi-domain data is too high. Therefore, it is very important and practical meaningful to improve the accuracy of text classification in multiple related domains. Multi-domain text classification (MDTC) [12] is proposed to solve above problems, it aims to utilize textual information in different domains to improve the performance of model architecture, but there is no need to train a separate classifier for each domain. In recent years, deep learning has been widely used in MDTC problems, and has achieved excellent results [22,23]. The method used in most studies is shared-private architecture. Private modules are used to capture domain-specific knowledge for each domain, and shared modules are used to capture domain-invariant knowledge [13]. However, these researches only pay attention to how to obtain the shared knowledge of multiple domains and domain-specific knowledge better, but ignore the representation of the samples in the representation space. In order to solve the problems above, in this paper, we propose Shared-Private Architecture based on Contrastive Learning (SPACL), which uses contrastive learning to improve the representations of different types of samples in the representation space, thereby improving the performance level of downstream tasks. Different from previous studies, our architecture can not only use conditional adversarial training to extract domain-invariant features, but also generate better sample representations for MDTC.

The contributions of this paper are summarized as follows: 1) In order to strengthen the alignment representations of data in different domains, we propose a shared-private architecture based on contrastive learning for multi-domain text classification which can improve both the accuracy and robustness of the text classfier. 2) We adopt a conditional adversarial network to interact domain-shared features and classification labels, which can be better adapted to multi-domain text classification. 3) Experiments are carried out on two public multi-domain datasets, and the experimental results compared with multiple baselines show that our proposed model architeture has achieved state-of-the-art results.

2 Related Work

2.1 Multi-domain Text Classification

Multi-domain text classification was proposed first to improve performance through fusing training data from multiple domains [12]. The biggest challenge of this task is that the same text may has different implications in different domains, and the cost of labeling each domain is too costly.

Some early studies mainly used domain transfer learning techniques for MDTC. The structural correspondence learning (SCL) algorithm was proposed to select source domains most likely to adapt well to given target domains [1]. Pan et al. [19] proposed a spectral feature alignment (SFA) method to align

domain-specific words from different domains into unified clusters, with the help
of domain-independent words as a bridge. Wu and Huang [22] proposed a novel
approach based on multi-task learning to train sentiment classifiers for different
domains in a collaborative way. Liu et al. [15] proposed a multi-task deep neural
network (MTDNN) for learning representations across multiple tasks, not only
leveraging large amounts of cross-task data, but also benefiting from a regularization effect that leads to more general representations to help tasks in new
domains. Liu et al. [14] proposed an adversarial multi-task learning framework,
alleviating the shared and private latent feature spaces from interfering with
each other.

The most recent prior works on MDTC include Meta Fine-Tuning (MFT) for
multi-domain text classification [21]. Dual Adversarial Co-Learning (DACL) for
Multi-Domain Text Classification [23], Conditional Adversarial Networks (CAN)
for Multi-Domain Text Classification [24] and Mixup Regularized Adversarial
Networks (MRAN) for Multi-Domain Text Classification [25]. MFT uses meta-
learning and domain transfer technology to learn highly transferable knowledge
from typical samples in various domains. Both DACL and CAN leverage adversarial training to obtain the shared domain features. MRAN adopts the domain
and category mixup regularizations to enrich the intrinsic features in the shared
latent space and enforce consistent predictions in-between training instances.
However, these methods ignore the distance of samples in the feature space when
learning multi-domain feature representations, which is an important guideline to
help classification. Furthermore, they did not consider the interaction between
the extracted features and class labels, which is often important to improve
their correlation. Different from the above studies, the work our proposed further advances the line of study by deploying contrastive learning. It can also
model the interactions between shared domain features and classes to enhance
their representations through a conditional adversarial network. We assume that
data in various domains is insufficient, and make full use of data from multiple
domains to improve overall system performance.

2.2   Contrastive Learning

Recently, related researches show that contrastive learning is an effective self-
supervised learning method. Chen et al. [3] proposed simple framework for contrastive learning of visual representations (SimCLR) to improve the quality of
the learned representations by contrastive learning.

Meng et al. [18] present a self-supervised learning framework, COCO-LM,
that pretrains Language Models by COrrecting and COntrasting corrupted text
sequences. Giorgi et al. [9] present Deep Contrastive Learning for Unsupervised
Textual Representations (DeCLUTR) to enclose the performance gap between
unsupervised and supervised pretraining for universal sentence encoders. One
of the key aspects of contrastive learning is the sampling of positive pairs. Gao
et al. [8] add dropout noise to keep a good alignment for positive pairs. Fang
et al. [6] uses data augmentation to generate positive pairs from the original
sentences.

We develop our model architecture with contrastive learning. In our experiments, we select a sample and combine it with itself to get a positive pair. And then combine it with other different kinds of samples to get negative pairs. A contrastive loss is used to control the distance between samples of different classes in the sample space so that enhance the ability of the text classifier.

3   Methodology

3.1   Model Architecture

In this paper, we consider MDTC tasks in the following settings.

Specifically, there exists M domains $\{D_i\}_{i=1}^M$. The labeled training collection of the m-th domain is denoted by $X_l^m = \{(x_j^m, y_j^m) \mid j \in [1, N_l^m]\}$, where x_j^m and y_j^m are the input texts and the label of the j-th sample of the m-th domain. N_l^m is the total number of the labeled samples of the m-th domain. The unlabeled training collection of the m-th domain is denoted by $X_u^m = \{(x_k^m) \mid k \in [1, N_u^m]\}$, where x_k^m and N_u^m are the input texts of the j-th sample and the sample size of the m-th domain. N_L represents the amount of labeled data for all domains and N_U represents the amount of unlabeled data for all domains. The goal of MDTC is to improve the overall system performance by utilizing the training sets of M domains. The classification performance of the system is measured by the average classification accuracy across M domains (Fig. 1).

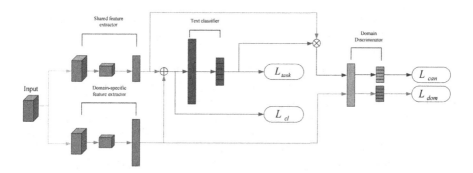

Fig. 1. The overall model atchitecture of SPACL. A shared feature extractor is used to capture the shared knowledge. Each domain-specific extractor is trained to extract the domain-specific knowledge. A domain classifier is trained to predict the domain label of the input sample. A text classifier is trained to predict the class of samples and calculate the loss of contrastive learning. L_{task} is the loss function of text classification. L_{cl} is the loss fuction of contrastive learning. L_{dom} is the loss function of domain classfication. L_{can} is the conditoning adverserial loss function which extracts the shared knowledge across domains.

3.2 Domain-Specific Representation Learning

In order to ensure the validity of our extracted domain-specific features, we add a simple and effective domain discriminator D_d, which takes the extracted domain-specific features as input and outputs the predicted domain category, so as to optimize the domain discrimination ability. The h_p is the output of the domain-specific extractor for the given instance X. The domain classifier $D_d(h_p; \theta_d) \rightarrow \hat{d}$ maps the domain-specific feature representation to a domain label prediction. θ_d denotes the parameters of the domain classifier D_d. The discriminator D_d is trained to minimize the prediction loss on labeled and unlabeled instances of multiple domains:

$$L_{\text{dom}} = -\frac{1}{N_U + N_L} \sum_{m=1}^{M} \sum_{j=1}^{N_l^m + N_u^m} d_j^m \log \hat{d_j^m} + \left(1 - d_j^m\right) \log \left(1 - \hat{d_j^m}\right) \quad (1)$$

where the $\hat{d}$ is prediction probabilities of domain labels of domain discriminator D_d and the d is the true domain label of input text.

3.3 Conditional Adversarial Network

Motivated by some previous works of domain separation learning [2,20], we adopt a conditional adversarial network for SPACL to extract domain shared features. After the domain-specific learning, we freeze the parameters θ_d of the domain discriminator D_d to ensure that the discriminator has good domain recognition capabilities. At the same time, in order to ensure that the features we extract can express shareability across domains, we also adopt a negative entropy loss so that the domain classifier cannot accurately identify the domain of the shared-representation the input text.

The h_s is the output of the shared extractor F_s for the given instance X. The h_s is the output of the shared extractor F_s for the given instance X. The h_p is the output of the shared extractor F_p for the given instance X. The final joint representations h is the concatenated vector of private features h_p and shared features h_s. The text classifier C outputs the probability distribution of the prediction labels which are denoted as h_c. The domain classifier $D_d(h_c \otimes h; \theta_d) \rightarrow \hat{d}$ maps the joint feature representation h and the class prediction h_c to a domain label $\hat{d}$. The loss can be defined as:

$$L_{\text{can}} = \frac{1}{N_U + N_L} \sum_{m=1}^{M} \sum_{j=1}^{N_l^m + N_u^m} d_j^m \log \hat{d_j^m} + \left(1 - d_j^m\right) \log \left(1 - \hat{d_j^m}\right) \quad (2)$$

where $h_c \otimes h$ denotes the cross-covariance of the two vectors which is calculated by multilinear conditioning [17].

3.4 Contrastive Learning

Intuitively, we hope that the distance between the final joint representation vectors of samples of different categories is as far as possible, so as to make the final text classifier C easier to distinguish. Therefore, we adopt a contrastive learning approach to generate better joint representation vectors. Specifically, assuming that given a batch of samples, we will sample a pair of positive examples and other sets of negative examples in the batch. The class label of every sample denotes y. Given a final joint representation h_i of a sample, from a batch we can get an positive pair (h_i, h_{pos}) and other negative sample pairs $\{(h_i, h_{neg}) \mid h_i \in y, h_{neg} \notin y\}$.

The loss of contrastive learning is defined as:

$$L_{cl} = -\frac{1}{N_b} \sum_{i=1}^{N_b} \log \frac{\exp\left(\text{sim}\left(h_i, h_{pos}\right)\right)}{\sum_{\{(h_i, h_{ne.g.}) \mid h_i \in y, h_{neg} \notin y\}} \exp\left(\text{sim}\left(h_i, h_n\right)\right)} \tag{3}$$

where $\text{sim}(u, v) = u^T v / \|u\|_2 \|v\|_2$ denotes the cosine distance between the two vectors u and v. N_b and $\|.\|_2$ denote the number of batch size and the L2 norm.

3.5   Objective Function

The multi-domain text classification task is a binary classification task. Therefore, we define the task loss is :

$$L_{task} = -\frac{1}{N_L} \sum_{m=1}^{M} \sum_{j=1}^{N_l^m} y_j^m \log \hat{y_j^m} + \left(1 - y_j^m\right) \log \left(1 - \hat{y_j^m}\right) \tag{4}$$

The text classifier C takes the final joint representation as input, and outputs the prediction labels which denote $\hat{y}$.

The final loss function is the combination of above losses:

$$L = L_{task} + L_{dom} + \alpha L_{can} + \beta L_{cl} \tag{5}$$

where α and β are hyperparameters for balancing different losses.

4   Experiment

4.1   Dataset

We evaluate SPACL on two standard datasets in our experiments: the Amazon review dataset [1] and the FDU-MTL dataset [15]. The Amazon review dataset contains reviews in four domains: books, DVDs, electronics, and kitchen. The data for each domain has 1000 positive samples and 1000 negative samples. This dataset is already preprocessed into a bag of features (unigrams and bigrams) which loses word order information. The FDU-MTL datasets contains a total of 16 domains: books, electronics, DVDs, kitchen, apparel, camera, health, music, toys, video, baby, magazine, software, sport, IMDB, and MR. Each domain of FDU-MTL dataset contains a development set of 200 samples, a test set of 400 samples, a training set of about 1400 samples, and about 2000 unlabeled samples.

4.2 Baselines

To evaluate SAPCL, we compare it with the following baselines.

The multi-task learning with bidirectional language (MT-BL) method utilizes extraction of task-invariant features by leveraging potential information among related tasks, which improves the performance of a single task [26]. The multinomial adversarial network (MAN) learns features that are invariant across multiple domains by resorting to its ability to reduce the divergence among the feature distributions of each domain [4]. This method trains the domain discriminator by two loss functions: the least square loss (MAN-L2) and the negative log-likelihood loss (MAN-NLL). Dual adversarial co-learning (DACL) deploys dual adversarial regularizations to align features across different domains, aiming to improve the classifiers' generalization capacity with the learned features [23]. Conditional adversarial networks (CANs) introduce a conditional domain discriminator to model the domain variance in both shared feature representations and class-aware information simultaneously and adopts entropy conditioning to guarantee the transferability of the shared features [24]. The collaborative multi-domain sentiment classification (CMSC) train the models by three loss functions: the least square loss (CMSC-LS), the hinge loss (CMSC-SVM), and the log loss (CMSC-Log) [22]. The adversarial multi-task learning for text classification (ASP-MTL) alleviates the shared and private latent feature spaces from interfering with each other [14]. All the comparison methods use the standard partitions of the datasets. Thus, we cite the results from [4,14,22–24,26] for fair comparisons.

Table 1. MDTC results on the Amazon review dataset

Domain	CMSC-LS	CMSC-SVM	CMSC-Log	MAN-NLL	MAN-L2	DACL	CAN	SPACL (proposed)
Books	82.10	82.26	81.81	82.98	82.46	83.45	83.76	**84.65**
DVD	82.40	83.48	83.73	84.03	83.98	**85.50**	84.68	85.20
Elec.	86.12	86.76	86.67	87.06	87.22	87.40	**88.34**	88.20
Kit.	87.56	88.20	88.23	88.57	88.53	90.00	90.03	**90.10**
Avg	84.55	85.18	85.11	85.66	85.55	86.59	86.70	**87.03**

4.3 Experimental Setting

In our experiment, we set the hyperparameters $\alpha = 0.001$, $\beta = 0.1$. The experiment uses the Adam optimizer with the learning rate of 0.0001. The vector size of the shared feature extractor is 64 while the vector size of the domain-specific feature extractor is 128. The dropout rate is 0.5. ReLU is the activation function. The batch size is 128. MLP feature extractors are the feature extractor of the experiment on the Amazon review dataset with an input size of 5000. MLP feature extractor is composed of two hidden layers, with size 1,000 and 500, respectively. CNN feature extractor with a single convolutional layer is the feature extractor of the experiment on the FDU-MTL review dataset. Each CNN

Table 2. MDTC results on the FDU-MTL dataset

Domain	MT-BL	ASP-MTL	MAN-L2	MAN-NLL	SPACL (proposed))
Books	89.0	84.00	87.6	86.8	**90.2**
Electronics	**90.2**	86.80	87.4	88.8	90.0
Dvd	88.0	85.50	88.1	**88.6**	88.5
Kitchen	**90.5**	86.20	89.8	89.9	90.0
Apparel	87.2	87.00	87.6	87.6	**88.0**
Camera	89.5	89.20	91.4	90.7	**91.2**
Health	**92.5**	88.20	89.8	89.4	90.2
Music	**86.0**	82.50	85.9	85.5	**86.0**
Toys	**92.0**	88.0	90.0	90.4	91.1
Video	88.0	84.5	89.5	**89.6**	88.7
Baby	88.7	88.20	90.0	**90.2**	89.9
Magazine	92.5	92.20	92.5	**92.9**	92.5
Software	**91.7**	87.20	90.4	90.9	89.5
Sports	**89.5**	85.7	89.0	89.0	88.2
IMDb	88.0	85.5	86.6	87.0	**88.7**
MR	75.7	**76.7**	76.1	**76.7**	76.5
AVG	88.6	86.1	88.2	88.4	**88.7**

Table 3. Ablation study on the Amazon review dataset

Method	Book	DVD	Electronics	Kitchen	AVG
SPACL w/o C	83.10	83.05	85.10	86.20	84.36
SPACL w/o CL	84.10	82.50	84.00	85.05	83.90
SPACL w/o D	83.05	80.01	82.05	83.17	82.07
SPACL (full)	**84.65**	**85.20**	**88.20**	**90.10**	**87.03**

feature extractor uses different kernel sizes (3, 4, 5) with input size of 1000. Text classifier and discriminator are MLPs with one hidden layer of the same size as their input (128 + 64 for text classifier and 128 for discriminator).

4.4   Results

We conduct the experiments on the Amazon review dataset and FDU-MTL dataset following the setting of [4]. A 5-fold cross-validation is conducted on the Amazon review dataset. All data is divided into five folds: three folds are used as the training set, one fold is used as the validation set, and the remaining one fold is used the test set. The experimental results on the Amazon review dataset are shown in Table 1 and the results on the FDU-MTL dataset are shown in Table 2. The best performance is shown in bold.

From Table 1, we can see that our proposed SPACL architecture is able to achieve the best average accuracy across multiple domains on the Amazon review dataset. This suggests our proposed model architecture is more effective than other baselines. From the experimental results on FDU-MTL in the Table 2, the average accuracy of our proposed SPACL is superior to the other methods. The experimental results once again demonstrate the effectiveness of our proposed method.

The reasons for the above results are as follows: 1) Our model utilizes a conditional adversarial network to correlate the extracted shared features and predicted class labels, thereby improving the overall generalization performance of the model architecture. 2) Our model architecture expands the distance between samples of different classes in the sample space and the distance of samples of the same class through the method of comparative learning. Therefore, our model performs better at multi-domain text classification tasks.

4.5   Ablation Study

To validate the contribution of conditional adversarial networks and contrastive learning in our model architecture, we conduct extensive ablation experiments on the Amazon review dataset. In particular, we studied two kinds of ablation variants: (1) SPACL w/o C, the variant model architecture of our SPACL without conditional adversarial learning on shared feature extractor; (2) SPACL w/o CL, the variant model architecture of our SPACL without contrastive learning on the final joint representation; (3) SPACL w/o D, the variant model architecture of our SPACL without domain-specific representation learning; The ablation experiment results are shown in the Table 3, where we can see all variants of produce poor results, the full model architecture provides the best performance. Therefore, this validated our model architecture of the components in the presence of necessity. From the results of the ablation experiments, we can see that using contrastive learning to improve the sample representation benefits the performance of our model.

5   Conclusion

In this paper, we proposed a shared-private architecture based on contrastive learning to use across different domains of all the available resources for multi-domain text classification. The model architecture expands the distance between shared-representations of samples of different categories in the sample space by introducing contrastive learning, thereby further improving the discriminative ability of the model architecture. In addition, the model architecture uses a conditional adversarial network to establish the correlation between domain shared features and classification prediction labels which improves the overall performance of the model architecture. The experimental results on two benchmarks show that the SPACL model architecture can effectively improve the performance of the system on the multi-domain text classification task. In the future, we will explore a better solution to transfer knowledge from different domains for multi-domain text classification.

Acknowledgement. This work has been supported by the Ministry of education of Humanities and Social Science project under Grant No. 19YJAZH128 and No. 20YJAZH118, the Science and Technology Plan Project of Guangzhou under Grant No. 202102080305.

References

1. Blitzer, J., Dredze, M., Pereira, F.: Biographies, bollywood, boom-boxes and blenders: domain adaptation for sentiment classification. In: Proceedings of the 45th Annual Meeting of the Association of Computational Linguistics, pp. 440–447 (2007)
2. Bousmalis, K., Trigeorgis, G., Silberman, N., Krishnan, D., Erhan, D.: Domain separation networks. Advances in Neural Information Processing Systems 29 (2016)
3. Chen, T., Kornblith, S., Norouzi, M., Hinton, G.: A simple framework for contrastive learning of visual representations. In: International Conference on Machine Learning, pp. 1597–1607. PMLR (2020)
4. Chen, X., Cardie, C.: Multinomial adversarial networks for multi-domain text classification. arXiv preprint arXiv:1802.05694 (2018)
5. Devlin, J., Chang, M.W., Lee, K., Toutanova, K.: Bert: pre-training of deep bidirectional transformers for language understanding. arXiv preprint arXiv:1810.04805 (2018)
6. Fang, H., Wang, S., Zhou, M., Ding, J., Xie, P.: Cert: contrastive self-supervised learning for language understanding. arXiv preprint arXiv:2005.12766 (2020)
7. Ganin, Y., et al.: Domain-adversarial training of neural networks. J. Mach. Learn. Res. **17**(1), 2030–2096 (2016)
8. Gao, T., Yao, X., Chen, D.: Simcse: simple contrastive learning of sentence embeddings. arXiv preprint arXiv:2104.08821 (2021)
9. Giorgi, J., Nitski, O., Wang, B., Bader, G.: Declutr: deep contrastive learning for unsupervised textual representations. arXiv preprint arXiv:2006.03659 (2020)
10. Hu, M., Wu, Y., Zhao, S., Guo, H., Cheng, R., Su, Z.: Domain-invariant feature distillation for cross-domain sentiment classification. arXiv preprint arXiv:1908.09122 (2019)
11. Lan, Z., Chen, M., Goodman, S., Gimpel, K., Sharma, P., Soricut, R.: Albert: a lite bert for self-supervised learning of language representations. arXiv preprint arXiv:1909.11942 (2019)
12. Li, S., Zong, C.: Multi-domain sentiment classification. In: Proceedings of ACL-08: HLT, Short Papers, pp. 257–260 (2008)
13. Liu, P., Qiu, X., Huang, X.: Recurrent neural network for text classification with multi-task learning. arXiv preprint arXiv:1605.05101 (2016)
14. Liu, P., Qiu, X., Huang, X.: Adversarial multi-task learning for text classification. arXiv preprint arXiv:1704.05742 (2017)
15. Liu, X., Gao, J., He, X., Deng, L., Duh, K., Wang, Y.Y.: Representation learning using multi-task deep neural networks for semantic classification and information retrieval. In: Proceedings of the 2015 Conference of the North American Chapter of the Association for Computational Linguistics: Human Language Technologies, pp. 912–921. Association for Computational Linguistics, Denver, Colorado (2015). https://doi.org/10.3115/v1/N15-1092, https://aclanthology.org/N15-1092/
16. Liu, Y., et al.: Roberta: a robustly optimized bert pretraining approach. arXiv preprint arXiv:1907.11692 (2019)

17. Long, M., Cao, Z., Wang, J., Jordan, M.I.: Conditional adversarial domain adaptation. Advances in Neural Information Processing Systems 31 (2018)
18. Meng, Y., Xiong, C., Bajaj, P., Bennett, P., Han, J., Song, X., et al.: Coco-lm: correcting and contrasting text sequences for language model pretraining. Advances in Neural Information Processing Systems 34 (2021)
19. Pan, S.J., Ni, X., Sun, J.T., Yang, Q., Chen, Z.: Cross-domain sentiment classification via spectral feature alignment. In: Proceedings of the 19th International Conference on World Wide Web, pp. 751–760 (2010)
20. Shen, J., Qu, Y., Zhang, W., Yu, Y.: Wasserstein distance guided representation learning for domain adaptation. In: Thirty-second AAAI Conference on Artificial Intelligence (2018)
21. Wang, C., Qiu, M., Huang, J., He, X.: Meta fine-tuning neural language models for multi-domain text mining. arXiv preprint arXiv:2003.13003 (2020)
22. Wu, F., Huang, Y.: Collaborative multi-domain sentiment classification. In: 2015 IEEE International Conference on Data Mining, pp. 459–468. IEEE (2015)
23. Wu, Y., Guo, Y.: Dual adversarial co-learning for multi-domain text classification. In: Proceedings of the AAAI Conference on Artificial Intelligence, pp. 6438–6445 (2020)
24. Wu, Y., Inkpen, D., El-Roby, A.: Conditional adversarial networks for multi-domain text classification. arXiv preprint arXiv:2102.10176 (2021)
25. Wu, Y., Inkpen, D., El-Roby, A.: Mixup regularized adversarial networks for multi-domain text classification. In: ICASSP 2021–2021 IEEE International Conference on Acoustics, Speech and Signal Processing (ICASSP), pp. 7733–7737. IEEE (2021)
26. Yang, Q., Shang, L.: Multi-task learning with bidirectional language models for text classification. In: 2019 International Joint Conference on Neural Networks (IJCNN), pp. 1–8. IEEE (2019)

Low-Resource Named Entity Recognition Based on Multi-hop Dependency Trigger

Peiqi Yan[1] and Jiangxu Wu[2(✉)]

[1] Guangzhou, Guangdong, China
[2] Shenzhen, Guangdong, China
wujx27@mail2.sysu.edu.cn

Abstract. This paper introduces DepTrigger, a simple and effective model in low-resource named entity recognition (NER) based on multi-hop dependency triggers. Dependency triggers refer to salient nodes relative to an entity in the dependency graph of a context sentence. Our main observation is that triggers generally play an important role in recognizing the location and the type of entity in a sentence. Instead of exploiting the manual labeling of triggers, we use the syntactic parser to annotate triggers automatically. We train DepTrigger using an independent model architectures which are Match Network encoder and Entity Recognition Network encoder. Compared to the previous model TriggerNER, DepTrigger outperforms for long sentences, while still maintain good performance for short sentences as usual. Our framework is significantly more cost-effective in real business.

Keywords: NER · Dependency trigger · Low resource

1 Introduction

Named Entity Recognition (NER) aims to detect the span from text belonging to the semantic category such as person, location, organization, etc. NER plays a core component in many NLP tasks and is widely employed in downstream applications, such as knowledge graph [1], question answering [2] and dialogue system [3]. The deep-learning based approaches have shown remarkable success in NER, while it requires large corpora annotated with named entities. Moreover, in many practical settings, we wish to apply NER to domains with a very limited amount of labeled data since annotating data is a labor-intensive and time-consuming task. Therefore, it is an emergency to improve the performance of the deep-learning based NER model with limited labeled data.

Previous work in low-resource NER mainly focused on meta-learning [6], distantly supervision [7], transfer learning [16], et al. Recently, [5] proposed an approach based on entity trigger called *TriggerNER*. The key idea is that an entity trigger is a group of words that can help explain the recognition process of an entity in a sentence. Considering the sentence "Biden is the president of _", we

---

P. Yan and J. Wu—These authors contributed equally to this work.

M. Sun et al. (Eds.): CCL 2022, LNAI 13603, pp. 325–334, 2022.
https://doi.org/10.1007/978-3-031-18315-7_21

are able to infer that there is a country entity on the underline according to "the president of". In this case, "the president of" is a group of triggers. Experiments reveal that the performance of utilizing 20% of the trigger-annotated sentences is comparable to that of exploiting 70% of conventional annotated sentences. However, crowd-sourced entity trigger annotations, which suffer from the same problem as traditional annotation, require labor costs and expert experience.

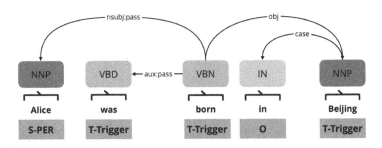

Fig. 1. The dependency parse results of "Alice was born in Beijing", "S-PER" is entity label, "T-Trigger" is trigger label, "O" denotes others.

Inspired by attribute triggers in Attribute Extraction [8], this paper presents an alternative approach to automatically annotate the trigger in a sentence by utilizing the syntactic parse. Figure 1 is the dependency parse result of the sentence "Alice was born in Beijing", the relation "nsubj:pass" shows that the subject of "born" is "Alice". According to the meaning of "born", we are capable of inferring that "Alice" is a person entity. Inspired by this fact, we propose a novel model, namley *DepTrigger*, which explore the structures of dependency trees and utilize the syntactic parser to annotate trigger in a sentence.

Naturally, we propose a simple yet effective framework for low-resource NER, namely *DepTriggerNER*. It includes a trigger semantic matching module (Trigger Match Network) and a sequence annotation module (Entity Recognition Network). The DepTriggerNER adopts two-steps pipeline mode: 1) we first trains the Trigger Match Network module for learning trigger representation; and 2) we combine trigger representation to train the Entity Recognition Network module. Our main contribution includes the new proposed "DepTrigger" model, which reduces the cost and complexity by using a syntactic parser to automatically annotate trigger.

We evaluate DepTrigger on CoNLL2003 [11] and BC5CDR [12], where Dep-Trigger outperforms the TriggerNER model on BC5CDR but slightly under-performs on CoNLL2003. Compared to TriggerNER, DepTrigger is particularly useful in its ability to automatically produce annotated triggers. Besides, the independent model architectures have a better performance. Our results suggest that DepTrigger is a promising alternative to the TriggerNER in low-resource NER tasks.

2 Model

2.1 DepTrigger

DepTrigger are prominent nodes relative to an entity in the context sentence dependency graph. We apply Stanford CoreNLP to the sentences to obtain dependency paths. The dependency paths is a directed graph with words as nodes and dependencies as edges. Figure 1 shows the dependency parse results of the sentence "Alice was born in Beijing". In Fig. 1, "born" is connected with the entity "Alice" by relation "nsubj:pass", so that "born" is a DepTrigger. Words have a one-hop relationship with entities are called primary triggers, and words have a two-hop relationship with entities are called secondary triggers.

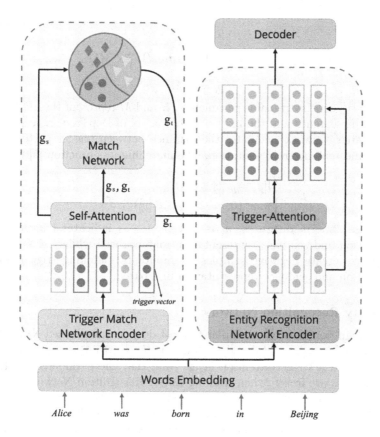

Fig. 2. The framework of DepTriggerNER. The left is the Trigger Match Network. The right is the Entity Recognition Network. The circle in the upper left corner is Trigger Pattern Prototype, it is a look-up table generated by Trigger Match Network after training.

2.2 Trigger Match Network

Each entity contains a group of DepTrigger, which form a trigger pattern. We assume that each sentence has an entity and contains a trigger pattern. In the training stage, the Trigger Match Network aims to learn the representation of trigger patterns and sentences. In the inference stage, the trigger pattern representation with similar semantics to the sentence representation will be selected from the Trigger Pattern Prototype.

In Fig. 2, each sentence is first transformed into a vector by the Words Embedding module. Then, the hidden state matrix is obtained through the Trigger Match Network Encoder. The self-attention layer is used to obtain sentence representation $\vec{g}_s$ and trigger pattern representation $\vec{g}_t$, [16] defined as follows:

$$\vec{\alpha}_s = Softmax\left(W_2 \times tanh\left(W_1 \times H\right)\right) \tag{1}$$

$$\vec{g}_s = \vec{\alpha}_s H \tag{2}$$

$$\vec{\alpha}_t = Softmax\left(W_2 \times tanh\left(W_1 \times M\right)\right) \tag{3}$$

$$\vec{g}_t = \vec{\alpha}_t M \tag{4}$$

W_1 and W_2 are the trainable parameters. H and M represent the hidden state matrix of the sentence and the hidden state matrix of DepTrigger, respectively.

The Match Network calculates the distance between trigger pattern representation and sentence representation. The matching loss function [5] is defined as follows:

$$L = \begin{cases} ||\vec{g}_s - \vec{g}_t||_2^2, t \in s \\ max\left(0, m - ||\vec{g}_s - \vec{g}_t||_2^2\right), t \notin s \end{cases} \tag{5}$$

$|| \cdot ||_2$ is L2-norm distances, m is margin. $t \in s$ indicates trigger pattern representation and sentence representation matches well while $t \notin s$ is on the contrary. We create negative samples by randomly matching trigger pattern representation and sentence representation in a batch.

2.3 Entity Recognition Network

Entity Recognition Network is similar to most deep-learning based NER models and consists of encoder and decoder. However, the Entity Recognition Network has been added a trigger-attention layer. Note that the parameters of Trigger Match Network are frozen when training Entity Recognition Network.

In training, each sentence passes through the Trigger Match Network Encoder and the Entity Recognition Network Encoder, respectively. Then, $\vec{g}_t$ is obtained from the self-attention layer. In the trigger-attention layer, $\vec{g}_t$ is used to calculate the weight of each vector in the Entity Recognition Network Encoder's outputs as follows [13]:

$$\vec{\alpha} = Softmax\left(\vec{v} \times tanh\left(U_1 \times H + U_2 \times \vec{g}_t\right)\right) \tag{6}$$

$$H' = \vec{\alpha} H \tag{7}$$

$U_1, U_2, \vec{v}$ are model parameters, and H is the Entity Recognition Network Encoder's outputs matrix. Finally, we concatenate the matrix H with the trigger-enhanced matrix H as the input ($[H; H']$) fed into the decoder.

2.4 Inference

After training, each sentence in the training set is re-input into Trigger Match Network to obtain trigger pattern representation. We then save these representations in memory, shows as the Trigger Pattern Prototype in Fig. 2. In the inference stage, We first obtain sentence representations $\vec{g}_s$ through Trigger Match Network and then retrieve the semantic similarity vector $\vec{g}_t$ from Trigger Pattern Prototype. Vector $\vec{g}_t$ is used as the attention query in Entity Recognition Network.

3 Experiments

3.1 Experiments Setup

Table 1. Data statistics.

Dataset	#Class	#Sent	#Entity
CoNLL'03	4	14986	23499
BC5CDR	2	4560	9385

CoNLL2003 [11] and BC5CDR [12] are used to evaluate our model. The statistics of these datasets are shown in Table 1. We choose BiLSTM-CRF [15] and TriggerNER [5] as baseline models. TriggerNER is the first trigger-based NER model. We choose BiLSTM as encoder and CRF as decoder in our model. To ensure a fair comparison, we use the same codebase and words embedding from GloVE [14], which used in baseline model. The hyper-parameters of the model are also the same. Our code and data are released[1].

We choose BIOES tagging schema for non-triggers, and triggers are all labeled with "T-trigger". In order to make the model learn the relation between entity and its trigger better, we repeat a sentence N times, and N is the number of entities in the sentence. Each sentence retains one entity and its trigger, other entities are marked as non-entities.

3.2 Results

As shown in Table 2, Our model achieves a similar performance as TriggerNER. More detailed, our model performs better on BC5CDR than TriggerNER, but slightly worse on CoNLL2003. We explain this phenomenon in terms of the

---

[1] https://github.com/wjx-git/DepTriggerNER.

number of triggers each entity has. Figure 3 shows the ratio of the number of sentences with the number of triggers an entity has in each dataset. The two yellow curves are very close when the abscissa value is greater than 3, and the yellow dotted line is larger than the solid line when the abscissa value is less than 3. This fact demonstrates that on CoNLL2003 the number of triggers annotated by our method is less than TriggerNER. In the two blue curves, the solid blue line is larger than the dashed line when the abscissa value is greater than 4, and the opposite is true when the abscissa value is less than 4. This shows that the number of triggers annotated by our method is more than TriggerNER on BC5CDR. We believe that an entity is easier to recognize when it has more triggers, which would explain why our model performs better on BC5CDR and slightly worse on CoNLL2003.

Table 2. F1 score results. "#sent" denotes the percentage of the sentences labeled only with entity label, "#trig" denotes the percentage of the sentences labeled with both entity label and trigger label.

CoNLL 2003					BC5CDR				
#sent	BiLSTM-CRF	#trig	Trigger-NER	Ours	#sent	BiLSTM-CRF	#trig	Trigger-NER	Ours
5%	69.04	3%	75.33	**77.42**	5%	71.87	3%	61.44	**63.37**
10%	76.83	5%	80.2	**80.26**	10%	72.71	5%	66.11	**66.92**
20%	81.3	7%	**82.02**	81.3	20%	69.92	7%	67.22	**69.27**
30%	83.23	10%	**83.53**	82.96	30%	73.71	10%	70.71	**71.42**
40%	84.18	13%	**84.22**	83.26	40%	72.71	13%	71.87	**73.17**
50%	84.27	15%	**85.03**	83.86	50%	75.84	15%	71.89	**74.35**
60%	85.24	17%	**85.36**	84.32	60%	75.84	17%	73.05	**75.08**
70%	86.08	20%	**86.01**	84.53	70%	76.12	20%	73.97	**76.44**

We analyzed the sentence length distribution in the two datasets to further understand why we annotate fewer triggers in CoNLL and more in BC5CDR than in TriggerNER. The statistical results of sentence length distribution in Table 3, show that sentences are shorter in the CoNLL dataset and longer in the BC5CDR dataset. From Table 3 and Fig. 3, it can be concluded that our method can label more triggers in long sentences but fewer triggers in short sentences compared to manual marking in TriggerNER. Therefore, our method is more suitable for datasets with longer sentences.

Table 3. Statistical results of sentence length distribution

Datasets	1~10	10~25	25~50	50~
CoNLL	52.32%	27.33%	19.93%	0.42%
BC5CDR	5.7%	50.64%	37.54%	6.51%

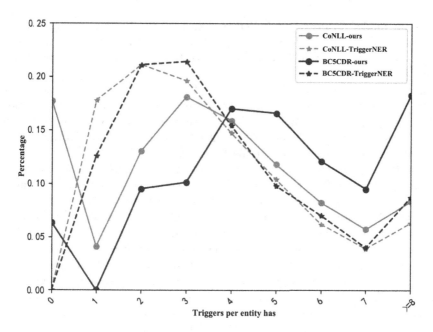

Fig. 3. Ratio of the number of sentences with the number of triggers each entity has in the dataset. The X-axis is the number of triggers of a entity has, and the Y-axis is the percentage. The solid lines represent the trigger of ours. The yellow line represents CoNLL datasets. (Color figure online)

Table 4. Comparative experiment F1 score results. **merge** means to merge Trigger Match Network encoder and Entity Recognition Network encoder. **separate** means to separate Trigger Match Network encoder and Entity Recognition Network encoder. The best results are in **bold**.

#trig	CoNLL 2003		BC5CDR	
	Merge	Separate	Merge	Separate
3%	76.36	**77.42**	61.3	**63.37**
5%	79.38	**80.26**	66.15	**66.92**
7%	80.37	**81.3**	68.02	**69.27**
10%	81.58	**82.96**	70.93	**71.42**
13%	82.55	**83.26**	72.7	**73.17**
15%	83.03	**83.86**	73.25	**74.35**
17%	83.51	**84.32**	74.95	**75.08**
20%	83.81	**84.53**	75.08	**76.44**

In our model, Trigger Match Network encoder and Entity Recognition Network encoder are independent, which is different from the TriggerNer. The main purpose of Trigger Match Network is to learn the representation of trigger patterns, and Entity Recognition Network is to learn entity representation. So we think we can not get an advantage by combining Trigger Match Network and Entity Recognition Network because they need to capture specific information. That is inspired by [17], and they observe that the contextual representations for the entity and relation models essentially capture specific information, so sharing their representations hurts performance.

We do a comparative experiment to test the performance of our model for merging and separating, respectively, while leaving everything else unchanged. The experimental results are shown in Table 4, **merge** means to merge Trigger Match Network encoder and Entity Recognition Network encoder. Separate means to separate Trigger Match Network encoder and Entity Recognition Network encoder. It shows that the performance is better when the Trigger Match Network encoder and Entity Recognition Network encoder are independent.

In order to compare the influence of primary and secondary trigger words on the model, we backup two datasets of CoNLL, and only the primary triggers are labeled in one dataset, and only the secondary trigger words are labeled in the other dataset, do the same for BC5CDR. Table 5 shows the F1 score on these datasets. Compared primary and secondary trigger, there is no evident show that one is better than the other. Combined with Table 1 and Table 4, the effect of using the primary trigger and the secondary trigger at the same time is significantly better than that of using them alone.

Table 5. Comparative experiment of primary and secondary trigger

#trig	CoNLL 2003		BC5CDR	
	Primary	Secondary	Primary	Secondary
3%	**63.4**	62.35	**52.3**	50.92
5%	**66.3**	**66.3**	54.17	**55.84**
7%	**70.37**	69.44	**58.92**	57.33
10%	**74.02**	73.44	**60.32**	60.24
13%	74.86	**74.91**	61.35	**62.01**
15%	**76.2**	75.46	64.26	**64.25**
17%	**77.36**	76.33	**64.51**	64.26
20%	**77.55**	77.53	65.94	**66.69**

4   Conclusion and Future Work

We have introduced dependency trigger to incorporate trigger information into NER method. The core of our method is using syntactic parser to automatically label the trigger of entities. Our model performs well for long sentences, while maintain similar performance as TriggerNER for short sentences. Thanks to automatically annotate trigger of entities, our framework is more practical in the real business. Future work with DepTrigger includes: 1) adjusting our model to encoder based on language model; 2) making a further analysis of trigger type; 3) developing models for improving the performance on short sentences.

References

1. Ji, S., Pan, S., Cambria, E., Marttinen, P., Philip, S.Y.: A survey on knowledge graphs: representation, acquisition and applications. IEEE Trans. Neural Netw. Learn. Syst. **33**, 494–514 (2021). https://doi.org/10.1109/TNNLS.2021.3070843
2. Mollá, D., van Zaanen, M., Smith, D.: Named entity recognition for question-answering system. In: Proceedings of INTERSPEECH 2004 - ICSLP, Jeju Island, Korea (2004)
3. Peng, B., Li, C., Li, J., Shayandeh, S., Liden, L., Gao, J.: SOLOIST: few-shot task-oriented dialog with a single pre-trained auto-regressive model. arXiv (2020)
4. Yuchen, B., et al.: Few-shot named entity recognition: a comprehensive study. arXiv (2020)
5. Yuchen, B., et al.: TriggerNER: learning with entity triggers as explanations for named entity recognition. In: Proceedings of the 58th Annual Meeting of the Association for Computational Linguistics, pp. 8503–8511 (2020). https://doi.org/10.18653/v1/2020.acl-main.752
6. Snell, J., Swersky, K., Zemel, R.: Prototypical networks for few-shot learning. arXiv (2017)
7. Yang, Y., Chen, W., Li, Z., He, Z., Zhang, M.: Distantly supervised NER with partial annotation learning and reinforcement learning. In: Proceedings of the 27th International Conference on Computational Linguistics, Santa Fe, New Mexico, USA, pp. 2159–2169 (2018)
8. Huang, L., Sil, A., Ji, H., Florian, R.: Improving slot filling performance with attentive neural networks on dependency structures. In: Proceedings of the 2017 Conference on Empirical Methods in Natural Language Processing, Copenhagen, Denmark, pp. 2588–2597 (2017). https://doi.org/10.18653/v1/D17-1274
9. Yu, D., Ji, H.: Unsupervised person slot filling based on graph mining. In: Proceedings of the 54th Annual Meeting of the Association for Computational Linguistics, Berlin, Germany, pp. 44–53 (2016). https://doi.org/10.18653/v1/P16-1005
10. Zhai, F., Potdar, S., Xiang, B., Zhou, B.: Neural models for sequence chunking. In: Proceedings of Thirty-First AAAI Conference on Artificial Intelligence (2017)
11. Sang, E.F., De Meulder, F.: Introduction to the CoNLL-2003 shared task: language-independent named entity recognition. In: Proceedings of the Seventh Conference on Natural Language Learning at HLT-NAACL 2003, pp. 142–147 (2003)
12. Li, J., et al.: BioCreative V CDR task corpus: a resource for chemical disease relation extraction. In: Database (2016)
13. Luong, T., Pham, H., Manning, C.D.: Effective approaches to attention-based neural machine translation. In: Proceedings of the 2015 Conference on Empirical Methods in Natural Language Processing, Lisbon, Portugal, pp. 1412–1421. Association for Computational Linguistics (2015). https://doi.org/10.18653/v1/D15-1166

14. Pennington, J., Socher, R., Manning, C.: Glove: global vectors for word representation. In: Proceedings of the 2014 Conference on Empirical Methods in Natural Language Processing (EMNLP), Doha, Qatar, pp. 1532–1543. Association for Computational Linguistics (2014). https://doi.org/10.3115/v1/D14-1162

15. Ma, X., Hovy, E.: End-to-end sequence labeling via bi-directional LSTM-CNNs-CRF. In: Proceedings of the 54th Annual Meeting of the Association for Computational Linguistics (Volume 1: Long Papers), Berlin, Germany, pp. 1064–1074. Association for Computational Linguistics (2016). https://doi.org/10.18653/v1/P16-1101

16. Lin, Z., et al.: A structured self-attentive sentence embedding. In: Proceedings of the 5th International Conference on Learning Representations (2017)

17. Zhong, Z., Chen, D.: A frustratingly easy approach for entity and relation extraction. In: NAACL (2021). https://doi.org/10.18653/v1/2021.naacl-main.5

Fundamental Analysis Based Neural Network for Stock Movement Prediction

Yangjia Zheng, Xia Li[⊠], Junteng Ma, and Yuan Chen

School of Information Science and Technology, Guangdong University of Foreign
Studies, Guangzhou, China
{yjzheng,xiali,juntengma,yuanchen}@gdufs.edu.cn

Abstract. Stock movements are influenced not only by historical prices, but also by information outside the market such as social media and news about the stock or related stock. In practice, news or prices of a stock in one day are normally impacted by different days with different weights, and they can influence each other. In terms of this issue, in this paper, we propose a fundamental analysis based neural network for stock movement prediction. First, we propose three new technical indicators based on raw prices according to the finance theory as the basic encode of the prices of each day. Then, we introduce a coattention mechanism to capture the sufficient context information between text and prices across every day within a time window. Based on the mutual promotion and influence of text and price at different times, we obtain more sufficient stock representation. We perform extensive experiments on the real-world StockNet dataset and the experimental results demonstrate the effectiveness of our method.

Keywords: Stock movement prediction · Fundamental analysis · Coattention mechanism

1 Introduction

Stock Movement Prediction aims to predict the future price trend of a stock based on its historical price or related information. Stock movement prediction can help investors, ordinary users and companies to predict the stock trend in the future, which has good application value.

The high randomness and volatility of the market make the task of Stock Movement Prediction a big challenge [1]. However, with the development of neural network technology, stock movement prediction has achieved good results in recent years [7,10,13,18,19,24,25]. Based on fundamental and technical analysis, existing methods can be roughly grouped into two categories, namely methods based on price factors only and methods based on price and other factors (e.g., news of the stock.). Nelson et al. [13] used the LSTM [9] network to predict future stock price trends based on historical price and technical analysis indicators. Feng et al. [7] used the adversarial training as perturbations to simulate

M. Sun et al. (Eds.): CCL 2022, LNAI 13603, pp. 335–350, 2022.
https://doi.org/10.1007/978-3-031-18315-7_22

the randomness of price variables, and trained the model to work well with small but intentional perturbations. They also extracted 11 related price features to effectively help the model to predict future changes.

According to the Efficient Market Hypothesis (EMH) [6], price signals themselves cannot capture the impact of market accidents and unexpected accidents, while social media texts such as tweets could have a huge impact on the stock market. Based on this idea, different models have been proposed to model relevant news texts to improve the overall performance of stock movement prediction. Hu et al. [10] proposed to use the hierarchical attention mechanism to predict the trend of stocks based on the sequence of recent related news. Xu et al. [24] integrated signals from social media which reflected the opinions of general users and used Variational Autoencoder (VAE) to capture the randomness of prices and the importance of different time steps by adding temporal attention. Sawhney et al. [18] introduced a novel architecture for efficient mixing of chaotic temporal signals from financial data, social media, and inter stock relationships in a hierarchical temporal manner through Graph Attention Neural Network.

Although previous studies have achieved good results, whether it is a purely technical approach based on historical prices or a fundamental approach based on multiple factors such as prices and news, they can be improved in terms of the full integration of the two important factors of texts and prices. We found that previous works usually encode news and prices separately according to time series, and then fuse them through simple concatenation operation, similar to the work of Sawhney et al. [18]. In fact, in practice, prices on a given day can be influenced by different news at different times (e.g., previous day or after two days). Similarly, some news about a stock on a given day may be influenced by stock prices at different times. As is shown in Fig. 1, if we can capture the context information of each price and text by different days, we can get more sufficient information for predicting the stock trend accurately.

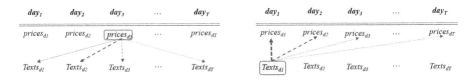

Fig. 1. Contexts of prices and texts across the history captured by coattention. Left shows each price representation of one day captures context of all news about the stock from day_1 to day_T by different attention weights. Right shows each text representation of one day captures context of all prices about the stock from day_1 to day_T by different attention weights.

To this end, in this paper, we propose a fundamental analysis based neural network for stock movement prediction. More specifically, we first use Bi-GRU to encode the original texts of each day. Then, we use text-level attention to get a text representation of each day. As for the prices of each day, we use the existing 11 indicator features and 3 indicators we proposed in this paper as price representation of each day. Then we use the coattention mechanism [23] to capture more information between texts and prices across every day within a time window. Finally, we incorporate a Bi-GRU to encode the fully integrated texts and prices representation according to the time window, so that it can obtain various prices and text-related information of the stock, and obtain the final effective representation of the stock.

The contributions of this work are as follows:

- We propose a fundamental analysis based neural network for stock movement prediction. The model introduces the coattention mechanism into text and price features of a stock to learn the effective context information of them. The method can obtain sufficient stock representation based on the mutual promotion and influence of texts and prices at different times.
- We also introduce three technical indicators based on raw prices in the financial field as their input features to better reflect the fluctuation information of the market. We perform multiple experiments on the StockNet dataset and the results demonstrate the effectiveness of our model.

2   Related Work

In this section, we will review the related work about stock movement prediction from technical analysis based approach and fundamental analysis based approach.

2.1   Technical Analysis Based Approach

Technical analysis based approach is to predict the trend of a stock based on its historical price features such as close price and movement percent of price, which follows the assumption that future price changes are the result of historical behavior. Most recent stock movement prediction methods are based on deep learning. Among them, recurrent neural networks such as LSTM and GRU have become a key part for capturing the temporal patterns of stock prices. This is because they can further capture long-term dependencies in time series. Nelson et al. [13] used LSTM networks to study future trends, predicting stock prices based on historical stock prices and technical analysis indicators. These indicators are mathematical calculations designed to determine or predict the characteristics of a stock based on its historical data. A total of 175 technical indicators are generated each period, and they are designed to represent or predict a very different set of characteristics of a stock, like the future price, volume to be traded and the strength of current movement trends. Feng et al. [7] proposed to use adversarial training and added perturbations to simulate the randomness of price variables, and trained the model to work well with small but intentional perturbations. In addition, they extracted 11 related price features that effectively help the model predict future changes. Feng et al. [8] proposed the Temporal Graph Convolution (TGC) model combining historical prices for predicting movement of stock, which dynamically adjusts the predefined firm relations before feeding them into Graph Convolution Network (GCN) [11]. As LSTM struggles to capture extremely long-term dependencies, such as the dependencies across several months on financial time series. Transformer-based employs multi-head self-attention mechanism to globally learn the relationships between different locations, thus enhancing the ability to learn long-term dependencies. Ding et al. [5] proposed various enhancements for Transformer-based models, such as enhancing locality of Transformer with Multi-Scale Gaussian Prior, avoiding learning redundant heads in the multihead self-attention mechanism with Orthogonal Regularization and enabling Transformer to learn intraday features and intra-week features independently with Trading Gap Splitter. However, in reality, it is often difficult to find clear pattern of change from the market historical data. Furthermore, it fails to reveal the rules governing market volatility beyond stock price data.

2.2 Fundamental Analysis Based Approach

Efficient Market Hypothesis tells that textual information can be used to extract implicit information for helping predict the future trend of stock prices, such as financial news and social media. Fundamental analysis based approach is able to capture information that is not available in traditional price-based stock prediction. A hybrid attention network [10] is proposed to predict stock trends by imitating the human learning process. In order to follow three basic principles: sequential content dependency, diverse influence, and effective and efficient learning, the model builds news-level attention and temporal attention mechanisms to focus on key information in news, and applies self-paced learning mechanisms to automatically select suitable training samples for different training stage improves the final performance of the framework. Different from the traditional text embedding methods, Ni et al. [15] proposed Tweet Node algorithm for describing potential connection in Twitter data through constructing the tweet node network. They take into account the internal semantic features and external structural features of twitter data, so that the generated Tweet vectors can contain more effective information. Financial news that does not explicitly mention stocks may also be relevant, such as industry news, and is a key part of real-world decision-making. To extract implicit information from the chaotic daily news pool, Tang et al. [19] proposed News Distilling Network (NDN) which takes advantage of neural representation learning and collaborative filtering to capture the relationship between stocks and news. Xie et al. [22] conducted adversarial attacks on the original tweets to generate some new semantically similar texts, which are merged with the original texts to confuse the previously proposed models, proving that text-only stock prediction models are also vulnerable to adversarial attacks. This also reflects that the model obtained only by text training is less robust, so it is still necessary to incorporate knowledge such as relevant historical price features and the relationship between stocks to better improve the performance of the model.

Therefore, some studies fuse price and text data to build models, and even add the relationship between stocks to improve the performance of the model. A novel deep generation model that combines tweets and price signals is proposed by Xu et al. [24]. They introduced temporal attention to model the importance of different time steps and used Variational Autoencoder (VAE) to capture randomness of price. Recent studies have attempted to simulate stock momentum spillover through Graph Neural Networks (GNN). Sawhney et al. [18] introduced an architecture for efficient mixing of chaotic temporal signals from financial data, social media, and inter stock relationships in a hierarchical temporal manner. Cheng et al. [4] proposed a momentum spillover effect model for stock prediction through attribute-driven Graph Attention Networks (GAT) [20], and the implicit relations between stocks can be inferred to some extent. Zhao et al. [25] constructed a market knowledge graph which contains dual-type entities and mixed relations. By introducing explicit and implicit relationships between executive entities and stocks, dual attention network is proposed to learn stock momentum overflow features.

Since stock prices have temporal characteristics, that is, the price of a day will be affected by the price and news text of previous days, in this paper, we propose to use coattention mechanism to obtain the context information of stock prices and news text under different timestamp, so as to improve the final representation of the stock and the prediction performance.

3   Our Method

3.1   Task Definition

Similar to the previous work [24], we define the stock movement prediction task as a binary classification problem. Given a stock s, we define the price movement of the stock from day T to $T + 1$ as:

$$Y_{T+1} = \begin{cases} -1, & p_{T+1}^c < p_T^c \\ 1, & p_{T+1}^c \geq p_T^c \end{cases} \tag{1}$$

where p_T^c represents adjusted closing price on day T, -1 represents stock price goes down and 1 represents the stock price goes up. The goal of the task is to predict the price movement Y_{T+1} of a stock s according to its historical prices collections P and news text collections L in a time sliding window of T days, where $P = \{P_1, P_2, ..., P_i, ..., P_T\}$, $L = \{L_1, L_2, ..., L_j, ..., L_T\}$, where P_i is the price features of the stock s on day i and L_j is the news text collection of the stock s on day j.

3.2   Overall Architecture

The whole architecture of our method is shown in Fig. 2. As is shown in Fig. 2, we first encode raw text for each stock across every day over a fixed time window. As for the price, the existing price features and the three new proposed indicators are concatenated together as the price representation. Then richer information will be captured by our introduced coattention mechanism. In order to obtain the integrated information of various prices and texts within the time window, we adopt a Bi-GRU for final encoding.

In the following sections, we will describe text and price features encoding in Sect. 3.3 and 3.4. And we will introduce temporal fusion to handle prices and text in Sect. 3.5 and introduce global fusion by sequential modeling in Sect. 3.6. Finally, model training will be introduced in Sect. 3.7.

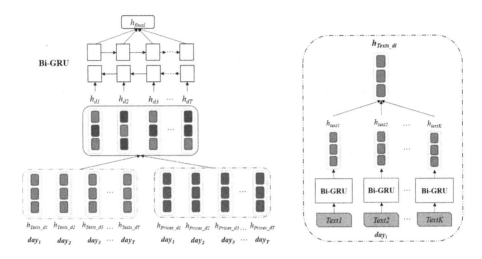

Fig. 2. Overview architecture of our method.

3.3   Text Encoding

As each text contains rich semantic information, we use a Bi-GRU to encode the text and get the representation of each text in one day. Besides, different texts within the same day about the same stock may also be different (e.g., one text contains important information about the stock while other texts don't have valuable information about the stock). For addressing that, we use a soft-attention operation to get the weighted representation of the texts of one day.

Following the work of Xu et al. [24], we incorporate the position information of stock symbols in texts to handle the circumstance that multiple stocks are discussed in one single text. Given stock s contains K number of related texts on day m, which is denoted as $L_m = \{l_{m_1}, l_{m_2}, ..., l_{m_i}, ...l_{m_K}\}$, where l_{m_i} denotes the i-th text of stock s on day m. For each text $l_{m_i} = \{w_1, w_2, ..., w_n\}$, suppose that the location where the stock symbol appears first is denoted as z, we use two GRUs to encode the words sequence from w_1 to w_z to get the hidden representations $\overrightarrow{h}_f$ and words sequence from w_z to w_n to get the hidden representations $\overleftarrow{h_b}$, respectively. We use the average of the last hidden states of the two GURs $\overrightarrow{h_z}$ and $\overleftarrow{h_z}$ as the hidden representation of the text $h_{l_{mi}}$:

$$\overrightarrow{h_f} = \overrightarrow{GRU}\left(e_f, \overrightarrow{h_{f-1}}\right) \tag{2}$$

$$\overleftarrow{h_b} = \overleftarrow{GRU}\left(e_b, \overleftarrow{h_{b+1}}\right) \tag{3}$$

$$h_{l_{mi}} = \left(\overrightarrow{h_z} + \overleftarrow{h_z}\right)/2 \tag{4}$$

Where e_f, e_b is the word embedding using pre-trained Global Vectors for Word Representation (GloVe) [17] for words of the text, $f \in [1, \ldots, z], b \in [z, \ldots, n]$. After that, we can get all the text representations $M_i = [h_{l_{m1}}, h_{l_{m2}}, \ldots, h_{l_{mK}}]$. Since the text quality is different, we use a text-level attention mechanism to identify texts that could have a more substantial impact on the market every day, and finally obtain a final representation of all texts. The calculation formula is as follows:

$$u_K = \tanh(M_i W_m + b_m) \tag{5}$$

$$\alpha_K = softmax(u_K W_u) \tag{6}$$

$$h_{Texts\_dm} = \sum_K \alpha_K h_{l_{mK}} \tag{7}$$

where α_K is the attention weight, W_m and W_u are the parameters to be learned, b_m is the bias terms. h_{Texts_dm} is the representation of the news text of stock s on m-th day(day_m). According to the time sliding window defined previously, the text data in the window is finally denoted as $H_t = [h_{Texts\_d1}, h_{Texts\_d2}, \ldots, h_{Texts\_dT}]$.

3.4 Price Features

As mentioned in Sect. 2.2, the models that predict stock trends only based on text are often fragile, while price features have been shown to effectively reflect market volatility. In this paper, we introduce three new relevant price features to be used in our method. The three new technical indicators are from financial domain and are used to describe fluctuation of stock, namely Average True Range (ATR) [3], Bias Ratio (BIAS) and Momentum (MTM) [12]. The detailed calculation of the three indicators is shown in Table 1. We describe the three indicators as follows:

- **ATR:** ATR is a volatility indicator that was developed by Wilder et al. [21] and is used to measure the volatility or the degree of price movement of security. It was originally designed for commodity trading, which is frequently subject to gaps and limit moves. As a result, ATR takes into account gaps, limit moves, and small high-low ranges in determining the true range of a commodity, and it also applies to the stock market.

- **BIAS:** BIAS is the deviation between the closing price and moving average. When the stock price moves drastically to deviate from the trend, the possibilities for a pullback or rebound increase; When the stock price movement does not deviate from the trend, it is likely that the trend will continue.
- **MTM:** MTM is an indicator that shows the difference between today's closing price and the closing price n days ago. Momentum generally refers to the continued trend of prices. Momentum shows a trend, staying positive for a sustained uptrend or negative for a sustained downtrend. An upward crossing of zero can be used as a signal of buying, and a downward crossing of zero can be used as a signal of selling. How high the indicator is (or how low when negative) indicates how strong the trend is.

Table 1. The three price features.

Features	Calculation
ATR	$EMA(max(high_t, close_{t-1}) - min(low_t, close_{t-1}), n)$
BIAS	$\frac{close_t}{\sum_{i=0}^{4} close_{t-i}/5} - 1$
MTM	$close_t - close_{t-1}$

Following previous work, We adopt 11 temporal price features based on the raw price [7], denoted as $F_1 = \{p_1, p_2, ..., p_{11}\}$ and our proposed three new price features, denoted as $F_2 = \{p_{atr}, p_{bias}, p_{mtm}\}$, as our final price features. The two are concatenated together to get the final price features of m-th day, recorded as $h_{Prices\_dm} = [F_1, F_2]$. According to the time sliding window defined above, the price features in the window are finally recorded as $H_p = [h_{Prices\_d1}, h_{Prices\_d2}, ..., h_{Prices\_dT}]$.

3.5 Temporal Fusion by Coattention Neural Network

After Sect. 3.3 and Sect. 3.4, the coding features of price and text were obtained as H_p and H_t respectively. To effectively blend text and price, we use the coattention mechanism [23] to learn the fusion between text and price to obtain richer implicit information. First, we use a nonlinear projection layer to convert the dimension of the price feature into the same dimension as the text with the following formula:

$$H'_p = \tanh\left(H_p W_p + b_p\right) \tag{8}$$

Applying the coattention mechanism to focus on both text and price, and learn about fusion. We first compute an affinity matrix that contains the corresponding affinity scores of all prices hidden states and texts hidden state pairs.

Then the affinity matrix is normalized by Softmax, attention weights are generated for text features by row, and attention weights of price features are generated by columns. The calculation formula is as follows:

$$L = H_t \left(H'_p\right)^T \tag{9}$$

$$A_t = softmax(L) \tag{10}$$

$$A_p = softmax\left(L^T\right) \tag{11}$$

Next, we calculate the attention context of price features based on the attention weight of text features. The calculation formula is as follows:

$$C_t = A_t H'_p \tag{12}$$

Meanwhile, we compute the attention context of the text features as $A_p H_t$ based on the attention weights of the price features. Following Xiong et al. [23], we also calculate $A_p C_t$ which maps text feature encoding into the space of price feature encoding. The calculation formula is as follows:

$$h_d = A_p \left[H_t, C_t\right] \tag{13}$$

where h_d is interdependent representation of the text and the price. The [ ] denotes for concatenation operation.

3.6 Global Fusion by Sequential Encoding

We input h_d obtained from Sect. 3.5 into the bidirectional GRU to obtain the hidden states for each time t. To capture past and future information as its context, we connect the hidden states from the two directions to construct a two-way encoding vector h_i with the following formulas:

$$\overrightarrow{h_i} = \overrightarrow{GRU}\left(h_d\right) \tag{14}$$

$$\overleftarrow{h_i} = \overleftarrow{GRU}\left(h_d\right) \tag{15}$$

$$h_i = \left[\overrightarrow{h_i}, \overleftarrow{h_i}\right] \tag{16}$$

In addition to its own information, h_i also contains information about its adjacent contexts. In this way, we encoded its time series. Since news releases on different dates contributed unequally to stock trends, we employed soft attention mechanism which is calculated as follows:

$$o_i = \tanh\left(h_i W_h + b_h\right) \tag{17}$$

$$\beta_i = softmax\left(o_i W_o\right) \tag{18}$$

$$h_{final} = \sum_i \beta_i h_i \tag{19}$$

where β_i is the attention weight, W_h and W_o are the parameters to be learned, b_h is the bias terms. Finally, h_{final} is input into a classic three-layer preceptron (MLP) to predict the future trend of stocks.

3.7 Model Training

We use cross entropy for model training, which is calculated by Eq. (20), where N is the total number of stocks, y_i^t and $\hat{y}_i^t$ represent the ground truth and predict stock trend of stock i at t day, respectively.

$$l = -\sum_{i=1}^{N}\sum_{t} y_i^t ln(\hat{y}_i^t) \tag{20}$$

4 Experiments

4.1 Dataset

We use the SotckNet[1] dataset [24] to train and validate the model. The dataset contains historical data on the high trading volumes of 88 stocks in the NASDAQ and NYSE stock markets. We annotate the samples based on the movement percent of the adjusted closing price of stock, and label the samples as up and down when movement percent $\geq 0.55\%$ or $\leq -0.5\%$, respectively. We split the dataset temporarily with $70/20/10$, leaving us with date ranges from 2014-1-1 to 2015-8-1 for training, 2015-8-1 to 2015-10-1 for validation and 2015-10-1 to 2016-1-1 for testing. Similarly, we adjust trading days by removing samples with missing prices or texts and further aligned data for all trading day windows to ensure that data is available for all trading days in all windows.

4.2 Experiment Settings

We use a 5-day trading day sliding window to build the samples. Following the setting of Xu et al. [24], we set the maximum number of texts in a day to 30, and each text has a maximum of 40 words. Glove word embedding is also used to initialize words into 50-dimensional vectors. We train the model using the Adam optimizer, with an initial learning rate set to 5e−5. The bidirectional GRU hidden dimensions for encoding tweets and sequential modeling were set to 100 and 64, respectively. Each model is trained for 40 epochs with a batch size of 32. We report the best average test performance of the model on the validation set at 5 different runs.

Following previous studies [18,24], we use Accuracy (Acc), F1 score, and Matthews Correlation Coefficient (MCC) as evaluation metrics for this classification task.

4.3 Compared Models

To demonstrate the effectiveness of our proposed model, we compare the results with the following comparative models.

---

[1] https://github.com/yumoxu/stocknet-dataset.

- **RAND.** A simple predictor to make random guess about the rise and fall.
- **ARIMA.** Autoregressive Integrated Moving Average, an advanced technical analysis method using only price signals [2].
- **Adversarial LSTM.** Feng et al. [7] proposed a deep model using an adversarial attention LSTM mechanism, which exploits adversarial training to simulate randomness during model training. They propose the use of adversarial training to improve the generalization of neural network prediction models, since the input feature for stock prediction is usually based on stock price, which is essentially a random variable that naturally changes over time. They added perturbations to their stock data and trained the model to work well with small but intentional perturbations.
- **RandForest.** Pagolu et al. [16] implemented a sentiment analysis model based on Twitter data. The authors used Word2vec to analyse the polarity of sentiments behind the tweets and directly assessed tweets related to stock and tried to predict the price of the stock for the next day.
- **TSLDA.** A new topic model, Topic Sentiment Latent Dirichlet Allocation (TSLDA), which can obtain new feature that captures topics and sentiments on the documents simultaneously and use them for prediction of the stock movement [14].
- **HAN.** A hybrid attention network that predicts stock trends by imitating the human learning process. Follows three basic principles: sequential content dependency, diverse influence, and effective and efficient learning. The model includes news-level attention and temporal attention mechanisms to focus on key information in news [10].
- **StockNet.** A Variational Autoencoder (VAE) to encode stock inputs to capture randomness and use temporal attention to model the importance of different time steps [24]. We compare with the best variants of StockNet.
- **MAN-SF.** Multipronged Attention Network (MAN-SF) jointly learns from historical prices, tweets and inter stock relations. MAN-SF through hierarchical attention captures relevant signals across diverse data to train a Graph Attention Network (GAT) for stock prediction. And the study considers one pre-built graph from Wikidata [18].

4.4 Experimental Results

We conduct several experiments to evaluate the performance of our method. In this section, we analyze the benchmark performance and the results of our model on the StockNet dataset. The experimental results of the different models are shown in Table 2.

First, we compare the first three baseline models presented in this paper. All three baseline methods use only historical price information, although Adversarial LSTM with more representative features and training with adversarial learning achieved better performance. Our model clearly exceeds these three methods in each evaluation indicator.

Second, our model is compared to models that only use textual information, such as RandForest, TSLDA, and HAN. Our model also significantly outperforms

Table 2. The results of different models.

Model	Acc	F1	MCC
RAND	50.9	50.2	−0.002
ARIMA [2]	51.4	51.3	−0.021
Adversarial LSTM [7]	57.2	57.0	0.148
RandForest [16]	53.1	52.7	0.013
TSLDA [14]	54.1	53.9	0.065
HAN [10]	57.6	57.2	0.052
StockNet [24]	58.2	57.5	0.081
MAN-SF [18]	60.8	60.5	0.195
Ours	**62.6**	**61.1**	**0.228**

these three methods, outperforming the best-performing HAN by 5, 3.9, and 0.176 in Acc, F1, and MCC, respectively. So far, we can find that the performance of the model using only price or text is not satisfactory enough.

Finally, compared to StockNet, which also uses texts and prices, our model is 4.4, 3.6 and 0.147 higher on Acc, F1 values and MCC, respectively. Compared to another MAN-SF using the same data, our model contains no additional knowledge of stock relations. But the result still demonstrates that our model is 1.8, 0.6, and 0.033 higher than the MAN-SF on Acc, F1 values, and MCC, respectively. Overall experimental results demonstrate the effectiveness of the proposed model.

4.5   Ablation Study

In order to better demonstrate the different effects of components of our method, we conduct ablation studies to investigate the different contribution of coattention mechanism and the three proposed financial indicators. The results are shown in Table 3. We mainly design two variants: ours w/o coattention and ours w/o ATR-BIAS-MTM.

For w/o coattention, we change the method of learning effective implicit information between price and text from the coattention mechanism to the direct concatenation of the two. This model drops 1.7, 0.7 and 0.014 compared to the full model on Acc, F1 value and MCC, respectively, proving that the coattention mechanism can effectively improve the performance of the model and obtain richer information between price and text.

For w/o ATR-BIAS-MTM, We remove the three features proposed earlier in this paper and only use the 11 features proposed in previous studies [7]. The experimental results of the model decreased by 0.3, 0.3 and 0.007 on Acc, F1 values and MCC, respectively, which also prove that these three features help the performance of the model by reflecting the volatility of the market. Here we take ATR as an example to analyze, it can simply be understood as the expectations and enthusiasm of traders. Large or increasing volatility indicates that traders may be prepared to continue buying or selling stocks during the day. A reduction in volatility indicates that traders are not showing much interest in the stock market.

Table 3. The ablation study of our method.

Model	Acc	F1	MCC
Ours	**62.6**	**61.1**	**0.228**
w/o coattention	60.9	60.4	0.214
w/o ATR-BIAS-MTM	62.3	60.8	0.221

4.6   Case Study

As mentioned before, we use the coattention mechanism in the model to capture richer information, which in turn help to learn more precise attention weights of intra-day tweets (Tweet-level attention) and inter-day of time slide window (Temporal attention). In order to investigate how the coattention mechanism guides the learning of attention weights, we conduct a case study on a sample of \$FB (FaceBook) between Nov 5th and Nov 9th, 2015, which is finally used to predict the rise or fall of Nov 10th, 2015.

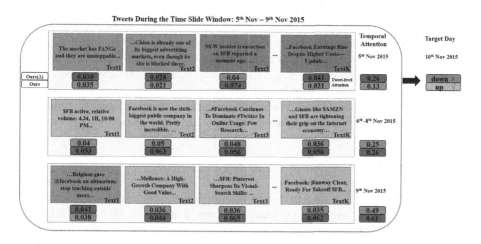

Fig. 3. Text-level and temporal attention weights learned by Ours and Ours (Δ) (as mentioned Ours w/o coattention) on a sample of \$FB (FaceBook). Numbers represent weight values and darker colors indicate greater weights. Text on green, red and grey backgrounds represent signals with positive, negative and neutral respectively.

As shown in Fig. 3, a row represents a day. For example, the first row represents texts of 5th. And we use the trading day alignment, because the 7th

and 8th are weekends, so the text data for the three days from the 6th to the 8th were merged together. Each rectangle inside each row represents the content of a text. All texts within a day are denoted as $[Text1, Text2, \ldots, TextK]$. And We present the attention weights learned by our model (Ours) and without coattention mechanism (denoted as Ours (Δ)).

First, we can see that the closer to the target day, the more weight Ours gives to that day. This is also in line with the laws of the real world, and the newer news can have a greater impact. Specifically, Ours pays more attention to the positive signals from the 6th to the 9th. On the 5th, it pays too much attention to a neutral $Text3$ whose impact is uncertain. However, because of giving it a lower weight on the day, it can help its correct prediction for the rise. On the contrary, Ours (Δ) has a greater weight than Ours on the 5th. At the same time, the tweet texts with negative signals in the 5th and 9th are more concerned by Ours (Δ), and finally make a wrong prediction.

Next we analyze the texts for each day in more detail. For a more intuitive understanding, we artificially add different background colors to each rectangle to represent different tendencies of the text, such as green, red and grey backgrounds representing signals with positive, negative and neutral respectively. On the 5th day, we can see that Ours (Δ) has higher attention than Ours on the two negative texts $Text1$ and $Text2$. During the period from the 6th to the 9th, Ours gives a higher weight value to the texts with positive signals than Ours (Δ), such as the $Text2$ from the 6th to the 8th and the $TextK$ of the 9th, which all reflect the good development prospects of FaceBook. In particular, Ours has a smaller weight than Ours (Δ) on the $Text1$ with negative influence in 9th. Although this negative news appears on the day closest to the target prediction, because the model combined with coattention can fuse the information of the entire window, and analyzes that Facebook stock is still showing an upward trend in general.

The observation shown in Fig. 3 indicates that the coattention mechanism can guide the model to pay more attention to texts with tendencies and can effectively model the temporal. With more accurate attention weights, Ours can capture more effective representation, thus it can achieve better performance than Ours (Δ).

5   Conclusion

To effectively fuse texts and prices to predict future stock movements, in this paper, we propose a fundamental analysis based neural network for stock movement prediction. Our model introduces the coattention mechanism to capture richer implicit information between text and price as a better representation of a stock. We also introduce three new technical indicators in the financial field as price features. We perform the extensive experiments on the StockNet dataset and the experimental results show the effectiveness of our proposed method. In the future, we plan to use more data other than stock prices, such as financial reports, relationships between stock, to better capture market dynamics. In addition, extracting features that can better reflect trend changes is still a direction worth exploring.

Acknowledgement. This work is supported by National Natural Science Foundation of China (No. 61976062).

References

1. Adam, K., Marcet, A., Nicolini, J.P.: Stock market volatility and learning. J. Financ. **71**(1), 33–82 (2016)
2. Brown, R.G.: Smoothing, Forecasting and Prediction of Discrete Time Series. Courier Corporation (2004)
3. Bruni, R.: Stock market index data and indicators for day trading as a binary classification problem. Data Brief **10**, 569–575 (2017)
4. Cheng, R., Li, Q.: Modeling the momentum spillover effect for stock prediction via attribute-driven graph attention networks. In: Proceedings of the AAAI Conference on Artificial Intelligence, vol. 35, pp. 55–62 (2021)
5. Ding, Q., Wu, S., Sun, H., Guo, J., Guo, J.: Hierarchical multi-scale Gaussian transformer for stock movement prediction. In: IJCAI, pp. 4640–4646 (2020)
6. Fama, E.F.: Efficient capital markets: a review of theory and empirical work. J. Financ. **25**(2), 383–417 (1970)
7. Feng, F., Chen, H., He, X., Ding, J., Sun, M., Chua, T.S.: Enhancing stock movement prediction with adversarial training. In: Proceedings of the Twenty-Eighth International Joint Conference on Artificial Intelligence, IJCAI-19, pp. 5843–5849. International Joint Conferences on Artificial Intelligence Organization (2019). https://doi.org/10.24963/ijcai.2019/810
8. Feng, F., He, X., Wang, X., Luo, C., Liu, Y., Chua, T.S.: Temporal relational ranking for stock prediction. ACM Trans. Inf. Syst. (TOIS) **37**(2), 1–30 (2019)
9. Hochreiter, S., Schmidhuber, J.: Long short-term memory. Neural Comput. **9**(8), 1735–1780 (1997)
10. Hu, Z., Liu, W., Bian, J., Liu, X., Liu, T.Y.: Listening to chaotic whispers: a deep learning framework for news-oriented stock trend prediction. In: Proceedings of the Eleventh ACM International Conference on Web Search and Data Mining, pp. 261–269 (2018)
11. Kipf, T.N., Welling, M.: Semi-supervised classification with graph convolutional networks. In: 5th International Conference on Learning Representations, ICLR 2017, Toulon, France, 24–26 April 2017, Conference Track Proceedings (2017). https://openreview.net/forum?id=SJU4ayYgl
12. Lin, T., Guo, T., Aberer, K.: Hybrid neural networks for learning the trend in time series. In: Proceedings of the Twenty-Sixth International Joint Conference on Artificial Intelligence, pp. 2273–2279 (2017)
13. Nelson, D.M., Pereira, A.C., De Oliveira, R.A.: Stock market's price movement prediction with LSTM neural networks. In: 2017 International Joint Conference on Neural Networks (IJCNN), pp. 1419–1426. IEEE (2017)
14. Nguyen, T.H., Shirai, K.: Topic modeling based sentiment analysis on social media for stock market prediction. In: Proceedings of the 53rd Annual Meeting of the Association for Computational Linguistics and the 7th International Joint Conference on Natural Language Processing (Volume 1: Long Papers), pp. 1354–1364 (2015)
15. Ni, H., Wang, S., Cheng, P.: A hybrid approach for stock trend prediction based on tweets embedding and historical prices. World Wide Web **24**(3), 849–868 (2021). https://doi.org/10.1007/s11280-021-00880-9

16. Pagolu, V.S., Reddy, K.N., Panda, G., Majhi, B.: Sentiment analysis of twitter data for predicting stock market movements. In: 2016 International Conference on Signal Processing, Communication, Power and Embedded System (SCOPES), pp. 1345–1350. IEEE (2016)

17. Pennington, J., Socher, R., Manning, C.D.: GloVe: global vectors for word representation. In: Proceedings of the 2014 Conference on Empirical Methods in Natural Language Processing (EMNLP), pp. 1532–1543 (2014)

18. Sawhney, R., Agarwal, S., Wadhwa, A., Shah, R.: Deep attentive learning for stock movement prediction from social media text and company correlations. In: Proceedings of the 2020 Conference on Empirical Methods in Natural Language Processing (EMNLP), pp. 8415–8426 (2020)

19. Tang, T.H., Chen, C.C., Huang, H.H., Chen, H.H.: Retrieving implicit information for stock movement prediction. In: Proceedings of the 44th International ACM SIGIR Conference on Research and Development in Information Retrieval, pp. 2010–2014 (2021)

20. Veličković, P., Cucurull, G., Casanova, A., Romero, A., Lió, P., Bengio, Y.: Graph attention networks. In: 6th International Conference on Learning Representations (2017)

21. Wilder, J.W.: New Concepts in Technical Trading Systems. Trend Research, Edmonton (1978)

22. Xie, Y., Wang, D., Chen, P.Y., Jinjun, X., Liu, S., Koyejo, O.: A word is worth a thousand dollars: adversarial attack on tweets fools stock prediction. In: Proceedings of the 2022 Conference of the North American Chapter of the Association for Computational Linguistics: Human Language Technologies (2022)

23. Xiong, C., Zhong, V., Socher, R.: Dynamic coattention networks for question answering. arXiv preprint arXiv:1611.01604 (2016)

24. Xu, Y., Cohen, S.B.: Stock movement prediction from tweets and historical prices. In: Proceedings of the 56th Annual Meeting of the Association for Computational Linguistics (Volume 1: Long Papers), pp. 1970–1979 (2018)

25. Zhao, Y., et al.: Stock movement prediction based on bi-typed and hybrid-relational market knowledge graph via dual attention networks. arXiv preprint arXiv:2201.04965 (2022)

Author Index

Printed in the United States
by Baker & Taylor Publisher Services